Madeline Dennis

Second Edition

Entrepreneurship
Creating a Venture

Authors

Lori Cranson

Madeline Dennis

Australia • Canada • Mexico • Singapore • Spain • United Kingdom • United States

Entrepreneurship: Creating a Venture
Second Edition
by Lori Cranson and Madeline Dennis

NELSON THOMSON LEARNING

Director of Publishing
David Steele

Senior Managing Editor
Nicola Balfour

Proofreader
Lisa Dimson

Production Coordinator
Sharon Latta Paterson

Cover Design
Peter Papayanakis

Printer
Transcontinental Printing Inc.

FIRST FOLIO RESOURCE GROUP, INC.

Program Manager
Fran Cohen

Developmental Editor
Brenda McLoughlin

Production Editor
Söğüt Y. Güleç

Interior Design/Art Direction
Tom Dart

Permissions
Erinn Banting

Photo Research
Robyn Craig

Composition
Claire Milne

Copy Editor
Tara Steele

Research
Matthew Gourlay
Amanda Stewart

Review Process
Natalie McKinnon

COPYRIGHT © 2001 by Nelson Thomson Learning, a division of Thomson Canada Limited. Nelson Thomson Learning is a registered trademark used herein under license.

Printed and bound in Canada
1 2 3 4 04 03 02 01

For more information contact Nelson Thomson Learning, 1120 Birchmount Road, Scarborough, Ontario, M1K 5G4. Or you can visit our Internet site at http://www.nelson.com

ALL RIGHTS RESERVED. No part of this work covered by the copyright hereon may be reproduced, transcribed, or used in any form or by any means—graphic, electronic, or mechanical, including photocopying, recording, taping, Web distribution or information storage and retrieval systems—without the written permission of the publisher.

For permission to use material from this text or product, contact us by
Tel 1-800-730-2214
Fax 1-800-730-2215
www.thomsonrights.com

National Library of Canada Cataloguing in Publication Data

Cranson, Lori
  Entrepreneurship: Creating a Venture

2nd ed.
First ed. written by M. Lily Kretchman, Lori Cranson, and Bill Jennings.
ISBN 0-17-620143-2

1. Entrepreneurship. 2. New business enterprises. I. Dennis, Madeline, 1948–
II. Kretchman, M. Lily, 1932–1993. Entrepreneurship. III. Title.
HD62.5.K74 2001   658.1′1
C2001-930414-5

The brand names and photos that appear in this book do not represent endorsements, but rather are business-related examples relevant to the content of the text.

Acknowledgments

We wish to thank the entrepreneurs who, through their ventures, provided a great deal of the direction for this book.

We also wish to acknowledge the help and support of staff at Nelson Thomson Learning as the work progressed. Our gratitude goes to David Steele for his continued commitment and support from the initial stages to publication, and to our editor, Fran Cohen, for her tireless efforts to ensure that the deadlines and quality standards were met. Special thanks are also due to the First Folio editorial and production team, without whose skills and cooperation this job would have been impossible.

In addition, we thank all our reviewers for their professional evaluations and thoughtful suggestions.

We also wish to acknowledge the work of Bill Jennings and Lily Kretchman who co-authored the first edition of this book with Lori Cranson.

We dedicate this book to the youth of Canada—may they catch the entrepreneurial spirit!—and to our families who gave up so much of their time with us while we worked on the book:

Steve, Dayna, Devon, and Brett (LC)
Jerry, Alicia, Robyn, Michael, Kymberley, and Jessica (MD)

In memory of Lily Kretchman—friend, mentor, and entrepreneur.

Reviewers

Fred Berg	Toronto District School Board, ON
Lennox Borel	University of Toronto, ON
Elizabeth Campbell	Bluewater District School Board, ON
Brian Childs	York Region District School Board, ON
H.G. Dichter	Toronto District School Board, ON
Paul J. Dwyer	Entrepreneurial Consulting Services, NF
Darryl Feener	Labrador School Board, District #1, NF
JoAnne Folville	Halton Catholic District School Board, ON
Bill Jennings	Formerly with Limestone District School Board, ON
Lauretta J.A. Jewell	Edmonton Public Schools Board, AB
Greg Kiesman	Winnipeg School Division #1, MB
Debra Lloyd	Toronto District School Board, ON
Shelley J. Lockhart	Royal Bank Financial Group, ON
Norah McGowan	Toronto District School Board, ON
David Sullivan	Avalon East School Board, NF
Betty Tamas	Halton District School Board, ON
Jacques Theriault	Saint John School District #8, NB

Preface

We live in a world of accelerating change. The need for young people to learn how to respond to this change in new and innovative ways grows ever more critical. Confident self-expression, positive personal development, and the ability to create and launch solutions—the hallmarks of the entrepreneur—become increasingly important. *Entrepreneurship: Creating a Venture* leads you through this changing, exciting world. The text provides a basis for you to discover opportunities for innovation that can be applied within an organization or to launch your own ventures.

Entrepreneurs and enterprising people are in demand today. They are needed on our farms, in our science labs, in businesses, hospitals, schools, government, and social agencies. Entrepreneurship and the need to be enterprising have become Canada's highest priorities. This text addresses the questions: "What can we do to develop more enterprising people?" and "What can we do to help young entrepreneurs create and launch successful ventures?"

Enterprising people and entrepreneurs make things happen! This book is about how you can make things happen. From the very first Venture Profile to the last Venturing Out, you will be actively involved in the dynamic process of entrepreneurship. You will learn to view problems as opportunities. You will generate and test your own ideas to meet these opportunities. You will become an entrepreneur or enterprising person!

The study of entrepreneurship is fun and exciting. Celebrate your successes, learn from your mistakes, gain experience from involvement in the entrepreneurial process, and make the most of the journey.

Catch the spirit! It will serve you well in the future!

A Note from the Publisher: The brand names and photos that appear in this book do not represent endorsements, but rather are business-related examples relevant to the content of the text.

Table of Contents

UNIT 1 Entrepreneurs: Made or Born? 1

Introduction 2
What Does Success Mean for You? 2
Venture Creation Wheel Model 2
Spokes in the Venture Creation Wheel 3

CHAPTER 1 What Is Entrepreneurship? 5

Successful Ventures 7
The Meaning of Entrepreneurship 9
Characteristics of Entrepreneurial Ventures 9
Technology and Change 11
Supply and Demand 13
Impact on the Community 15
Job Creation 15
New Ideas 15
Economic Benefits 15
Political Benefits 15
Entrepreneurship and Demographics 16
Intrapreneurship 17
Approaches to Entrepreneurship 18
Entrepreneurs: Made or Born? 19

CHAPTER 2 Entrepreneurs and Enterprising People 23

Entrepreneurs 27
Characteristics of Successful Entrepreneurs 28
Entrepreneurial Skills 30
What Makes an Entrepreneur Tick? 32
Enterprising People 35
Enterprising Employees 36
What Motivates You to Excel? 37
Supporting Enterprising Employees 38

CHAPTER 3 Assessing Your Entrepreneurial Potential 43

First Steps: Young Entrepreneurs 45
Challenges Facing Young Entrepreneurs 46
The Value of Experience 47
Setting Goals 47
Why Set Goals? 48
Flexibility Is the Key 51
Goal Setting and Commitment 51
Knowing Yourself 53
Are You an Edison or an Einstein? 56
Assessing Your Skills 57
Classifying Your Skills 58
Strategies for Entrepreneurial Success 60

UNIT 2 Preparing the Way 65

Preparing the Way 66

CHAPTER 4 Challenges and Changes in the Labour Market 67

Labour: Past and Present 69
The Information Age 71
Current Labour Market Trends 72
What Employers Are Looking For 73
Work-Life Balance 74
Home-Based Employment 77
Opportunities for Enterprising Employees 79
The Changing Workplace 84
Rewards for Enterprise 84

CHAPTER 5	Invention, Innovation, and the Creative Edge	87

Ideas and the Creative Edge	**89**
Ways to Find New Ideas	90
How Well Do You Observe?	90
Looking for Patterns	91
Developing Your Ideas	91
Invention and Innovation	**94**
Protecting Your Ideas	95
The Problem-Solving Process	**100**
Stages and Skills in the Problem-Solving Process	100
Lateral Thinking	102
The Six Thinking Hats	102
How Do You Interpret Information?	106
More than One Solution	106
Advantages of Teamwork	107
The Left and Right Brain and Problem Solving	107
More Ways to Generate Ideas	110
The Ideas Spoke of the Venture Creation Wheel	111

CHAPTER 6	Opportunities, Ideas, and the Enterprising Work Environment	114

Ideas and Opportunities	**116**
Which Comes First—an Idea or an Opportunity?	118
Looking for Opportunities	119
Following Market Trends	**120**
Forecasting Trends	120
Current Global Trends	121
The Time-Series Forecast	123
Using Research	128
Primary Research	128
Designing a Questionnaire for Primary Research	130
Secondary Research	131
Steps in Marketing Research	131
Evaluating Your Ideas	**134**
Blue Hat Thinking	134
The Enterprising Workplace	**137**
Encouraging Innovation	138

CHAPTER 7	The Venture Plan	143

Life Cycle of a Business	**145**
Prestartup Stage	146
Development Stage	146
Growth Stage	146
Comfort Stage	147
Turnaround Stage	147
What Is a Venture Plan?	**147**
The Mission Statement	148
The Research Assistance Grid: a Basic Planning Tool	148
Six Reasons to Prepare a Venture Plan	150
Sections in a Business Venture Plan	**151**
Section 1: Executive Summary	151
Section 2: Market Analysis	152
Section 3: Resource Analysis	154
Section 4: Operating Strategy	155
Section 5: Financial Strategy	157
Mentorship	**160**
The Importance of the Venture Plan	**163**

UNIT 3 Moving into Action	167
What Does "Moving into Action" Mean?	168

CHAPTER 8 Analyzing Your Market — 169

Knowing Your Market	171
Advantages of Marketing Research	173
Knowing Your Product or Service	173
Knowing Your Customers	174
Forms of Marketing Research	174
Purposes of Marketing Research	175
Conducting Marketing Research	**176**
Primary, Secondary, and Internal Research	176
Selecting a Sample	177
Identifying a Marketing Strategy	**180**
The Marketing Mix	**181**
The Four Ps of Marketing	181
Confirming a Target Market	182
Market Segmentation	**182**
Common Market Segments	183
Life Cycles and Competition	**184**
Stage 1: Introduction	184
Stage 2: Growth	184
Stage 3: Maturity	184
Stage 4: Decline	184
The Six Ps of Entrepreneurship	**185**
Profit	185
Price	187
Production, People, and Productivity	189
Promotion	190
Customer Expectations	**193**

CHAPTER 9 Rolling Up Your Sleeves: Resource Allocation and Management — 196

Resources for a Successful Venture	198
Material Resources	199
Technological Resources	199
Financial Resources	199
Human Resources	200
Finding and Keeping Good Employees	**201**
Choosing the Best Person for the Job	202
Building Employee Loyalty	203
The External Venture Team	204
The Functions of Management	**209**
Planning	209
Organizing	210
Leading	211
Controlling	211
Effective Leadership	**214**
Motivating Others	214
Facilitating Communication	215
Resolving Conflicts	217
Managing Personal Stress	217
Choosing the Right Form of Ownership	**219**
Sole Proprietorship	219
Partnership	220
Corporation or Limited Company	221
Franchises	**224**
Laws and Regulations	**225**

CHAPTER 10	**Financing Your Dream**	**229**
Planning a Financial Strategy		**231**
Step 1: Establishing Financial Objectives		231
Step 2: Preparing a Personal Budget		235
Step 3: Estimating Revenue and Expenses		237
Step 4: Preparing a Cash-Flow Projection		239
Step 5: Calculating Startup Costs and Operating Expenses		242
Step 6: Preparing a Personal Balance Sheet		242
Step 7: Preparing Income Forecasts and Projected Balance Sheets		244
Ways to Raise Capital		**247**
Equity Financing		247
Debt Financing		251
Why Plan a Financial Strategy?		**254**

CHAPTER 11	**Vision to Action: Writing the Venture Plan**	**258**
The Venture Planning Process		**260**
Step 1: Decide What Sections to Include in Your Plan		261
Step 2: Find the Information You Need		263
Step 3: Summarize Your Research		264
Step 4: Analyze Your Critical Risks		264
Step 5: Make a Go/No-go Decision		265
Step 6: Prepare a Draft Plan		268
Step 7: Ask for Advice		271
Step 8: Edit and Proofread Your Plan		272
Step 9: Polish Your Plan		273

CHAPTER 12	**Venturing as a Way of Life**	**278**
Why Some Ventures Fail		**280**
Recognizing the Warning Signals		280
Minimizing Risks		285
The Importance of Development Tasks		**286**
Growing a Venture		**291**
Harvesting a Venture		**293**
Financial Harvest		293
Personal Harvest		295
Ethics, Integrity, and the Law		**297**
Ethics and Integrity		297
Ethics and the Law		298
Business and Personal Ethics		299
Integrity and the Entrepreneurial Venture		300

Glossary   **304**

Index   **310**

Credits   **317**

UNIT 1

Entrepreneurs: Made or Born?

Introduction

Entrepreneurs make things happen! In this book, you will learn to become a more enterprising person, perhaps even an entrepreneur. Unit 1 introduces the qualities that enterprising people possess and will help you become more aware of some of these qualities in yourself.

As you gradually explore who you are and what you love to do, you may discover a passion that will give you the strength and commitment to face the challenges of starting a new venture. Learning to become an enterprising person may be a rocky road at times, but you are sure to gain pleasure from what you learn along the way, and you will thrive as you work toward achieving your goal.

Successful entrepreneurs and enterprising people do not always earn a lot of money, but they do enjoy a feeling of pride in who they are and what they do. Their success is measured in how well they balance family and work, in the contributions they make to the community and the economy, and in how they take care of their employees.

What Does Success Mean for You?

As you work through this unit, you will begin to formulate an answer to this question. Your notion of success will likely change as you journey toward your goals, but it will always be aligned closely with the things you value most. As with any journey, enjoy and learn from the experiences along the way. In the end, they may prove to be even more important to you than your ultimate destination.

Unit 1 of *Entrepreneurship: Creating a Venture* starts you on a road that may well continue throughout your life. The Venture Creation Wheel, which appears in each chapter, will guide you on your journey.

In the Venture Profiles that appear throughout the book, you will read about real entrepreneurs and their ventures to see how their experiences reflect some of the ideas shown on the Venture Creation Wheel.

In Unit 1, you will explore

- the characteristics of entrepreneurs and their ventures
- the role of entrepreneurship in the community
- the role of entrepreneurship in wealth creation
- the importance of intrapreneurship to a successful business
- your own potential as an entrepreneur or enterprising person

At the beginning of each chapter, you will also find a list of "Learning Opportunities" that describes what you will learn from the chapter.

Venture Creation Wheel Model

The process of entrepreneurship, using entrepreneurial skills to create a new venture, involves ability, a set of values, and an overall plan or procedure for action. Venture creation needs more than knowledge: It requires appropriate skills and attitudes to bring about positive results. The Venture Creation Wheel helps explain the entrepreneurial process. It is a good model to consult when undertaking a new entrepreneurial venture.

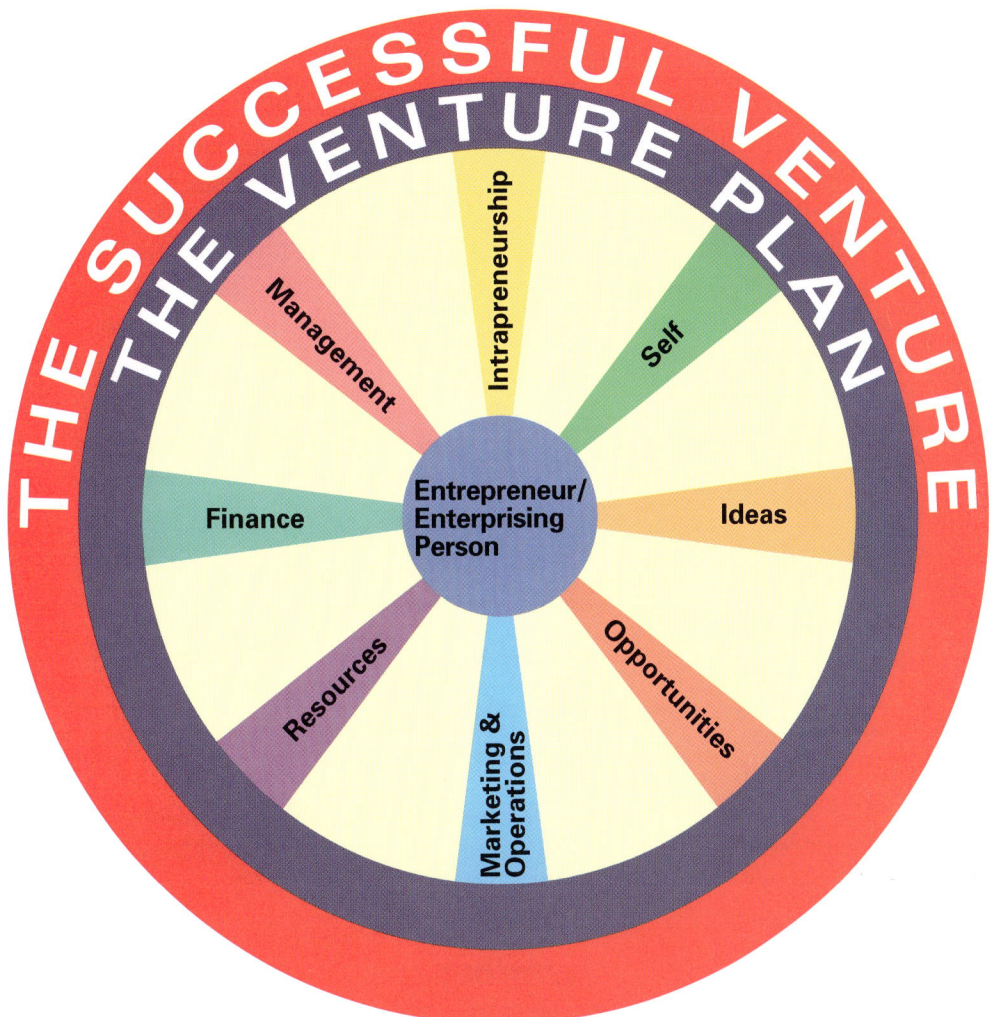

The model itself should not be followed in a linear way. The process of venture creation involves a great many variables. It combines seemingly chaotic creative thinking and behaviour with highly disciplined critical thinking and decision making. For these reasons, venture creation cannot be described as a set of step-by-step instructions.

The process of venture creation looks more like a bicycle wheel. In a bicycle wheel, there is a hub with many spokes. Each spoke is connected to and supports the rim. The rim is the part that holds the spokes in place and gives strength to the rest of the wheel.

Spokes in the Venture Creation Wheel

The foundation of the venture is created by the hub and the spokes. Just as it takes many spokes to give a bicycle wheel strength and stability, so it is with the Venture Creation Wheel. The success or failure of the venture depends on how well the entrepreneur at the hub performs the tasks represented by the spokes.

There are eight spokes in the wheel: **Self**, **Ideas**, **Opportunities**, **Marketing and Operations**, **Resources**, **Finance**, **Management**, and **Intrapreneurship**.

The first two chapters look at the Venture Wheel as a whole. The hub of the wheel is the entrepreneur or enterprising person at the centre of the venture creation process. In Chapter 3, the **Self** spoke represents you, the prospective entrepreneur. Starting a venture requires effort and skill. It entails commitment and persistence. For these reasons, it is important for aspiring entrepreneurs to question themselves continually. What are my interests? my strengths? my needs? What do I enjoy doing? What are my goals? What do I know? What can I do?

Asking these questions begins the process of self-assessment that will help determine what an individual is trying to achieve and what kind of venture he or she is best suited to.

In Chapter 4, the spoke of **Intrapreneurship** deals with being an enterprising person, even if you are not pursuing a venture of your own.

The **Ideas** spoke generates and evaluates ideas for a venture. Generating ideas requires the entrepreneur to use the right side of the brain—the creative side. Learning to be a creative thinker takes practice. In Chapter 5, you will learn some techniques to help unlock the right side of your brain.

The **Opportunities** spoke identifies entrepreneurial opportunities by examining and tracing trends and changes in society that give rise to opportunity. Entrepreneurs or enterprising employees can recognize these opportunities. In Chapter 6, you will discover how to identify and evaluate opportunities.

> *The venture planning process is essential to the success of any entrepreneurial endeavour, within an existing organization or in a startup.*

The **Marketing and Operations** spoke of the Venture Creation Wheel represents marketing methods and organizational resources used by successful entrepreneurs on a day-to-day basis. Details about marketing and operations are included in Chapter 8.

Knowing how to mobilize and allocate resources is an important skill for any entrepreneur. The **Resources** and **Management** spokes are explained in more detail in Chapter 9.

Raising capital and planning the finances of the venture over the short and long term are essential to the success of the venture. The **Finance** spoke demonstrates how to organize a financial strategy for the venture. This process is described in Chapter 10.

Once the venture is started, it is crucial for the entrepreneur to develop management strategies for the survival of the venture.

The venture planning process is essential to the success of any entrepreneurial endeavour, within an existing organization or in a startup. Chapters 7, 11, and 12 provide a road map for the successful planning and writing of the venture plan.

Once the venture is successfully on its way, Intrapreneurship can help it grow. Intrapreneurs will need to draw on all the other spokes of the wheel to stimulate and manage changes that will help the business run more efficiently and responsively or extend its reach.

Turn the Venture Creation Wheel to begin your journey.

CHAPTER 1

What Is Entrepreneurship?

LEARNING OPPORTUNITIES

By the end of this chapter, you should be able to
- understand the meaning and role of entrepreneurship
- describe the characteristics of entrepreneurial ventures
- describe how technology and globalization are changing the Canadian workplace
- describe the impact that entrepreneurs have on a community
- explain the connection between entrepreneurship and the creation of jobs and wealth
- describe the contributions that intrapreneurs can make in the workplace

Entrepreneurial Language

- market niche
- venture
- entrepreneur
- need
- want
- entrepreneurship
- profit
- not-for-profit
- good
- service
- virtual business
- e-commerce
- globalization
- gross national product (GNP)
- demographics
- downsize
- rightsize
- incubator
- networking
- demand
- supply
- multiplier effect
- intrapreneurship
- market share

These terms are introduced in this chapter. Which ones are you familiar with? Try to figure out what the unfamiliar terms mean. Read the chapter to confirm your understandings.

Venture Profile

THREE BLONDES COOK UP SWEET SUCCESS

Donna Korchinski, The Globe and Mail

After two decades of marriage, Nadja Piatka had been left with two children and thousands of dollars of debt. She was almost unemployable, she recalls. Seven years later, Ms. Piatka worries more about dough than bills. She is a partner in Three Blondes and a Brownie Inc., an Edmonton-based low-fat cake and muffin maker that's starting to make the transition from a highly publicized startup to an established business.

Founded in 1993, Three Blondes and a Brownie recently negotiated orders for its Fat Wise products—in this case, coffee cakes and brownies—from 220 Safeway supermarkets through Western Canada, and from 124 Federated Co-operative and Calgary Co-operative grocery stores in the West.

The three blondes are Ms. Piatka, 49, and her two partners, former Miss Canada Terry Lynn Meyer, 47, and onetime bank manager Candace Brinsmead, 40. In this team, Ms. Meyer is the communicator, Ms. Brinsmead the "bean counter," and Ms. Piatka the visionary, the partners say.

Even through her dark, cash-starved days, Ms. Piatka says she held on to an entrepreneurial vision. She could imagine a parade of huge trucks rolling down the highway carrying her products to market. Those original products were fat-reduced muffins that she developed in her Edmonton kitchen, test-marketed on her two teenaged children, and delivered to small stores and coffee shops.

Ms. Piatka's fortunes took an upturn when she appeared as a guest on an Edmonton-based morning television show hosted by Ms. Meyer. Ms. Piatka was talking about her low-fat recipes. Together, they saw a business opportunity and recruited Ms. Brinsmead, the finance-minded best friend of Ms. Meyer.

Three Blondes started on the fast track. Four months after incorporating in mid-1993, the company persuaded McDonald's to test its Fat Wise muffins in the Edmonton market. McDonald's tested the product in Vancouver as well, and then went nationwide with it. The company's **revenue** hit $100 000 the first year. By 1998, it was up to $2.3 million.

By 2005, they believe that they can reach almost $7 million, if projected expansion throughout Canada goes ahead. After that, there is the U.S. market.

There are unwritten principles that contribute to the company's success. The first is they have no debt. Ms. Brinsmead, who runs the day-to-day operations, admits to a "cautious approach to financing."

Each partner works out of her home—Ms. Meyer and Ms. Brinsmead in Edmonton, Ms. Piatka in Calgary. They have no employees other than themselves and they outsource all the baking.

CONTINUED➡

One marketing plus has been the company's name. They had called their first efforts "Nadja-approved Low Fat Desserts—a Division of Three Blondes and a Brownie." Then they realized that the Three Blondes tag was getting all the attention. The company also avoids the label "low fat." "People get sick of the word," Ms. Piatka says. "They think low fat is no taste."

> ### *Exploring*
>
> 1. Briefly state the vision that Ms. Piatka had.
> 2. How did Ms. Piatka achieve her vision?
> 3. What needs or wants were addressed in this venture? (See the definitions of "needs" and "wants" on page 9.)
> 4. A **market niche** is a specific segment of the market. What niche did this venture focus on?
> 5. Why do you think the name of a company is so important to its success? Can you name other companies that have catchy or inventive names? Have these names affected the success of their ventures?

SUCCESSFUL VENTURES

Throughout this text, you will read about a number of **ventures**—business startups or undertakings—that have had an impact on people's lives. Each venture is profiled as a case study. Through reading, discussing, and exploring these Venture Profiles, you will learn to understand entrepreneurship. In the first Venture Profile, Nadja Piatka recognized the need for low-fat goodies and coupled that with her skill at baking cakes and muffins. Nadja knew less about promotion and finance and took in partners to fill the gaps.

Venture Profile

THIRST FOR JOCK WATER ... OXYGENATED DRINK TOUTED AS THE EVIAN OF JOCKS

David Steinhart, Financial Post

First the hyperbaric chamber, then the nose patch, and now along comes an Ontario company with a product it says will soon dominate the sporting world. And while pro athletes and officials usually stick to what's helping them score goals, hit home runs, or make the big call in a tight game as a matter of superstition, Woodbridge, Ontario's

CONTINUED➡

Chapter 1 ◆ What Is Entrepreneurship? 7

Oxyl'Eau Inc. has designed a product that adds a splash of science to the mix.

Oxyl'Eau is marketing spring water said to contain 400% more oxygen than most varieties. Although not yet available on the open market, Oxenergy is starting to become a force. So much so that National Hockey League referee Kerry Fraser swears by it.

"Once I started to use the product, I found that I had more jump in my legs from period to period," he said yesterday. "The big thing with the water is that it shortens post-game recovery time by a lot. When I use it, I have no muscle soreness the next day." Mr. Fraser drinks five bottles of Oxenergy on game day and three on days when he's not officiating.

Tom Mohr, vice president of Oxyl'Eau, said the drink can significantly raise an athlete's blood oxygen levels. In a recent issue of *Sports Illustrated*, Dallas Stars centre Mike Modano is quoted as saying that the water helped him recover better after shifts. "I'd get a second wind," he said.

However, Doug McKenney, strength and conditioning coach for the NHL's Buffalo Sabres, called Oxenergy a "placebo-type" drink with no real merit. "There is no research to suggest that it improves performance," he said. "There may be some floating around here, but to my knowledge our guys don't use it."

Oxenergy runs about U.S. $48 per case, with 24 half-litre bottles in each. Right now, the product is only available to professional and amateur sport organizations.

Mr. Mohr, who is marketing his water toward big-name teams such as the NHL's Stars and the NFL's Denver Broncos and Dallas Cowboys, said the product's only known side effect is lightheadedness if too much is consumed too quickly. He said a comparison between Oxenergy and the hyperbaric chamber—a pressurized bath of pure oxygen, usually at triple the outside air pressure—is often made.

Mark Scappaticci, a Niagara Falls, Ontario, chiropractor who works with professional and Olympic athletes, said Oxenergy has been well received. "Athletes have said that it gives them more energy and better recovery," he said. "And I have not heard any negative things from users, except that maybe they didn't feel any different."

Although Oxyl'Eau is still relatively unknown, confidence is building that the product will some day become the Evian of the jock crowd. "There will come a time when every athlete in the world will be drinking this water," Mr. Mohr said.

Exploring

1. What is Oxenergy?
2. What market niche is Oxenergy being marketed to?
3. What might the future hold for this venture? Why do you think so?
4. What are the positive and negative features of this venture?
5. Compare the first two Venture Profiles.
   a) What change or new idea was brought about by each venture?
   b) Create a Venn diagram such as the one below to show the similarities and differences between the ventures.

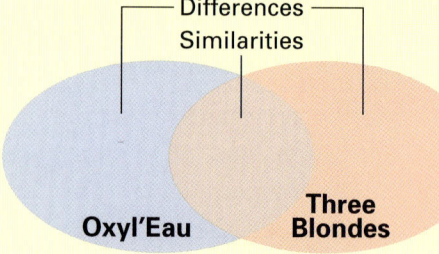

   c) Which of these entrepreneurial ventures has the best chance for long-term success? Why do you think so?

Starting Up

What people do you know who have started a business? What impact has their business had on them and on their community?

The Meaning of Entrepreneurship

Many people dream of owning their own business. The idea of becoming an **entrepreneur** has been around for centuries. The word "entrepreneur" is descended from the Latin word, *prendere*, and later, the French word *prendre*, which means "to take." Entrepreneurs are people who take hold of opportunities when they see them. They are willing to assume calculated risks as they look for ways to satisfy the needs and wants of others through innovation. **Needs** are essential for human survival. They can be classified as "real" or as "psychological." Real or basic needs, such as food or shelter, are tangible. Psychological needs, such as companionship and security, are emotional. **Wants** are human desires that go beyond basic needs and are not essential for survival. They make people feel good or help them achieve a goal. Both needs and wants can be met through, and provide a market for, the goods and services that entrepreneurs supply. The essence of **entrepreneurship** is the creation and building of a venture to fill a market niche.

Worth Repeating

"Fortunately, Canadians are really quite entrepreneurial, as about half of us are willing to consider starting our own businesses. Apart from business entrepreneurship, entrepreneurial values can permeate every sector of society where contribution and success are rewarded and self-reliance is encouraged as a value."

Goldfarb Consultants, CFIB, and Scotiabank, Study on Workplace Satisfaction in Private, Public Sectors

Discuss the second sentence of this quote with a partner. Can you restate it in your own words?

CHARACTERISTICS OF ENTREPRENEURIAL VENTURES

Entrepreneurial ventures are business ideas that are conceived, initiated, and operated by a person or group. Most ventures fit into one or more of the following categories:

FOR-PROFIT/NOT-FOR-PROFIT

A business venture is usually undertaken for **profit**, that is, to make money. However, entrepreneurial ventures are sometimes created for social or community service purposes. **Not-for-profit** organizations such as Greenpeace, Save the Children, the Salvation Army, Big Sisters, Boy Scouts of Canada, the Heart and Stroke Foundation, and the United Way may be involved in fundraising initiatives. Their goal is not to make a profit but rather to raise the money they need to deliver a special service or satisfy a specific need in society.

LARGE SCALE/SMALL SCALE

Entrepreneurship is not dependent on the size of the business. Large business corporations or large not-for-profit organizations seek to satisfy needs or wants on a large scale, usually at a national or an international level. Smaller companies or not-for-profit organizations may work at satisfying a need or a want at a smaller, more local level.

The Cancer Society, for example, annually mounts an international appeal for funds and then directs money raised to large-scale research initiatives. A smaller community service organization in your own neighbourhood, on the other hand, might initiate a smaller fundraising campaign to help a local community centre.

SERVICE PRODUCTION/GOODS PRODUCTION

Entrepreneurial ventures can be organized either to produce a **good** (a product) or to provide a **service**. The good might be something that will be sold eventually for profit at a store or on the Internet; or it might be something that a not-for-profit organization will produce and distribute free of charge, such as hand-knitted mittens for people in need. The service can be anything from the work that a mechanic or repairperson would do for a price, to the advice provided by a lawyer for a fee, to the fundraising efforts of a community organization, provided by volunteers for no pay.

PHYSICAL/VIRTUAL

In the past, most businesses provided **bricks-and-mortar** locations that customers could visit to make their purchases. Shopping malls and car dealerships are examples. However, innovations in communications technology have made it possible for today's entrepreneurs to operate very successfully without a store or showroom. This **virtual business** is conducted electronically through **e-commerce** over the Internet, though traditional locations are still the primary places to do business.

LOCAL/PROVINCIAL/NATIONAL/INTERNATIONAL

Within Canada, entrepreneurship exists in your school, in your local community, throughout your province, and on a national scale. A local enterprise is confined to one community. Provincial entrepreneurship exists when an entrepreneurial venture grows beyond its starting location to other towns and cities within a single province. A national enterprise operates in more than one province.

An international enterprise operates in more than one country. There has been a recent trend to **globalization**, with increased markets throughout the world for large and small businesses. With instantaneous communication by telephone, fax, and computer, individuals from all over the world can communicate, collaborate, and trade in real time.

Since consumers in many other countries provide a market for Canadian goods and services, Canada exports a large percentage of its gross national product. The **gross national product (GNP)** is the total of all the goods and services produced in Canada in one year.

E-Bits & Bytes

"Results of a national survey reveal that 69% of the 9246 small- and medium-sized businesses surveyed are now connected to the Internet. More than one third of small firms have entered into the arena of e-commerce."

Canadian Federation of Independent Business

What advantages and disadvantages might these companies have experienced after they were connected to the Internet?

Cargo is loaded onto a freighter for export to the United States.

> ### Worth Repeating
>
> "Market opportunities to over 350 million consumers were opened to Canadian businesses as a result of NAFTA."
>
> D. Wesley Balderson, Canadian Entrepreneurship and Small Business Management

In order to compete more effectively, many countries have entered into trade agreements. These agreements outline which goods and services can travel easily between countries and which ones will have a tariff or a tax added. Entrepreneurs in Canada benefit from trade agreements such as GATT (General Agreement on Tariffs and Trade) and NAFTA (North American Free Trade Agreement). GATT regulates and reduces tariffs among more than 100 countries around the world, including Canada. It also provides a way for member countries to resolve any trade disputes that may occur. NAFTA benefits North American businesses by gradually reducing trade tariffs to encourage the trade of goods and services flowing between Canada, the United States, and Mexico.

■ Technology and Change

We are living in a period of rapid technological development. One important change is that the growth of e-commerce has made it possible for small businesses to compete with much larger ones. As **demographics** (data about groups of people including age, ethnic

> ### Worth Repeating
>
> "The only job security is between your ears, and the only secure job is the one you create yourself."
>
> *The Only Secure Job, Richard Worzel, Canadian futurist*

origin, religion, family size, income, etc.) change and consumer buying habits change, small businesses have the flexibility to adapt to trends, while larger ones may be bogged down by a lengthy decision-making process.

Another change is that information technology has revolutionized the way we do business. Entrepreneurs now have access to large data banks and search engines that used to be available only to large companies. In this way, small businesses can gain information that can translate into further opportunities for success.

Inexpensive software packages developed for small enterprises include tools for accounting, marketing research, financing, marketing, sales, and more. These tools, along with quality computer technology, greatly increase the small venture's competitive advantage.

The past few years have brought about an entrepreneurial revolution. As the number of new ventures increases, more and more entrepreneurs are able to achieve their dreams of owning their own business. At the same time, our economy is evolving and society is changing. All these trends open up new opportunities for business startups.

A less positive effect of technological change is job loss. As new technological opportunities made it possible for companies to **downsize** or **rightsize**, many Canadians lost their jobs and were forced by necessity to become entrepreneurs.

Today, many Canadian residents are small business owners. These entrepreneurs are increasingly important to society. As a result, government, banks, and other community-based organizations have a keen interest in helping entrepreneurs succeed by providing excellent resources, education, and support for individuals starting a venture.

Incubators are organizations whose sole purpose is to give a new entrepreneur a place to share office space, equipment, or other resources. They also offer training and **networking** opportunities. Networking is the ability to interact with people in a positive way. Whether you meet people in a social or business setting, you never know who can help you grow your business using their knowledge and connections.

Look up "incubator" in the dictionary. How does the meaning fit in this context?

Supply and Demand

Entrepreneurship is not a new idea. In ancient Babylon, business was regulated by the oldest set of written commercial laws. Named for the king, this document was called the Hammurabi Code. Some of the laws in the code are similar to laws we still have today. For example, one of King Hammurabi's laws says, "If a merchant gives an agent corn, wool, oil, or any other goods to transport, the agent shall give a receipt for the amount and compensate the merchant therefor. Then he shall obtain a receipt from the merchant for the money that he gives the merchant."

Entrepreneurship has a long history in Canada as well. The oldest company in Canada, the Hudson's Bay Company, was founded to supply furs to people in Europe. Today, this entrepreneurial venture has become a large national corporation employing 70 000 people and contributing great wealth to the Canadian economy.

In Hammurabi's time, people bought corn, wool, and oil. When the Hudson's Bay Company was founded, customers in Europe wanted to buy furs. An alert entrepreneur takes advantage of consumer **demand** (what the consumer needs and wants) by providing a **supply** of goods or services. When the supply is greater than the demand, the price of the good or service goes down. When the demand is greater than the supply, the price goes up. An entrepreneurial venture that can achieve the right balance between supply and demand is destined for success.

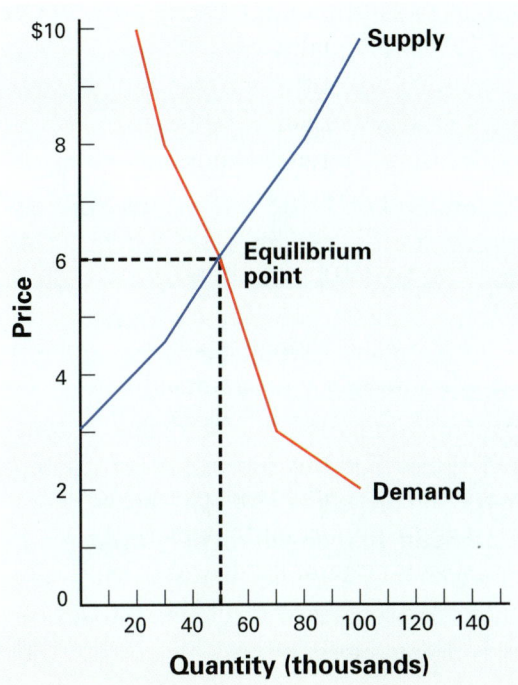

Figure 1.1 Basic Supply and Demand Curve Chart

Agents of Change

In 1913, automobiles were outrageously expensive because they were built one car at a time. They were custom-made machines. Henry Ford saw the potential demand for them, and he thought of a solution to make the manufacturing process more efficient. His solution was to invent a moving-belt production line. Employees could then build cars one piece at a time for many cars rather than one car at a time. This new system, which is called **mass production**, allowed workers to focus on doing one thing very well. These factories produced cars quickly and efficiently. As a result, the prices dropped to a level that the average consumer could afford. A radical concept created an exciting change: An ordinary person could own a car.

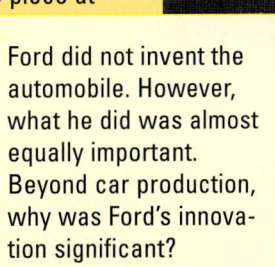

Ford did not invent the automobile. However, what he did was almost equally important. Beyond car production, why was Ford's innovation significant?

Chapter 1 ◆ What Is Entrepreneurship? **13**

Venture Profile

AWARD-WINNING ENTREPRENEUR

Rotman School of Management, University of Toronto,
Canadian Woman Entrepreneur of the Year Awards

In 1989, the closure of the Canadian Forces Base in Summerside on Prince Edward Island resulted in the loss of 1200 jobs and, to the people of the town, the future looked grim. Jo-Anne Schurman decided that her business idea might be exactly what was needed to ignite a spark in the local economy and put people back to work.

The owner of a gift shop since 1979, Jo-Anne was determined to build an inn that would attract tourists to the beautiful area. In spite of the difficulty in securing funding, the decision in 1990 to build the Loyalist Country Inn proved to be the vote of confidence the community needed. The fact that a local family would invest considerable dollars in its own community during a period of great uncertainty and create 72 new jobs seemed to be a turning point and encouraged other projects to go forward. Approximately 125 local tradespeople worked on the construction of the Loyalist Country Inn, which now employs an in-season staff of over 100. The inn offers 103 rooms, a lavishly appointed dining room, banquet and meeting rooms, and a tavern.

The Loyalist Country Inn is noted for a taste of heritage and Island hospitality. Jo-Anne has marketed the inn locally, nationally, and internationally through Rendez-Vous Canada and other trade shows, as well as through a series of trips to Japan. The response has been so good that a $4.6 million expansion has been completed. Tourists and corporate travellers have ensured that the inn maintains a high occupancy.

The community as a whole has readily acknowledged that the Loyalist Country Inn was one of the projects that led to the recovery of Summerside. In recognition of her outstanding achievement, Jo-Anne won the Canadian Woman Entrepreneur of the Year: Impact on Local Economy Award in 1997.

Exploring

1. What evidence is there that the Loyalist Country Inn venture had a positive impact on the local community?
2. What happens in a community when jobs are lost?
3. Why is the creation of new jobs so critical to a community's well-being?
4. Find out more about Summerside, Prince Edward Island. If you lived in Summerside, what venture would you consider starting? Why?

Impact on the Community

Entrepreneurs can have a powerful impact on a local economy in terms of job creation, new ideas, and economic and political benefits.

Job Creation

Jo-Anne Schurman was able to employ 125 tradespeople to build the Loyalist Country Inn and 72 more people to operate it. When entrepreneurship creates jobs in the local community, it has a **multiplier effect**. Those who are employed by the business have money to buy goods and services. If these goods and services are provided in the local community, people will likely spend their money there and more jobs will be created. If the business grows and needs more employees, more people may move into the community, and more goods and services will be needed.

New Ideas

Another benefit to the community is that entrepreneurship often generates new ways of doing things. It encourages the creation of a broader range of goods and services than would otherwise exist. Many of us now take innovations such as the Internet, cell phones, CDs, or microwave ovens for granted.

Economic Benefits

Through competition, entrepreneurs not only help lower prices, but also improve a society's standard of living. When more wealth is distributed throughout the society, everyone enjoys the benefits. The success of one new business venture can produce a variety of additional entrepreneurial and investment opportunities, which will in turn bring more wealth. For example, the successful introduction of the personal computer brought with it a number of opportunities, including software, hardware, training, repair services, computer magazines, journals, advertising, e-commerce, and more.

Political Benefits

A society that wants to encourage entrepreneurship needs to provide a supportive environment. Entrepreneurship is strong in countries where financial and legal institutions provide a strong

---

International NEWS

Adherex Technologies Inc., an Ottawa-based biotechnology company, announced that it has received investment financing from Fujisawa Investments for Entrepreneurship, L.P., a venture capital fund based in Osaka, Japan. Fujisawa is committed to helping provide innovative products that contribute to the health and welfare of people all over the world. Adherex's prime focus is to develop anticancer drugs. It will use the investment to assist in bringing a promising new treatment approach for cancer to clinical trials with human cancer patients.

In what ways might this investment have an impact in Canada?

> *Entrepreneurs who study the demographics of their customers will be better able to predict what these people might want to buy.*

foundation; where money for starting a new venture is easily accessible; where education and training are widely available; where laws and regulations do not deter new venture creation; and where free and open trade exists. It is strong where lobby groups (support groups) in government, business, and education are available to collaborate, advise, and encourage entrepreneurs.

Entrepreneurship and Demographics

Demographics is the study of the characteristics of people in a population. Entrepreneurs who study the demographics of their customers will be better able to predict what these people might want to buy.

Between the end of World War II and the early 1960s, there was a sharp increase in the number of babies born in Canada. These people, called "baby boomers," represent an important market for entrepreneurs. It has been estimated that the boomers have the largest percentage of disposable income and earned wealth of all Canadian age groups. As they grow older, they are choosing to spend their money on leisure lifestyles, on health care and related products, on services that make their lives easier, and on their families. Ventures that cater to the demands of the baby boomer population will create significant jobs in a community.

Immigration has also created a positive impact on local economies. Immigrant populations have their own ethnic and cultural interests that local entrepreneurs can support. Ventures such as an Asian food market in a predominantly Asian neighbourhood or an Italian bakery in an Italian neighbourhood are examples of businesses that meet cultural needs while supporting the local economy. These ventures often go from the local to the general community, thereby increasing sales even more.

As the baby boomers grow older, they spend more money on leisure activities.

YOUR TURN

1. What is the difference between "wants" and "needs"? How do these terms relate to "demand"? Do you think having a job is a need or a want? Explain.

2. Give examples of two trade agreements Canada has signed. How do countries benefit from trade agreements?

3. Work with a partner to create a short survey asking older people in your community about changes they have seen during their lifetime. Include questions about transportation, the business world, leisure activities, technology, cost of living, and housing. With your partner, interview one or two seniors using your survey. Then, work in teams of four to six to compare results.
   a) What entrepreneurial ventures have had the greatest impact on their lives?
   b) If you wanted to start an entrepreneurial venture that would serve people like those you interviewed, what would it be? Why?

■ Intrapreneurship

Intrapreneurship is entrepreneurship that occurs within an existing organization or corporation. More and more organizations are encouraging intrapreneurial activity in order to become more competitive, improve their productivity, or keep pace with changing markets, technology, and new opportunities.

These corporations use a variety of methods to stimulate intrapreneurship. Some have restructured their organizations into smaller, more innovative teams and then challenged each team to turn a particular idea into a new product, service, or process. Others are inviting customers to give them ideas about needed changes in a product or service. Still others are devising ways to reward innovation and recognize their intrapreneurs.

Organizations that are not intrapreneurial today are at a disadvantage. The fast pace of business means that organizations must respond to, and even anticipate, market demands or they will quickly lose their **market share**. With the increased availability of instant information and worldwide access to goods and services, consumers will be loyal only to local ventures that respond to their needs.

In the late 1960s, the Swiss watch industry was the leader in the world, with over 65% of market share and 80% of profits. By 1980, their share had dropped to less than 10%, with over 50 000 jobs lost. Why? Because the world changed. Swiss employees invented the quartz watch movement, but their companies did not see the value of it and did not patent it for protection. As a result, these inventors went to Japan where Seiko Corporation bought the rights. Seiko is now one of the largest watch manufacturers in the world.

Joel Barker, Future Edge: Discovering the New Paradigms of Success

Approaches to Entrepreneurship

> **Worth Repeating**
>
> "Any new businessperson has to be totally consumed by his or her operation to be successful. You have to eat, sleep, and breathe it."
>
> Colette Nap, Canadian architect

Some people start their businesses from scratch. Others prefer to buy an existing business in which they see potential for growth. This does not make a person any less entrepreneurial. In fact, some of the most successful entrepreneurial ventures stem from **modifications** or changes that one person has made to another person's idea. One such success story is that of the founder of the McDonald's chain of fast-food restaurants. In 1954, a salesman named Ray Kroc visited a hamburger stand in California owned by Dick and Mac McDonald. He was very impressed by the quality and speed of service—he knew that this type of restaurant could be successful all over the country. In 1955, Ray obtained franchising rights from the brothers. This agreement allowed him to open other, similar restaurants under one central management. Eventually, he bought out the McDonald brothers and in 1965, McDonald's went public. The rest is history.

Paul Dumas, of Terrebonne, Quebec, is a franchisee of five McDonald's restaurants. He not only runs a successful franchising venture, he also applies his entrepreneurial skills to raise money for local children's charity. He believes that you need to put something back into the community that gives you business. As a result of Paul's efforts, $177 000 has been raised by his staff for charity in 2000, and he was presented with one of the company's most prestigious international awards in recognition of his extraordinary efforts.

YOUR TURN

1. What is intrapreneurship? How does it help an organization gain market share?

2. What organizations in your community encourage intrapreneurship? What services in particular do they provide?

3. In pairs, identify an entrepreneurial venture operating in your local community.
    a) Is this venture a for-profit or a not-for-profit initiative?
    b) Does it provide a product or service? What is it?
    c) Is it large or small scale?
    d) Is it local, provincial, national, or international in scope? Why?
    e) In what ways does it take advantage of innovations in technology?

4. In a small group, share your research results about local entrepreneurs. Prepare a summary chart describing entrepreneurship in your community.

5. With your group, prepare a map or community directory to show the variety of entrepreneurial ventures operating in your community. Present your work to another group.

6. How can organizations benefit from intrapreneurship? Give examples.

Entrepreneurs: Made or Born?

Studies of entrepreneurs indicate that individuals whose parents or grandparents are self-employed are more likely to start their own businesses than individuals born into other families. This leads some people to the conclusion that entrepreneurs are born, not made. However, another possible conclusion is simply that these entrepreneurs were influenced by their family environment. Did they get caught up in the excitement of business-related talk around the dinner table? Did they share the satisfaction of success with a parent or other family member? Did they work for the family business when they were young?

Whether entrepreneurs are born or made is likely still to be debated many years from now. Even though heredity is important in establishing basic entrepreneurial traits, the influences of environment cannot be dismissed. These two factors often work together in shaping a future entrepreneur.

Although some entrepreneurs come from entrepreneurial families, many others do not. What all entrepreneurs do share, however, is a vision for the future and the willingness to take the risk of starting a venture.

Think About It

Do you think having parents who are entrepreneurs would contribute to the likelihood of becoming one yourself?

Venture Profile

YOU'RE HACKED—NOW HIRE ME

Julie Alnwick, Canadian Business

In March 1999, Curtis Penner, Steve Skoronski, Wil Hutchins, and Corey Auger began to check Calgary-based International Properties Group's computer system—from the outside. Realizing that the system was weak, they contacted company security and mocked the network's "hackability." Unimpressed, International Properties Group Ltd. (IPG) staff challenged them to hack into the network. In less than a week, the hackers produced IPG financials, databases, and scores of personal e-mails. IPG hired them on the spot.

It was the first contract for efinity Inc. The company's founders had just dropped out of the University of Calgary. They pooled their tuition funds to rent an office for a startup whose mission is ethical hacking—breaking into corporate information systems to find weaknesses. After a year and a half of taunting, being challenged, and hacking into other firms, efinity grew into a 10-person firm with clients like CIBC World Markets, Westcorp Inc., and CDL Systems Ltd. "That approach has worked again and again for us because there's not a lot to lose," says Penner, efinity's president. Taunts lead to contracts for security audits (including hacks) for which efinity charges up to $25 000. Profits last year totalled $125 000, and Penner anticipates revenue of $750 000 this year.

To better simulate a real breach of network security, efinity doesn't tell its clients exactly when it will attack. "We want to come across as a skilled attacker rather than someone who's just doing it from their home," says Skoronski. Audits test a company's defences, its reaction to apparent virus infection, and its susceptibility to denial-of-service (DOS)

attacks, in which many infected computers automatically ask for Web pages from a targeted site so fast that the system freezes. An audit includes a first check, risk assessment, and another check after fixes are made.

Skoronski swears efinity has hacked ethically since day one—if not earlier. At university, Skoronski hacked into a server, but didn't ferret out the juicy data; instead, he told the network administrator and helped fix the security hole. Now, that's an ethical hacker.

Exploring

1. What niche does efinity respond to?
2. How did the founders get their first client? Why did their strategy work?
3. Which characteristics of efinity make it an entrepreneurial venture?
4. Do you think that the venture has a chance for a successful future? Why or why not?
5. What impact has this venture had on the business community?

ACTIVITIES

FLASHBACKS

Choose four of the following concepts to explain to a partner. Then switch roles.

- Entrepreneurship involves the recognition of opportunities (needs, wants, and problems) and the gathering of resources in order to create a successful venture.
- Entrepreneurship is about finding a niche in the market.
- Entrepreneurship is important for the well-being of society.
- Entrepreneurial ventures can have many characteristics.
- Entrepreneurial ventures benefit from technology.
- Entrepreneurship is an increasingly common way of earning a living.
- Intrapreneurship helps larger companies be creative, responsive, and competitive.
- Entrepreneurship can come from modification of existing market concepts.
- Entrepreneurs are shaped by both inherited characteristics and experience.

LESSONS LEARNED

1. What does "entrepreneurship" mean?
2. What is the relationship between entrepreneurship and supply and demand?
3. Give an example of a market niche. Describe an enterprise that serves this niche.
4. Distinguish between the following characteristics of entrepreneurial ventures:
   a) for-profit and not-for-profit
   b) service and goods production
   c) local and national
   d) physical and virtual
5. How has NAFTA affected entrepreneurial opportunities?
6. What effect has changing technology had on entrepreneurial activities?
7. What is the oldest entrepreneurial venture in Canada?
8. Why do entrepreneurs need to keep track of demographic changes?

9. How does entrepreneurship create wealth in our society?
10. What is the relationship between intrapreneurship and entrepreneurship?
11. Are entrepreneurs born or made? Explain your answer.

Venturing Out

1. Form groups of five. Each member selects one of the following industries:
    a) music
    b) sports equipment
    c) fashion
    d) fast food
    e) media

    Suggest a number of ways in which a company within your chosen industry could encourage and benefit from intrapreneurship.

2. Work with a small group or in pairs. Search the Internet or newspapers and magazines to find information about three entrepreneurial ventures, each in a different industry sector or community. Prepare a profile of each venture using the characteristics of entrepreneurial ventures that you learned about in this chapter.

3. With a small group, prepare a list of ten successful ventures in your community. Choose from a variety of fields such as athletics, entertainment, music, community service, and home decorating. Create a chart that shows the venture characteristics of each business you chose.

4. Survey five students in your class to determine if they would like to own and operate a venture. Ask what kind of venture they would launch and why they would make this choice.

5. Use an Internet search engine to find five Web sites that offer entrepreneurial advice. List these sites and compare them.

> **E-Bits & Bytes**
>
> To do your research, visit www.business.nelson.com and follow the links to "entrepreneurial ventures."

Point of View

1. Select one of the entrepreneurial ventures from Question 3 in Venturing Out. Why might the person who began this venture feel proud of the impact his or her business has had on the community? Prepare a monologue from the entrepreneur's point of view.

2. How would starting a business change your life?

3. Is it better to start a large new venture or a small one? Why? Under what circumstances would you change your answer?

CHAPTER 2

Entrepreneurs and Enterprising People

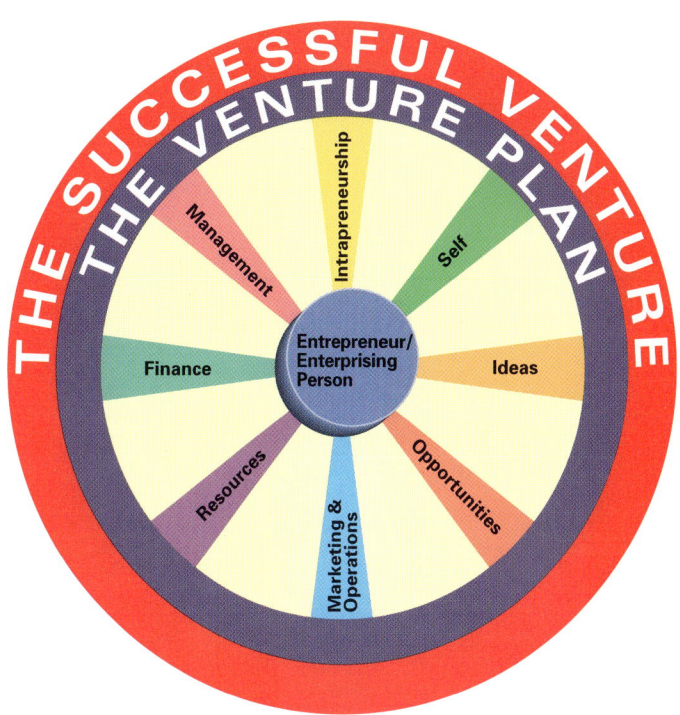

LEARNING OPPORTUNITIES

By the end of this chapter, you should be able to
- explain the entrepreneurial characteristics that play a role in successful entrepreneurial ventures
- compare the characteristics of an entrepreneur with those of an enterprising person
- identify factors that motivate entrepreneurs and enterprising people
- explain how an organization can encourage an enterprising spirit in its employees

Entrepreneurial Language

- value-added
- proprietary
- just-in-time
- mentor
- trade-off
- internal motivator
- external motivator
- workplace culture
- diorama

Talk with a partner about what you think each term might mean in a business context. Then check your predictions by looking at the Glossary.

Venture Profile

TALKING SUCCESS

*Susanne Baillie,
Profit magazine*

Need to call an overseas client but don't speak the language? Perhaps you need to read a menu in a foreign restaurant? Maureen Mitchells and her company, CanTalk Canada Inc., are aiming to put an end to such communication challenges. The Winnipeg-based firm offers rapid, on-demand, over-the-phone language interpretation and fax translation: **value-added** services, says Mitchells, to help customers open up new global markets, break down communication and cultural barriers, and improve customer relations. Mitchells, a former CBC-TV journalist and international marketing consultant, first got the idea after hearing a radio interview about a U.S.-based company that provided emergency translation services. Canada has a rich multicultural and linguistic makeup, she mused: "I thought why not throw it into hospitality, finance, or even tourism?" But five years ago, those industries weren't yet ready to embrace the global marketplace or her translation services. Instead, Mitchells found a niche providing telecommunications companies, such as Teleglobe Inc., with foreign-language operator services, including international collect calling and directory assistance. The demand for these language services was growing, and Teleglobe's in-house divisions couldn't keep pace. CanTalk stepped in, offering third party translation services through its certified interpreters and translators. CanTalk's edge? Says Mitchells: "We are nimble, quick, and highly customized."

CONTINUED

CanTalk has another key advantage: **proprietary** software that helps track, analyze, and then forecast call volumes and the different languages that come into CanTalk's call centre. The tool allows CanTalk to staff and schedule employees on a **just-in-time** basis, thereby cutting costs and improving services.

The concept is working: CanTalk's 150 employees manage more than 300 000 calls a month, offering services in 93 languages to 160 countries. And CanTalk is still looking forward. The company is now developing new methods of service delivery, including applications for wireless communication devices, Internet conferencing, and other new services. Mitchells foresees CanTalk as a virtual global network of translators and interpreters capable of translating any language into any other.

"The combinations are staggering," says Mitchells. "But it's nothing more complex than helping people communicate."

Venture Profile

THEY ARE IT

Sharlene Azam, The Toronto Star

What would you do if you could do anything you wanted? Jennifer Corriero, 20, and Michael Furdyk, 18, asked that question, and they are now taking their answer global.

"We were in Ottawa, rollerblading on Parliament Hill, when we decided that, if we could do anything we wanted, we would work together to create a global network for young people who have an idea they want to develop or who want the opportunity to work on someone else's project."

They have already secured the initial round of funding for their not-for-profit company, TakingITGlobal. TakingITGlobal is meant to help young people use technology to achieve their goals by providing **mentors**, technical resources, and help from their peers. Corriero and Furdyk hope that it will provide a learning option that complements traditional schooling.

The pair credit their success to simply following their curiosity. "I got interested in the Internet when my friend's dad asked me to set up his e-mail," says Furdyk. "I was in grade 8 and I didn't know how to do it, but I told him I could figure it out and I did."

That was in early 1996. By the end of that year, Furdyk had started MyDesktop.com with two other young partners, Michael Hayman and Albert Lai. Last year, they sold their startup, which provides information about computer sites, for more than $1 million.

Furdyk and Hayman have started a new company called BuyBuddy.com which provides consumer-oriented computer product information.

CONTINUED→

Corriero thinks of herself as a late bloomer when it comes to technology, unlike Furdyk. She isn't even a millionaire yet.

"It wasn't until I was hired at a multimedia company in 1997 that I learned about the Internet. My first project was to work with four older techie guys to develop a Web site for a client. I led the group and the project by being the first to learn Flash," she says.

Corriero and Furdyk met while working together on a project.

Her fearlessness and skills helped her snag the opportunity to design and facilitate the GirlsAreIt conference in 1998. The conference was a Canada-wide government- and industry-backed project to encourage girls to get familiar with the Internet.

Soon after, Corriero met Canadian feminist and philanthropist Nancy Ruth. "She hired me and a few other girls to create the Web site coolgirls.org, an adjunct to coolwomen.org, a site Ruth started about amazing women, past and present." Amid these projects, Corriero was still in high school.

"There are opportunities for people to make a difference," Corriero says. "It's not as much about the technology as it is about the purpose and vision behind it."

Exploring

Compare these two technology-based ventures:
1. What need or want is being addressed in each of these ventures?
2. How is TakingITGlobal similar to CanTalk? How is it different?
3. What innovation or new creation was involved in each venture?
4. Use information from the articles and photographs to write a character sketch of Maureen Mitchells, Jennifer Corriero, or Michael Furdyk. Include the risks or chances each person took, and why the person was motivated to take these risks.

Starting Up

Make a checklist of the qualities you think successful entrepreneurs have. As you read this chapter, add to your list. Put an ✗ beside those qualities you feel you have. Put a ✓ beside those qualities you would like to work on.

"Striving for success requires individuals to stretch themselves, reach outside their comfort zone, and challenge their own limits."

Entrepreneurs

The individuals described in the Venture Profiles share characteristics that are common to many entrepreneurs. Each person saw an opportunity to satisfy a need or want, and responded by initiating a change. In the process, they brought together the resources they needed to start a venture.

Maureen Mitchells's experiences as a journalist and international marketing consultant helped her become aware of people's need to communicate in many languages. As she pursued the idea of offering translation services, she adjusted her vision to meet market demands and took advantage of developing technology to provide a highly valued service.

Jennifer Corriero and Michael Furdyk noticed that other young people had good ideas but needed technological help to develop them. Corriero and Furdyk decided what they wanted to accomplish and brought together the resources they needed to achieve their vision.

Entrepreneurs are often agents of change. Because of Maureen Mitchells, international telecommunications companies are now able to offer their customers quick service in the language of their choice. Because of Jennifer Corriero and Michael Furdyk, young people interested in starting a technology-based project have a "one-stop shop" that offers them assistance.

These entrepreneurs identified, measured, and then minimized the risks associated with their ventures. By taking controlled and calculated risks, they were able to increase their chances for success. Striving for success requires individuals to stretch themselves, reach outside their comfort zone, and challenge their own limits. Every time an individual succeeds in an entrepreneurial or intrapreneurial activity, it is because they took a calculated risk. The risk is often perceived by others to be much greater than it really is. Entrepreneurs and enterprising people have done their homework, have put their safeguards in place, and are prepared to take a controlled risk. Many individuals are immobilized by the possibility of failing and are not prepared to take any risk.

Entrepreneurs must set goals to help themselves stay on track. Maureen Mitchells's goal was to help people communicate across language barriers. Jennifer Corriero and Michael Furdyk's goal was to provide technological assistance to other young people interested in working on a project. To identify their goals, entrepreneurs look for something unique that will meet a need, satisfy a want, or solve a problem. They spend a lot of time asking "What if?" and "Why not?"

They question and explore every aspect of an idea until they can see its potential. Then, they develop a vision and work diligently, continuing to ask and answer questions even after the venture is launched.

CHARACTERISTICS OF SUCCESSFUL ENTREPRENEURS

Although no two entrepreneurs are exactly alike, they may share common traits. Many of the characteristics identified in the Venture Wheel below can be learned and developed by individuals who want to become successful entrepreneurs.

International NEWS

When Karl Ulrich, a professor at The Wharton School, Philadelphia, started Nova Cruz Products, he had no idea the worldwide demand for his scooters would grow so quickly. The Internet provided a level playing field for his new startup to build customer relations all over the world.

How did the invention of the Xootr "meet a need, satisfy a want, or solve a problem"?

ENTREPRENEURIAL CHARACTERISTICS

- Self-confident
- Perceptive
- Hard-working
- Motivated
- Resourceful
- Able to manage risk
- Creative
- Goal-oriented
- Optimistic
- Flexible
- Independent
- Visionary
- Able to get along with others

Entrepreneur/Enterprising Person

SELF-CONFIDENT

Successful entrepreneurs are realistic about what they can accomplish. They believe in themselves and in their ability to succeed. They set attainable goals and approach them with confidence.

PERCEPTIVE

Entrepreneurs are intuitive. They know what is going on. They are able to identify problems as they arise and find creative solutions.

■ HARD-WORKING

Entrepreneurs work long and hard to achieve success. A successful entrepreneur needs the stamina that comes from good physical and mental health. To maintain energy, entrepreneurs must carefully balance their commitment to work with their commitment to other aspects of their lives, such as family and friends.

■ MOTIVATED

Entrepreneurs are driven by an internal need for accomplishment. They will actively seek opportunities for success, both at work and elsewhere.

■ RESOURCEFUL

Entrepreneurs explore, ask questions, and generally use all their resources to find ways to achieve their goals. They often develop a broad network of associates who can help them find ways to overcome obstacles in their paths.

■ ABLE TO MANAGE RISK

Entrepreneurs view risk as a challenge to be overcome. They calculate and measure it and look for ways to gain control over the outcome. Entrepreneurs will take a risk if it is a calculated one—where the chances for success are greater than the chances for failure. They are willing to take on a certain degree of risk because of the potential rewards involved in being agents of change.

■ CREATIVE

Entrepreneurs look at the world in new and different ways. They enjoy challenges and feel comfortable with ambiguity. They do not sit and wait for things to happen. Instead, entrepreneurs take charge of shaping the world around them in a way that benefits them and others.

■ GOAL-ORIENTED

Entrepreneurs work determinedly toward goals they have set for themselves. Once their initial goals are achieved, they set new goals and begin the process again. Personal satisfaction and the need for accomplishment give them momentum as they continue to move forward.

■ OPTIMISTIC

Entrepreneurs have a positive mental attitude. Minor setbacks or roadblocks do not discourage them. They believe they can touch the future and are enthusiastic about what it holds.

Worth Repeating

"Whether you think you can or you can't, you're right."

Henry Ford, founder of the Ford Motor Company

What does this quote mean? Do you agree with Ford? Give an example from your own experiences.

▌ FLEXIBLE

Entrepreneurs are able to adjust to the changing marketplace, to technology, and to competition. If one idea doesn't work the way they expect, they look for other options.

▌ INDEPENDENT

Entrepreneurs need the freedom to make their own decisions and their own mistakes. They do not respond well to being managed by others. For this reason, they often leave secure jobs to move out on their own. Being the person in charge gives them control over their own destiny.

▌ VISIONARY

Entrepreneurs have a vision of how things should be in the future. This is what gives them the strength to continue step by step toward their goals. To bring about the changes they foresee, they must not only understand their vision themselves but must also be able to communicate it to others.

▌ ABLE TO GET ALONG WITH OTHERS

Entrepreneurs seldom work alone. Most gather a team around them, carefully choosing team members who will help them realize their goals. Successful entrepreneurs have insight into the abilities and personalities of others, which enables them to build an effective team.

▌ ENTREPRENEURIAL SKILLS

In addition to entrepreneurial characteristics, entrepreneurs require certain skills to ensure the success of their ventures. These skills can all be learned. Successful entrepreneurs are able to

- communicate—listen, speak, and write
- generate ideas
- identify opportunities
- plan
- organize
- make decisions
- solve problems
- negotiate
- network
- market their ideas
- keep records (financial and others)
- lead others

Agents of Change

Twenty-six-year-old Chris Piché began his entrepreneurial career at age 12. An avid computer whiz, Piché developed custom accounting software for his father, a financial adviser, and for his dad's friends and clients. He not only earned a few thousand dollars selling his software but also gained the confidence to tackle bigger projects. Says Piché: "It's always fun, when you are 12, to be smarter than adults." He is now CEO of Eyeball.com Network Inc., one of Canada's fastest-growing startups.

Rick Kang, Profit magazine

Because of his age, what challenges do you think Chris Piché might have faced as an entrepreneur?

E-Bits & Bytes

"Economies around the world are undergoing a wholesale rejuvenation; businesses are reinventing themselves. In this new economy, the Internet and technologies like the Java platform have helped businesses streamline business processes, have helped companies compete in new ways, and have engendered altogether new types of business opportunities. It is clear we are on the cusp of a new era."

Dr. Alan Baratz, President, Java Software, Sun Microsystems, Inc.

What do you think business might be like in the "new era" anticipated by Dr. Alan Baratz?

Although all of these skills can be learned, many entrepreneurs recognize that it is sometimes more effective to hire talented, enterprising people with the skills they lack to complement their own skills.

Entrepreneurs are explorers, adventurers, and conquerors. They are always analyzing and conceptualizing. Observant of their surroundings, they are pulled in the direction of new opportunities.

Some people are drawn into entrepreneurship by a vision of the creative possibilities. Others are fascinated by the prospect of being their own boss. Sometimes, people are pushed into entrepreneurship. They may have experienced a lack of power and influence in their work environment, or they may have been unable to find work in their chosen field.

In starting and operating their own ventures, entrepreneurs take on many roles:

- inventor
  They develop new ideas for products, processes, or services.
- innovator
  They improve existing products, processes, or services.
- manager
  They set goals and develop a plan to achieve them.
- administrator
  They implement the plan to achieve the goals.
- leader
  They create the vision and communicate it to others.

YOUR TURN

1. Review the entrepreneurial characteristics and skills you have just read about. Identify situations in your own life where you have demonstrated any five of these.

2. Construct a database of entrepreneurs you have met in Venture Profiles so far. Include each person's name and venture. List the entrepreneurial characteristics and skills each person has demonstrated. Give evidence from the Venture Profiles to support your opinion. Add to the database as you read other profiles.

3. With a partner, brainstorm the names of some entrepreneurs in your community. Choose one person from your list and record all the entrepreneurial characteristics and skills this person demonstrates. If you do not know the person, you might want to call or visit him or her at work to conduct an interview. Support your ideas with examples.

WHAT MAKES AN ENTREPRENEUR TICK?

Entrepreneurs are motivated by a number of different factors. The following lists indicate those motivating factors that entrepreneurs consider to be most important and those they consider to be least important.

MOST IMPORTANT

- to achieve a sense of personal accomplishment
- to be my own boss
- to have an element of variety and adventure
- to make better use of my training and skills
- to have considerable freedom to adopt my own approach to work
- to be challenged by the problems and opportunities of starting and growing a new business venture

LEAST IMPORTANT

- to continue a family tradition
- to do the only thing I could
- to contribute to the welfare of my ethnic group
- to leave an insecure work environment
- to follow the example of a person I admire

Although the individual characteristics and motivations of each entrepreneur contribute to the success of his or her venture, additional influences—such as education, family background, values and attitudes, political structure, and competition—also play an important role. Entrepreneurial initiative will arise from the various environments, experiences, and educational opportunities afforded to an individual. The more supportive the family, society, and the current government, the greater the likelihood that the venture will succeed.

Worth Repeating

"It's important that entrepreneurs set goals and go for what is important to them and makes them happy. When you are enthusiastic and love what you do, success is obtainable."

*Tracey Aylward,
Aylward Group of Companies*

Cool Stuff

Canadians are moving toward high-speed Internet access faster than any other country in the world. At the end of 1999, 606 000 Canadians had high-speed access. By 2002, this number is expected to reach 3.3 million. Experts predict that an important result of this change will be the universal adoption of online marketing, online shopping, and Webcasting, or online television. In fact, it will be possible to conduct all transactions and make all payments online.

How might Webcasting change the nature of television?

Venture Profile

THE MARATHON OF HOPE

Leslie Scrivener, excerpted from Terry Fox: His Story

September 1, 1980—it was a dull day in Northern Ontario when Terry Fox ran his last miles. For 3339 miles [5372 km], from St. John's, Newfoundland, he had run through six provinces and now was two-thirds of the way home. He had run close to a marathon a day, for 144 days. No mean achievement for an able-bodied runner, an extraordinary feat for an amputee.

Terry's left leg was strong and muscular. His right was a mere stump fitted with an artificial limb made of fibreglass and steel. He had lost the leg to cancer when he was 18.

He was 22 now, curly haired, good looking, sunburned. He was strong, willful, and stubborn. His run, the Marathon of Hope as he called it, a quixotic adventure across Canada that defied logic and common sense, was his way of repaying a debt.

Terry believed that he had won his fight against the illness, and he wanted to raise money, $1 million perhaps, to fight it. Certainly, he showed there were no limits to what an amputee could do. He changed people's attitude toward the disabled, and he showed that while cancer had claimed his leg, his spirit was unbreakable.

His Marathon of Hope had started as an improbable dream—two friends, one to drive the van, one to run, a ribbon of highway, and the sturdy belief that they could perform a miracle.

The administrators of the Canadian Cancer Society were skeptical about his success, when Terry approached them. They doubted he could raise $1 million and, as a test of his sincerity, told him to earn some seed money and find some corporate sponsors. They believed they would never hear from him again.

But Terry persevered, earning sponsors and the promise of promotion from the Cancer Society. On April 12, 1980, he dipped his artificial leg in the murky waters of St. John's harbour and set off on the greatest adventure of his life.

CONTINUED→

"I loved it," Terry said. "I enjoyed myself so much and that was what other people couldn't realize. They thought I was going through a nightmare running all day long. Even though it was so difficult, there was not another thing in the world I would rather have been doing."

Donations poured in. Reading of Terry's goals, Isadore Sharp, President and CEO of Four Seasons Hotels and Resorts, was also caught up in the dream of the Marathon of Hope. He pledged $10 000 to the marathon and challenged 999 other Canadian corporations to do the same.

If $1 million toward cancer research was within reach, why not $1 from every Canadian, why not a goal of $23 million? The money came in many ways. People waited for hours on the roadside to watch Terry pass. Sometimes a stranger would press a $100 bill into his hand as he ran by.

"How many people do something they really believe in? I just wish people would realize that anything's possible, if you try; dreams are made, if people try. When I started this run, I said that if we all gave $1, we'd have $23 million for cancer research, and I don't care, man, there's no reason that isn't possible. No reason. I'd like to see everybody go kind of wild, inspired with the fundraising."

Terry's run ended at Thunder Bay, Ontario, when doctors discovered that cancer had spread from his legs to his lungs. In less than 48 hours, the CTV television network arranged a special telethon and by the end had raised more than $10 million.

Isadore Sharp sent a telegram that Terry pinned to his hospital bed. He said that Terry's marathon was just the beginning and that a fundraising run would be held in his name every year to continue his fight against cancer. "You started it. We will not rest until your dream to find a cure for cancer is realized."

In 1980, donations to Terry's Marathon of Hope had reached $23.4 million. The marathon continues to raise huge sums of money every year.

Copyright © 2000 The Terry Fox Foundation. All rights reserved.

E-Bits & Bytes

For links to The Terry Fox Foundation, visit www.business.nelson.com. Review their Web site and any other literature you can find about Terry Fox. Write a letter to the organization outlining how Terry's vision has made a difference in your community.

Exploring

1. What characteristics did Terry Fox display?
2. How are these characteristics like or different from those of Maureen Mitchells, Jennifer Corriero, and Michael Furdyk?
3. Describe Terry's vision. How did he communicate it to others?
4. What motivated Terry?
5. Isadore Sharp is also mentioned in this profile. What characteristics does he appear to have? Conduct research to find out more about him, or another enterprising person from your community who helps others, and prepare a class presentation.

Worth Repeating

Wisdom comes from good judgment.
Good judgment comes from experience.
Experience comes from mistakes.
Mistakes come from bad judgment.

Chinese proverb

How does this proverb apply to an entrepreneur or to an enterprising person?

Enterprising People

Terry Fox was an enterprising person. He had many of the same characteristics and skills that entrepreneurs have. Enterprising people are like entrepreneurs in many ways. They are

- self-confident
- perceptive
- hard-working
- motivated
- creative
- goal-oriented
- optimistic

Entrepreneurs usually begin as enterprising people. However, not all enterprising people become entrepreneurs. Some enterprising people do not like to take financial risks. They may pursue their visions as intrapreneurs, or they may try to accomplish their goals in their spare time. Only those who are prepared to assume the financial risk involved in starting a business venture will become true entrepreneurs.

Like Terry Fox, many enterprising people are agents of social change. They respond to needs and wants in order to improve the lives of others or to contribute to the community.

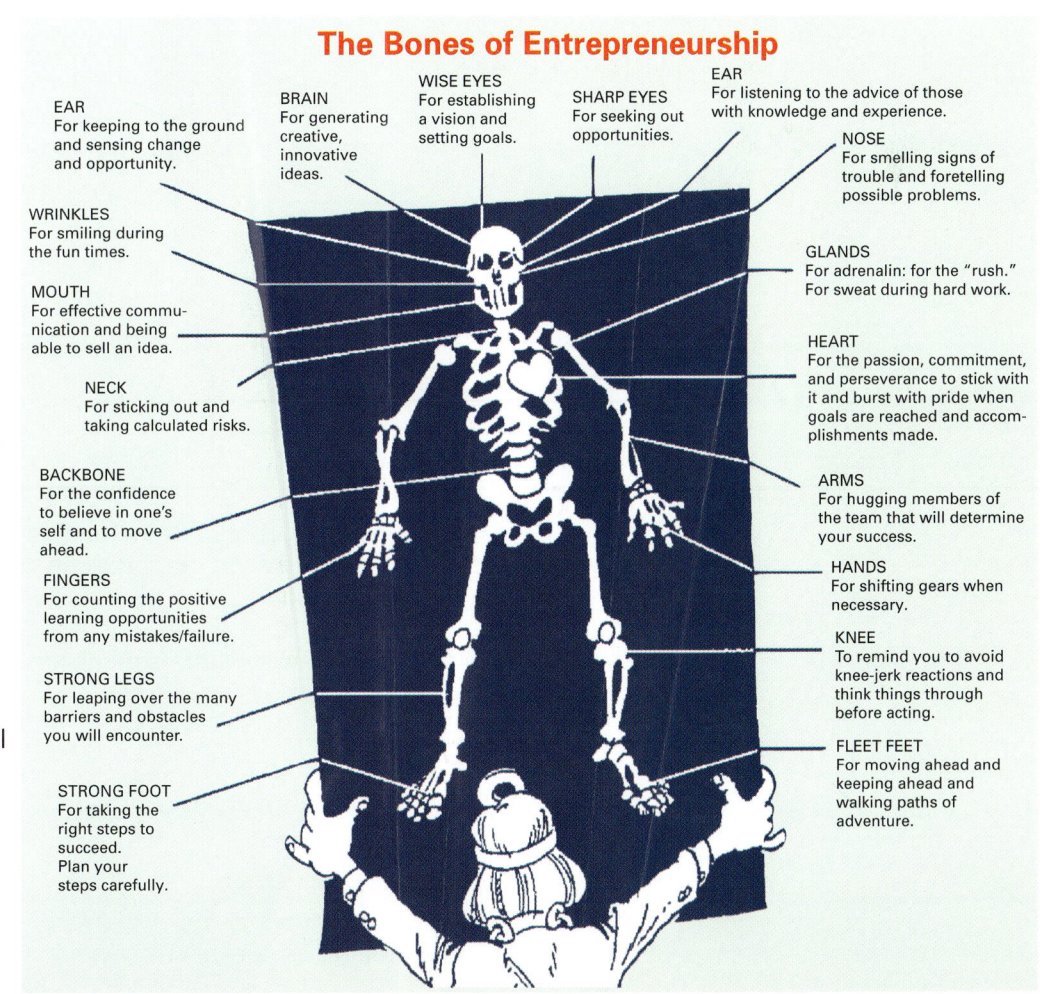

The Bones of Entrepreneurship

EAR For keeping to the ground and sensing change and opportunity.

WRINKLES For smiling during the fun times.

MOUTH For effective communication and being able to sell an idea.

NECK For sticking out and taking calculated risks.

BACKBONE For the confidence to believe in one's self and to move ahead.

FINGERS For counting the positive learning opportunities from any mistakes/failure.

STRONG LEGS For leaping over the many barriers and obstacles you will encounter.

STRONG FOOT For taking the right steps to succeed. Plan your steps carefully.

BRAIN For generating creative, innovative ideas.

WISE EYES For establishing a vision and setting goals.

SHARP EYES For seeking out opportunities.

EAR For listening to the advice of those with knowledge and experience.

NOSE For smelling signs of trouble and foretelling possible problems.

GLANDS For adrenalin: for the "rush." For sweat during hard work.

HEART For the passion, commitment, and perseverance to stick with it and burst with pride when goals are reached and accomplishments made.

ARMS For hugging members of the team that will determine your success.

HANDS For shifting gears when necessary.

KNEE To remind you to avoid knee-jerk reactions and think things through before acting.

FLEET FEET For moving ahead and keeping ahead and walking paths of adventure.

Figure 2.1 Bones, the entrepreneurial person, illustrates many of the characteristics and skills possessed by entrepreneurs and enterprising people.

Agents of Change

When famous pop singer Sarah McLachlan was told she could not choose a female opening act for her show because her promoters thought that fans would not pay to see two female singers on stage, she set out to prove them wrong. She created Lilith Fair by putting 12 women on one bill. It played 139 concerts in three years, grossing more than $60 million.

How was Sarah McLachlan an "agent of social change"?

Enterprising Employees

All entrepreneurs are enterprising people but not all enterprising people are entrepreneurs.

Statistics point to the fact that the need for enterprising people is growing. As large organizations continue to look for leading-edge employees who are flexible and responsive and can deliver services more effectively and efficiently, there will be opportunities for enterprising people to move into leadership positions.

Enterprising employees work for someone else for a variety of reasons. They may not be willing or able to take personal financial risks. When an enterprising employee is hired, the employer bears the financial risk in return for the value the enterprising person will bring to the organization.

Enterprising employees may not view job security as the most important consideration. They take responsibility for their own career paths and believe that frequent job changes are important in career growth.

They work for the following reasons:

- to feel connected and belong to a group with a common goal
- to make a living
- to gain a sense of personal accomplishment
- to experience a sense of self-worth
- to be identified with a vocation or organization
- to structure their time
- to impose a rhythm on their lives
- to achieve feelings of satisfaction and well-being
- to shape and influence the world around them

Think About It

What might happen if a person allowed one of the five choices—meaningful work, leisure time, learning new skills, money, or security—to become *too* important?

Enterprising people make choices about the kinds of work they do, and the organizations and individuals they work for. They seek jobs that offer

- meaningful work—often something that contributes to the well-being of others
- leisure time to spend with friends and family, and on activities they enjoy
- a chance to learn new skills
- money
- security

Enterprising people make **trade-offs** among the five choices. The trade-offs reflect what each individual values most.

One enterprising person may choose to work for a not-for-profit organization doing important work for the community but earning less money than in the private sector. Another enterprising person may opt to work for a large corporation that offers flextime, making it possible to spend more time with family.

What Motivates You to Excel?

Most people need to earn money to live, but money is not usually what motivates employees to excel. An abundance of research tells us that employee recognition is a key factor in motivating enterprising employees.

Think about how you feel when someone you respect gives you a compliment. Receiving this recognition helps you feel good about yourself, increases your confidence, and encourages you to try even harder to do a good job.

Self-esteem, or how you feel about yourself, is an **internal motivator** that lasts a lifetime. Money is an **external motivator** that is never lasting. Even if you manage to earn a consistently high income throughout your working career, this earning power will decrease when you retire. Your self-esteem, on the other hand, will never leave you.

Worth Repeating

"Many people fail to achieve their goals because they have grown so comfortable in their job that they are afraid to meet the challenges of a new one."

Harvey Mackay, business motivational speaker

What does "growing comfortable in a job" mean? In what other ways might it be a negative thing for an employee?

Chapter 2 ♦ Entrepreneurs and Enterprising People 37

Worth Repeating

"Experience is that marvelous thing that enables you to recognize a mistake when you make it again."

Franklin P. Jones, former president of American Management Assoc.

Enterprising employers encourage their employees to treat mistakes as opportunities. How might a mistake have positive results for an employee? for the employer? How can a mistake at school have positive results for you?

SUPPORTING ENTERPRISING EMPLOYEES

Enterprising employees contribute to the success of their employers. They behave in ways that propel the organization forward. They are flexible, responsible, customer-focused, and achievement-oriented. Enterprising people have a greater comfort with ambiguity and uncertainty. The challenge for employers is to create an environment that empowers employees to reach their full potential and to communicate a compelling vision of the future.

To meet this challenge, employers need to

- create a **workplace culture** where employees feel their input is valued and where it is safe to make and learn from mistakes
- provide the tools needed to achieve desired results
- offer meaningful work that adds value to society
- provide alternate work arrangements, such as flextime or telecommuting, so employees can balance their work with other aspects of their lives
- support employees with benefit packages that meet their needs at various life stages

YOUR TURN

1. Draw a Venn diagram, such as the one below, to compare the factors that motivate an entrepreneur and an enterprising person. Do you see yourself more as an entrepreneur or an enterprising person? Explain.

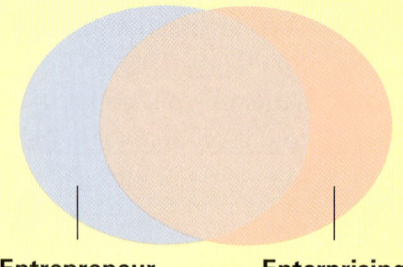

   Entrepreneur / Enterprising Person

2. Enterprising people often make trade-offs that reflect their personal values. Refer to the Venture Profiles at the beginning of this chapter. What trade-offs did each person make?

3. Why do companies need enterprising employees? Why do enterprising people like ambiguity and uncertainty?

4. How can employers motivate enterprising employees?

5. Think about a time in your life when you had to make a trade-off. Describe the situation. What choice did you make? Why?

6. Prepare a two-column chart. Label the first column "Internal Motivators" and the second column "External Motivators." List at least three factors that motivate you to achieve your goals in each column. Compare your list with a partner's.

7. Why do you think self-esteem is such an important ingredient in the success of an enterprising person?

8. Suppose you are an enterprising employee at an international corporation. Next week, you will receive a visit from a customer who lives in another country. With a partner, decide what country or cultural group this customer is from, and why she or he is visiting your workplace. Use the Internet, library, and current periodicals to conduct research that would assist you in preparing for the visit. Consider the following in your research: customs and traditions of their home country, normal business hours and practices, status of women in business, entertainment expectations and concerns. Share your findings with the class. Do you think your research reflects the approach of an enterprising employee rather than that of just any employee? What might be the differences between the two approaches?

Venture Profile

TECHNOLOGICAL INNOVATOR

Printed with acknowledgment to Ontario Prospects

At 21, Wade Cachagee and his partner, Kevin Linquist, established CREE-TECH Inc. Based in the Fox Lake Reserve in Northern Ontario, the company uses Geographical Information Systems (GIS) technology to provide to its clients computer-generated information for resource management.

Three years later, with Wade as president, CREE-TECH's clients included forestry companies, Aboriginal organizations, and the Ontario government. One of CREE-TECH's clients is one of the world's largest pulp and paper companies, as well as one of the largest users of recycled paper. CREE-TECH's prosperity does not come without great effort—Wade works an average of 65 hours a week.

As a member of the Chapleau Cree First Nation, Wade is especially pleased that his technology helps people make decisions that support "sustainable" forestry development. "Within forestry management, GIS technology now largely replaces manual mapping techniques to project future growth and manage our land. We analyze and project how the trees that are cut down can be replaced by new growth."

Protecting Native values and culture is also important to CREE-TECH. To do this, the company does cultural value inventories. For example, "We look at the current state of parts of the ecosystem, such as the nests of eagles, sites of other endangered or protected species, trapping lines, and the growth of plants used in traditional medicine, to ensure they are protected." CREE-TECH's motto sums it up: "Use tomorrow's technologies to manage today's resources."

Wade studied at Algonquin and Mohawk Colleges. Kevin was a professional forester

CONTINUED➡

who had his own business before they teamed up. Wade makes it a point to continually seek advice from other business people. "My mother and father have both served as chief of our First Nation for several years. I am lucky to have the mentorship of my parents to guide me through my career."

Has his age ever been a barrier?

"In a few cases, when I have met with new clients, I've sensed some hesitation which is soon overcome when they see the professionalism that comes out of our offices."

Why is CREE-TECH so successful?

"As a younger, smaller company we focus on innovation and technological expertise to compete with more established companies."

Exploring

1. Using evidence from the Venture Profile, show how CREE-TECH is an enterprising work environment.
2. How did Wade ensure the success of the venture?
3. What characteristics and skills does Wade demonstrate? Give evidence from the profile.
4. Create a piece of art that captures CREE-TECH's vision for the environment. For example, you might choose to paint a picture, present a poem you have written in a dramatic reading, or write and record a song. If you wish, you could design an interactive computer presentation that incorporates visuals and sounds.

ACTIVITIES

FLASHBACKS

Using the statements below as guidelines, discuss with a partner how entrepreneurs and enterprising people are alike and different.

- Entrepreneurs bring together the resources needed to initiate change in response to an identified need or want.
- Entrepreneurs have the characteristics and skills to act on their vision.
- Entrepreneurs take controllable risks.
- Entrepreneurs are goal-oriented and self-confident.
- Enterprising people have many of the same characteristics and skills that entrepreneurs have.
- Enterprising employees are in high demand.
- Employers of enterprising employees need to create a culture that supports them.

LESSONS LEARNED

1. Identify the characteristics that entrepreneurs share.

2. What are the most important motivating factors for entrepreneurs? the least motivating?

3. In a table such as the following, list the advantages and disadvantages of being an entrepreneur. Then, compare and contrast your findings with a partner.

Advantages	Disadvantages
independence of being your own boss	lack of people to confide in

4. Hold a class debate on this topic: "It's great to make mistakes."

VENTURING OUT

1. Identify three Canadian entrepreneurs. Research them using the Internet, library, and current periodicals, or conduct personal interviews. Concentrate on the characteristics that contributed to each entrepreneur's success. Add these entrepreneurs to your database.

2. Choose one of the entrepreneurs you researched for Question 1. Write a Venture Profile about this person.

> Whenever you are planning to conduct an interview, start by making an appointment or arranging to send the interview questions by e-mail. Be sure to follow up with a thank-you note.

3. With a group, prepare a list of 10 achievers from a field such as athletics, art, music, community service, or business. Identify the personal characteristics of each individual. Compare these to the attributes of a typical entrepreneur or enterprising person.

4. Suppose you have been asked to hire a marketing manager for a large corporation. With a partner, brainstorm a list of interview questions that will help you determine whether or not a candidate is an enterprising person.

   Change partners and conduct your interview. Record the answers. Then, let your partner interview you. Change partners again to interview someone else. Compare the answers you heard. Which person would you hire? Why?

5. Assume you are going to be an entrepreneur. Describe what your life will be like. Consider hours of work, income, family needs, leisure time, commitment to your employees, business travel, leisure travel, household responsibilities, and community responsibilities.

6. Why do you think individuals become entrepreneurs? Talk to two entrepreneurs in your community and ask why they chose to start their own business ventures.

7. In groups of four, brainstorm the characteristics of a workplace that would encourage employees to behave in enterprising ways. Write a short profile of this company describing its key features, or create a **diorama**. Be prepared to explain how your diorama demonstrates these key features.

8. List the characteristics of successful entrepreneurs and the advantages of being an entrepreneur. What connections can you find between the two lists?

E-Bits & Bytes

Visit www.business.nelson.com to find out about the youth programs on entrepreneurship in your area.

POINT OF VIEW

Select a book or movie about an entrepreneur or an enterprising person. After reading the book or viewing the movie, prepare a multimedia presentation for your classmates about the person. After you have completed your presentation, answer the following questions in your journal or portfolio.

1. What did you learn from the book or movie that you did not already know?

2. How does what you learned connect with what you already knew, including what you learned in this chapter?

3. How and for what purpose could you use what you learned?

CHAPTER 3

Assessing Your Entrepreneurial Potential

THE SUCCESSFUL VENTURE — THE VENTURE PLAN

Entrepreneur/Enterprising Person — Self, Ideas, Opportunities, Marketing & Operations, Resources, Finance, Management, Intrapreneurship

LEARNING OPPORTUNITIES

By the end of this chapter, you should be able to
- explain the strategies young entrepreneurs may undertake to overcome challenges and take advantage of opportunities
- understand the importance of goal setting and planning to successful entrepreneurial activity
- identify and classify your own goals
- recognize that entrepreneurial success involves a wide range of skills
- assess your own enterprising/entrepreneurial qualities and describe situations in which you have been enterprising
- recognize the importance of the entrepreneur to the venture creation process

Entrepreneurial Language

- credit history
- collateral
- red tape
- infrastructure
- goal
- steppingstone
- milestone
- target date
- SWOT analysis
- incremental problem solving
- out-of-the-box thinking
- interpersonal skills
- critical-thinking skills
- creative-thinking skills
- practical skills

Sometimes a prefix can help you figure out what a word means. Use a dictionary to find the meaning of each of these prefixes: col-, infra-, in-, inter-. Tell what each prefix has to do with the meaning of one word on this list.

Venture Profile

TURNING A PROBLEM INTO AN OPPORTUNITY

Brett and Devon Cranson were 14 and 12, respectively, when they spotted an opportunity. Both passionate hockey players, they got tired of having to end their shinny games on the street at sunset, instead of playing through to the end of the game. One day their mother said, "Stop complaining and do something about it!"

That's exactly what they did. Brett and Devon turned this problem into an opportunity. They decided to start a roller hockey league for other hockey enthusiasts in the community. They surveyed friends, neighbours, and classmates to see if others were interested in paying for this service. The response was overwhelmingly positive. In the first year, they had 130 players. Since then, the league has grown over 30% each year so there are now over 1000 players.

It wasn't all easy, though. In that first year, they had to register players, confirm locations, buy insurance, open a business account at the bank, and deal with customers who weren't always easy to get along with.

Because of their ages, Brett and Devon had to have their father cosign for the insurance. No insurance company would sign a contract with someone under the age of 18, and the boys couldn't run the league without liability and accident insurance because of the potential risks.

Dealing with customers proved to be another challenge and a valuable learning experience. Once the teams were made up, the hockey politics began. Parents called to have their child play on a different team and, of course, that was not always possible. Brett and Devon learned from firsthand experience how to satisfy their customers without always giving the customers exactly what they thought they wanted.

The business has since expanded and Brett and Devon have brought their sister, Dayna, into the business, as well as many of their friends. The prospects look good. Roller hockey continues to be one of the fastest-growing sports. The obstacles faced by the Cranson brothers as teens are gradually dissipating as the boys gain experience, wisdom, and age.

Exploring

1. What challenges did Brett and Devon Cranson face? Which challenges were a result of their youth?
2. What helped the boys overcome these challenges?
3. What might Brett and Devon have learned from being young entrepreneurs?
4. Brett and Devon succeeded partly because of their passion for roller hockey. What hobbies or interests are passionate about? How could you turn one of these into a venture?

Starting Up

Everyone has goals. Thinking, talking, and writing about your goals will help you gain more control over your future. Talk with a partner about some of the goals you plan to achieve.

First Steps: Young Entrepreneurs

Many young people today choose to bet on themselves rather than taking a chance on a job. Becoming an entrepreneur offers independence, flexibility, and the potential for a great deal of satisfaction. According to a recent study called "New Perspectives on Nexus Generation" (Royal Bank of Canada, 1997), work is still an important factor in defining who a person is, but where and how work happens is changing dramatically. The Royal Bank uses the term Nexus Generation to refer to Canadians aged 18 to 35 in 1997. Figure 3.1 indicates the professions most desired by young people today.

Most Desirable Professions

Entrepreneur	32%
Filmmaker, artist, musician	28%
Executive at a large company	27%
Teacher	26%
Lawyer	23%
Doctor	20%
Director of a not-for-profit venture	18%
Stockbroker	8%
Politician	6%
Commissioned salesperson	5%

Figure 3.1 Nearly one-third of the 18- to 35-year-olds surveyed rated entrepreneurship as the most desirable profession.

According to the results of the survey, being an entrepreneur ranked as the most desirable profession for this group. It is important to note that the other career choices on the graph also require enterprising qualities like the ones illustrated by Bones on page 35 of Chapter 2. Enterprise is becoming an increasingly desired characteristic in the new economy. The concept of new economy will be examined in more detail in Chapter 4.

Brett and Devon Cranson nurtured their enterprising skills by starting and operating their own venture. The road to the success of the roller hockey league had its ups and downs, but their commitment to and passion for the vision sustained them through the rough parts.

Starting and operating a business at a young age poses significant challenges but offers significant benefits as well. For example, Brett and Devon learned firsthand about creative problem solving, financial and risk management, and customer service. In many ways, their experience has given them a head start. No matter what Brett and Devon choose to do in the future, they will use these skills and continue to develop them.

Entrepreneurs come from widely different backgrounds. They could be your friends, members of your family, your neighbours, or you. Entrepreneurs may be male or female, single or married, with or without business experience. What they do have in common is an idea, and a strong desire to develop that idea into a successful venture.

CHALLENGES FACING YOUNG ENTREPRENEURS

The greatest challenge facing young entrepreneurs is the lack of experience and knowledge they bring to a venture. Traditionally, young entrepreneurs have been viewed with caution by more experienced businesspeople. Fortunately, media interest in young entrepreneurs is at an all-time high. Coverage of entrepreneurial success stories has helped raise confidence in young entrepreneurs and their capacity to develop and operate successful ventures. Media interest also helps young entrepreneurs market their ventures with free publicity that adds credibility to their efforts.

Young entrepreneurs typically have no **credit history**, no **collateral**, and no track record in paying off debt. This makes financing the venture a real challenge. Obtaining suitable financing often requires people to complete a great deal of administrative work, commonly called **red tape**. There are many business startup programs available to help young entrepreneurs manoeuvre through the red tape. Most of these programs are free of charge and offer a range of services such as consulting, mentoring, and administration.

Worth Repeating

"You miss 100% of the shots you never take."

Wayne Gretzky, former NHL hockey player

How does Wayne Gretzky's advice apply to entrepreneurs?

Agents of Change

At 12, Scott Painter launched his first startup—a car-detailing business. Today, almost 20 years later, he and partner Bill Gross have found a way to take the misery out of car buying with their venture CarsDirect.com, a one-stop shop for car purchasing. Purchasers can research different cars, compare them, and buy them over the Net. Once the purchase or lease is made, buyers can add deals for car insurance, maintenance, and roadside service—all without ever having to leave home.

How might starting up so young have affected Scott's life/career as an entrepreneur? What might be the advantages and disadvantages of starting so early?

Think About It

What experiences have you had that might help you become an entrepreneur?

Working part-time or full-time will give you the opportunity to develop your enterprising and entrepreneurial skills.

THE VALUE OF EXPERIENCE

Part-time and summer work, volunteer opportunities, and school leadership positions offer young people opportunities to develop their enterprising and entrepreneurial skills. In each context, they can learn the importance of reliability, develop the ability to complete work quickly and accurately, and hone interpersonal skills as they deal with others.

If you plan to launch your own venture, working part-time or full-time in a related industry will give you the opportunity to

- learn about the **infrastructure**
- develop a positive reputation in the industry
- build a network of contacts
- earn money you can save for the future
- learn firsthand about the industry

Worth Repeating

"Obstacles are those frightful things you see when you take your mind off your goals."

Anonymous

The quotation above calls obstacles "frightful" things. Do you think this means that obstacles are bad things, or just that some people are afraid of them? Explain.

Setting Goals

A **goal** is the purpose of your work—the objective you wish to reach. To see how you are progressing toward the goal, you need to measure smaller steps along the way. You might think of these small steps as **steppingstones** and **milestones**. Each steppingstone can be achieved in a relatively short time. Milestones are more significant events that you reach by completing a number of steppingstones. For example, if your goal is to graduate from high school, the steppingstones might be the passing grades you earn for individual assignments and tests, while the milestones would be the credits you earn for passing courses. Goals should always follow the SMART principle—they should be Simple, Measurable, Achievable, Realistic, and Timely.

Chapter 3 ◆ Assessing Your Entrepreneurial Potential   47

> *Goals should always follow the SMART principle— they should be Simple, Measurable, Achievable, Realistic, and Timely.*

■ SIMPLE

Goals should always be stated simply and written down. This ensures that you know exactly what commitment you have made to yourself. Your written list of goals also serves as a constant reminder of where you are headed.

■ MEASURABLE

If your goal is measurable, then it's easy to tell when you've achieved it. Passing a course is a measurable goal. Becoming a wiser person is not. Often, the progress you can't measure happens naturally as you pursue a path toward more measurable objectives.

■ ACHIEVABLE AND REALISTIC

Goals should also be both achievable and realistic. If you set a goal for yourself, but you don't have the resources to make it happen, the result will be frustration and failure. At the same time, if the goals you set are too easy to achieve, you won't make much progress. Goals should be challenging enough to require some effort, but not too challenging.

■ TIMELY

Setting **target dates** for achieving your goals will help you get started and progress steadily. If your progress toward your goal is slower than you expect, you can either increase your resources to meet the target date or alter the target date.

■ WORTHWHILE

As well as being SMART, your goals should also be worthwhile. Only you can determine the personal value you place on your goals. The question you need to ask yourself is "Is this achievement important to me?" If the answer is "yes," pursue it wholeheartedly. If your answer is "no," take some time to reflect on why you're pursuing it. Pursuing a goal with a personal meaning is always more worthwhile than adopting a goal simply because others are pursuing it.

■ WHY SET GOALS?

Everyone has more than one goal. You may have financial goals, entrepreneurial goals, family goals, social goals, intellectual goals, spiritual goals, or a combination of these. It is much easier to talk about goal setting than it is to actually set goals. Day-to-day activities often prevent us from taking the time to sit down and set our goals. Being too busy is a typical excuse. If people don't have enough time to deal with the present, how are they supposed to find time to deal with the future? The problem is that the future eventually arrives in the present, whether you plan for it or not.

Worth Repeating

"If you
- care more than others think is wise
- risk more than others think is wise
- dream more than others think is practical
- expect more than others think is possible

then you dramatically increase your chances of reaching your goals."

Anonymous

It is important to recognize that goal setting ultimately results in change. It can lead to happiness, a different lifestyle, or more money. On the other hand, change comes hand in hand with risk, and sometimes frustration. Goal setting is a way of managing change, to minimize the negative possibilities. It allows people to look into the future and choose the path that looks best. Recognizing that the present is a steppingstone to the future can help people become more effective and efficient in their personal and business lives.

YOUR TURN

1. Name two challenges facing young entrepreneurs.
2. Why is experience important for young entrepreneurs?
3. Prepare a wish list of as many things as you can think of that you would like to have or do. (Don't worry if your wishes aren't realistic.) Rank your wishes in order of priority and set a target date for the achievement of each. Now go through the list and cross out the ones that you think are impossible to attain. Take the wishes that are left on your list and rewrite each one as a goal.
4. Picture your life as a series of events. Draw a timeline for your life, including the milestones you've already reached and those you think you might achieve in the future.

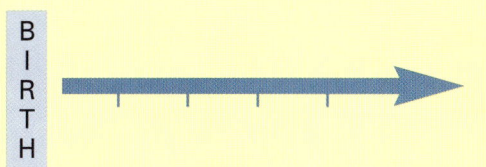

5. Write a letter to yourself about your goal(s). Draw a timeline for each one that shows the steppingstones and milestones you expect to encounter along the way. Put the letter in a sealed envelope with your name on the outside and give the envelope to your teacher. You'll use it again in Chapter 12.

Venture Profile

YOUNG AT HEART

Paul Delean, The Gazette

Roméo & Juliette is a labour of love for Tony Bacile. After stints in banking and real estate, the Cartierville native has his own company, a fast-growing designer and manufacturer of children's clothing based in St. Laurent, Quebec, and he couldn't be happier.

"I was 30, wondering what to do with the rest of my life," said Bacile, 36. "The money was good, but [real estate] wasn't gratifying any more. I decided to start from scratch, and build my own enterprise."

Bacile's first idea was to get into the water business. He'd already started collecting bottle samples when he crossed paths one day with friend Josée Madore. A freelance clothing designer, Madore was also itching to get into business for herself.

CONTINUED→

Anne Lavergne and Tony Bacile

They kicked around the idea of a children's clothing company and, within months, Roméo & Juliette was born in 1995.

The name was Madore's idea, Bacile said. "We were looking for a name with international reach. And it's a name that people remember."

He still recalls the first time he saw someone wearing a Roméo & Juliette original. "It was in Varennes, a little boy in one of our jackets. We were used to seeing the children of friends and family wearing our things, but this was different, a stranger. My heart was really pumping."

Housed in Bacile's basement for the first six months, the company began with a total staff of two. Madore looked after the designs, while Bacile was in charge of administration and sales.

"We started with a line of children's sleepwear. Right off the bat, we got into specialty stores," Bacile says. "We sold about $30 000 worth the first season and then worked on expanding our line."

From the start, all production was contracted out. "Here, we do only design, administration, and distribution," Bacile said. Most of the company's clothing is manufactured in Canada, but about 10% comes from Asia.

About 18 months after its debut, Roméo & Juliette had its first crisis. Madore left the company for family reasons, selling Bacile her shares.

"If Anne Lavergne hadn't accepted the offer to take her place, there wouldn't be any more Roméo & Juliette," Bacile said.

Lavergne, a friend of Madore, had joined Roméo & Juliette a few months before as a pattern maker. "I was attracted by the opportunity to work with a smaller group in more of a family setting," she said.

The collection, which includes jackets, coats, pyjamas, raincoats, dresses, mitts, hats, and pants, is sold through more than 500 retail outlets in North America. "Ideally, we'd love to have our brand known all over the world. Imagine selling clothing to the French or Italians."

Exploring

1. What goals did Bacile and Madore each have?
2. What skills did each person bring to the venture?
3. What evidence is there that Bacile and Madore cared a great deal about the work they were doing?
4. If Bacile had gone into the water business, do you think he would have been successful? Why?
5. In what ways did Bacile have to be flexible as his business developed?

Worth Repeating

"Behold the turtle; he makes progress only when he sticks his neck out."

James B. Conant, American educator and scientist

James Bryant Conant suggests that entrepreneurs need to be like turtles in order to be successful. What other animal characteristics might be useful to an entrepreneur? Why?

■ FLEXIBILITY IS THE KEY

People need to believe in themselves if they are to realize the goals they set. When you're setting goals and making plans, it's important to keep an open mind. Your chances of success will be greater if you can remain flexible in your attitude and change your plans as needed. Flexibility doesn't diminish the importance or worth of a goal. Instead, it increases its worth by making it more attainable.

■ GOAL SETTING AND COMMITMENT

Achieving a goal is hard work that depends on sound strategy. Once you've identified the goal, you'll need to plan for each steppingstone and milestone you will encounter on your journey. If you make a good plan and have the persistence to follow it through, your goals will be within your reach.

To reach your destination, you need to make a total commitment and believe in your success. When you encounter obstacles, don't despair. Most obstacles can be overcome, and you will gain knowledge and experience in the process of overcoming them. When people view challenges in a positive way, they are motivated to develop new strengths and abilities that will help them prevail.

YOUR TURN

1. Suggest several reasons why people might have to revise or replace a goal as they get older and acquire more education.

2. In the previous Your Turn section, you listed unrealistic personal goals along with those you might someday attain.
   a) Why is it important to think about unattainable goals, even though you may never reach them?
   b) If a friend has set a goal that seems unattainable, what advice would you give?

3. How should career goals relate to personal goals? Explain.

4. Learning to know yourself is a lifelong process that can help bring you success, particularly as an entrepreneur or enterprising person. You can use this activity to find out more about who you are now. Just remember that as circumstances change, so will you.

   a) Draw three vertical lines to divide a large piece of paper (28 cm x 35.5 cm) into fourths. In the first section, write your name and three facts about yourself. In the second, list ten questions another person should ask you to get to know you better. In the third, list five people you admire, and in the fourth, list three pastimes you enjoy.
   b) Choose a partner and exchange pages. Ask each other the questions you wrote in the second section. Then explain to each other why you selected the five people you admire.
   c) Join another pair to form a group of four. Talk with your group about what you learned from this activity. Together, discuss this question: How can talking with others help people get to know themselves better?

Venture Profile

FATHER KNOWS BEST

Curtis Sittenfeld, Fast Company magazine

Some parents dream that one day their son or daughter will join them professionally, allowing them the opportunity to work with their kids. For Paul Furdyk, that dream has been inverted. In March 2000, at the age of 45, Paul left his job at NCR Canada Ltd. in order to become V.P. of sales for BuyBuddy.com—a startup of which his 18-year-old son is the founder.

"I'm sure that I'm not the first parent, nor will I be the last, to be in this type of situation," Paul says. "Technology has made it possible for youth to innovate very rapidly. We're seeing earlier adoption, we're seeing faster exploitation, and as a result, we're seeing quicker entry into the business world for younger people. There will be a significant number of people who will be as successful as Michael is early on in their lives."

For Paul, the decision to take a job with BuyBuddy.com, a consumer information and shopping Web site, was an easy one. "They wanted someone more mature to come on board and help them with sales and marketing development," he says. "It just seemed like it would be a good fit for me."

Yet working with one of your children is not without complications. BuyBuddy's management style is intentionally loose and casual. But, as Paul himself observes, "Parenting is a lot more hierarchical in nature." However, Paul says that this contradiction has not been a problem for him at all. "There's a delineation—with parenting on one side and business on the other. From a business perspective, Michael and I are on a peer level."

No matter how professional the two Furdyk men are able to act, Paul is still Michael's father. "I'm very, very proud," admits Paul. "Every so often, I kind of pinch myself on the shoulder to make sure that this is real. I have to tell myself, yes, I am standing here beside my son."

Michael Furdyk

Exploring

1. What challenges do Paul and Michael face as they work together?
2. In Chapter 2, you met Michael Furdyk who cofounded a company called TakingITGlobal. Here, you've learnt about another of his ventures. What challenges might leading two ventures at the same time pose? What characteristics and skills will Michael need to overcome them?
3. What do you think Michael's goals are?
4. Paul says that technology is making it easier for young entrepreneurs to enter the business world. Discuss his idea with a partner. What evidence have you seen in the news or in your community that he is correct?
5. How might technology assist you in achieving your goals?

■ Knowing Yourself

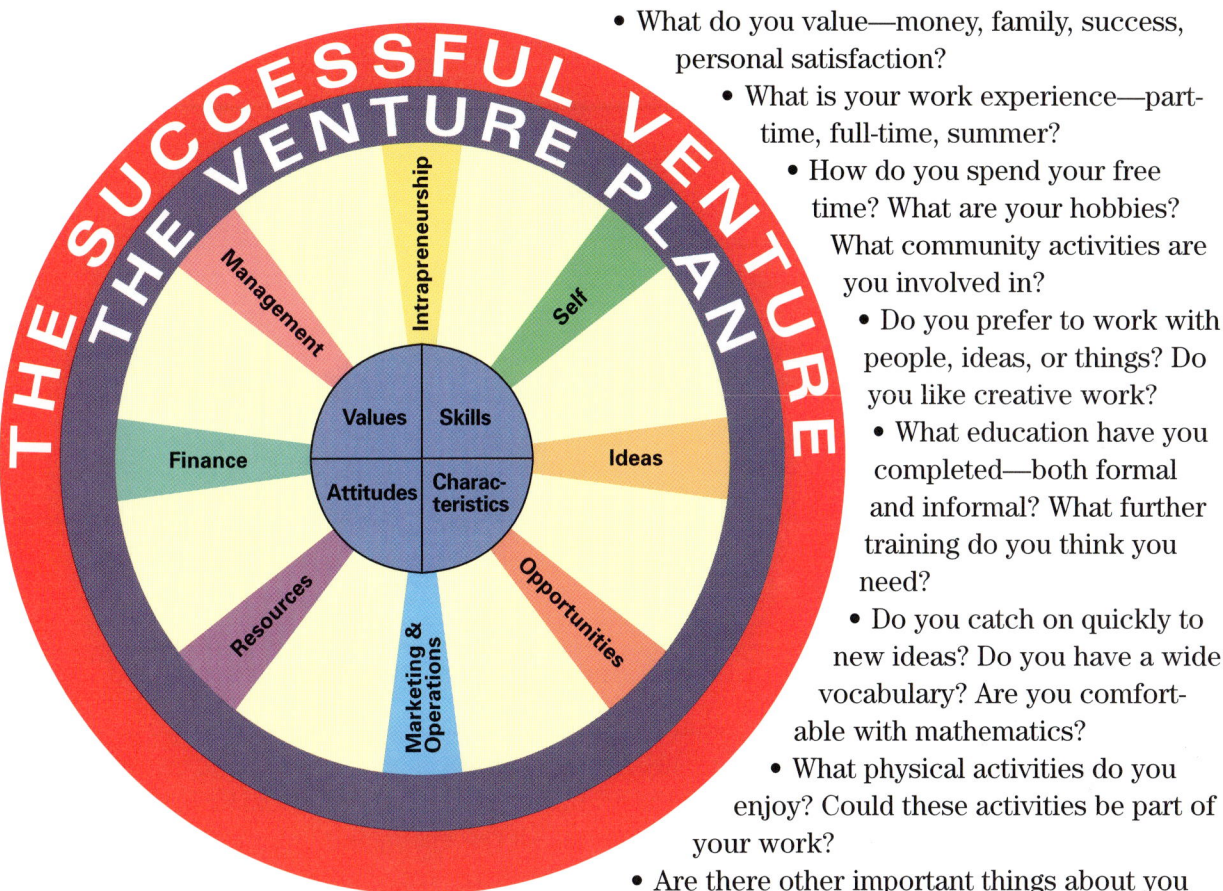

THE SUCCESSFUL VENTURE • THE VENTURE PLAN •

Inner wheel sections: Intrapreneurship, Self, Ideas, Opportunities, Marketing & Operations, Resources, Finance, Management

Center: Values, Skills, Attitudes, Characteristics

- What do you value—money, family, success, personal satisfaction?
- What is your work experience—part-time, full-time, summer?
- How do you spend your free time? What are your hobbies? What community activities are you involved in?
- Do you prefer to work with people, ideas, or things? Do you like creative work?
- What education have you completed—both formal and informal? What further training do you think you need?
- Do you catch on quickly to new ideas? Do you have a wide vocabulary? Are you comfortable with mathematics?
- What physical activities do you enjoy? Could these activities be part of your work?
- Are there other important things about you that should be considered?

Being an entrepreneur is probably one of the hardest things you will ever do. It will demand your personal attention and energy 24 hours a day, seven days a week. To be successful, you will need to reach inside yourself to find the enthusiasm and commitment that will help you move forward.

Everything you undertake will take longer than you anticipated and cost more. Sometimes unanticipated problems will arise. You have to be honest and ask yourself if you have the qualities needed to be an entrepreneur or an enterprising person. Are you comfortable living with unpredictability? Are you willing to take calculated risks?

An assessment of your Strengths, Weaknesses, Opportunities, and Threats is sometimes called a **SWOT analysis**, and can be applied to any situation. After you read the Venture Case that follows, you will have the opportunity to conduct a SWOT analysis of your own entrepreneurial potential.

Worth Repeating

"Watch your thoughts;
they become words.
Watch your words;
they become actions.
Watch your actions;
they become habits.
Watch your habits;
they become character.
Watch your character;
it becomes your destiny."

Frank Outlaw, writer

Venture Case

DO YOU HAVE THE SKILLS OF AN ENTREPRENEUR?

Chips Klein, The Globe and Mail

Doing a job and running a business are two entirely different activities. To be entrepreneurial, you have to be aware of the difference. Entrepreneurs have almost all of the following abilities:

Ability to Formulate and Articulate a Vision

This entails knowing exactly what the venture will look like, what business it is going into, and what products and services will make the enterprise viable. It also involves being able to visualize a direction for the business and establishing plans that will take it from a startup to a self-sufficient entity.

Equally important is the ability to communicate the vision to others. This requires people skills to deal with investors, employees, customers, and suppliers, as well as the ability to construct teams and delegate.

Ability to Spot Talent

Recognizing strengths, capabilities, and performance levels in others is another characteristic. Those who possess this skill know when to praise people around them, and when to go out and acquire the missing links, which may include personnel with complementary skills, or an executive coach.

Willingness to Take Risks

There has to be a willingness to take chances while knowing the limits in terms of budget, lifestyle, and time, as well as a sharp eye and mind to differentiate between positive and negative risk.

Starting a new venture with all the necessary elements in place (financing, marketing strategy, and so on) can be viewed as taking a positive risk. Conversely, rushing blindly into a project and throwing money around without having done the homework certainly classifies as negative risk.

When things go wrong, an entrepreneur must have the self-confidence to cope with rejection and bail out if necessary. Many see these times not as failures but as opportunities, and have the self-assessment skills to revisit the vision and modify it.

Ability to Stay Focused

It is crucial to maintain the enthusiasm and determination to follow through on what has been started. This can be a major challenge for some. To be able to set a course for the business and stick to the plan, even when there are roadblocks, requires skill and nerve.

So draw up a list of your skills and traits to determine whether running a business is right for you.

Exploring

1. Write a brief description of a time when you demonstrated each of the four qualities described in the article.
2. Which of the four qualities described do you think is the most critical quality for an entrepreneur to have? Why?

Conduct Your Own SWOT Analysis

1. In your notebook, copy the chart below and respond to each statement by checking "most of the time," "sometimes," or "hardly ever."

	Most of the time	Sometimes	Hardly ever
I have a great deal of energy.			
I am confident that I can do what I set out to do.			
I can plan for the future.			
Money is important to me.			
I take responsibility for my own actions.			
Achieving my goals is more important to me than financial security.			
I see problems as challenges that make daily life interesting.			
I am able to set goals for myself.			
I am comfortable with risk.			
I am able to learn from my mistakes.			
I am willing to seek help when I need it.			
I strive for excellence in everything I do.			
I am flexible.			
I am reliable.			
I have the ability to be creative and innovative.			
I interact well with others.			

2. Select four statements to which you responded "most of the time." Write a paragraph to describe a time when you demonstrated each quality.
3. Draw a small circle and draw yourself in the centre. Then, draw a larger circle around the small one and mark it off in eight sections. In each section, write the answer to one of the questions shown with the Venture Creation Wheel on page 53.
4. Review the entrepreneurial qualities outlined starting on page 28 of Chapter 2 and in the article by Chips Klein on page 54. Which of these qualities do you already have? Which ones do you still need to develop?
5. Remember that SWOT stands for Strengths, Weaknesses, Opportunities, and Threats. You have already considered your strengths and weaknesses. Now use the list of less-developed qualities that you wrote for Question 4 to help you think about opportunities. Write a plan that explains how you could develop each quality. Consider how you might find opportunities to develop these qualities at school (in class or through extracurricular activities), through a part-time job, or through volunteer work.
6. What threats might you face in your quest to become a more enterprising/entrepreneurial person? How could you cope with each one?

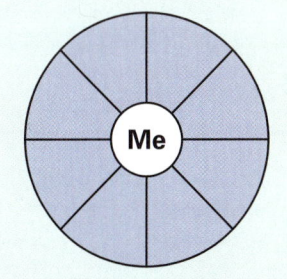

YOUR TURN

1. What did you learn from completing the SWOT analysis? Discuss the results with a partner.

2. In what ways did sharing your answers with another person add insight to what you learned about yourself?

3. Select one thing about yourself that you would like to change. Write it down so that you can refer to it later.

3. Collect pictures and articles from newspapers, magazines, or the Internet. Create a "Wall of Excellence" in your classroom to promote young enterprising people.

ARE YOU AN EDISON OR AN EINSTEIN?

As you explore your personal strengths and weaknesses, it is important to know what type of thinking style you prefer. Some enterprising people and entrepreneurs think like "Edisons," while others think like "Einsteins."

Thomas Edison invented the light bulb by applying a logical step-by-step process. In his hundreds of attempts, Edison used **incremental problem solving** to achieve his goal. Albert Einstein developed the theory of relativity in a completely different way. His predictions stemmed from **out-of-the-box thinking** rather than hands-on experiments. In fact, most of Einstein's ideas were not proven by experiments until years later. Both Edison and Einstein made exceptional contributions to how we live today. They were agents of change who thought and worked in very different ways.

The world needs both Edisons and Einsteins. Edisons are the people who think about ways to make existing ideas better. Edison used existing knowledge to develop his inventions, and then spent a long time gradually improving them through experimentation. Einsteins are the people who come up with fundamentally new ideas. They look beyond existing knowledge to find solutions to problems.

If all the people in a workplace were Edisons, the focus would be on making existing systems better. The Edisons might not notice external challenges, and this could lead to the demise of the organization in the face of global competition. On the other hand, if all the people were Einsteins, there would be plenty of ideas, but no one to carry them through to completion. Einsteins like to think creatively about entirely new systems, but they are not very interested in the details of implementation. For a team to be successful, the members need to have diverse thinking styles.

Worth Repeating

"Genius is 1% inspiration and 99% perspiration."
Thomas Edison

"The most beautiful thing we can experience is the mysterious. It is the source of all true art and all science."
Albert Einstein

Imagine that Edison and Einstein held a debate about the process of human discovery. What might each person have to say?

YOUR TURN

1. Meet with a small group to study and discuss the chart below. What advantages and disadvantages are there to each approach?

Impact of Style Preferences on Group Process and Output

Edisons		Einsteins
• Treats problem as defined.	**Problem Definition**	• Treats problem definition as part of the problem (instinctively reshapes).
• Uses rules and regulations to solve problems.	**Rules and Regulations**	• Ignores or breaks rules to solve problems.
• What group thinks is important.	**Group Consensus**	• Challenges group thinking.
• Masters detail.	**Attention to Detail**	• Sheds detail.
• Less is more—2 or 3 well-defined ideas.	**Types of Ideas**	• Generates many ideas.

Edisons: Make existing systems better.
Einsteins: Make existing systems different.

Diane Blair, Bank of Montreal, Institute for Learning, adapted from Adaptors and Innovators by Michael Kirton

2. Conduct research on either Edison or Einstein. Develop a portrait that illustrates his personal qualities. Your portrait can be visual, or you might prefer to present it in the form of a dramatic monologue or multimedia presentation. Would you describe the person you portrayed as an entrepreneur, an enterprising person, or neither? Give reasons for your choice.

3. The "Change at Work" chart that follows shows how the Edison and Einstein approaches can bring about positive changes in the workplace, in the community, at school, and at home. Discuss the chart with your group. How could you use the ideas shown here to improve your performance at school? to develop your entrepreneurial potential?

Change at Work:
7 possibilities for making change

Incremental (Edisons)

Do things right.
(Efficient—right procedures.)

Do the right things.
(Effective—right priorities first.)

Do things better.
(Improvement—analysis, fine tune.)

Do things others do.
(Copy ideas—think beyond our box.)

Fundamental (Einsteins)

Do away with things.
(Cut—stop doing low yield things.)

Do things not yet done.
(Different perspective—new box.)

Do things that can't be done.
(Breakthrough—do the impossible.)

Adapted from Adaptors and Innovators by Michael Kirton

4. Are you an Edison or an Einstein? Or are you like another famous person? Write a short essay that explains your choice. Describe how you could make your style preference work to your advantage.

E-Bits & Bytes

To do your research for Your Turn Question 2, visit www.business.nelson.com and follow the links to "Edison" and "Einstein."

ASSESSING YOUR SKILLS

To succeed as an entrepreneur or as an enterprising person, you must develop skills and characteristics that will help you achieve clearly defined goals. For example, if you've used the Internet to look up information for a school research project, then you've developed a valuable research skill. Now you can transfer this specific research skill into a more general skill that you can use in the workplace.

Table 3.1 outlines how some familiar activities can help you build skills that you can apply to a venture or within an organization.

Table 3.1 Identify and Reflect

My Activities	My Skills
When I	I demonstrate my ability to
take a telephone message	communicate effectively
name my computer files and store them in an appropriate directory	manage information
sort out my personal relationships	think and solve problems
balance my chequebook	use numbers
turn off the iron when I am finished using it; look after someone who is sick	look out for the health and safety of others
ask for help when I do not understand something	learn continuously
show up for work on time, or call if I am going to be late or absent	deal with people, problems, and situations with honesty and integrity
make time in my schedule for homework and socializing	balance work and personal life
juggle time commitments when something comes up	be adaptable
play volleyball	work with others
do my share of the household chores	carry out tasks from start to finish

Orbit magazine

CLASSIFYING YOUR SKILLS

For an entrepreneur to be successful, **interpersonal skills**, **critical-** and **creative-thinking skills**, and **practical skills** are all essential in varying degrees. Remember that even if some of these skills don't come to you naturally, they can still be learned.

INTERPERSONAL SKILLS

Interpersonal skills include

- the willingness and ability to talk to others, especially those different from ourselves
- the ability to listen to and understand what others are saying
- the ability to motivate and encourage others
- skills for negotiating and resolving conflicts
- caring for yourself and others

Worth Repeating

"I am a great believer in luck, and the harder I work the more I have of it."

Stephen Leacock, Canadian humorist, author, and educator

Do you believe in luck? Can it be gained by working hard? What does Stephen Leacock mean?

E-Bits & Bytes

Communication is an important interpersonal skill, but sometimes people communicate *too* well. "In a recent survey to determine how many people kept in touch with the office while on vacation, a full 83% of respondents admitted to checking messages via e-mail, voice mail, cell phone, or pager while lounging on the beach. For better or for worse, the technology that keeps us wired to the world can also keep us connected to our jobs 24/7."

Tim Walker, htc - Canada's HiTech Career Journal

Why is it important for people to take time every once in a while to be out of touch with the office?

Worth Repeating

"When one door closes, another opens. But we often look so regretfully upon the closed door that we don't see the one that has opened for us."

Alexander Graham Bell, inventor of the telephone

Explain this quote to a partner in your own words. Why would entrepreneurs and enterprising people be more likely to recognize a new opportunity?

CRITICAL- AND CREATIVE-THINKING SKILLS

Critical- and creative-thinking skills include

- the ability to solve problems by evaluating a variety of solutions
- having the confidence to make a decision and act on it
- the ability to set goals, plan how to achieve them, and carry out the plan
- keeping records and being accountable for all actions undertaken
- the ability to generate ideas and identify opportunities

PRACTICAL SKILLS

Practical skills involve the ability to use special tools designed for a specific job. For example, someone who works with digital media or in telemarketing needs to know how to use the appropriate equipment for the job.

Cool Stuff

People around the world have names for their cell phones that reflect their love for a communications tool that has become indispensable to many. Here are just a few, along with their literal meanings.

Why do you think communications skills are listed in the top two positions on the "Interpersonal Skills" list on page 58?

China	da ge da ("big brother")
Finland	kanny ("extension of the hand")
Germany	das Funktelefon ("radio telephone")
Iran	telefon dasti ("hand telephone")
Israel	pelephone ("wonder phone")
Italy	telefonino ("little phone")
Netherlands	draagbare telefoon ("portable phone")
New York City	cellies
Turkey	cep ("pocket")

Chapter 3 ◆ Assessing Your Entrepreneurial Potential 59

Strategies for Entrepreneurial Success

A number of strategies can help you increase your chances of entrepreneurial success.

Think First
Planning is crucial to any enterprise. If you take time to think before you act, and to consider problems from different perspectives, you can anticipate and overcome obstacles before they arise. Remember that reflective decisions are typically better than impulsive ones.

Believe in Yourself
Resist the pressure to conform. Be confident in your own abilities and set goals for improving your own performance rather than competing with others.

Entrepreneurial insight is a unique way of seeing opportunities. Entrepreneurs and enterprising people often see things that others do not see and then seek a way of demonstrating the viability of the opportunity to others.

Know Yourself
When planning your venture, take time to consider your own abilities, character traits, skills, and goals. If your plan is to become an enterprising employee, you'll need to assess opportunities within the organization you work for and consider how these opportunities fit with what you have to give, and what you expect in return.

Enjoy the Challenge
To be worth your time and effort, a venture should challenge your abilities, encourage your creativity, suit your personality, and be compatible with your vision of yourself. When obstacles arise, as they inevitably do, try to look at them as opportunities rather than threats. The feeling of accomplishment that comes from meeting these challenges, and the lessons you learn from them, are a gift your venture will give you in return for your investment of time and effort.

International NEWS

According to a study conducted by 10 universities in 10 countries, Canada, the U.S., and Israel rank highest in entrepreneurship. The study examined the percentage of entrepreneurship activity in the setup of independent businesses, startup companies, and other businesses. The study indicates that 6.9% of the Canadian population is currently in the process of forming a business, compared to 7% in the U.S., 5.4% in Israel, and 1.8% in each of Germany, France, and Japan.

Find out what Canada's current population is. How many people does 6.9% represent?

YOUR TURN

1. Classify the skills in Table 3.1 on page 58 as interpersonal skills, critical- or creative-thinking skills, or practical skills.

2. Are your strongest skills your interpersonal skills, your thinking skills, your practical skills, or a combination of all three? Explain.

3. Identify one interpersonal skill, one thinking skill, and one practical skill that you would like to improve. Briefly list strategies you could use to improve each one. Present your ideas in the form of a chart or diagram.

Venture Profile

COMPUTER PROFESSIONALS WITH A SOCIAL CONSCIENCE

Lorne Chase, htc - Canada's HiTech Career Journal

Ask Susheel Gupta, chair of the Canadian chapter of Computer Professionals for Social Responsibility (CPSR), how the organization first got started and he'll tell you it was due to Star Wars. Not the famous sci-fi film, but the U.S. space defence initiative proposed by President Reagan in the early 1980s.

"The people who started CPSR looked at Reagan's plan and basically said, 'Hold on a minute, technology is not infallible and there's plenty of room for errors,'" recalls Gupta, who is also a federal prosecutor for the Department of Justice. "As the organization evolved, it started looking at other social issues related to technology, like privacy and civil liberties."

CPSR is a public-interest alliance of computer scientists and others concerned about the impact of computer technology on society. They meet regularly to discuss issues related to their profession and keep the public informed through newsletters, public forums, and press releases. When they become concerned about an issue, like the space defence initiative, they bring their concerns to the attention of the people involved.

The grassroots organization—begun by computer professionals from California's Xerox Palo Alto Research Centre and Stanford University—has grown in the past two decades to include worldwide chapters and an international membership.

Gupta was instrumental in bringing together over 100 Canadian members to form their own chapter, most of them from the academic community. But any high-tech professional is welcome to join for a nominal fee.

Gupta believes the CPSR has a role to play in Canada in speaking out about the impact technology has on society. He says there are a number of issues the organization can address including online privacy, censorship, free speech, and the digital divide.

For instance, it was the CPSR that alerted the public to faults in filtering software being used in many library computers connected to the Internet. Members discovered that the

CONTINUED

software used to protect children from viewing objectionable Web sites also prohibited them from accessing legitimate educational sites.

"There was a good reason to have the filtering, but it took technical people to realize that the software was also depriving children of information on serious community issues," notes Gupta.

"It's an example of the type of issues high-tech professionals feel the public should know about."

Gupta wants the Canadian chapter of CPSR to connect members via the Internet.

"Right now it's important for us to spread the word and engage our members in a discussion of the themes and issues we want to cover here in Canada," says Gupta. "Then we can coordinate our activities around that."

Exploring

1. What need did the CPSR founding group identify?
2. What can the CPSR accomplish as a group that they might not be able to accomplish as individuals?
3. What other not-for-profit ventures can you name? Describe the purpose of each one. What other characteristics do these ventures have in common?
4. Describe an issue that concerns you. If you were going to start a not-for-profit venture to address this issue, what would it be like?
5. The Xerox Palo Alto Research Centre (mentioned in the article) is considered to be an incubator for innovation. Use the Internet, periodicals, or an interview with someone who works at Xerox to find out what other innovations first came from there.

Agents of Change

David Suzuki is a scientist, a teacher, an award-winning broadcaster, a conservationist, and someone who can be counted on to speak out for the causes he holds dear. He is committed to helping people understand how important it is for them to live in harmony with their environment. In 1990, he established the David Suzuki Foundation to find and communicate ways to achieve balance among social, economic, and ecological needs. The Foundation focuses its efforts primarily on climate change, on ecosystems along the Pacific coast, and on the Canadian rainforest. It is funded mainly through donations, although some money is also raised through the sale of merchandise. The purposes of the Foundation are to

- define a vision of society in harmony with the environment
- study the causes of, and alternatives to, environmental threats
- inform the public and decision makers about sustainable solutions
- participate in projects and initiatives that serve as models for an ecologically balanced future

Find out more about David Suzuki's life. What experiences helped him develop the skills and ideas that he needed to start the David Suzuki Foundation?

ACTIVITIES

FLASHBACKS

Read the following statements. Discuss the last one with a partner in relation to the others. You might review the work you did in Chapter 2 on the similarities and differences between entrepreneurs and enterprising people.

- Young entrepreneurs face unique challenges.
- Determining one's own future is a key reason why young people become entrepreneurs.
- Enterprising skills can be learned.
- Work experience, volunteer experience, and experiences at school all help people develop enterprising and entrepreneurial skills.
- People travel toward their goals by reaching a series of small "steppingstones" and larger "milestones."
- Accurate self-assessment is the first step toward becoming an entrepreneur or an enterprising person.
- A firm belief in yourself and a commitment to that belief are the keys to success for any entrepreneurial venture.
- A positive, confident, and creative attitude helps the entrepreneur/enterprising person overcome obstacles.
- There are many different ways to make a contribution to the workplace. Not everyone needs to be an entrepreneur or an enterprising employee.

LESSONS LEARNED

1. What are some advantages and disadvantages of being a young entrepreneur?
2. Differentiate between a steppingstone, a milestone, and a goal.
3. What characteristics should a goal have before you adopt it as your own?
4. Why is it easier to talk about goal setting than it is to set goals?
5. In what ways are flexibility and commitment important in the goal-setting process?
6. What do entrepreneurs and enterprising people need to know about themselves to be successful?
7. How can people develop specific skills into general ones? Explain.
8. Explain how interpersonal skills, critical- and creative-thinking skills, and practical skills are important for the enterprising person and for the entrepreneur.

9. Reread the Venture Profiles of Jo-Anne Schurman in Chapter 1 and Maureen Mitchells in Chapter 2. Write a paragraph to describe the interpersonal skills, thinking skills, and practical skills demonstrated by one of these entrepreneurs. Share your ideas with someone who wrote about the other person.

10. How are "Edisons" and "Einsteins" different in their approaches to problem solving? What impact does this have on the workplace?

VENTURING OUT

1. Interview a young entrepreneur in your community or look on the Internet to find information about a young entrepreneur. Find out
   a) what challenges this person faced in starting the business
   b) what advantages and disadvantages there are to being your own boss

   Add the information you found to the database of entrepreneurs you began in Chapter 2.

2. In this chapter, you considered plans for the future that could be stated in the form of goals. List two personal goals that you could take action on in the next month.
   a) How do you plan to achieve each goal?
   b) What challenges stand in your way?
   c) How can you overcome these challenges?

3. Contact a volunteer leader in your community. Ask what skills this person has developed as a result of volunteering and how these skills might be transferable to the workplace.

4. Earlier in this chapter, you did a SWOT analysis of your personal skills. Write a short essay to explain why you do or do not wish to become an entrepreneur or an enterprising employee. These questions may help you frame your answer.
   a) What entrepreneurial strengths and weaknesses do you have?
   b) Which weaknesses could you compensate for by hiring others to work for you?
   c) What type of life do you want for yourself?
   d) How comfortable are you with taking responsibility for all the decisions that will be made where you work?
   e) Do you have a passion for a certain business idea?
   f) What vision do you have for what a workplace could be like?

> Remember to update the database you began in Chapter 2 to include the people you met in Chapter 3. Continue to update the database as you read each new chapter.

POINT OF VIEW

As you worked through this chapter, what did you learn about yourself that you did not already know? How will you use what you have learned?

UNIT 2

Preparing the Way

Preparing the Way

The new economy is a knowledge economy supported by employees who make effective use of both information and rapidly changing technology. The Information Age is revolutionarily different from the Industrial Age, and is changing almost daily.

This rapid rate of change will present many opportunities for entrepreneurs and enterprising people. In Chapter 3, you assessed your own enterprising/entrepreneurial skills. Now, you will have a chance to reflect on how these skills can help position you for success in the new economy. You will discover how to identify and seize opportunities, find the best idea, and develop a plan of action.

Many good ideas are simple ones that make you wish you'd thought of them yourself. John Archibald Wheeler expressed this thought when he said: "To my mind there must be, at the bottom of it all, not an equation, but an utterly simple idea. And to me that idea, when we finally discover it, will be so compelling, so inevitable, that we will say to one another, 'Oh, how beautiful! How could it have been otherwise?' "

Planning and preparing for your journey will help keep you on the right track. As you move along the way, remember to look after yourself, to build a network of people who can help and support you, and to celebrate your successes.

In Unit 2, you will think about possibilities for enterprise, match those possibilities with your own interests, and begin the planning process. You already have a good sense of who you are, and what characteristics and skills you bring to the planning process. You know that the skills and characteristics of entrepreneurs and enterprising people can be learned, and you understand how these skills and characteristics can benefit the community and society at large.

Chapter 4 will focus on the history of the new economy and the importance of the **Intrapreneurship** spoke in the Information Age. You will explore how developing technologies, globalization, and the rapid pace of change have affected the workplace and given rise to many opportunities for entrepreneurs and enterprising people.

Chapter 5 will deal with the **Ideas** spoke. You can try out strategies people use to generate ideas and identify opportunities for entrepreneurial ventures.

In Chapter 6, the **Opportunities** spoke of the wheel will show you how to spot trends and fads in the marketplace and to assess the ones that you are best suited to pursue.

The inner rim of the Venture Creation Wheel is the **Venture Plan.** Chapter 7 outlines the components of a successful plan so you can put your plan into action in Unit 3.

Good luck, and enjoy the journey!

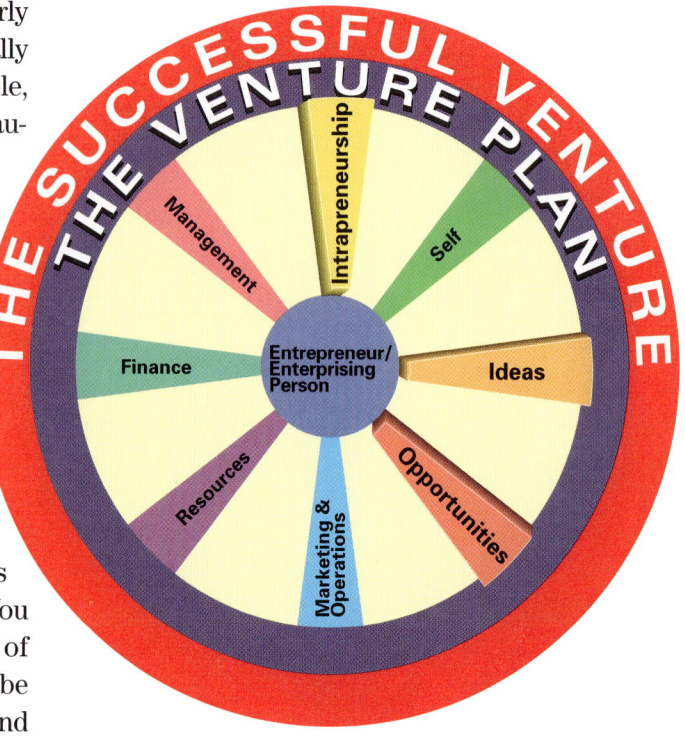

CHAPTER 4

Challenges and Changes in the Labour Market

LEARNING OPPORTUNITIES

By the end of this chapter, you should be able to
- explain the major factors affecting Canada's labour market
- describe current trends in the labour market and their causes
- describe the changes that are affecting people's work and workplaces
- explain the factors affecting workers' employability

Entrepreneurial Language

- Agricultural Age
- merchant
- Industrial Age
- labourer
- intangible asset
- goodwill
- command and control
- trade union
- strike
- new economy
- Information Age
- trend
- labour market
- attrition
- war for talent
- telecommuter
- teleconferencing
- intellectual capital
- competency
- hierarchy

These terms are listed in the order in which they appear in the chapter, but this doesn't really show that some words belong together, or explain how they are related. Create a diagram that presents the words in a way that makes it easier to see relationships. If you are not sure what a term means, check to see how the word is used in the chapter, or refer to the Glossary.

Venture Profile

THE NIKE STORY? JUST TELL IT!

Eric Ransdell, Fast Company

When most people think of Nike, they think of superstar athletes like Michael Jordan, Mia Hamm, and Tiger Woods. When Nike's own employees think of their company, they think of a retired university track coach, an Olympic runner whose career ended tragically in a 1975 car crash, and a so-so athlete whose achievements as an entrepreneur far outpaced his accomplishments as a runner.

Most people have heard of Nike CEO Phil Knight, a middle distance runner who turned selling shoes out of his car into a footwear-and-apparel colossus. But few know of Nike cofounder Bill Bowerman, Knight's coach, or of Steve Prefontaine, the now-deceased runner, who was also coached by Bill Bowerman and whose crusade for better equipment inspired Bowerman and Knight to build the Nike empire. Yet, inside Nike, those three figures are more relevant to the company's sense of identity than any of its superstar spokespeople.

Why? Because Nike has made understanding its heritage an intrinsic part of the corporate culture. Think of this approach as internal branding—the stories that you tell about your past shape your future.

And, like all great stories, the ones about Nike offer archetypes that people can learn from. When Nike's leaders tell the story of how Coach Bowerman, after deciding that his team needed better running shoes, went out to his workshop and poured rubber into the family waffle iron, they're talking about the spirit of innovation.

Over the past couple of years, Nike experienced the roller coaster that lots of other companies ride: euphoric periods of growth followed by setbacks and public backlash. But through all these ups and downs, winning companies hold on to their values. "To survive those downtimes," explains Nelson Farris, Nike's director of corporate education, "You have to understand what real teamwork is—keeping promises and keeping commitments."

To foster that kind of understanding, the company launched its corporate storytelling program. An orientation in company history is given to new employees and to tech reps who attend a nine-day Rookie Camp at Nike headquarters in Beaverton, Oregon. Storytellers are also responsible for telling the Nike story to salespeople at large retailers that carry the Nike product line. At a Nike store in Eugene, Oregon, a Heritage Wall includes everything from the shoe moulds that Bowerman made with his family's waffle iron to the first pair of Nike running shoes ever to cross a finish line.

Bill Bowerman, the cofounder of Nike

CONTINUED→

As Nike gets even bigger, its storytellers feel that their mission becomes even more critical. "Every company has a history," says Dave Pearson, a training manager and storyteller. "But we have a little bit more than a history. We have a heritage, something that's still relevant today. If we can connect people to that, chances are that they won't view Nike as just another place to work."

Exploring

1. Why is it important for Nike employees to view working at Nike as special?
2. How does storytelling contribute to the development of this view?
3. What other activities could Nike undertake to reinforce this notion?
4. What can other organizations learn from Nike's corporate storytelling program?

Starting Up

It is said that we live in the Information Age. What is meant by this term? Discuss this with a partner and give examples.

Labour: Past and Present

The economy has experienced significant changes over the past few thousand years. For many years, people lived a nomadic lifestyle, moving from place to place in search of food and water. Gradually, they learned to gather seeds and plant them in cleared land, and the **Agricultural Age** began. As the Agricultural Age developed, most people became **merchants**, craftspeople, farmers, or farm workers. Some merchants and craftspeople were entrepreneurs who brought their goods or services directly to their customers. In other cases, where tools and equipment were less mobile—a blacksmith's forge, for example—one entrepreneur could supply the needs of a town or village, and its surrounding farms.

Entrepreneurs such as this blacksmith served a small local market.

The Agricultural Age gradually evolved into the **Industrial Age**, a period when people began to build equipment they could use to produce standardized goods in large quantities. The equipment was too big and heavy to carry around, and was so expensive that only a few people could afford to purchase it. For the first time, the majority of people who produced goods were not self-employed, but were **labourers** employed by the few people who could afford to be business owners. This was a significant change to the way goods were produced.

In the Industrial Age, organizations were formed to produce goods and services. Their assets included their equipment, their **capital investments**, and the **intangible asset** of **goodwill**. Most organizations operated under a **command and control** model—the labourers were expected to follow the exact instructions of the managers. Since most of the jobs were routine, workers who demonstrated enterprising characteristics were often discouraged from approaching their work in a creative way, and were sometimes even terminated.

Employees with new and innovative ideas grew frustrated with jobs like these, and sought out jobs with more thoughtful employers who could see the long-term benefits of innovative ideas.

In the late 18th and early 19th centuries, workers began to form associations called **trade unions**. Through bargaining with their employers as a group, unionized employees were able to gain better wages and improved working conditions. Occasionally, when a trade union failed to reach an agreement with the employer, the workers opted to **strike**. This means that they refused to work until they had achieved their objectives. Today, trade unions negotiate arrangements that deal with wages, hours, working conditions, and benefits. They may also use political power to lobby for government legislation that benefits and protects workers.

Labourers on an assembly line usually had little input into how the business operated.

Agents of Change

In 1872, 18-year-old Thomas Watson went to work for a telegraph instrument maker in Boston as a machinist's apprentice. Bored with his repetitive job, Watson developed jigs that could be used to turn out a number of identical pieces with less work. Watson's employer, Charles Williams, encouraged him to work with an inventor who leased space from the company—Alexander Graham Bell. As a result, Charles Williams became the first person ever to have a telephone line between his home and his business, and his firm manufactured all the equipment for Bell Telephone until the demand grew beyond the company's capacity.

Agents of change often begin by solving an immediate problem. They might not foresee all that their work will lead to, or the changes it will bring. Find another example in this book that demonstrates how a solution to an immediate problem led to bigger and lasting changes.

Worth Repeating

"The illiterate of the 21st century will not be those who cannot read and write, but those who cannot learn, unlearn, and relearn."

Alvin Toffler, futurist author

Describe something you have recently unlearned or relearned.

THE INFORMATION AGE

The **new economy** has ushered in the **Information Age**. The Information Age is distinctly different from the Agricultural and Industrial Ages, because, for the first time, information and knowledge are explicitly valued. This age is prime for entrepreneurs and enterprising people.

Information is not dependent on expensive equipment and large factories, but is readily available to anyone who wants it. The people who will succeed in the Information Age are those who seek out new information, or new ways of handling information, and turn it into practical knowledge that can be applied in new and different ways.

YOUR TURN

1. How is the Information Age different from the Agricultural Age and the Industrial Age?

2. How did the attitude of employers toward their enterprising employees change over time?

3. With a partner, brainstorm key concepts or words that are associated with the Information Age. Choose three of the words or concepts and enter each one in an Internet search engine. What do the results tell you about the Information Age?

4. Through discussion, reduce the list you made for Question 3 to four or five main concepts. With your partner, brainstorm entrepreneurial opportunities that might develop because of these concepts.

5. Work with a partner or small group to create a short multimedia presentation about a business in your community that opened in the 21st century. How did the business get started? How does it use information technology?

Chapter 4 ◆ Challenges and Changes in the Labour Market

Agents of Change

By the mid-1800s, cable wires were still unreliable because they could not withstand the ocean's salt. Frederick Gisborne of Nova Scotia developed a method of insulating these wires from the salt, opening the door to transcontinental communication by telegraph. An important step toward the Information Age was taken.

Why was this invention important for the communication sector? for globalization?

Worth Repeating

"If the 20th century was the time of the large integrated industrial corporation, the 21st century is becoming the time of entrepreneurship."

Don Tapscott, authority on the new economy and the author of Growing Up Digital

What evidence can you offer to support Tapscott's view of the 21st century?

Current Labour Market Trends

Nike is representative of many long-established organizations. Enterprising people and entrepreneurs like Phil Knight, Bill Bowerman, and Nelson Farris watch changes in the marketplace and take note of **trends** or movements. They act on what they see to ensure their organizations remain competitive as the economy evolves. They particularly watch for labour market trends. The **labour market** is the supply of, and demand for, workers in the economy. In Chapter 1, you learned how supply and demand are shaped by people's needs and wants. Supply and demand in the labour market refer to the number of available workers and the number of current or predicted job openings. Job openings occur when there is an increase in market activity or when there is **attrition**.

Table 4.1 Trends in the New Economy

Trend	Opportunities for Entrepreneurs	Opportunities for Enterprising People
• rapid growth in global economy	• imports and exports	• more jobs for people with international experience and/or a second language
• increase in the number of small- and medium-sized businesses	• political and economic climate is ripe to support the startup and growth of entrepreneurial ventures • growing opportunities to share experiences, pool resources, and make referrals	• increased employment opportunities for employees who can multitask and approach each day with a creative and positive attitude
• rapid change and growth in the technology sector	• as new technologies are developed, opportunities emerge in the areas of information technology, medical technology, environmental technology, and communications technology	• opportunity to learn and grow as new businesses develop and business practices change
• increasing use of contract labour	• entrepreneurs can set up consulting practices with professionals who can work for a variety of clients	• opportunity to become self-employed while working for a large organization on a contract-by-contract basis

72   Unit 2 ◆ Preparing the Way

E-Bits & Bytes

The high technology industry could create 500 000 more jobs in Canada if it could solve its skill-shortage problem.

Statistics Canada

What is meant by "skill-shortage problem"? How can Canada solve it?

The Information Age economy has prompted an increase in market activity, creating jobs that did not exist a decade ago. It encourages enterprising organizations and entrepreneurship, and has led to an increase in the demand for enterprising employees.

Attrition occurs when more people leave their jobs voluntarily, for example, due to relocation or retirement, than are hired to replace them. Statistics Canada estimates that, because of the age of Canada's population, over 60% of job openings over the next decade will arise because of attrition.

Enterprising people search out information about labour market trends that will help them pursue work in an industry that is likely to have opportunities. Entrepreneurs use this same information to explore opportunities for new ventures.

What Employers Are Looking For

The type of work available to any one individual depends on that person's skills and knowledge level. Education and training play an important role. In the new economy, individuals who do not graduate from high school are at a disadvantage because there are fewer and fewer job opportunities available to them.

Figure 4.1 shows that the number of new jobs is increasing for people with postsecondary education, and decreasing for those who left school at or before the completion of high school. Postsecondary education includes college and university programs, apprenticeship, and technical programs offered in areas such as hairdressing, art, or business.

In addition to education, today's employers require other work-related skills. An Employability Skills Profile developed by The Conference Board of Canada says that employees will be required to have academic skills that "provide the basic foundation to get, keep, and progress in a job and to achieve the best results." The Profile shows that, to succeed, employees will need a combination of academic skills, personal management skills, and teamwork skills.

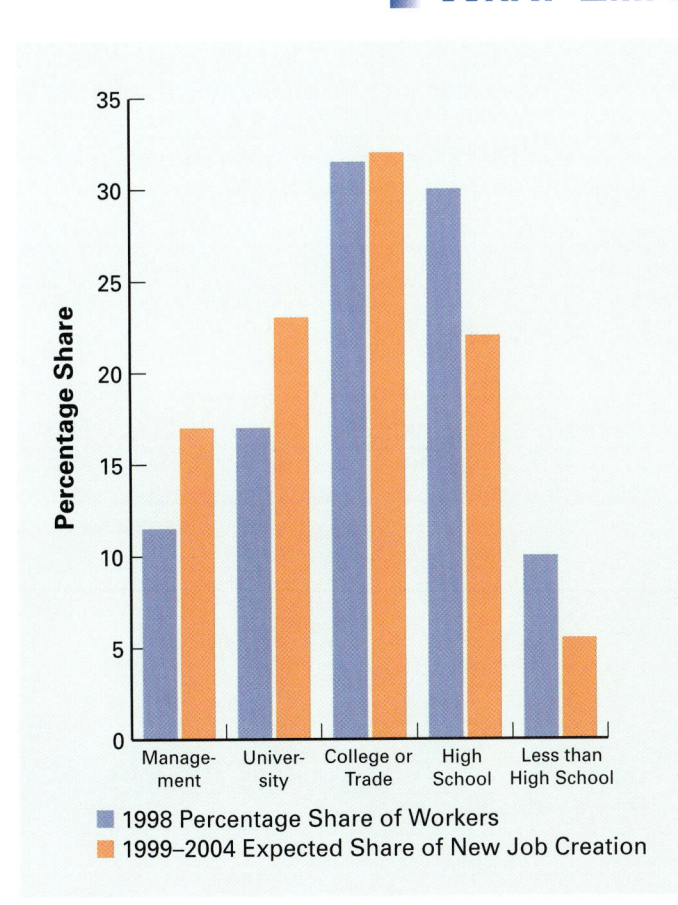

Figure 4.1 Share of New Job Creation by Skill Level (1999–2004)

It is clear that the more skills and education a person has, the greater his or her choice of jobs will be in the Information Age labour market. The workplace is using highly adaptable technology to replace low-skilled and unskilled work formerly done by employees, or sending these jobs to other countries where the labour costs are significantly less than in Canada. The new economy no longer needs assembly-line-style workers. Instead, it needs employees who can think, work in teams, make decisions, communicate, and learn.

YOUR TURN

1. What are labour market trends? Why do entrepreneurs and enterprising people watch these so closely?

2. What is attrition? Why will it result in so many job openings over the next decade?

3. The E-Bits and Bytes comment on page 73 indicates that Canada's technology industry is experiencing a shortage of skilled workers. To see if this is true, look for information about the technology industry on the Internet or in newspapers and magazines. If possible, ask someone who works in the industry what job opportunities are available for skilled workers. Work with classmates to create a class "job board" that lists available jobs in the technology industry and the qualifications a person needs to do each one.

WORK-LIFE BALANCE

As an antidote to the increased demands being placed on them by the labour market, employees are looking for ways to balance their commitment to work with their family commitments. In the long run,

A balance of work and family life helps reduce stress.

Worth Repeating

"We have to keep operating outside of the organization's comfort zone. It's a difficult challenge, but for somebody who thrives on challenge, you couldn't find a better zone to work in."

Thor Ibsen, Chief Internet Activist, Ford Motor Company

What is meant by "comfort zone"? Why is it important for a company to operate outside the comfort zone? What kind of an employee thrives on challenge?

a person who can successfully balance work with family needs is likely to be less stressed and more productive. Employers are becoming acutely aware of this need for flexibility as they try to hire and retain high-quality staff.

Employers know that their human resources are the key to their competitive advantage. Nike implemented their corporate storytelling program as a way to help employees feel connected to the organization. In this way, they encouraged people on the Nike team to make a commitment to their jobs—to do their best work and to remain with the company longer. The **war for talent** is emerging as the single factor most critical to organizational growth and competitiveness in the Information Age. Employees are aware of their value to an organization and will choose to work for organizations that meet their workplace expectations. To attract and hold enterprising employees, workplaces must be flexible in ways that will help their employees balance their work with other aspects of their lives.

What Motivates Talent?

Percentage of top 200 executives rating factor absolutely essential

Great company (brand)

Values and culture	58
Well managed	50
Company has exciting challenges	38
Strong performance	29
Industry leader	21
Many talented people	20
Good at development	17
Inspiring mission	16
Fun with colleagues	11
Job security	8

Great jobs (products)

Freedom and autonomy	56
Job has exciting challenges	51
Career advancement and growth	39
Fit with boss I admire	29

Compensation and lifestyle (price)

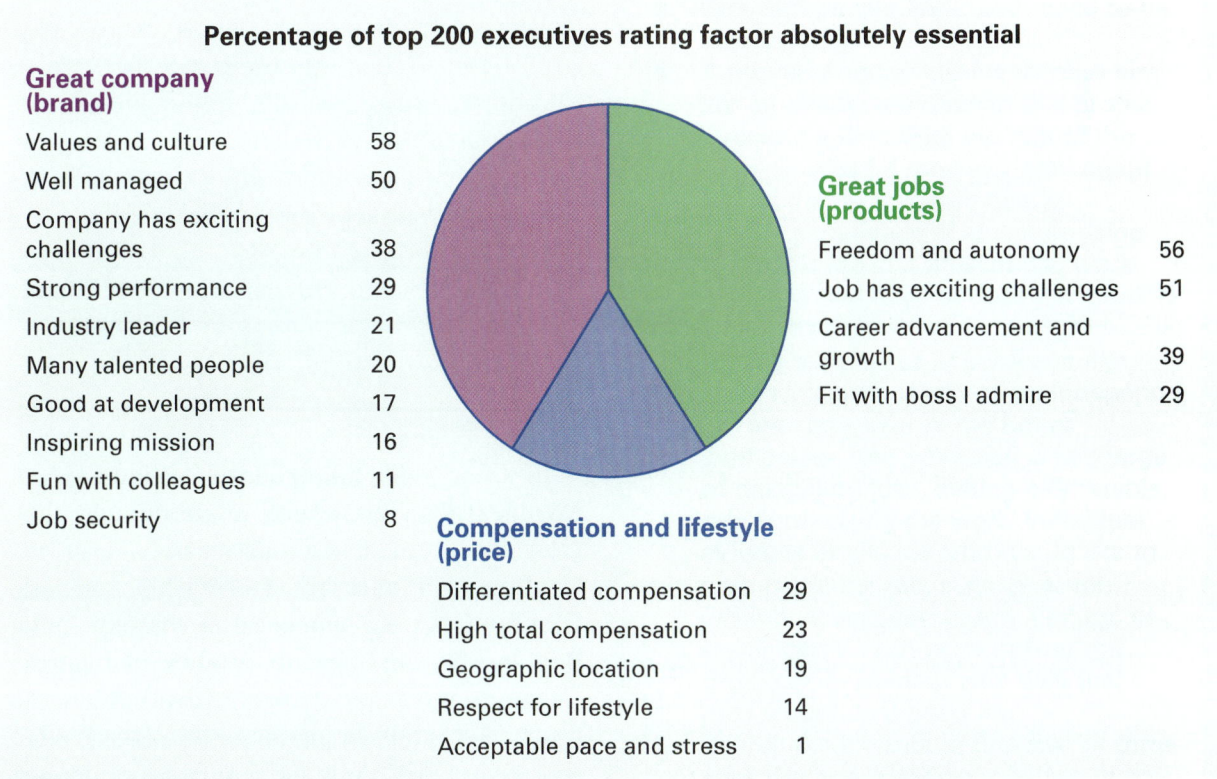

Differentiated compensation	29
High total compensation	23
Geographic location	19
Respect for lifestyle	14
Acceptable pace and stress	1

Figure 4.2 *The McKinsey Quarterly* surveyed more than 6000 top executives from its list of "top 200" companies. It wanted to determine factors that motivate these executives to work for an organization. The data shows that for top executives, a company's culture and the types of jobs offered are more important than compensation and lifestyle issues.

Venture Profile

HOME-BASED KNOWLEDGE IN CANADA'S ARCTIC

Darrell Greer, Home Business Report

Nestled in his Eastern Arctic home of Rankin Inlet in the Kivalliq Region of the new territory of Nunavut, John Hickes started his home-based business, Nanuk Enterprises Ltd., more than 26 years ago.

"Basically, I'm hired to set up and assist in the development of training components for Inuit organizations and government agencies," says Hickes. "If, for example, Nunavut Tourism was looking for a company to train guides, I would bid on it. Another scenario I would be interested in would be if a mining company wanted a traditional knowledge study completed as part of its land or site assessments."

Hickes's company is also directly involved with the tourism industry through its Rankin Inlet-based Tumie Tours which provides "a unique Arctic adventure experience." The company's offerings include weekend seminars on living on the land and living in igloos, and photo safaris of the wondrous Eastern Arctic landscape.

The company also works with movie and production companies requiring assistance in lining up guides, outfitters, and other services indigenous to the Arctic climate.

Hickes has learned from his mistakes over the past three decades and, although a tireless worker with a positive outlook, he fully appreciates the dangers of overzealousness to the home-based business owner.

"Through my confidence in being able to resolve any issue that presented itself, I have gotten myself involved in ventures that were not financially successful because, in retrospect, I did not fully understand the venue," he says. "The best advice I could give to anyone with their own home-based business is to involve themselves with undertakings they truly enjoy and have a positive impact on."

Due to the uniqueness of his business, Hickes often plays where he works, explaining that he's learned the importance of balance. "Having your own home-based business requires strict discipline, but I think that's what makes it work. You don't quit working just because it is five o'clock. That said, you need to make time away. For me, my weekends are

CONTINUED→

sacred. You need time for yourself, your family, your hobbies—and things that take your mind away from business."

As for the future, Hickes sees promise in the continuing need for the training and consulting aspects of his business, especially those primarily tied to his Inuit citizenship.

> ### Exploring
>
> 1. What services are offered by Nanuk Enterprises Ltd.?
> 2. What characteristics of his business make it possible for John Hickes to work from home?
> 3. What other kinds of jobs might lend themselves to working from home?
> 4. Hickes says, "Having your own home-based business requires strict discipline, but I think that's what makes it work." Why might it take self-discipline to work at home?
> 5. What do you think Hickes likes about his job?
> 6. How are his priorities different from those of the executives surveyed by *The McKinsey Quarterly*? (See Figure 4.2.) How are they similar?

HOME-BASED EMPLOYMENT

The advance of computer technology has made fundamental changes not only to how people work, but also to where they work. **Telecommuters** can work from home with computer access to files, collaborating with others via e-mail and software programs, and **teleconferencing** with colleagues, customers, and suppliers.

Work-at-home employees are generally more productive, having eliminated travel time and office distractions. They are often happier as well, since they have more time to concentrate on their families and personal goals. Employers benefit from this increased productivity and employee satisfaction, and, at the same time, reduce their office costs.

In order to retain talented and committed employees, organizations must recognize that staff members need different types of support as they try to balance work and family responsibilities. This need can be met by offering a variety of alternative work arrangements. See Table 4.2 for descriptions of alternative work arrangements on page 78.

Increasingly, people are juggling family demands, professional requirements and goals, and personal needs and goals. Employees whose needs are not met by their employers will tend to leave. Some will leave to join another organization that might meet their needs more effectively, while others may try to gain more control over their time and priorities by starting their own ventures.

Worth Repeating

"Time is precious. You cannot get back the time you wasted yesterday. Those who can extract value from their excess time will have a huge impact on their business."

Timothy Fong, Founder, Lassobucks.com

Today, everybody seems to be busy all the time. What strategies do you use to get the most out of the time you have?

Table 4.2 Alternative Work Arrangements

Work at home	
Description	The employee is given equipment such as a computer and a fax machine to use to set up a home office.
Benefits	• reduces travel time and costs • benefits the environment by reducing traffic congestion and pollution • employer saves money on office costs
Compressed work week	
Description	The employee condenses the normal work week by working fewer days, with longer hours each day.
Benefits	• employee has more time for family or personal goals, such as completing additional education
Flexible work schedules	
Description	The employee works a full week but selects start and end times to fit a personal schedule.
Benefits	• employee can work at those times when he or she is most productive, even if those hours are not between 9:00 a.m. and 5:00 p.m. • families with young children can schedule work so one parent can take the children to school and the other can supervise them after school
Job share arrangements	
Description	Two employees share the same job and organize their work schedule to ensure that someone is on the job at all times.
Benefits	• employees may opt to work partial weeks, alternate weeks, alternate months, or six months at a time • allows employees to respond to other demands in their lives such as caring for a family member
Part-time work	
Description	Employees may choose to work fewer hours each day or fewer full days each week.
Benefits	• employees have the flexibility to schedule personal commitments • employees may be offered benefits that full-time workers receive on a pro-rated basis
Personal leave programs	
Description	In addition to legislated maternity leave, employers may also offer paternity leaves, elder-care leaves, and leaves to pursue personal interests such as travel or education.
Benefits	• enhances the organization's skill base • reduces employee burnout

Opportunities for Enterprising Employees

Trends toward globalization, advances in technology, and deregulation open the door to new opportunities and create new challenges. New occupations are being created every day. Ten years ago, there were no Web masters, robot technicians, or cyber café managers. Ten years from now there will be jobs that we cannot even imagine today—jobs that may require completely new skills.

Today's jobs are going to talented and skilled employees who are not afraid of new ideas. Organizations that once were locally based are now more globally focused, with loyalties that extend far beyond the boundaries of a single community. There is a demand for workers who can generate innovative ideas and communicate them to others —for enterprising employees.

In the Information Age, **intellectual capital** has become an important asset to any organization. Employees who build their knowledge and skills on the job are critically important to any organization's success—even more important than those who come to the job with highly developed skills. Skills become outdated over time, but enterprising employees are able to compensate by learning new skills and adapting to new ways of doing things.

Enterprising employees, sometimes called intrapreneurs, continually reinvent how they work, and continually reinvent themselves in the process. Their ability gives rise to new opportunities as they meet problems, find solutions, and carry their organizations forward with them.

The skills that enterprising employees use to succeed within an organization are somewhat different from the skills a person needs to start a venture.

Cyber cafés are a creation of the Information Age.

E-Bits & Bytes

Sixty-three million people are in the online consumer population and, of those, 83% consider the computer the most important product of the 20th century.

The American Online/Roper Starch Cyberstudy, 1999

Do you agree with these consumers? Explain. Why is the computer an important symbol of the Information Age?

Cool Stuff

Profit magazine published this list of what's hot and what's not for today's enterprising employees.

Work with a partner to create and role-play a brief scene depicting each item.

HOT!	NOT HOT!
• Team play: working effectively with others, sublimating the self for the good of the team.	• Blind faith operators: incapable of independent thought or action, they instead follow others with single-minded compliance.
• Entrepreneurial: the ability to see opportunities and capitalize, take risks, and make decisions.	• The super-specialist: one-dimensional employees who are unable to satisfy today's demand for broader job descriptions and a wide range of skills.
• Networking skills: the ability to connect with others for mutual gain and to understand political relationships, both in and outside the company.	• Change resisters: individuals who refuse to expand their skills through training, avoiding opportunities for personal growth.
• Influence: the ability to negotiate successfully with coworkers, employees, customers, and superiors.	• Lone wolves: people who insist on working alone, unwilling to cooperate to meet today's complex business challenges.
• Time management: plus the confidence to say "no".	

YOUR TURN

1. Why do you think top executives are more motivated by the nature of the company and the job than by compensation and lifestyle issues? (See Figure 4.2.)
2. How has technology helped employers offer more flexible work arrangements?
3. Study Table 4.2. With a partner, try to imagine any drawbacks of each type of work arrangement.
4. Interview someone who is involved in a flexible work arrangement, either as an employee or as an employer. Ask this person to describe the impact of this work arrangement on both the individual and the organization.
5. What is intellectual capital? How is it related to a business's success?
6. The average age of workers is changing, with a large number expected to retire in the next decade. What impact might this change in the work force have on the new economy?

Venture Case

THE BATTLE ESCALATES FOR ALL LEVELS OF TALENT

Brian Orr, Canadian HR Reporter

When **capital** was the limiting factor in organizational growth, finance and treasury functions moved to the forefront in many organizations. Now that people are becoming the scarce resource, human resources departments are moving to the forefront in an increasing number of organizations.

The growing shortage of qualified staff is forcing many organizations to change their thinking. These organizations are beginning to realize they cannot afford to lay off highly skilled staff as a cost-saving measure, because they will need these staff in the future when the organization turns around.

Increasingly, HR departments are focusing their efforts on attracting new staff. One significant development has been the move toward Internet recruiting as organizations seek ways to broaden their search options, as well as seeking tools to increasingly automate and speed up the recruiting process.

Another growing development is to adopt a continuous recruiting strategy when an organization requires a large number of staff with similar qualifications. In continuous recruiting, the organization seeks out and hires qualified candidates before it has identified vacancies. In essence, it prehires in anticipation of future vacancies.

Along with more aggressive recruiting, organizations are revisiting their compensation, benefits, and quality of work-life practices. As in any sellers' market, job candidates are putting more emphasis on what the organization is offering them.

The flip side is retaining needed staff. Organizations are now beginning to pay more attention to why staff members leave. There is an increasing focus on evaluating turnover and the use of exit interviews. This is now becoming a topic of discussion at board meetings.

Although employees leave for many reasons, organizations are beginning to understand that the single most common reason for an employee leaving is having to work under a bad manager or supervisor. The quality of the leader has a significant impact on performance. Indeed, excellent leadership can be at least as important as talent in determining the level of a group's performance.

Exploring

1. What impact does the skill and talent shortage have on organizations?
2. What strategies are being used by enterprising organizations to attract and retain talented employees?
3. If you were a human resources manager hiring a staff recruiter for your company, what skills would you look for? In pairs, prepare a job description for this person. Include responsibilities as well as **competencies**, or abilities.
4. What leadership qualities do you think are needed to motivate talented employees?

Venture Profile

2020 VISION: HOW WILL PEOPLE WORK IN THE FUTURE?

Richard Worzel, adapted from The Next 20 Years of Your Life

Individuals working on their own will become the "virtual corporations" of the future. They'll stay away from hiring employees wherever possible and they'll spread their names, reputations, and talents through a mixture of technology, personal contacts, self-promotion, and gumption. This is the way many people work already—but it doesn't mean that such people will spend their working days alone. In the future, as now, some will work together, share office and equipment expenses, assist and promote each other in business, subcontract work to each other—but, legally, they will work for themselves and will not share ownership in their companies.

There will still be big businesses because some enterprises require large amounts of capital and large-scale coordination. However, there will be fewer employees than in the past, and more outsourcing for specific purposes. As a result, whether they work for a large organization or for themselves, more and more people are going to be responsible for their own success and failure.

What, then, might a working day in the life of someone who has just left school today be like in 20 years' time?

November 29, 20 years in the future

"Yes, we can handle that. I'll get on it right away," 45-year-old Judith Maxim agrees, then hangs up. To her genie, Hobbes, she says: "Commence a new database search on the subject of life insurance sales to individuals over 65 in North America. Search the following databases: Canadian Life Health Insurance Association, Statistics Canada, U.S. Library of Congress, Toronto Reference Library, National Insurance Association. End List. Discover possible additional databases. Limit fees paid to U.S. $20 per database, $100 total all databases. Where the cost would exceed these limits, ask me for permission. Begin search."

Judith then instructs her genie to reach one of her regular subcontractors on the phone. He appears shortly as an image in her Looking Glasses. "Hi, Judith! What's up?"

"What's the name of the graphic artist you used on the cough syrup ads we worked on last August? You know, the one that was so good at creating an old-fashioned, image-of-yesteryear kind of look?"

"Carolyn Kranz—why, do you have something for me?"

"Not this time, Ken. I'm on a tight deadline for a proposal, and my margin's too thin to include you. Next time. Do you have Carolyn's phone number?"

Ken looks uncertain, then says, "You're not going to make a habit of going around me to my people, are you?"

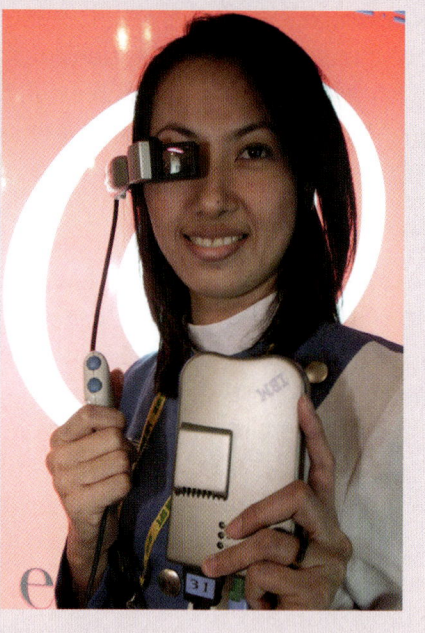

"No, Ken; we work well together, and we will again in future. But this is a rush job on a tight budget to impress a new client. If we land them, there'll be other work for all of us."

"Okay—just so long as you still love and appreciate me." He instructs his genie, "James, give Hobbes Carolyn's number."

Next, Judith spends an hour surfing the Net, looking for ideas that others have used successfully with mature consumers. Newspaper accounts call what she's doing "just-in-time learning," but she still thinks of it as "research." She can't delegate the task to her genie, because she isn't quite sure what she's looking for until she sees it.

The assignment has come to her from one of the outsourcing specialists of an insurance group. Judith had met the specialist at a conference in Vancouver last year and had added her to the distribution list of newspaper and magazine articles that she writes. This yearlong warm-up had resulted in a small, but potentially significant request to propose a marketing strategy for the sale of life insurance to the mature market.

Judith's working world is an unstructured one based on research, a constant, steep learning curve, a network of friends and connections, and a reputation carefully built and nurtured over time. Judith responds with great speed to new challenges, and she is always looking for ways to expand her network of both suppliers and clients.

She follows a marketing path that was uncommon when she started out in business in the late 1990s, which she calls "paid advertising," whereby other people pay her for advertising her abilities through the articles and books she writes, and the speeches she gives. The profile these activities give her cause people to remember her when they have a new and as yet vaguely defined marketing task to address.

Judith is still a one-person show, even though her annual gross billings now exceed $10 million. She has no employees, and only Hobbes, her genie, to assist her. What she does have is a network of people who are very talented, who trust her and her judgment, but who aren't quite as adept at self-promotion and marketing as she is. They are, therefore, quite content to subcontract work for her. For her part, Judith knows the strengths and weaknesses of all her subcontractors, which ones work best under pressure, and which ones need a slower, more relaxed pace.

Exploring

1. What do you think a "genie" might be?
2. What skills will people like Judith need to be successful?
3. Why will people like Judith need to be enterprising?
4. A movie producer uses a process similar to what's described in this profile to create a film. With the rest of the class, produce a movie or play about one of the topics listed below.
   a) the experience of an enterprising employee in a present-day workplace that does or does not support enterprise
   b) the experience of someone like Judith, who works as an independent contractor in the future

   One person, the producer, is in charge of delegating jobs, setting a timetable, and supervising the work. Individual students or groups who would like to do a particular job, such as scriptwriting, acting, set design, filming, or music can submit proposals to the producer, explaining why they feel they would do a good job.
5. Search the Internet to find two or three sites that bring people together to collaborate on projects. Write a brief description of each site.

Think About It

If you ran a small company, what would you offer to entice enterprising employees away from a larger competitor?

■ The Changing Workplace

The new economy is forcing workplaces to change the way they operate if they want to be successful. Factors influencing these changes include

- globalization
- competition
- applications of new technology
- concerns for human rights
- e-commerce
- the focus on quality
- the needs of employees
- changing customer demands

In reaction to rapid change, organizations are flattening their **hierarchies** and encouraging all employees to be leaders. Globalization has made it necessary for businesses to be ready to respond to customers around the world 24 hours a day, and smart technologies have made it possible. In the future, large organizations will likely use networks like Judith's more frequently, although the work may be done on a larger scale.

Technology also means that competition is coming from new and unexpected places. Large, long-established organizations like Nike are finding themselves in competition with small- and medium-sized enterprises. These smaller companies are attracting talented, enterprising employees from larger organizations.

■ REWARDS FOR ENTERPRISE

The workplace of tomorrow is likely to offer enterprising employees increased flexibility and more opportunities for self-fulfillment in return for greater productivity and a commitment to learning. Already, many workplaces have staff in place who are capable of thriving in the new economy. The challenge for managers is to find ways to foster and develop the enterprising potential of each employee.

Enterprising managers encourage their employees to take up the challenge of lifelong learning and to help achieve the goals of the organizations they work for. They praise employees who search for solutions using the latest information technology.

The rewards for enterprising employees are many. Through their efforts, they can gain respect from their managers and coworkers, the opportunity to pursue personal goals, and perhaps financial rewards as well. But more importantly, they gain the confidence, serenity, and self-respect that comes from discovering that they have the resources to deal with the challenges that confront them at work and elsewhere in their lives.

International NEWS

"The storm that is arriving—the real disturbance in the force—is when the thousands and thousands of institutions that exist today seize the power of this global computing and communications infrastructure, and use it to transform themselves. That's the real revolution."

Louis V. Gerstner, Jr., Chief Executive Officer, IBM

ACTIVITIES

FLASHBACKS

Choose two of the statements below. Using examples, make a small presentation to your group to demonstrate your understanding of the chapter.

- We are living in the Information Age, in which technology has a major impact on our lives.
- Entrepreneurs, enterprising employers and employees watch for changing trends in order to identify opportunities.
- The supply of and demand for workers are related to job creation and attrition.
- The new economy presents multiple opportunities for entrepreneurs and enterprising people.
- Working in the new economy requires higher education, job skills, and interpersonal skills.
- Enterprising employees are motivated by a variety of factors including the opportunity for work-life balance.
- Telecommuting, or working from home, is increasingly popular among entrepreneurs and enterprising employers.
- The changing workplace demands new methods for recruiting staff, managing work, and understanding the competition.

LESSONS LEARNED

1. Describe the three ages through which the economy has evolved and list the changes that occurred at each stage. Include information about where and how people worked, and what was valued in the economy.

2. How are jobs created in the new economy?

3. What questions should you ask as you decide how you will educate yourself to prepare for a job in the new economy?

4. What is the "war for talent" and how might it affect your life?

5. Describe some of the advantages and disadvantages of telecommuting.

6. Think of a situation in which an employee might wish to take advantage of one of the six types of alternative work arrangements presented in Table 4.2 on page 78. Develop your situation into a short story.

E-Bits & Bytes

Visit www.business.nelson.com and follow the links to The Conference Board of Canada. Review its list of employability skills. Select five of these skills, and in your notebook, briefly describe a situation in which employees might demonstrate each of them. Explain how each skill benefits both the employer and the employee.

7. What different points of view might a small company and a large company have about how competition is changing the way business is done in the new economy?

8. What would you say are the key ideas presented in this chapter?

VENTURING OUT

1. The new economy depends on people who can find and interpret information and turn it into new ideas. For example, "frequent flyer" programs were developed because someone looked at information about ticket sales and flight patterns, realized that frequent flyers represented value for an airline, and created the idea of rewarding repeat customers with travel points. In small groups, brainstorm other examples of situations where people successfully turned information into business opportunities.

2. With the whole class, list all the careers you might someday like to have. Find and list the education requirements that would be needed for each job.

3. Work-life balance is an emerging trend in the new economy. What impact might this trend have on individuals, families, and organizations?

4. Review the work you did in Chapter 3 to determine your own enterprising and entrepreneurial skills. How well do your skills match the employability skills outlined by The Conference Board of Canada? Design a poster using words and pictures to illustrate your personal employability skills.

5. With a partner, brainstorm job titles that might exist in the future. Select one title from your list and write a job description. Include the responsibilities the person would have and the competencies and support network she or he would need to do the job.

6. With a small group, prepare a timeline that starts 10 years in the past, continues through the present, and for 20 years into the future. Use your timeline to show changes in the workplace that have occurred or are likely to occur.

E-Bits & Bytes

Visit
www.careers.nelson.com
and follow the links to
other Web sites about
careers.

POINT OF VIEW

Review the comment by Louis Gerstner in International News on page 84. Explain what you think he meant. How might institutions transform themselves? What evidence of this transformation are we already seeing today? (Suggest an example of a company that has transformed itself. How is it different today from what it was?)

CHAPTER 5

Invention, Innovation, and the Creative Edge

LEARNING OPPORTUNITIES

By the end of this chapter, you should be able to
- understand and use research skills and critical- and creative-thinking skills
- identify and explore the sources of an entrepreneurial idea
- compare invention and innovation
- describe how to obtain patent, copyright, and/or trademark protection
- identify and apply each stage in the creative problem-solving process
- analyze the creative-thinking, problem-solving, and decision-making processes that help entrepreneurs find opportunities to create new ventures
- demonstrate ways in which different creative-thinking techniques (e.g., brainstorming, mind mapping) can be applied to generate new ideas
- identify significant Canadian inventions and innovations, and summarize the impact that these have had on people's lives

Entrepreneurial Language

- invention
- innovation
- intellectual property
- patent
- copyright
- trademark
- industrial design
- proprietor
- Integrated Circuit Topography
- criteria
- lateral thinking
- Thinking Hats
- right brain
- left brain
- word clustering
- mind mapping
- brainstorming
- visualizing

With a partner, think of as many words as you can that have to do with creative thinking or problem solving. Which words from this list could you include on your list?

Venture Profile

HARMONIZE YOUR LIFE, HOME, AND BUSINESS

Paul Ng's venture, called Geomancy, takes its name from the ancient science of creating harmony between people and their surroundings—a science more commonly known by the Chinese name "Feng Shui." Although Paul Ng was trained and employed in computer science and business administration in Canada, he also studied geomancy, astrology, and life charting, which have strong Chinese influences.

Paul says, "Ever since my childhood, I have always been searching for the meaning of life. There had to be a purpose for living in this world. Yet no philosopher in history had really given me a satisfactory answer—until I had my own life charted. The accuracy of timings and events surprised me. From then on, I began my research into both Chinese and Western philosophies. After reading many books, fate brought me to several retired masters who taught me the fundamentals of Feng Shui. Suddenly, everything clicked."

After 12 years of research, Paul decided that he should leave his job in corporate management in order to pursue his passion full-time. Money was not the issue. Instead, he left to pursue his desire to help people look at and harmonize their lives. Through his company, Paul works with real-estate developers and builders to provide advice on ways to harmonize houses or businesses. In 1994, the *World Journal Newspaper* proclaimed Paul Ng one of the top people in his field in Canada.

In 1996, Paul was invited by the United Nations World Conference of Mayors to speak at their annual meeting in Kingston, Jamaica. Paul says, "I spoke about city development, because I wanted people to discover that they can use ancient knowledge to help cities in the world become more peaceful and prosperous."

Paul advises young entrepreneurs: "Even old knowledge may be adapted to the new world. We need to remember to learn from our mistakes, and then to look for a new and better approach to our problems. We are here to create a way for tomorrow. Instead of talking about what hasn't worked in the past, we need to look at how it might work in the future."

CONTINUED→

Paul currently teaches Feng Shui for the Real Estate Council of Ontario and writes a column for several specialty newspapers in Canada, including: *Ming Pao Daily News*, *World Journal Daily News*, *Singtao Daily News*, the *Great Wall Newsmagazine*, and *Royal LePage Magazine*.

Exploring

1. The prefix "geo-" indicates that a word has something to do with the Earth.
   a) What does "geomancy" have to do with the Earth?
   b) What other words can you find with the same prefix?
2. What are some of the services offered by Paul Ng's business?
3. Who are Paul Ng's customers?
4. What motivated Paul to leave his job in corporate management?
5. Make a chart or diagram to show the characteristics illustrated by Paul Ng in this profile. Give evidence from the profile for each characteristic you list.
6. Summarize the advice Paul has for young entrepreneurs.
7. Use the Internet or the library to research the term "Feng Shui." What does it mean? Where did it come from?

Starting Up

In your own words, define the terms "invention" and "innovation." How do you think they relate to entrepreneurs?

Ideas and the Creative Edge

Every venture starts with an idea—but where does the idea come from? Entrepreneurs and enterprising people are always on the alert. Whenever they meet someone new, open a newspaper or magazine, watch television, or surf the Internet, their minds store information that might help them get closer to a venture goal or even start them in a new direction.

Good ideas come in many forms, but the ones that turn into ventures have two features in common:

- They are innovative—often offering something that no one has thought of before, or that has never been made to work before.
- They suggest a way to satisfy a need.

There are plenty of places to look for ideas. Government agencies, community and professional associations, hobby groups, and trade shows are only a few possibilities. Sometimes the new idea you need is only one step beyond an idea someone else has already had. Or it may be one someone else has tried and abandoned. Perhaps the only missing ingredient for success is you!

Ways to Find New Ideas

Here are some of the sources you can use to find new ideas that might lead to new ventures.

Newspapers
- Newspaper articles contain information about local and global business trends.
- Classified advertising can indicate local needs and wants, and list available jobs.
- Business Opportunities ads describe businesses for sale, including their locations and prices.
- Business Services ads can help you find out what services are in demand.

Magazines
- Consumer magazines predict and report changes in consumer buying.
- Trade magazines describe trends in specific industries and report new products and services.
- Specialty magazines offer advertisements and articles about goods and services that appeal to their target markets.

Attending trade shows is a way of finding new ideas.

Trade Shows
- At trade shows, manufacturers and distributors display their newest products and services for others in similar businesses or for potential customers. These shows are sometimes open to the public.
- At craft or hobby shows, individuals and small businesses can sell products or services to interested customers, often at low prices chosen to attract new customers.

How Well Do You Observe?

To become aware of the business ideas that surround you every day, you need to be a good observer. You might be surprised at how much you can see when you take the time to look.

90 Unit 2 ◆ Preparing the Way

> ## Observation Test
>
> Take this test with a partner and discuss the results. What kinds of things are you good at observing? not so good? With your partner, discuss techniques people can use to improve their observation skills.
>
> 1. If you were looking for an odd-numbered address, would you look on the north or the south side of the street?
> 2. What colour are the walls in the hallway outside your classroom?
> 3. How many cupboard doors are there in your kitchen at home?
> 4. Describe what your teacher wore to class yesterday.
> 5. How many places are there to buy coffee within 1 km of your school?
> 6. Name 10 things you can see from your locker.
> 7. About how many steps is it from one end of the school gym to the other?
> 8. Name one new business that recently opened in your community.
> 9. When you enter the main office at school, does the door swing in or out?
> 10. Look carefully around your classroom. Name one feature of the room that you never noticed before.

Being a good observer means being aware of what is going on around you.

LOOKING FOR PATTERNS

Once you become more aware of your surroundings, you will likely begin to notice what the people in your community are doing. Where do they like to shop? eat? have fun?

The most important thing to watch for is change because change can spur an idea for a new venture. For example, if the price of a popular item just increased, there might be room for a competitor to step in. Or, if people are just beginning to buy a new product or service, there might be related products or services they would also be interested in buying.

You never know when you will get an idea for a new venture. You might be at the movies or waiting in line to pay for groceries. Start an ideas journal and keep it handy so you can jot down possibilities as they occur to you. From time to time, review the journal to look for patterns that might help point you in the right direction.

DEVELOPING YOUR IDEAS

Not all good ideas make good ventures. Once you've found an idea that interests you, the research begins. Talk to people and discuss your idea. Who will your customers be? What problems might you encounter? Try to pursue a range of related ideas so, if one stalls, you'll have others to fall back on.

Look for help from experienced businesspeople, and from people whose job it is to support new entrepreneurs. Information is available

> ### Worth Repeating
>
> "Those who say that something cannot be done should get out of the way of those who are doing it."
>
> *Anonymous*

What differences in character distinguish those who say something cannot be done from those who are actually doing it?

from a variety of agencies and organizations. Keep records of all your findings. Information that doesn't seem valuable now may be useful later, so you'll need to keep track of everything. Use a notebook or an electronic recording device when you're away from your desk, and file the information on a computer when you return. Some enterprising people like to keep a pen and paper at their bedside so they can record ideas that come to them at night or when they first wake up.

Table 5.1 Where to Go for Help

Government Agencies and Departments
• Both the provincial and federal governments offer programs that support business startups. Look for "Business Information" in the blue pages index in a telephone book. • Statistics Canada gathers and organizes data about business- and lifestyle-related issues. You can access this information on their Web site by following the links at www.business.nelson.com. • Municipal governments often have economic development departments that work to attract and encourage new business. • Community colleges and other educational institutions offer courses in various aspects of small business development and management.
Community Organizations
• Many not-for-profit and volunteer organizations exist to help people find jobs or start their own businesses.
Business Associations
• Business people often form groups to exchange ideas and welcome new business development. These associations include chambers of commerce, economic development councils, industry and trade associations, and business clubs.

YOUR TURN

1. What are the advantages of being a good observer?

2. Why is it important to talk about your ideas with other people?

3. With a small group, select one of the products or services listed below.
   - snack foods
   - travel
   - automobiles
   - hair accessories
   - video games
   - home repair

   See page 110 to learn about brainstorming. Brainstorm possible sources of ideas for related business ventures. To get started, refer to "Ways to Find New Ideas" on page 90 and "Developing Your Ideas" on page 91. When you finish brainstorming, make a "Top 10" list of your idea sources. Present the results to the class.

4. Work with a group to develop and present a skit that shows why it is helpful to be a good observer.

Venture Profile

MADE TO MEASURE

Dawn Calleja, Canadian Business

AC Dispensing Equipment Inc. began as a quest for the perfect cup of coffee. Every morning, Michael Duck would stop at Tim Hortons on his way to work at a Lower Sackville, Nova Scotia, dairy. And every morning, Duck would complain to his coworkers that there was either too much cream in his coffee or too little. His boss finally got sick of hearing him: He challenged Duck to do something about it.

The high school dropout and lifelong tinkerer spent night after night in his basement, trying to build a machine that would pour the perfect amount of cream into a steaming cup of java. He offered the first one—an electronically souped-up milk fridge—to the local Tim Hortons owner and told him if it didn't work, he didn't have to pay. "I did that for quite a while," says Duck, 42. "But eventually everyone paid up because the dispensers worked so well." He also built a sugar dispenser to complement his popular cream machine—both of which are now standard equipment in all new Tim Hortons franchises.

The company finally grew too big for Duck's basement, and AC Dispensing moved into a 6100 m^2 building in 1997. Duck's staff of more than 20 (headed by his former boss from the dairy, now AC Dispensing's general manager) have built and sold thousands of machines to doughnut and fast-food franchises across North America. Revenue doubled in each of the last three years.

Now that the company is doing so well, Duck has gone back to concentrating on his passion: research and development. And who knows, maybe one of these mornings, as he sips his perfect, predictable Tim Hortons coffee—one cream, one sugar—Duck will figure out how to turn another pet peeve into his next big moneymaker.

Exploring

1. Why do you think Michael Duck hired his former boss to be general manager of AC Dispensing?
2. After he created his cream dispenser, Michael Duck took marketing courses at night school to learn how to sell it. What did he do initially to get his product noticed? Why do you think that was an effective strategy?
3. Many Canadians drink coffee every day. What impact do you think Duck's invention has had on the industry? With a partner, create a collage of inventions that have a daily impact on our lives. Share it with the class.
4. Michael Duck was irritated by something; his boss challenged him to fix it. Write down three things that bother you. Trade your list with a partner. Try to find at least two possible solutions for each problem.

E-Bits & Bytes

Visit www.business.nelson.com and follow the links to "inventors" to find out more about Canadian inventions and innovations. Choose one example to investigate in more detail. Present your findings to the class in an inventive way.

Invention and Innovation

Invention and innovation are closely linked for the successful entrepreneur or enterprising person. An **invention** is the creation of something new, while an **innovation** is a change to something that already exists.

The word "invention" originates from the Latin word *invenire*, which means "to come upon." An inventor "comes upon" a new idea. Some inventions happen by accident. When James Wright, an engineer, was asked to find a way to make synthetic rubber, he tried mixing different chemicals to see what would happen. He tried combining boric acid with silicone oil. The result was stretchy and bouncy—too stretchy to work as a rubber substitute. But when some engineers at a party got hold of the samples, they started stretching it and tossing it around the room. Another party guest, an advertising man named Paul Hodgson, recognized the potential of this material as a toy. When he thought of packaging it in plastic egg-shaped containers, Silly Putty was born.

Other inventions happen because someone takes the time to look for a solution to a problem. Jacques Plante, a goalie in the NHL, was concerned about the injuries goalies suffered when they were hit in the face with the puck. He decided to work with Fibreglass Canada to develop the first-ever goalie mask. Today, a mask is an essential part of every goalie's equipment.

Former NHL goalie Jacques Plante (below) asked, "What if I wear a mask to protect my face?"

94 Unit 2 ◆ Preparing the Way

> **Worth Repeating**
>
> "Do not follow where the path may lead. Go instead where there's no path and leave a trail."
>
> Muriel Strode, writer

Innovations happen the same way inventions do—by accident or by design. Just ask Ruth Wakefield, the creator of the chocolate chip cookie. In 1933, Ruth and her husband owned the Toll House Inn, a restaurant near Boston. One day, she was in a rush and changed the chocolate cookie recipe she always used. Instead of using melted chocolate, she broke a semisweet chocolate bar into pieces and tossed the pieces into the batter. To everyone's astonishment, the chocolate chunks didn't mix with the rest of the batter as the cookies baked, and her customers loved the results!

Most new ideas begin with a "What if…?" question. Michael Duck asked, "What if I could come up with a better way to dispense cream?" Paul Hodgson asked, "What if we market this as a toy instead of a rubber substitute?" Jacques Plante asked, "What if I wear a mask to protect my face?" And Ruth Wakefield asked, "What if I substitute chocolate chunks for melted chocolate?"

"What if…?" questions stimulate your imagination and shake up your perspective. Think about a product or service you use. Ask yourself, "What if I shrank it? enlarged it? made it lighter? changed its shape? reversed it? added something? subtracted something? sold it in another place? sold it in a different way? changed its name?"

PROTECTING YOUR IDEAS

Once you've come up with an idea, an invention, or an innovation, there are a number of ways to protect it so potential competitors can't take advantage of it. In Canada, there are several ways to protect your **intellectual property**. You can find information about each of these topics by viewing the Canadian Intellectual Property Office Web site by following the links at www.business.nelson.com, or by looking under the heading "Business" in the blue pages of your phone book.

PATENTS

A **patent** is a grant made by the government that gives the creator of an invention the sole right to make, use, and sell the invention for a set period of time. This provides an incentive for people to explore and do research, and makes it safer for people to discuss their work. Anyone can apply for a patent through the federal government.

COPYRIGHTS

A **copyright** protects literary works, musical works, artistic works, and software. By law, all Canadians hold the copyright to any original work they have created unless they were hired or employed to create it. (In that case, the employer who paid for its creation owns it.) Under the Copyright Act, no one can publish, perform, translate,

> **Agents of Change**
>
> Can you imagine driving a car without windshield wipers? Until 1903, that's exactly what you would have had to do. Mary Anderson of Alabama decided to do something about it and created one of the first windshield wipers for cars. Mary hit upon an idea that's still helping us today.
>
> Were Mary Anderson's windshield wipers an invention or an innovation? Explain.

or adapt another person's work without permission. If the copyright holder dies, the copyright is transferred to the holder's heirs for a period of 50 years and then expires unless the heirs take steps to renew it. Items that might be copyrighted include books, maps, song lyrics, music, sculptures, paintings, photographs, films, tapes, computer programs, databases, performances, sound recordings, and communication signals.

How are the designs of these products distinctive? How might a distinctive design help sales?

TRADEMARKS

Trademarks are words, symbols, or designs—or a combination of these—used to identify a product or service and distinguish it from its competitors. Trademarks are valuable because they have come to represent the reputation of the producer as well as the products that bear them.

Trademarks come in three basic categories: **Ordinary marks** are words or symbols that distinguish the wares or services of a specific firm or individual. **Certification marks** identify wares or services that meet a defined standard. They are owned by one person but licensed to others to identify acceptable wares or services. **Distinguishing guises** refer to the unique shape of a product or its package—such as the distinctive design of a Coke bottle.

INDUSTRIAL DESIGN ACT

In Canada, **industrial designs** are protected by the Industrial Design Act. An industrial design is anything made by hand, tool, or machine that has distinctive features, such as the shape of a chair or the decoration on the handle of a spoon. Once a design is registered, the designer, called the **proprietor**, has exclusive rights to the design for a 10-year period.

INTEGRATED CIRCUIT TOPOGRAPHY ACT

Integrated Circuit Topographies (ICT) are electronic integrated circuits or **IC products** that are configured and interconnected. These creations are protected in Canada by the Integrated Circuit Topography Act, which gives the creator exclusive rights for a period of ten years after registration. Because products containing these circuits are often exported outside Canada, Canada has reciprocal agreements with other countries that also protect the design for ten years.

Worth Repeating

"Creativity is thinking up new things. Innovation is doing new things."

Theodore Levitt, management thinker and author

Suggest examples of creativity and innovation that demonstrate the differences between them.

Cool Stuff

A corporate logo can instantly communicate an organization's message. In a recent poll to select the top 50 logos of all time, the one for the Red Cross came second (after the Michelin Man). The Red Cross symbol, adopted in 1863 as a globally recognized symbol for medical personnel, is now "one of the most widely recognized and understood symbols of all time."

R.O.B. Magazine

Design a logo that conveys a message about the ideals of your school.

YOUR TURN

1. Explain the difference between an invention and an innovation. Give an example of each.

2. Outline the five ways to protect your ideas and inventions.

3. Choose three Canadian inventors or inventor teams from the list that follows:
   - Sam Jacks
   - James Naismith
   - Reginald Fessenden
   - Olivia Poole
   - Sir Sandford Fleming
   - Arthur Sicard
   - Rachel Zimmerman
   - Chris Haney/Scott Abbott
   - Dr. Elsie MacGill/Dr. Inge Russel

   Conduct research with a partner or small group to find out more about these people and their inventions. Which inventors are also innovators? Explain your reasoning.

4. Complete the sentence stem "What if…?" with an idea for a business venture. Do this several times until you have a page full of ideas. Don't be afraid to include crazy ideas along with the rest.
   a) Compare your ideas to look for any common threads.
   b) What did you discover about yourself as you looked for patterns in your ideas?

Venture Profile

IMPROVE WITH !MPROV

Andy Burnham makes his ideas work with his venture, !mprov at work. Andy began looking for alternatives when he grew dissatisfied with his marketing job at a Montreal electronics firm. He felt that his employers put more emphasis on seniority than on new ideas. After reading *Do What You Love, The Money Will Follow: Discovering Your Right Livelihood* by Marsha Sinetar, Andy began to ask himself, "What if…?"

Andy's idea blossomed from his passion for comedy. He went to Toronto to try his hand at improvisational comedy and acting. In a moment of inspiration, Andy realized that many of the skills needed for improv are the same skills that help people become creative and innovative problem solvers and communicators. He took his idea one step further and reasoned that a comedy-based approach would be an attractive option for companies looking for corporate training.

"What a perfect match!" Andy says. "I saw a way to combine my love of comedy with a need out there in the world. I worked for a year installing windows and doing extra work while I wrote my business plan and analyzed the competition."

Andy's first contract in January 1999 was a 90-minute experiential keynote address for The Law Society of Upper Canada.

As the business developed, Andy had to overcome obstacles such as operating on a shoestring budget, finding ways to promote his business, and facing his own fear of failure. Sometimes he looked to other people for help. Since he could only call a certain number of companies each day, he wondered, "What if I didn't *have* to sell myself and my programs directly? What if I found others to offer my services for me?"

The answer was to contact speakers' agencies, brokers, and entertainment agencies. "I leveraged my time. Now I was contacting people who could sell my ideas to hundreds of people with whom I had no prior relationship."

!mprov at work's target customers are teams in mid- to large-sized corporations that want to find new ways to generate ideas and solve problems. The business grew 75% in each of its first two years by adding a Web site, focusing more attention on marketing, and setting up strategic partnerships with other organizations.

!mprov at work is constantly looking for new markets, but Andy still finds time to focus on the design and delivery. He says, "If you can focus on your passion and get others to do the essential tasks that help your business grow, you can have success."

Andy's advice to young entrepreneurs?

"Don't say something will never work. This is self-defeating because so many ideas start off as absurd or crazy notions. Build on ideas by accepting their possibilities. Be willing to let go of your original idea so it can grow and change."

Exploring

1. Would you say Andy Burnham is an inventor or an innovator? Why?

2. What motivated Andy to create his venture?

3. Once people have an idea, Andy recommends that they should develop an insatiable curiosity about it. "Creativity starts with questions," he says. "If you share your idea with others and use their experience and knowledge, there's a better chance that your idea will work."

    With a small group, choose a business currently operating in your community. Brainstorm and record as many questions as you can about the business.

4. Choose a few of the questions you generated in Question 3. To find the answers, talk with someone who works at the business you chose. Share your findings with the rest of the class.

5. Andy Burnham uses an activity called "The Gibberish Translator" to help people learn to pick up information from nonverbal cues, such as body language, facial expressions, and tone of voice. Here is how it works:

    a) Form a circle so each student can see everyone else.

    b) One student takes a step into the circle, acts out some imaginary action (such as looking through binoculars), and creates a short phrase in Gibberish (e.g., "Bloo, mack slock tor winga mont!") to go with the action.

    c) The next student in the circle repeats both the Gibberish phrase and the action as accurately as possible.

    d) The third student repeats the action and translates the Gibberish into English. (There are no right and wrong translations, but the meaning should reflect the action as well as any emotions suggested by body language or tone of voice.)

    e) The next person makes up a new action and Gibberish phrase, and the activity continues until everyone has had a turn.

    If you have trouble making up Gibberish, try taking a few deep breaths and then saying whatever occurs to you. Gibberish comes from your feelings, not from your thoughts.

The Problem-Solving Process

Michael Duck and Andy Burnham are both creative people. Each one had an idea, and then organized the resources needed to create a venture. To be successful, enterprising people and entrepreneurs not only need to be creative thinkers, they also need to be good problem solvers.

STAGES AND SKILLS IN THE PROBLEM-SOLVING PROCESS

The problem-solving process involves three stages: the problem-finding stage, the idea-finding stage, and the solution-finding stage. It also requires both creative-thinking skills and critical-thinking skills.

Figure 5.1 The Creative Problem-Solving Process

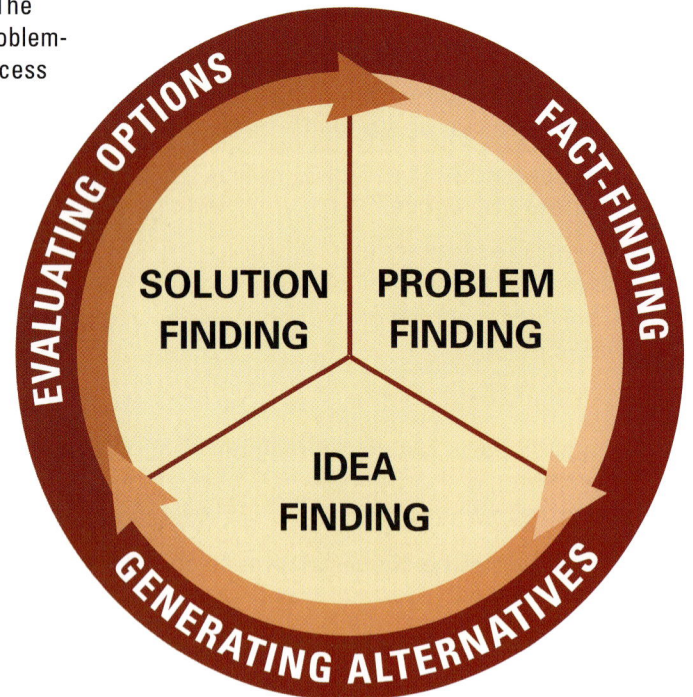

PROBLEM FINDING

In the **problem-finding** stage, the entrepreneur tries to define the problem by gathering observations, feelings, and impressions about the situation. Attitudes are very important since they influence how the problem is perceived. The inventive individual will see a problem as an opportunity that might lead to the creation of a venture.

Fact-finding is also an important feature of this stage. Facts help the entrepreneur define the problem and may provide information that can be used in the solution.

IDEA FINDING

At the **idea-finding** stage, the entrepreneur tries to come up with different alternatives or different ways of solving the problem. Creativity is the key! Some ideas may turn out to be absurd, but no alternative should be dismissed at this stage. All ideas should be evaluated. Sometimes the craziest ideas lead to the best ventures, so record every alternative you generate.

Figure 5.2 Steps to Problem Solving

1. Think about the problem.
2. Generate lots of possible solutions.
3. Establish criteria for evaluating ideas.
4. Use your criteria for evaluating ideas.
5. Rank your ideas and select the best one.
6. Try out your idea.
7. Is the problem solved? If not, choose another idea and try again.

SOLUTION FINDING

The final step in the process is the **solution-finding** stage, when the entrepreneur will evaluate each of the ideas created earlier. Before this can happen, the entrepreneur needs to establish the **criteria** that will be used to evaluate each option. Criteria are the standards or measures that will be used to evaluate the strengths and weaknesses of each idea. Those ideas that do not meet the criteria are tossed out. The remaining ideas are ranked until it becomes possible to choose the best solution.

The process is not complete until a solution has been tried and evaluated to make sure that the problem has, in fact, been solved. If the solution does not turn out as expected, the entrepreneur has to go back a few steps to generate more ideas or select a different solution.

Agents of Change

In 1922, 15-year-old Joseph-Armand Bombardier had a problem. He wanted to design a vehicle that would run on skis, to help people travel through the snow. He tried exchanging the front wheels of a car for skis and adding extra wheels in the back—it didn't work. Over the next few years, he tried adding propellers, belts, and lots of small wheels. By 1935, he had designed a wooden sprocket wheel with 12 cogs, and covered it with a track made of rubber belting and cross-links. This time, it worked! Armand patented his idea and the resulting venture, Bombardier, is now a world leader in manufacturing not only Ski-Doos and Sea-Doos, but also aerospace technology.

When Bombardier introduced his 1959 model snowmobile, he called it the Ski-Dog. Suppose you were hired to help the company come up with a better name for the snowmobile. Use the problem-solving steps shown in Figure 5.2 to come up with the perfect name. (No fair choosing the same name Bombardier eventually decided to use: Ski-Doo!)

LATERAL THINKING

Lateral thinking means generating ideas by being flexible and creative. Lateral thinkers break away from standard solutions and solve problems in unique and different ways. Lateral thinking moves sideways rather than forward or up and down. This allows the problem solver or venture planner to look at a problem from a unique perspective.

Lateral thinking involves a number of different perceptions and methods, including provocation, in order to get us to think "outside the box"—that is, to think about things in a new way.

For example, a horse trainer noticed that her horses always licked the salt from the cars of farm visitors, and often scratched the paint. Since the horses roamed the farm freely, guests were asked to drive their cars into the corral and close the gate after them to keep the horses out. Lateral thinking helped the trainer see that the corral could be used to keep things out, as well as to keep them in.

> *Lateral thinking moves sideways rather than forward or up and down. This allows the problem solver or venture planner to look at a problem from a unique perspective.*

THE SIX THINKING HATS

Edward De Bono is an expert on creative thinking. According to him, there are six modes of thinking. To explain his idea, De Bono uses the analogy of six metaphorical **Thinking Hats** that can be put on and taken off at will by the idea creator or problem solver.

These hats do not reflect the wearers or their characteristics. The hats are colour-coded to help people remember which type of thinking is associated with each one.

Figure 5.3 The Six Thinking Hats

Worth Repeating

"So what's in a name anyway? According to naming experts—everything. Granted, as Shakespeare's Juliet noted, a rose by any other name would smell as sweet ... but name it a thugwhistle and see if it sells half as much. There is power in a name."

Lindsay Elliott, Realm magazine

What does this quote reveal about the wisdom of Bombardier's decision? (See Agents of Change on page 101.)

THE WHITE HAT

White hat thinking is concerned with gathering facts, figures, and objective information. It does not allow opinions to interfere. The white hat thinker should think like a computer, without emotion. White hat thinking sounds like

- Give me the facts and figures, please!
- How many? How often? How much? When?
- What is the problem?
- What are the needs?

THE RED HAT

The red hat recognizes that emotions and intuition influence thinking. The red hat thinker uses hunches and feelings to generate information without judgment or logic. Red hat thinking sounds like

- I have a hunch that this ...
- This is how I feel about ...
- I think this is terrible!

THE GREEN HAT

The green hat indicates a form of lateral thinking that includes creativity, alternatives, and proposals. The colour green represents nature and things that grow from seeds. Like plants, creativity also grows from seeds—the seeds of ideas. Green hat thinking encourages provocations and change, and sounds like

- Aha! I've got an idea!
- So, that's what you mean!
- How else can this be done?

THE BLACK HAT

The black hat represents the use of judgment and caution. This thinker must present a logical case against the idea. The black hat always provides negative feedback that is objective and free from emotions. Black hat thinking sounds like

- This idea won't work because ...
- This could pose a problem.
- Yes, but ...

Agents of Change

During the 1930s, the Kraft company tried selling packages of low-priced cheddar cheese powder. No one wanted them. Left with cases of the stuff, one salesman tied packages of cheese powder to boxes of macaroni and started selling the two together. He called the new item Kraft Dinner.

How are the salesman's solution to the cheese powder problem and the trainer's solution to the salt-licking problem (on page 102) examples of lateral thinking?

E-Bits & Bytes

"WebCT, a University of British Columbia spinoff, and now the Canadian arm of an American company, makes Web course development software including tools that can create a kind of virtual classroom. Students can talk together online in real time, download assignments, and even listen in on guest lectures. The company's learning products are used by more that 4.3 million students at more than 1000 institutions."

*Wendy Stueck,
The Globe and Mail*

Meet with a small group to discuss the implications of online learning for traditional schooling. What are the problems students encounter? Use all of the Thinking Hats in turn to find possible solutions to these problems. When you're finished, share your recommendations with the class.

THE YELLOW HAT

The yellow hat is also logical, but in a very constructive way. The yellow hat looks for positive outcomes, and reasons why the idea will work. Put on the yellow hat when you want to assess the benefits of a situation. Yellow hat thinking sounds like

- This fits together well.
- I want to explore this further.
- This idea has some value.

THE BLUE HAT

Put on the blue hat and think about how the hats are working together to solve the problem, not the problem itself. Blue hat thinking is used to lead and pull the other hats together. The blue hat thinker is the one who makes things happen. Blue hat thinking sounds like

- Focus!
- Let's get started!
- It's your turn!

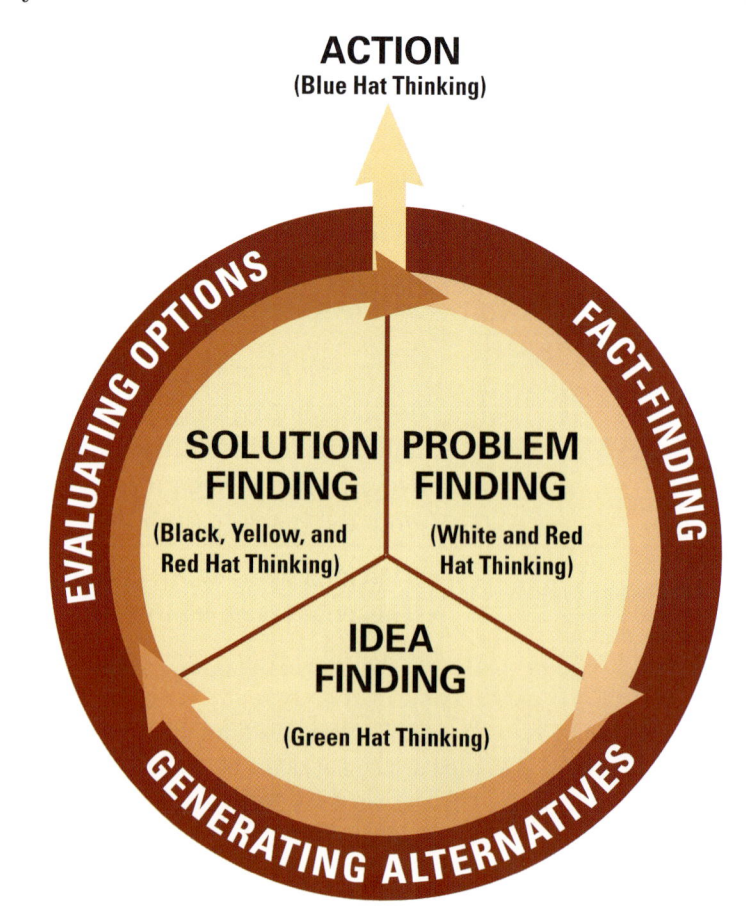

Figure 5.4 How De Bono's Hats Fit the Problem-solving Model

Cool Stuff

HOW DO YOU GATHER INFORMATION?

When it comes to gathering information, what's your personal style? For each row in the table, select either Column A or B, depending on which statement describes you best.

A		B
I enjoy looking at details and proof that things are really as they appear to be.	or	I tend to skim over details and look for hidden meanings in things.
I enjoy checking, inspecting, and reading the fine print, finding out all the information I can.	or	I become impatient with routine and repetition, and with slow, precise activities.
I enjoy things as they are, recall past events, and learn from the combination of these two in a "common sense" sort of way.	or	In a flash of insight, I go with my hunches on many things.
It would be fairly accurate to describe me as realistic and practical.	or	It would be fairly accurate to describe me as imaginative and inventive.
I rarely rely on inspiration to keep me going.	or	I have many bursts of energy with slack periods in between.

If most of your choices are from Column A, you prefer a fact-based white hat approach. If you chose more from Column B, you prefer to rely on hunches and intuition, like the red hat.

C.M. Mamchur, Insights: Understanding Yourself and Others

YOUR TURN

1. What skills do effective problem solvers demonstrate?

2. Review your self-assessment from Chapter 3 to determine which of these skills you have and which you need to develop. Organize the information in a chart and write a brief conclusion.

3. With a small group, discuss the difference between problem finding and fact-finding. Give an example of each.

4. Which of the Six Thinking Hats would you be wearing when you make each of these statements?
   a) I like your idea.
   b) I need all the statistics first.
   c) That is just too expensive to do.
   d) I just know that this is going to be great.
   e) Let's see if we can make it fit into a smaller space.
   f) Get all the stuff we need so we can start tomorrow.

5. Think of a problem currently in the news in your community. Meet with a small group and use De Bono's "thinking hat" approach to see what solutions you can generate. When you're finished, share your recommendations with the class.

Chapter 5 ◆ Invention, Innovation, and the Creative Edge

How Do You Interpret Information?

Psychologists have learned that people may interpret the same thing or event in many different ways. To explore how you interpret information, try these exercises with a partner.

1. How many squares do you see in this figure? Compare your answer with your partner's.
2. Six volumes of an encyclopedia are lined up on a shelf. The pages in each volume are 2 cm thick and the covers are each 0.3 cm thick. If you could measure a straight line from the centre of the first page of Volume 1 to the last page of Volume 6, how long would this line be?
3. With a partner, cut some shapes out of coloured construction paper. (The shapes and colours do not matter, but you and your partner will need matching sets.) Set up a barrier, such as a book standing on end, so you and your partner each have a work surface the other person can't see. One person arranges the shapes to form a design, and then describes the design so the other person can make it without looking. Compare the results. Do your designs look the same? If not, what differences were there in how each person perceived the instructions?

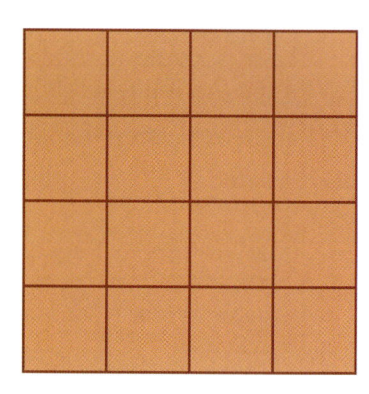

More than One Solution

Most math problems, like the encyclopedia problem above, have only one solution. (Don't feel bad if you got the wrong answer, though; only about one person in ten is able to solve it on the first try.) In real life, there are usually many ways to solve a problem. The more ideas you have, the more options you have. And options mean better solutions.

Smart entrepreneurs and intrapreneurs do not stop thinking when they find one right answer. Instead, they look around for more. To become a better problem solver, cultivate your curiosity. The best problem solvers are constantly searching, looking, and probing. They absorb and remember a wide variety of information, and have an ability to notice details without losing their perspective on the larger issues.

HOW TO FIND MORE ANSWERS

When you're looking for solutions to problems, here are some strategies you might try:

- Change your routines.
- Talk to and listen to people.
- Make lists and don't be afraid to change them.
- Daydream.
- Try to look at things from different perspectives.
- Read something you've never read before.
- Try something you've never tried before.
- Invite ideas from others and think of ways to improve or combine them.
- Write down all your new ideas before you forget them.

ADVANTAGES OF TEAMWORK

Some ventures are developed by individuals; sometimes they grow from the combined efforts of a group. Creative inventors and innovators may not have the time or energy needed to develop their ideas on their own. Like Andy Burnham, good problem solvers seek out people who can help them.

Sometimes people with good ideas are nervous about sharing their ideas. They may be afraid that their ideas will be laughed at, or that someone else will take advantage of their creativity. By trying to do it alone, they risk running out of energy and ideas before the venture gets off the ground.

Other creative people enjoy generating ideas, but don't want to put in the work it would take to see their ideas transformed into ventures. These individuals are motivated by the excitement of problem solving. They may be inventors or innovators, but they are not entrepreneurs.

The advantage of teamwork is that it builds on people's strengths, and provides support for their weaknesses. Sometimes, it takes inventors, entrepreneurs, and others, working together, to bring a venture to life.

THE LEFT AND RIGHT BRAIN AND PROBLEM SOLVING

The human brain is divided into two hemispheres—the **right brain** and the **left brain**. Brain research indicates that each half functions differently. The left brain is sequential, analytical, and linear. It contains the function of language and all language-related activities. The

---

International NEWS

Huntsville, Ontario, resident Bob Hutcheson operates Hutcheson's Sand and Gravel, which exports specialty sand worldwide. Hutcheson sends sand to beach resorts in Las Vegas and tested the sand for the beach volleyball court in Sydney, Australia, for the 2000 Olympics. Hutcheson's Sand and Gravel also provides sand for golf courses and bunkers in Canadian communities. Canadian initiative—and sand—goes a long way around the globe.

Roberta Avery, The Toronto Star

How can you tell that Bob Hutcheson is a creative problem solver?

right brain works with the left brain and is the portion that is creative, imaginative, emotional, and intuitive.

Figure 5.5 We possess a single brain, but it is made up of two hemispheres.

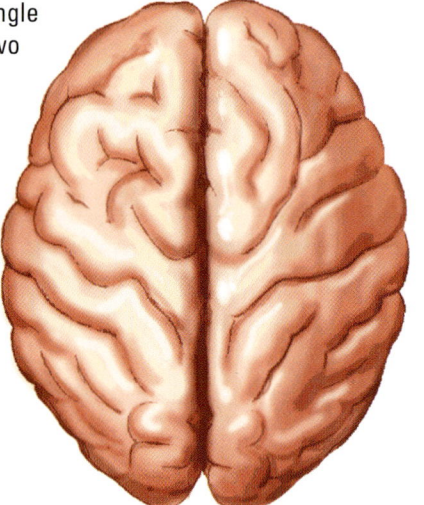

This creative side of our brain often gets forgotten in the rush of everyday life. However, with the right brain, we often get sudden insight into something, and everything falls magically into place. The two brain hemispheres work together like teammates, supporting each other and producing results that neither one could attain on its own. When the creative potential of the right brain is combined with the linear thinking of the left brain, the power of an individual's creativity can increase dramatically.

Exercising the right brain helps people become more creative. How can you exercise your right brain? Try reading out loud! This type of reading grabs the attention of the right brain and the sound stimulates it into action—creative action. The next time you have homework to do or a problem to solve, try reading it aloud. The results may surprise you!

Think About It

Study Figure 5.6 and consider the differences it suggests. How is the right hemisphere different from the left?

Figure 5.6 Left and right hemispheres process information in very different ways. This figure presents them in the form of an image.

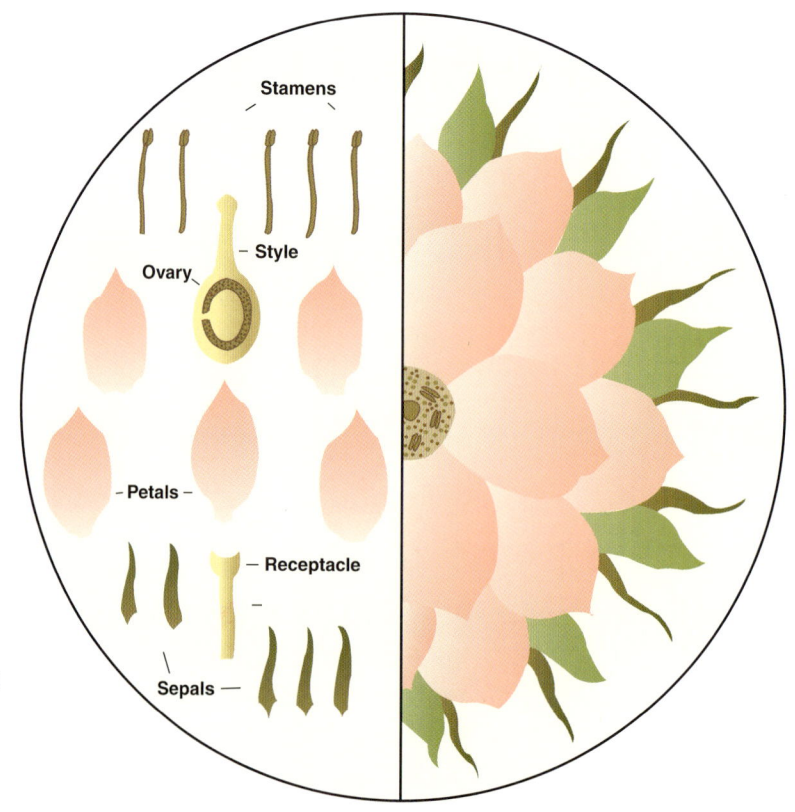

108 Unit 2 ◆ Preparing the Way

Figure 5.7 Verbal and visual representation of the differences between the processing styles of the two hemispheres

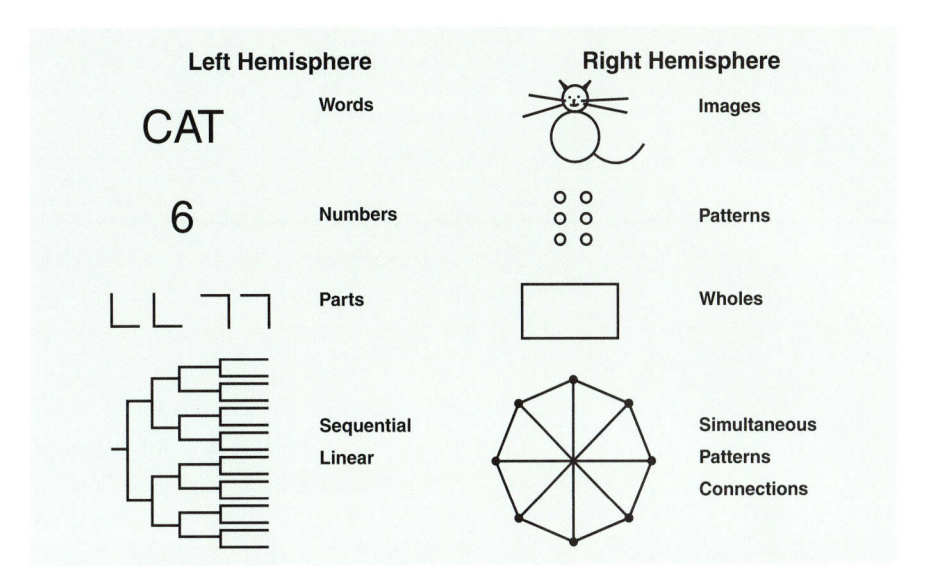

Left Hemisphere

CAT — Words
6 — Numbers
⌐⌐ ¬¬ — Parts
(tree diagram) — Sequential / Linear

Right Hemisphere

(cat drawing) — Images
(dot pattern) — Patterns
(rectangle) — Wholes
(star/web diagram) — Simultaneous Patterns Connections

Agents of Change

Gutenberg observed the operation of the coin punch and the wine press, and conceived the idea of the printing press. Picasso saw the handlebars of a bicycle and sculpted the horns of a bull.

What connections might each man have made between the objects he observed and the ideas that came to him as a result?

YOUR TURN

1. What are the functions of each of the two hemispheres of the brain?

2. Make a list of the ways in which your experiences at school have developed the left and right sides of your brain. What experiences have taught you to think critically? creatively?

3. Which side of your brain do you feel most comfortable using? To find out, think about how you prefer to learn to play a new game. Do you read the directions or do you figure it out as you play?

4. What could you do to exercise the side of your brain that you feel less comfortable using?

5. In what situations do you find that you do your best creative thinking?

6. What do you think of when somebody says the word, "pizza"? Take a few minutes to write down everything you can think of about pizza, including anything that you associate with it— uses, properties, emotions, and so on. Now use some of the items on your list to help you find at least three solutions to the following problem: Homelessness is on the upswing in Canadian cities, and winter is approaching. What can Canadians do to help?

Chapter 5 ◆ Invention, Innovation, and the Creative Edge   109

More Ways to Generate Ideas

As human beings, we have many ways to use our brains for generating ideas.

Word Clustering

Word clustering is the free association of ideas and words. It helps stimulate the right brain into action. Begin by writing a word or phrase at the centre of a page. Circle your word or phrase. Then write other words or phrases that come to mind as you consider the idea at the centre. Circle each new idea. Draw lines between the circles that are connected in your mind. When you finish, look for patterns that will increase your understanding of the first idea. This is a great activity to use when you're studying for a test, when you're looking for new ideas, or when you need to make a decision.

Mind Mapping

Mind mapping is a more visual way of organizing and relating ideas using pictures and key words. Again, start at the centre of a page. Instead of writing a word, draw a picture that captures the main idea for your map. (With mind maps, the more pictures you can substitute for words, the better.) Work your way out from the centre by linking words or pictures that represent subthemes to the central focus. Print key words along the connecting lines to reinforce ideas. Use colours, icons, and arrows to link related ideas or make things stand out. Balance is not necessary, but fun and creativity are. If you run out of ideas on one branch, start working on another one. If you run out of space, extend your map by attaching extra sheets of paper.

A mind map works in the same way a brain does to associate key words and images, and make connections. Using pictures as well as words helps the flow of ideas and makes them easier to remember. Starting in the centre of the page allows lateral thinking in all directions.

The more you use mind maps, the more fluently your ideas will flow. Mind maps make great study aids because they are easy to follow and they stimulate your memory. You could use them for brainstorming, note taking, generating ideas, making decisions, solving problems, planning, and presenting information.

Brainstorming

Completing a word cluster or a mind mapping exercise with other people is a form of **brainstorming**. Brainstorming, or productive thinking, as it is sometimes called, can generate a large number of new and unusual ideas. As with word clustering and mind mapping, there are a few simple rules to follow. The most important rule is to

---

Worth Repeating

"It is the function of creative [people] to perceive the relations between thoughts, or things, or forms of expression that may seem utterly different, and to be able to combine them into some new forms—the power to connect the seemingly unconnected."

William Plomer, author and poet

Worth Repeating

"If you can't imagine it, you can never do it. In my experience, the image always precedes the reality."

Marilyn King, two-time Olympic Pentathlete

How do you think imagining or visualizing helps an athlete achieve his or her goals?

International NEWS

The Canadian founder of iGrocer.com woos busy, dual-income Japanese families. Duane Sandberg is convinced that rice, sushi, and seaweed can be served up on the Internet.... In May 2000, the Edmonton native launched Tokyo-based iGrocer.com as an upscale supermarket on the Net.

Tyler Hamilton, The Globe and Mail

How is Duane Sandberg an innovator? What problems will he likely need to find creative solutions for?

---

record every single idea you generate, even the zany ones, and not to be judgmental. You never know when an idea that may seem implausible can lead to another idea that is sensational. Evaluation comes *after* the brainstorming, not during it.

People can think more creatively when they are not concerned about finding *the* right answer. In a good brainstorming session, the ideas are flying almost as fast as you can write them down, and people are piggybacking their own ideas onto those of others. In fact, brainstorming may be one situation where quantity is better than quality.

VISUALIZATION

Closing your eyes and **visualizing** different scenarios in your mind can help you become more comfortable with new ideas. Many professional athletes visualize their new routines before they actually try them. See things the way you want them to be and visualize the idea becoming a reality. Visualize yourself in your venture.

"Just imagine!" is a very catchy phrase that is used to sell all sorts of things, but it also has a fundamental wisdom. People who can imagine are people who can create.

THE IDEAS SPOKE OF THE VENTURE CREATION WHEEL

Every successful venture starts out as an idea. Creative thinkers are good at seeing possibilities and generating alternatives.

Entrepreneurs develop and apply these new ideas to satisfy a need or solve a problem. They organize their resources and build teams in order to nurture and develop the idea, and bring it to maturity.

Some enterprising people are creative themselves, while others rely on having a network of creative people around them; yet Ideas remains an important spoke in the Venture Creation Wheel.

With today's ease of access to the Internet and other communications technology, the possibilities for invention and innovation are greater than ever. E-commerce has opened the door to a multitude of fresh ideas. It has reinvented the way we do business and has enabled new products and services to emerge at a rapid rate. Creativity, or access to creative people, has become an indispensable commodity for anyone who expects to flourish in the new economy.

ACTIVITIES

FLASHBACKS

The following statements express main ideas in this chapter. Study them for five minutes. Then, without looking at them, see how many you can tell to a partner in your own words.

- Every venture starts with an idea.
- Asking "What if…?" is a powerful tool in idea creation.
- Invention means creating something new while innovation means looking at something familiar in a new way.
- The creative problem-solving process involves problem finding, idea finding, and solution finding.
- Lateral thinking involves viewing problems from different perspectives.
- Edward De Bono's Six Thinking Hats model helps create ideas and solve problems.
- The human brain is divided into two parts: the creative brain on the right side and the logical, rational brain on the left side.
- Word clustering, mind mapping, and brainstorming are all strategies people can use to generate ideas and solve problems.
- Many inventors need entrepreneurs to bring their inventions to the world's attention.

LESSONS LEARNED

1. Name seven possible sources of venture ideas.

2. What does being a good observer have to do with generating ideas for a venture?

3. Why do enterprising people and entrepreneurs tend to seek the support of inventors and innovators?

4. Identify a problem that you have encountered. Explain how a solution might develop through each of the seven steps in the problem-solving process.

5. Outline five ways in which Canadians can protect their ideas and inventions.

6. What is the purpose of wearing De Bono's yellow and black hats? Why are both these hats necessary?

7. Which of De Bono's coloured hats is the most important for idea creation? Why?

8. Describe how your left brain and your right brain work together to help you generate ideas.

9. Explain the relationship between innovation and technology.

VENTURING OUT

1. Think of a problem that affects your school.
   a) Work with a small group to generate as many "What if…?" questions as you can about the problem.
   b) Choose one of your questions and apply the seven problem-solving steps to the problem. What solutions can you suggest?

2. Choose one of the following topics to brainstorm with a small group. Use word clustering or mind mapping to organize your ideas.
   a) How could I find startup capital for a venture?
   b) How could we help people who live in seniors' homes in our community?
   c) How can we make more efficient use of our time each day?

3. All these inventions were created by Canadians or by people who have lived in Canada:
   - Pablum
   - the Canadarm
   - Skydome's retractable roof
   - Java Script
   - microfilm
   - the telephone
   - the electronic synthesizer
   - the cardiac pacemaker

   Choose two of these inventions to find out
   a) who invented each one, and when and how it was invented
   b) how the invention developed into an entrepreneurial venture
   c) to what extent the inventor was involved in, or gained from, the production and use of the new invention
   d) how people have benefited from each invention

4. List five inventions or innovations in goods, services, or technology that have changed the way we do things.

E-Bits & Bytes

Visit www.business.nelson.com and follow the links to "ideas" to find Web sites that will help you learn more about creative thinking. Choose one site to investigate in more detail. Write a short guide to this Web site that can be included in a class "Creative Thinking" directory.

POINT OF VIEW

1. Andy Burnham uses this exercise, called "The Could Exercise," to help people think about what they *could* do.
   a) Write down three things you could do right now with the skills you have.
   b) What would you do if you could do anything you can imagine with your life?
   c) What help could you get from teachers, friends, and family?
   d) What could you do to help someone else?
   e) What financing could you get from the government or other agencies and organizations?
   f) How could you translate what you love to do into a business?

2. Create a mind map to show as many aspects as you can of an entrepreneurial venture that you might like to start some day. Remember to begin in the middle of the page, to use as many pictures as possible, and to have fun!

CHAPTER 6

Opportunities, Ideas, and the Enterprising Work Environment

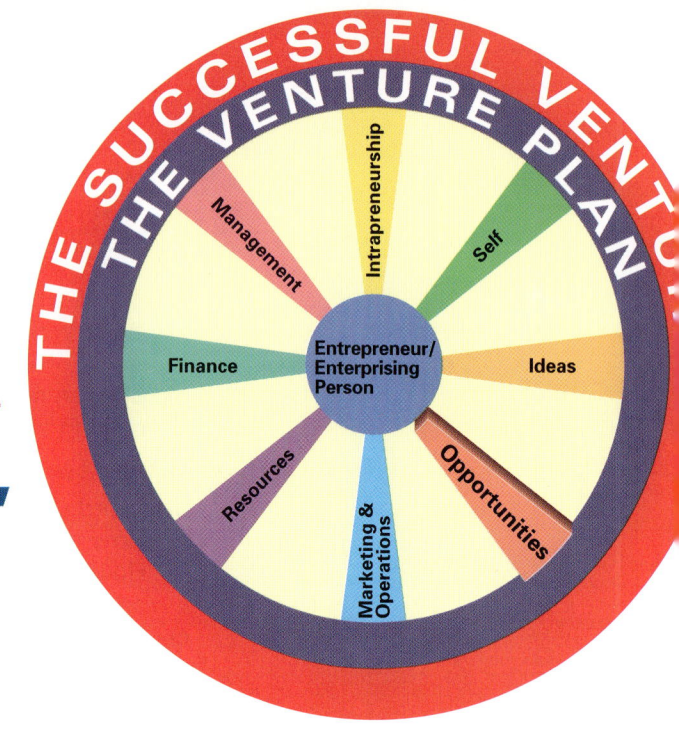

LEARNING OPPORTUNITIES

By the end of this chapter, you should be able to
- identify the relationship between opportunities and ideas
- distinguish between fads and trends
- analyze current economic and social trends
- use research techniques to determine trends, and to identify and evaluate opportunities
- evaluate the factors that influence the creation of an enterprising work environment

Entrepreneurial Language
- opportunity
- syndicated
- market-pulled entrepreneurship
- product-driven entrepreneurship
- service-driven entrepreneurship
- fad
- forecast
- time-series forecast
- growth trend
- stable situation
- declining trend
- linear
- curved
- irregular
- cyclical
- primary research
- secondary research
- research instrument
- multiple-choice question
- attitude scale
- open-ended question
- customer profile
- window of opportunity
- opportunity cost
- European Union
- mission statement

This chapter is about recognizing and capitalizing on opportunities. Look up the word "opportunity" in a dictionary and record the definitions you find. Then, choose six other words from this list, look them up in the dictionary, and think about what each one might have to do with an opportunity.

Venture Profile

BACK TO THE FUTURE: FIVE SISTERS USE WEB-OF-MOUTH TO ENERGIZE THE RADIO BIZ

Alissa MacMillan, Working Woman

Their concept was simple: conversation. And their medium, equally quaint. But for the originators of the popular American radio show *Satellite Sisters*—Julie, Liz, Sheila, Monica, and Lian Dolan—their labour of love has put a new spin on old-fashioned chat. "Radio is the medium of the future," says Liz, 43, who notes the average household has five sets. "We wanted to marry what's great about radio and the Web."

By linking their weekly show with their Web site (www.satellitesisters.com)—and without any previous experience in radio or the Internet—the sisters have created a new form of exchange that has momentum of its own. The topics they discuss in their show also appear on their Web site, and listeners or viewers can e-mail the sisters or post their views on the site's board about these topics any time they want. "The conversation can go on without us," says Liz. "Moving people back and forth between the radio and the Web allows for a much higher level of dialogue." In partnership with Oregon Public Radio and WNYC, the show premiered in April 2000, went national on Public Radio International two months later, and is now on more than 25 stations. Every week, from New York, Portland, Oregon, Bangkok, Thailand, and Pasadena, California, the sisters talk about everything from childcare to phobias to elephants.

"I'm really impressed with my sisters' foresight," says 45-year-old Julie of the family venture. "I always knew they were good, but I never knew how good."

Exploring

1. What opportunity did the Dolan sisters see?
2. What "new form of exchange" have the sisters created? What are some of the advantages and disadvantages of this approach?
3. On their Web site, the sisters describe their show this way: "For one hour a week, we think that radio can be about something other than issues or judgments or news or sports, sports, sports. For one hour a week, we want to talk about the things people really talk about every day. So far, we've talked about going to a college reunion, clearing up bad credit, finding a lump, tracking a lost dog, fixing the disposal, and raising trout." Would this venture, or one like it, appeal to a Canadian audience? Explain.
4. In groups of four, use green hat thinking to brainstorm possible growth opportunities for *Satellite Sisters*.

Starting Up

In this chapter, you will learn how it is possible to predict what people will do in the future by looking at trends. What trends do you notice at your school? How do you think these trends might develop in the future?

Ideas and Opportunities

The Dolan sisters had a great idea, but ideas are only a small part of entrepreneurial success. With no want, no need, no market, and no perceived **opportunity**, *Satellite Sisters* might no longer be on the air, let alone **syndicated** around the world. Once the sisters identified an opportunity—a market—they made a major breakthrough. By linking radio and the Internet, *Satellite Sisters* found a way to market the show to computer users as well as radio listeners—an idea that other broadcasters are already adopting.

People frequently confuse entrepreneurial opportunities with ideas. For the Dolan sisters, the idea for the radio show came during a "sisters only" weekend getaway, when Liz persuaded the others to take advantage of their talent for conversation. The opportunity came when they pitched their idea successfully to a network of public radio stations. A venture can succeed only when a good idea and an opportunity come together.

Cool Stuff

Technology made it possible for the Dolan sisters to link their radio show to a Web site. This chart from *Canada Prospects* magazine shows some other ways in which technology is changing our lives.

How does technology influence the way you live? the way you learn?

Technology keeps changing the products we buy for everyday use.

In the 1900s	In the 1950s	In the 1990s	In 2025?
Corsets	Girdles	Pantyhose	Pantyhose that won't run
Stereoscopes that allowed viewers to see pictures in 3D	Black and white television	Colour digital television with "screen within screen" technology	Virtual reality television that puts the viewer in the picture
Wax cylinder records for gramophones	Vinyl long-playing records	MP3 format and MP3 players that allow listeners to download music off the Internet	Microsound technology with ear-plug sized stereo systems
Wood stoves	Electric and gas stoves	Microwaves and convection ovens	Laser cookware pots that cook on their own
Gas lamps	Electric lights	Halogen high-intensity lights	Glow walls created by electrified paint that illuminates a room

Venture Profile

THE METHOD BEHIND THE MAGIC

Tod Jones, The Costco Connection

Begun in 1984 by Guy Laliberté, a former accordion player, stilt walker, and fire-eater from Quebec City, and an eclectic group of street performers, Cirque du Soleil was born with the assistance of the Quebec government, as part of the celebrations surrounding the 450th anniversary of Jacques Cartier's arrival in Canada. The company debuted in the small Quebec town of Gaspé and then performed in 10 other cities throughout the province. The first blue-and-yellow big top seated 800.

"In the beginning, we had no fear," says Laliberté. "We just jumped in."

Today, Cirque du Soleil's presence can be felt on several continents. Not only does the organization have a solid footing in its native Quebec, with its new $30 million Montreal headquarters, but it also has offices in Amsterdam, Singapore, and Las Vegas. Its travelling big top shows, which tour the globe annually, delighted and startled about 6 million spectators in 2000. All told, Cirque has become a financial juggernaut, bringing in close to $200 million annually with an annual profit of 15 to 20%.

And Cirque has grown no less fearless. Not content, as it deservedly could be, to simply rest on the laurels of its groundbreaking style, the artists, performers, and designers insist each year on upping the ante, giving themselves new and unique challenges, pushing the envelope of creativity, and testing the limits of what they can accomplish physically, emotionally, and technically.

"Acrobatics, tumbling, and trapeze have existed for a long time," says Lyn Heward, vice president of creation in Montreal. "Our mandate is to give old things a new perspective."

Every concept and scenic element in a Cirque du Soleil show begins in the Cirque du Soleil International Headquarters in Montreal. The studio was designed to meet the special requirements of Cirque artisans, with two huge training rooms, as well as set and costume shops bustling with creators, designers, artists, and craftspeople. More than 500 employees work in the building on floor space exceeding 15 300 m^2.

"The creative process is very organic," says Heward, adding

> **E-Bits & Bytes**
>
> Visit www.business.nelson.com and follow the links to "circuses" to find out more about the Cirque du Soleil and some other circuses. What qualities make the Cirque du Soleil unique?

CONTINUED➡

that it takes about two years to take a performance from idea to completion. "Each person brings something to the table. The set designer, each coach, each and every artist brings his or her vocabulary of movement, and a unique spirit, to the creative process. Then the creative director puts the magic touch, the wand, on it. He's the head chef who pulls the whole meal together and brings out the best that each person has to offer."

The challenge is to find the right combination. "We are always trying to find the true balance between that which can be considered theatrical and that which is exciting," Heward says. "We don't consider a show to be really successful unless it's able to invoke the imagination of the spectators."

Because, no matter how it's dressed up, the performance still has to engage the audience. With Cirque du Soleil, you get the sizzle and the steak. At the heart of every performance, underneath all the elaborate staging, the remarkable costumes, the ingenious and slightly demented atmosphere, beats the heart of a true circus—something that has the ability to evoke a sense of wonder from even the most jaded viewer.

The maxim is "never to repeat ourselves," says Heward. "Always to surprise."

And that is why Cirque du Soleil succeeds.

Exploring

1. *Satellite Sisters* began when Liz Dolan came up with an idea and persuaded her sisters to help her look for an opportunity to put it into action. How is this different from the way the Cirque du Soleil began?
2. What evidence is there that Cirque du Soleil encourages enterprise in its employees?
3. Would you like to be the vice president of creation at Cirque du Soleil? Explain.
4. What was the idea that led to the beginning of Cirque du Soleil? What was the opportunity?

WHICH COMES FIRST—AN IDEA OR AN OPPORTUNITY?

This question is a little like "Which came first, the chicken or the egg?" Regardless of which comes first, the idea or the opportunity, it is important to realize that both are central to the venture creation process.

Sometimes an entrepreneur will identify a problem, see an opportunity, and then come up with an idea to take advantage of the situation. This process is referred to as **market-pulled entrepreneurship**. The opportunity provides the pull that sparks the development of ideas.

Guy Laliberté recognized an opportunity when the Quebec government was granting financing for a celebration of the 450th anniversary of Jacques Cartier's arrival in Canada. When he proposed his idea for a new type of circus, he received an enthusiastic response to his idea.

The Dolan sisters, on the other hand, came up with an idea first, and then went to look for a marketing opportunity. This process or pattern of entrepreneurship is often called **product-driven** or **service-driven entrepreneurship**.

Worth Repeating

"Luck is what happens when preparedness meets opportunity."

Anonymous

Agents of Change

Whenever Kerry Adler logged on to the Net, he could never find what he wanted; links often failed; and there was no one to ask for help. Instead of getting mad, the former customer service manager got creative and launched Webhelp.com. Through chat technology, the site provides users with real-time person-to-person search services.

Was Kerry Adler's enterprise market-pulled or service-driven? Give reasons for your choice.

Profit magazine

LOOKING FOR OPPORTUNITIES

Imagine the range of opportunities that were available to Guy Laliberté—a street entertainer with a great deal of talent. He could have become a promoter for other street entertainers. He could have gathered his friends and put on a show at a local theatre. He could have organized a street troupe to play at corporate functions. What he chose to do was to create Cirque du Soleil, an innovative venture that has grown into an internationally renowned organization.

Connecting ideas with viable opportunities is both a reward and a challenge for entrepreneurs and enterprising employers. For the entrepreneur, each idea needs to be evaluated to see what needs and wants it can satisfy. For the enterprising employer, opportunities to put good ideas into action can help advance the mission of the organization.

Successful entrepreneurs and enterprising people look for opportunities in a purposeful and systematic way. Opportunities can be found in many ways and in many places. Look for them where the population is changing, where knowledge and technology are advancing, or where people are struggling with a problem. You learned in Chapter 4 that the world is changing more rapidly now than it has at any other time in our history, so opportunities are being created at an unprecedented rate. Many people see opportunities, but only enterprising people and entrepreneurs act on them.

It takes a great deal of effort to act on an idea. It also takes preparation, planning, networking, selling, and resource acquisition and allocation.

Worth Repeating

"An opportunity is as real an ingredient in business as raw material, labour, or finance—but it only exists when you can see it. Just before it comes into existence, every business is an opportunity that someone has seen."

Edward De Bono, creative-thinking expert

YOUR TURN

1. Review the Venture Profiles from previous chapters in this book. Which ones describe market-pulled entrepreneurship? Which ones describe product- or service-driven entrepreneurship?

2. From the list you made in Question 1, select one market-pulled and one product- or service-driven enterprise. Create a Venn diagram to show the similarities and differences in the way each enterprise is marketed.

3. Look around your community. Describe three opportunities you can see for market-pulled entrepreneurship. Explain what the market need is and how an entrepreneur could satisfy it.

Following Market Trends

In the previous chapters, you learned that entrepreneurs watch what is going on around them. They study trends, identify potential changes in needs and wants, and seek out opportunities for new ventures. Changes trigger opportunities, and entrepreneurs are excited by opportunities.

Changes in society can develop over a long time, or they can emerge and disappear in a matter of weeks or months. The long-term changes are trends. Changes that lead to temporary or short-term adjustments in the way we live are called **fads**.

Fads usually make quick entrances and quick exits, but they do occasionally develop into trends. Examples of fads include mood rings, Pokémon games and toys, and Furbies. In-line skating started out as a fad, but has since developed into a trend, and is now the fastest growing sport in North America.

Entrepreneurs can take advantage of fads for a short time, but only trends provide opportunities for a business to thrive over the long term. Learning to tell a fad from a trend is an important skill for an entrepreneur who wants to stay in business.

FORECASTING TRENDS

A **forecast** is a prediction about the future. Although it is difficult to predict the future with any degree of accuracy, a careful analysis of past events can help you make educated guesses about what's most likely to occur.

Accurate forecasting depends on your ability to organize data in a way that will help you see patterns. Being able to chart data or plot it graphically, and to analyze the results, will help you identify trends that represent opportunities for entrepreneurship.

A few years ago, a number of entrepreneurs noticed that people's work was becoming less physically active. They accurately predicted a growing interest in physical fitness and good health, and capitalized on opportunities to develop fitness clubs, health foods, exercise equipment and clothing, personal training services, and even specialized newsletters and magazines related to this new trend. Many of these businesses have expanded their services throughout the community, the province, the entire country, and, in some cases, internationally.

Worth Repeating

"Opportunities are never lost. Someone will take the one you miss."

Anonymous

What opportunities might a fad present for an entrepreneur who wants to stay in business over the long term?

Forecasting can be a complicated and sophisticated process or it can be relatively straightforward. For example:

- Newspaper business sections and specialized financial, business, or investment-related publications use trained statisticians to report a variety of forecasts related to the gross national product, unemployment figures, inflation rates, and other changes likely to affect the Canadian community.
- Financial experts sometimes use computer programs to simulate future events and to predict general economic trends.
- Magazines and newspapers employ staff writers to study forecasts and trends, and to make predictions that will interest their reading audience.
- Large industries use opinion polls and attitude surveys to predict consumer tastes, employee preferences, and political choices.
- Accounting, legal, and management consultants regularly produce newsletters or journals to draw attention to trends, helping their clients take advantage of related opportunities.

CURRENT GLOBAL TRENDS

At a recent international conference called the Global Meeting of Generations, the following major population trends were identified:

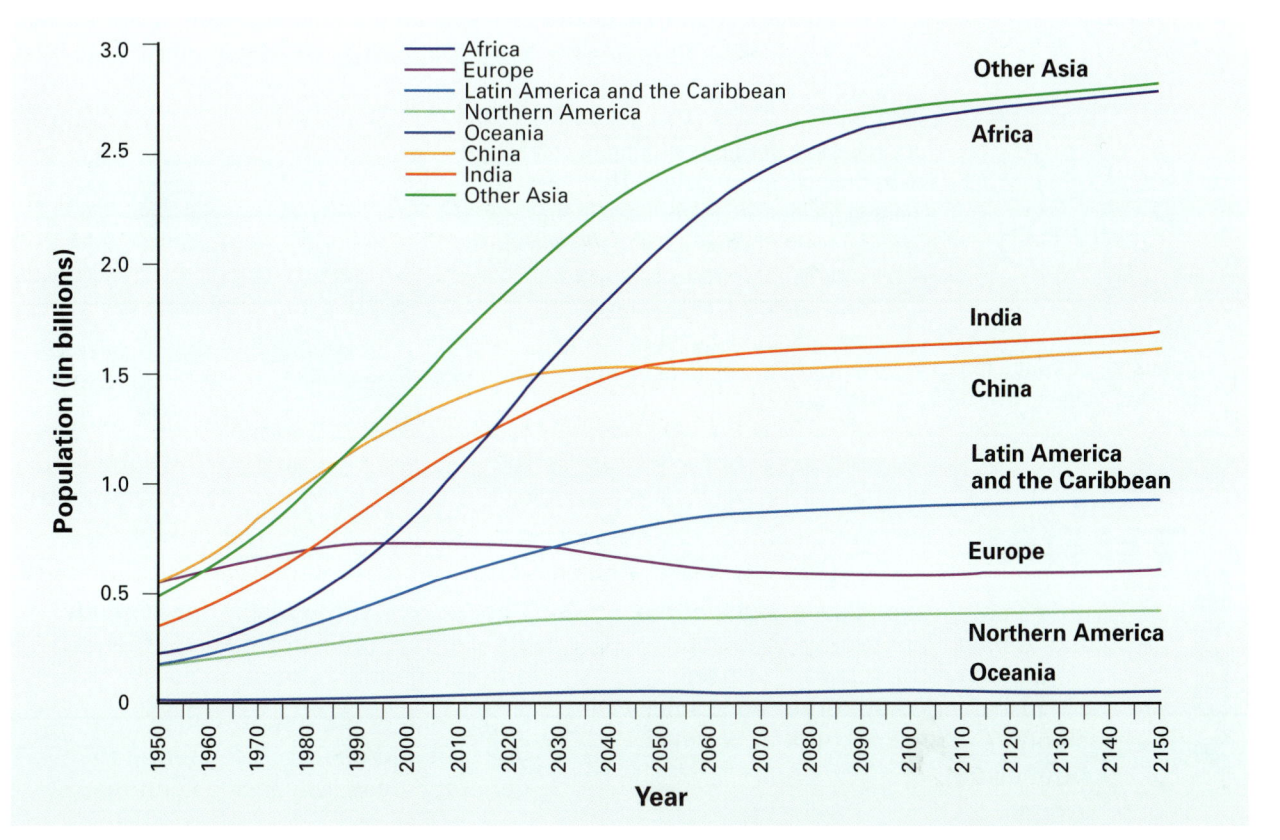

Figure 6.1 The World Population Trends by Continent

Think About It

In groups of four, discuss the trend shown in Figure 6.1. Use De Bono's Six Thinking Hats to examine the possible implications of this trend.

1. The world population is at an all-time maximum and is continuing to grow. According to research conducted by the United Nations, the total populations of developed countries, like Canada, will decrease from 20% of the world's population to 10% by 2100. (See Figure 6.1.)

2. More than 50% of people in the world are under 25 years of age. The number of young people who will enter the work force in the next 10 years will be greater than the number of people who made up the entire work force of the developed world in 1990.

3. By 2150, the average life expectancy is likely to be 86 for males and 92 for females. Today, for the first time in history, the population over 65 is greater than the population under 15, and seniors are expected to represent 25% of the total population by 2050. Individuals between 60 and 80 are viewed as generally self-sufficient and able to make contributions to society. The older population, over 80, is in need of social services, medical care, and housing.

4. Families are shrinking in size. Two-income families, city living, crowding, and social pressures are contributing to smaller numbers of children per family in most countries. This is important: If family size does not shrink, the world will not be able to sustain the resulting population of 300 billion people by 2150.

5. People are moving away from rural communities and into cities and towns. By 2025, about 66% of the world's population will likely live in towns and cities. This will allow people more varied choices as they pursue work and entrepreneurial opportunities.

Agents of Change

Tom and Mike Corbin are trying to solve the traffic pollution problem. They have invented an electric motor vehicle that is environmentally friendly and economical. The Sparrow is a single-passenger car that plugs in to any electrical outlet to get the power it needs to drive up to 100 km.

Is this the right time for the Corbins to introduce the Sparrow? Why or why not?

YOUR TURN

1. With a small group, discuss each of the global trends. Find examples in your community, on the Internet, or from other research to support or contradict each one. Create a poster that outlines your findings.

2. Choose one of the major trends. With your group, brainstorm a list of related entrepreneurial opportunities.

3. Select one of the opportunities from your list and use word clustering to generate ideas for specific ventures.

The Time-Series Forecast

There are a number of different methods people can use to forecast accurate information about possible venture opportunities. The easiest method for beginners to use is called the **time-series forecast**. In a time-series forecast, you plot data from the past and present on a chart. Then you analyze the trends you see, make comparisons to other trends, and use this information to project information about the future.

A **growth trend** will be indicated by a line on your chart that is increasing or sloping upward over time.

Figure 6.2 Growth Trend

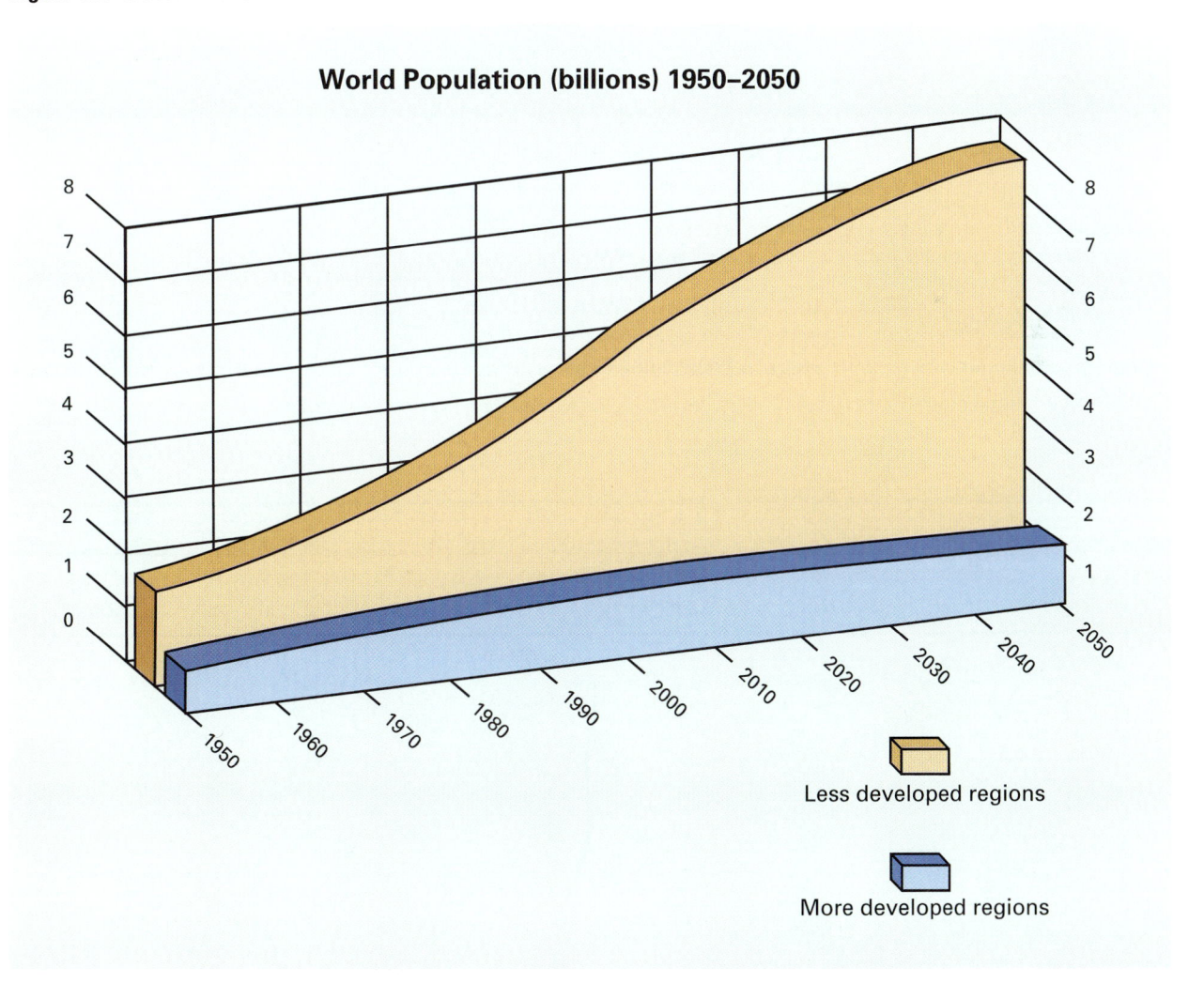

World Population (billions) 1950–2050

- Less developed regions
- More developed regions

A **stable situation** will be indicated by a line that is neither increasing (sloping upward) nor decreasing (sloping downward) over time.

Figure 6.3 Stable Situation

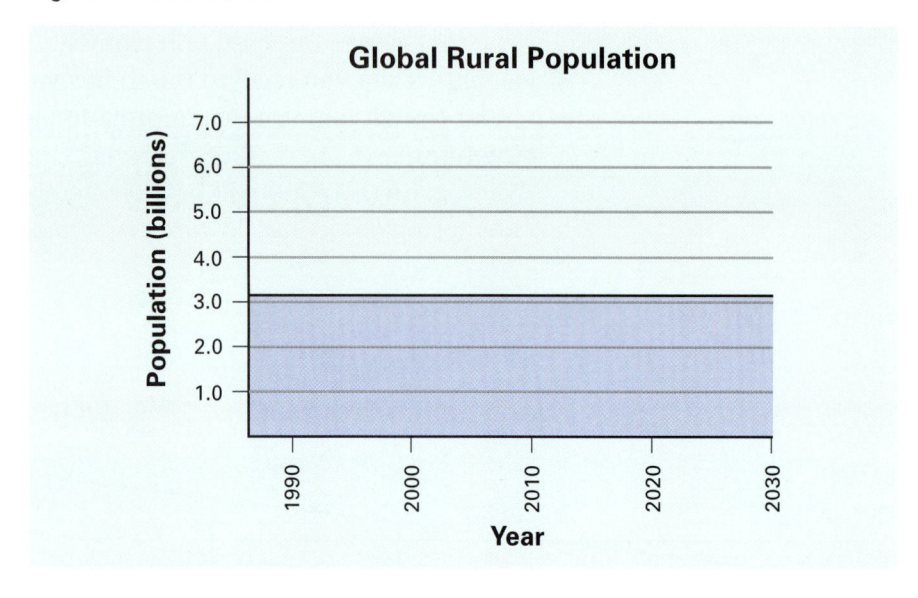

Global Rural Population

(Line graph showing population in billions from 1990 to 2030, remaining constant at approximately 3.0 billion)

A **declining trend** will be indicated by a line that is decreasing or sloping downward over time.

Figure 6.4 Declining Trend

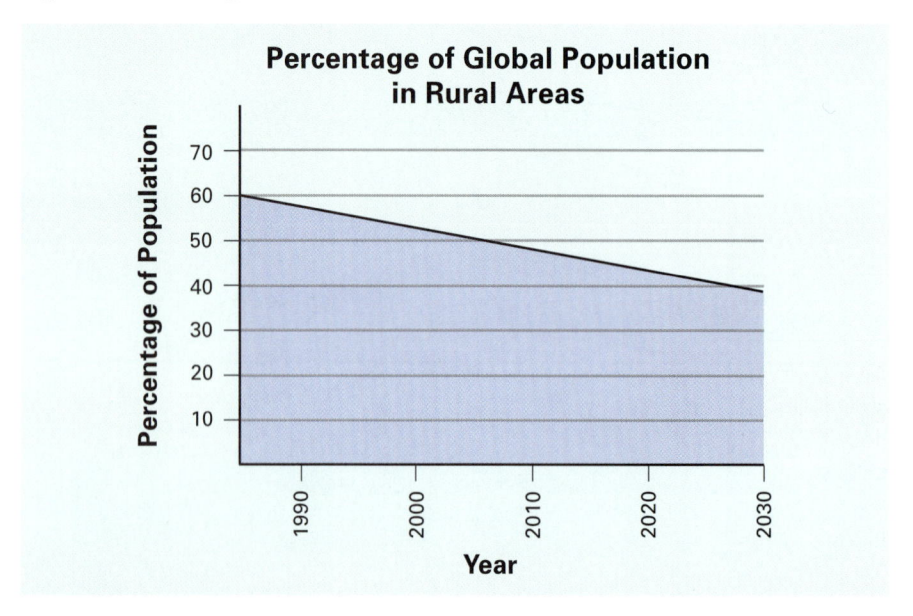

Percentage of Global Population in Rural Areas

(Line graph showing percentage of population declining from about 60% in 1990 to about 40% in 2030)

Lines plotted for any of these three situations (growth, stable, or declining) may be **linear** (a straight line), **curved** (a line curving up or down), **irregular** (indicating an irregular up and down movement), or **cyclical** (indicating a regular pattern of increases and decreases).

E-Bits & Bytes

Ten million young people (ages 16 to 22) account for $4.5 billion in online sales. About 84% of these young shoppers use a parent's credit card when buying online.

What are the negative and positive implications of this trend in e-commerce for bricks-and-mortar retail stores?

A linear graph shows a steady rate of increase or decrease.

Figure 6.5 Linear Line

Subscribers with Mobile Devices

A curve shows that the rate of increase or decrease is speeding up or slowing down.

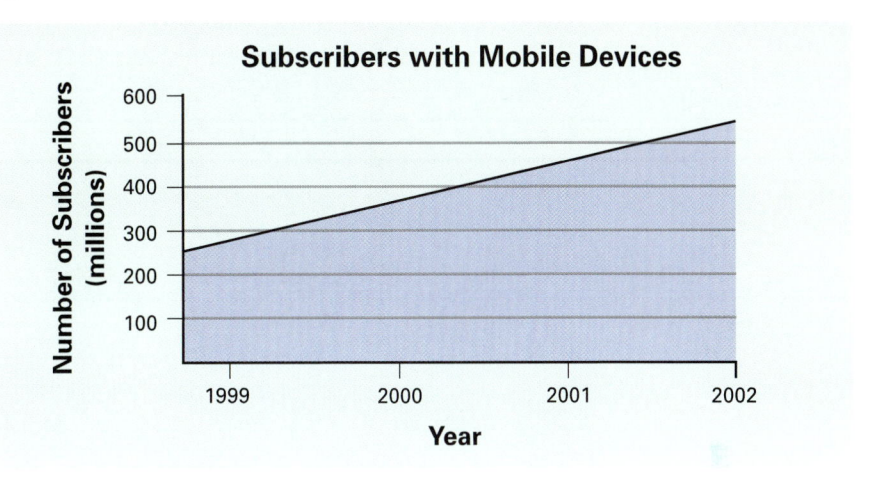

Figure 6.6 Curved Line

Number of Personal Computers Worldwide

An irregular graph shows that something both increases and decreases, although you may still see a gradual trend up or down if you follow the pattern of the maximum points.

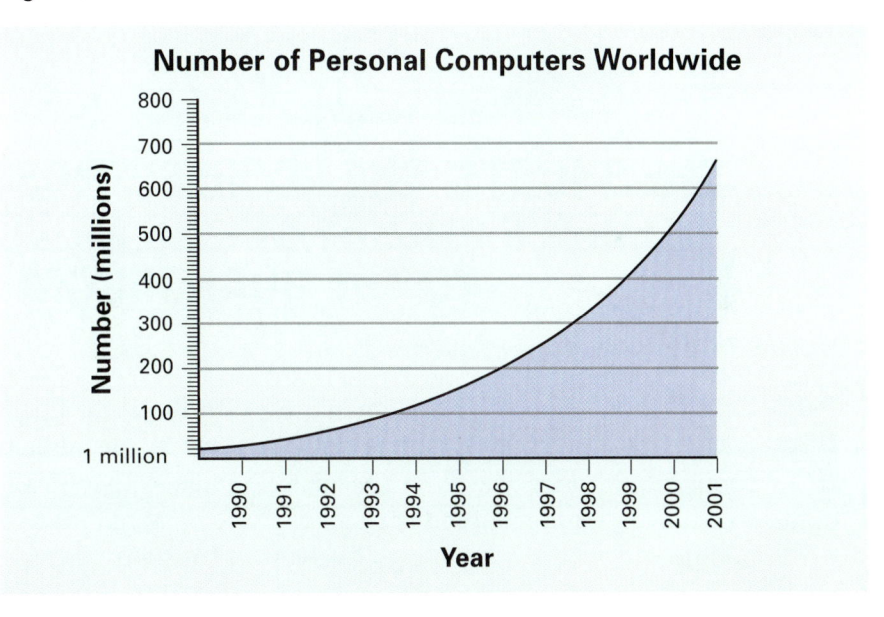

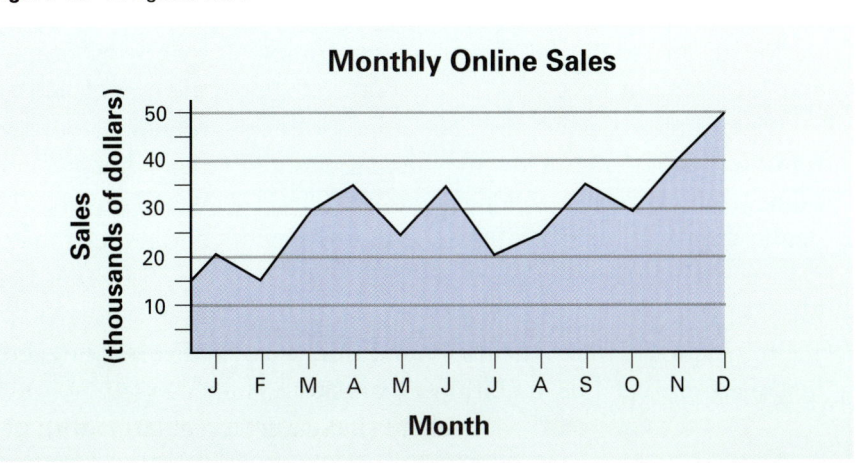

Figure 6.7 Irregular Line

Monthly Online Sales

Chapter 6 ♦ Opportunities, Ideas, and the Enterprising Work Environment **125**

Figure 6.8 Cyclical Line

A cyclical curve shows that there is a repeating cycle of increases and decreases.

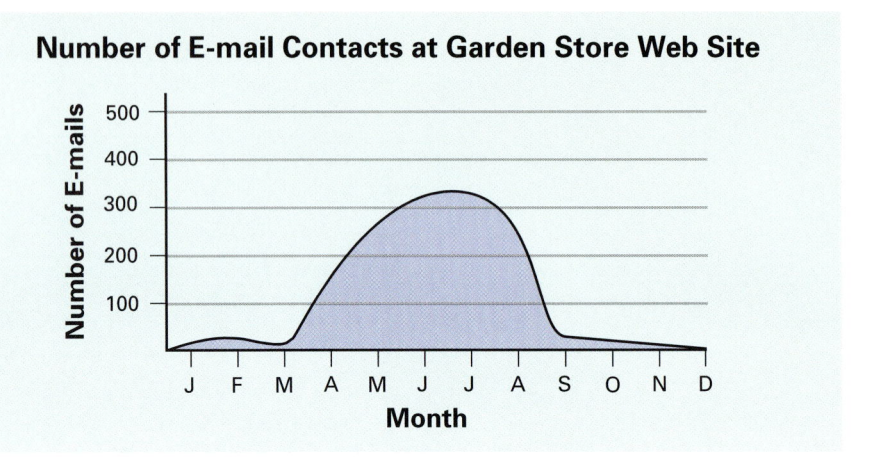

Number of E-mail Contacts at Garden Store Web Site

(Graph showing Number of E-mails (0–500) vs. Month (J F M A M J J A S O N D), with a bell-shaped curve peaking around June–July at approximately 330.)

Venture Profile

SHE SHOOTS, SHE SCORES: "FIRST LADY" OF WOMEN'S HOCKEY MAKES MOVE FROM ICE TO THE BOARDROOM

Wayne Karl, Hockey Business News

First she broke the ice for women in professional hockey, now Manon Rheaume promises to make waves in the male-dominated hockey equipment industry.

In addition to winning an Olympic silver medal in 1998 and two World Championships, Rheaume is perhaps most famous for being the first woman to play in an NHL game—one period of an exhibition game for the Tampa Bay Lightning in 1992.

Frustrated by what she calls a lack of attention to women's hockey by equipment suppliers, the former Canadian national team goalie vows to make a difference in her new role as global director (women's category) at Mission Hockey.

In August 2000, Rheaume and Mission began executing this ambitious mandate by introducing the Betty Flyweight, which they say is the industry's first high-end skate designed specifically for women.

"My job is to care about the girls and to be out there and to give them the stuff on time, and listen to their needs and be able to make changes for their needs," says Rheaume.

"The Mission approach is very much a teamwork concept," she says. In preparing for the launch of the Betty Flyweight, most of the technical work was done by skate development manager, Frederick Aird. "I bring ideas based on what I think and what the girls need, and he tells me whether it is possible."

Now that the company has introduced its first women's product, much of Rheaume's time is spent preparing sales materials, writing

CONTINUED

labour on the ice inspires her and pushes her to achieve more.

"At hockey, I was always the first one on the ice, and the last one to leave. When I'm committed to something, and I really believe in it, I go at it with 100% interest. I don't do it halfway."

Despite being fully aware of her place in hockey history and her iconic status, Rheaume is most loyal to her first love: the game.

"And this is the perfect company to work with, since they're looking for new ideas and innovations. With Mission Hockey, the name, colours, and marketing—everything is so creative. It's a good match."

business plans, and mapping out marketing strategies.

"We really want to promote the growth of women's hockey," she says. "Our mission is to produce the best product for the girls, but the cause of that is the growth of women's hockey. Women's hockey wins, no matter who gets the gold."

In Betty Flyweight promotional materials, Mission Hockey cites figures from U.S.A. Hockey and the Canadian Hockey Association that show participation levels in women's hockey doubling between 1998 and 2002.

With a few months of experience in the industry under her belt, the "First Lady" of women's hockey has a slightly different view of the game now. Seeing the fruits of Mission's

E-Bits & Bytes

Visit www.business.nelson.com and follow the links to "women's hockey" to conduct your research for Question 5.

Exploring

1. What evidence is there in the profile that Mission Hockey is an enterprising employer?
2. What evidence is there that women's hockey is a growing trend?
3. How does Rheaume's passion for the game influence her work at Mission?
4. How have Rheaume's efforts benefited Mission? How have they encouraged the growth of women's hockey?
5. Suppose you were hired to help Mission Hockey develop marketing strategies for its equipment. Conduct online research to assess Mission's current products, the competition, and the size of the market. Present your findings and your recommendations in a short report.

Using Research

You have now learned to identify trends by plotting and analyzing data. Another way to identify trends is to conduct research. The research process should be designed so that it will provide the kind of information you need to help identify opportunities or evaluate ideas effectively. To find the right information, you will need to know exactly what it is you're looking for.

If you are planning a venture, you might want to know about trends that affect your customers. You can find this information by using either **primary research** or **secondary research**.

Primary research involves interviewing customers and potential customers directly. It can be conducted by mailing out questionnaires, conducting telephone surveys or personal interviews, or by posting surveys on the Internet. Secondary research uses data that has already been collected by someone else. When you conduct research by reading books or articles or searching a Web site, you are using secondary research.

Primary Research

If you decide to use primary research to find out about market trends, you'll need to design a **research instrument** that will help you collect the data in a consistent and objective way.

This instrument will vary depending on what information you need and how you intend to gather it. For research about existing customers, you may only need a chart with spaces where a clerk can enter or check off data obtained from company files or from customers as they respond in person. If the instrument is to be mailed, you will need an attractive, easy-to-read questionnaire and perhaps a coupon or other incentive that will encourage potential customers to complete it.

In either case, the administrative costs will be relatively low. For a mail-out survey, the costs would include printing the questionnaire, labelling and mailing the envelopes, and providing self-addressed, postage-paid envelopes for responses. If you post your questionnaire on the Internet, the costs will be even lower, and you will reach a broader base of potential customers, but it may take longer to assess and interpret the data.

If you use a telephone survey, you will need to provide telephone lines, interviewers, and supervisory personnel. Personal interviews are the most expensive to conduct because interviewers need to be hired, trained, and supervised, and you may have travel expenses to pay. Because services like these are required by many organizations, there are companies available that will conduct telephone surveys or personal interviews for you and report on the results.

Think About It

What careers might there be for people who know how to conduct and analyze marketing research? Check with a university, college, or business school to find out more. Share your findings with the rest of the class.

Table 6.1 Methods of Primary Research

By Mail

Respondents are most likely to complete a questionnaire that fits on one page. Questionnaires can include **multiple-choice questions**, **attitude scales**, or **open-ended questions**.

Have you ever eaten a pizza from Boomers?
☐ Yes   ☐ No

Please rate Boomers Pizza on the following qualities:

Taste	Poor 1 2 3 4 5 Excellent
Amount of Cheese	Poor 1 2 3 4 5 Excellent
Temperature	Poor 1 2 3 4 5 Excellent
Price	Poor 1 2 3 4 5 Excellent
Delivery Service	Poor 1 2 3 4 5 Excellent

Would you order from Boomers again? Why or why not?

_____
_____
_____

In Person

In a personal interview, the interviewer needs to be friendly and polite, but must be very careful not to influence people's responses with comments, body language, or facial expressions.

By Telephone

If you are conducting a telephone survey, you may need to include alternative ways to word the question in case the person being interviewed has trouble understanding something.

On the Internet

For Internet surveys, you may wish to use shortcuts that will make it easier for people to enter data, such as the name of the province or country where they live.

* Enter your own: _____
* Your Answer: _____
* Retype Answer: _____

3. Your Personal Information

* First Name: _____
* Last Name: _____
Company Name: _____
Title: _____
* Email: _____
* Address: _____
_____
* City: _____
* Province/State: [Not Applicable ▼]
* Postal/Zip Code: _____
* Country: [Canada ▼]

[Done] [Clear Form] [Cancel]

In any form of primary research, you will need to ensure that your questions will

- motivate people to respond
- be easy to understand but not so simple that the questions lose their significance
- be brief enough to hold the attention of the respondent
- provide complete and accurate data
- allow researchers/respondents enough room to record complete answers
- be objective and not encourage people to answer in a predetermined way

DESIGNING A QUESTIONNAIRE FOR PRIMARY RESEARCH

A questionnaire that is to be mailed or used to collect data from a telephone or Internet survey should include each of the following sections:

SECTION 1: STATEMENT OF PURPOSE

An introductory statement should explain the purpose of your research and establish a positive relationship with the respondent. With a questionnaire, this statement might appear in a covering letter. In a telephone survey, the caller can use the statement as an introduction and to invite the listener's participation.

SECTION 2: PERSONAL INFORMATION

In this section, the respondent will fill in his or her name, address, e-mail address, and any other information that you might need for your records or to help validate the survey data.

SECTION 3: QUESTIONS

In a survey about a product or service, the questions should elicit information about the customer's perception of features such as quality, price, and availability, and how the respondent might react to different kinds of advertising. If the research is exploratory in nature, use open-ended questions. If you're looking for specific information, multiple-choice questions, which are easier to tabulate, might be a better choice. Attitude scales, where respondents use numbers to rate a feature along a scale from poor to excellent, are commonly used in these situations.

If you want to find ways to improve a product, include questions that will help you understand why consumers might purchase a

---

Worth Repeating

"Treating others fairly, and with kindness and respect is critical. People do business with those they know, like, and trust."

Verna Korkie,
VEK Rehabilitation Liaison

competitor's product instead of yours. If you want to determine how much potential customers are prepared to pay for your product or service, identify several price ranges and ask which range best describes the amount respondents would be prepared to pay.

The way you sequence the questions can help motivate respondents to keep working through the questionnaire. Go from easy questions to more difficult ones, and then back to easier ones again. Try to avoid questions that might influence answers to later questions. For example, a question such as "Boomers Pizza has recently added more cheese to its regular pizza. Have you enjoyed this extra cheesy taste?" may influence a later question such as "What did you enjoy most about the new Boomers Pizza?"

SECTION 4: DEMOGRAPHIC INFORMATION

Include questions that will provide **customer profiles**, including information such as age, education level, and household income. Since many people may be reluctant to give specific answers, which are difficult to tabulate anyway, it's better to indicate a series of ranges for each category and ask respondents to indicate which range they fit into. Always close with a simple but friendly "thank you" to convey your appreciation.

SECONDARY RESEARCH

Mission Hockey used data from U.S.A. Hockey and the Canadian Hockey Association to determine the potential of the women's market. This is an example of secondary research.

Secondary research can provide useful information about what has happened in the past, for example, how much money women hockey players spent for equipment and accessories in a given year. Once the information has been gathered, researchers can identify trends and make predictions.

You can conduct secondary research by reading articles in trade journals, magazines, or newspapers, watching movies and television shows, or studying advertisements. Your school or community librarian can help you locate reading material that you can use to evaluate an idea or identify an opportunity.

STEPS IN MARKETING RESEARCH

Marketing research usually follows a systematic procedure that helps researchers gather information in an effective and objective way.

1. Identify objectives.
   What do you need to know? Why?

International NEWS

"English isn't managing to sweep all else before it.... Native speakers of English are already outnumbered by second-language and foreign-language speakers, and will be more heavily outnumbered as time goes on."

Barbara Wallraff, Atlantic Monthly

Many people in Canada speak languages other than English. What are the implications of this fact for marketing researchers?

2. Plan the research program.
   Will you use primary or secondary research? Why?
3. Select a sample.
   Whose opinions will you sample? How many people will you contact?
4. Collect the data.
   How will you collect the data? How do you plan to organize it?
5. Analyze the data.
   How will you interpret the information?
6. Draw conclusions.
   Prepare a summary of your findings.
7. Decide how to proceed.
   What decisions can you make based on your findings? What contingency plans can you make in case your first choices don't work out?

YOUR TURN

1. With a small group, identify one of the following stores in your community: a specialty shop, a department store, a variety store, a catalogue store, or a discount store. Visit the store you chose and use an instrument designed for primary research to answer the following questions:
   a) What are the characteristics of a typical customer?
   b) What do you notice about the store?
   c) What do you notice about the merchandise? Which items are on sale? new? dusty? missing? featured in promotional materials?
   d) If there are several departments at the store, which ones are busiest?
   e) What conclusions can you draw about trends and business opportunities at the store?

2. Use secondary research to develop some spreadsheets and graphs that present information about one of the following topics.
   a) Canadian spending on automobiles and related products
   b) the percentage of households with an income exceeding the national average in various cities or provinces
   c) distribution by age of the population in several cities or provinces

   To do your research, use periodicals or visit www.business.nelson.com and follow the links to "automobile expenditures," "average income," and "population by age." Draw conclusions about any trends in the data and how these might lead to venture opportunities.

3. Suppose you work for a company that is about to introduce a new game or toy. Describe the product and explain how you could use the seven marketing research steps to predict how well your item will sell, and how much it should cost. Include a copy of the research instrument (questionnaire or survey) you will use to gather your data.

Venture Profile

CHARTING A NEW COURSE

Caron Hawco, New Shoes magazine

Looking at the big picture is what CHART is all about. The big picture in this case is satellite imagery of coastlines that tells you what plants and animals are living in the surrounding waters. This information is important in protecting the environment.

Dr. Elisabeth Deblois, president of CHART (Coastal Habitat Assessment Research Technology) in Newfoundland, believes that if we want to protect our environment, in particular our coastal waters, we have to take into consideration the economy, society, ecology, and biology. And through the use of satellite images and databases, CHART is collecting information related to all these areas. So when governments and marine-based companies such as offshore oil and gas companies are developing environmental plans, they will draw upon CHART's scientific and technological capabilities and database of information.

Normally, scientists do not move into the private sector. Governments and academic institutions tend to attract many young graduates. But after working as a freelancer for five years, Elisabeth decided she wanted to make things happen, and work in a challenging and more creative environment.

"I took a look at my skill set, conducted research on the Internet (in particular I went to Industry Canada's site), and came up with a business plan. With 1998 being the Year of the Ocean, and integrated coastal zone management garnering a great deal of attention, I saw an opportunity and identified the area in which I would specialize."

Taking into consideration her extensive academic background, Elisabeth recognized that she knew very little about the private sector. So she surrounded herself with key people from the scientific and business community and set up a board of advisers who regularly meet to advise her on operating a business. Nothing CHART has done or accomplished is by chance. According to Elisabeth, everything has been researched and planned.

"By receiving valuable input from business and scientific experts, my work is validated and I feel confident in my decisions. It's important that I maintain my ideals, do good work, and contribute to the environment."

Exploring

1. What business opportunity did Elisabeth see?
2. What steps did she take to evaluate her ideas before she developed the business?
3. Why is it important to ask for expert advice about your ideas when you're planning to launch a business? after your business becomes successful?

Worth Repeating

"It's a little like a roller coaster. From knowing the difference between a good idea and a lame one to figuring out the financing, starting a business can encompass both the wind-in-your-hair thrills and the terrifying descents of the scariest amusement park ride."

Ron Sparling, Realm magazine

Evaluating Your Ideas

Before you enter into a venture, it's important to consider how your venture will fit into the larger picture. This process is sometimes referred to as looking at the **window of opportunity**. Timing your venture so that it will fit into the window, whether big or small, is crucial to success. Windows of opportunity can be predicted using the research skills or trend analysis skills outlined earlier in this chapter.

Here are some steps that will help you evaluate your venture ideas. To find the information for each step, you'll need to do research, talk to people, seek advice from other businesspeople, and look for a mentor who can help you through the early stages of your business's development.

What Will Your Venture Be Like?

Steps to Evaluate Your Ideas

1. List and describe the features/benefits of your product or service.
2. Define the main geographic area you intend to sell to during your first year.
3. What price do your competitors charge? Estimate the maximum price you can charge and still remain competitive.
4. List and briefly describe trends in your market or industry.
5. How are you going to let your customers know that you exist?
6. Estimate your sales for the first year.
7. List any government approvals necessary to launch your idea.
8. Make a list of potential suppliers.
9. Make a list of resources that you will require to start your venture.
10. List your financial strengths and weaknesses.

Adapted from the Canada Business Service Centres Web site

BLUE HAT THINKING

After you have an idea of what your venture will be like, you can use blue hat thinking to evaluate the practicality of your plans. Every venture is different, but you can use questions like those listed here to tailor a checklist to your personal venture plan.

Cost

- Will your venture cost more than you can afford, or more than you will be able to obtain? Over time, will your costs decrease, stay the same, or increase?
- Will your customers be able to afford your product or service?
- What marketing costs need to be covered?
- What personnel or labour costs need to be covered?

Worth Repeating

"There are numerous ideas floating around. What is needed is the desire and determination to turn those ideas into opportunities.... The key is to recognize those opportunities and to be prepared to follow a new path."

Sandra C. Kelly, Minister of Industry, Trade, and Technology, Government of Newfoundland and Labrador

OPPORTUNITY COST
- How much of your time will this venture take?
- What personal commitments or pleasures will you have to give up as part of the **opportunity cost**?
- How stressful is your venture likely to be?

TIME
- Do you have the resources to start your venture right away? If not, when will you be ready?
- What is the window of opportunity for your venture? Can you be ready before it closes?
- Will you have a long-lasting or a short-term venture?
- When should you get out of the venture?

FEASIBILITY
- Is your idea going to work?
- Will it be manageable?
- What procedures can you put in place to make sure your venture is managed effectively?

ACCEPTABILITY
- Will your venture serve a specially targeted market?
- Have you carefully considered what your customers will be like?
- How will you ensure your product or service meets your customers' needs or wants?
- Is your product or service consistent with accepted values and attitudes?

USEFULNESS
- Will your product or service meet a real need?
- Why will people want to buy your product or service instead of a competitor's?

YOUR TURN

1. Select one product or service idea from the list below and take it through the Steps to Evaluate Your Ideas on page 134.
   Products:
   glow-in-the-dark scooters
   washable silk shirts
   gourmet pizza
   easy-to-collapse walkers
   Services:
   house cleaning/nanny service
   Internet-based résumé writing
   health spa

2. By now, you probably have some ideas for ventures that you might want to start now or in the future. Use the questions on pages 134 and 135 to evaluate one of your ideas.

3. If you don't plan to start a venture of your own, use the evaluation steps and blue hat thinking questions to evaluate a venture that has recently begun in your community.

Venture Profile

GOT FIT?
YOUNG ENTREPRENEUR HELPS NEW COLLEGE GRADS FIND THEIR WAY INTO THE WORKING WORLD

Debbie Selinsky, Success magazine

When Jennifer Floren graduated from Dartmouth College with a psychology degree in 1993, she wasn't quite sure what to do next. Her college internships had been in media-related jobs, and she'd learned enough to be unsure she wanted to begin the race down that path.

So Floren, who describes her education as being "as liberal arts as liberal arts gets," joined a management consulting firm in Boston. Three years and a couple of dozen clients later, she was still trying to find where she "fit in the working world."

A gabfest with her siblings led to the initial idea behind experience.com—putting together resources that help young people coming out of college determine where they fit. "Graduating from college feels like jumping off into the great beyond," Floren says. "That's how I felt. So I wanted to provide the kind of resource I wish I'd had when I graduated."

What was missing was the kind of information that's difficult for people who are unfamiliar with a field to find on their own, she says. "For example, if you go to the job boards and type in, say, 'advertising in Boston,' what comes back is a list of classified ads. Well, if you're just starting out and you don't have any perspective, you don't know what these jobs are and what they mean. Listing available jobs is important, but having your contacts understand their path and what's right for them is critical."

Floren used savings to start the career-advice/job-matching business in her Boston apartment and soon began to forge relationships with university career centres that could serve as sources of information for Web site visitors. Floren then started fundraising—and reeled in U.S. $10 million in her first round of venture capital.

Three years into the business, the company has 100 employees across the country, according to its 28-year-old president and CEO.

The company also has a client base of 300 schools in the United States and abroad, and is in rapid growth mode, Floren says. "The key for us is building an army of career service professionals who add value to our service. We'll be working with more top-tier schools, and we're getting the word out to employers who want to recruit our talent."

CONTINUED➡

So what has Floren learned about business? "People are everything, absolutely everything," she says. "Our business is looking at organizations that offer mentoring and coaching opportunities, and we're finding that the degree to which an organization focuses on people as individuals is directly related to its success."

"We're not reinventing the wheel—just the information gap. We're helping people get experience through us instead of having to learn it the hard way."

Exploring

1. What is the key idea in this Venture Profile?
2. How did Floren initially identify the opportunity for her venture?
3. What similarities can you find between Jennifer Floren and the Dolan sisters?
4. How do you think experience.com could assist you? Visit the company's Web site to find out more.
5. What characteristics of experience.com might influence a potential investor?

International NEWS

Many countries outside North America are using a new, innovative keyboard design that allows people to input information more rapidly. International companies can transfer information by satellite to these countries and have documents produced rapidly at considerable savings.

■ The Enterprising Workplace

Mission Hockey encourages Manon Rheaume and its other employees to generate ideas for products that will suit their customers. Jennifer Floren says that she's finding that "the degree to which an organization focuses on people as individuals is directly related to its success." By encouraging innovation among their employees, Canadian businesses are becoming more competitive at local, national, and international levels.

To compete against small entrepreneurial businesses in a global market, it is essential for larger companies to come up with new and better ideas. By allowing their employees the freedom to experiment and make mistakes, they are nourishing and encouraging these ideas.

The North American Free Trade Agreement (NAFTA) has opened up new markets for Canadian entrepreneurs, but it has also increased competition. The **European Union** has given rise to free trade across Europe and a single currency. All citizens of the Union are free to relocate from one country to another depending on where their expertise is required. Products and services can now cross borders without tariffs (duties or taxes), resulting in new opportunities and markets for entrepreneurs and intrapreneurs.

The Pacific Rim countries—especially Japan, Singapore, Thailand, Korea, and the Philippines—will continue to compete with North American businesses by offering lower costs, an abundant labour force, and sophisticated technology.

Agents of Change

Art Fry was a researcher for 3M who was fed up with continually losing the paper scraps he used as bookmarks. To find a solution, Fry took advantage of the 3M company's policy which allows scientists to spend a portion of their time on projects of their own choice. Fry remembered an adhesive, invented by another 3M scientist, that had been rejected because it didn't stick very well. When he applied the adhesive to paper strips, the result was a bookmark that could be stuck to the page and then removed. Fry continued to experiment until he came up with the idea of putting a strip of the adhesive at the top of each sheet of paper in a notepad. Today, Post-it Notes are used in homes and offices around the world.

How does the Post-it Note story show why it is important for enterprising employers to create a climate where it's possible for employees to make mistakes?

Encouraging Innovation

Companies that recognize employee innovation as their greatest asset have learned to train their employees to be creative thinkers. Some companies, such as 3M, provide time for personal projects and reward creative thinkers for their ideas. By helping, encouraging, and rewarding their innovative employees, these companies develop enterprising people within the organization. Enterprising employees, in turn, improve a company's productivity and generate ideas that help the company outdistance its competition.

Many companies ask their customers, as well as their employees, to suggest improvements. Doing so helps make the company more competitive and innovative.

In the enterprising workplace, employers recognize people's efforts and celebrate their achievements. They invite new ideas and are willing to try them. Open lines of communication are vital to success.

To create a climate that fosters new ideas, companies need to create a supportive environment, encourage employees to talk to each other, set time aside for groups of employees to get together to brainstorm, and reward the innovations that are developed.

The enterprising workplace can only exist where the leader knows how to manage both the process of innovation and people who bring it about. The successful leader will

- provide support to employees
- allocate resources effectively
- evaluate ideas objectively
- encourage innovation
- foster passion and commitment
- reward efforts and results
- support employees who have tried something new and failed
- provide freedom that is balanced by responsibility

Enterprising people are attracted to companies where they can share in the decision-making process, and where the company executives show a personal commitment to innovation that supports their **mission statement**. You can find out more about mission statements in Chapter 7. Enterprising people want to feel that they are a part of a team, and that they have a say in the way that team will grow and develop. A company that wants to attract employees like these will often offer compensation packages that include rewards for productivity and personal contributions to the company's well-being.

> ### Worth Repeating
>
> " 'Competence' doesn't mean being perfect, knowing everything, doing everything yourself, or … being an expert. 'Competence' means knowing how to use resources to get the job done."
>
> *Valerie E. Young, professional speaker*

YOUR TURN

1. With a partner, contact one of the larger corporations in your community and arrange to interview one of the managers about innovation and intrapreneurship within the organization. As you plan your interview, you might consider questions such as the following:
   a) How is your industry changing? How have these changes affected your organization?
   b) In what ways has your organization been innovative?
   c) What aspects of your business have you been paying close attention to?
   d) In what ways do you communicate the importance of innovation to your employees?
   e) How does your company celebrate or reward employee achievement?
   f) What do you do to encourage team building and collaborative problem solving?
   g) How will innovation and intrapreneurship help your company compete in a global market?

2. Examine the job descriptions in the classified ads section of a newspaper. Choose some examples of advertisements that you think would appeal to enterprising employees and explain why you think so.

Venture Profile

TRAVIS KEITH BRUCE, FOUNDER OF TK WORM FACTORY

Mark Richard Moss, Black Enterprise magazine

The lowly earthworm has helped raise the business IQ of Travis Keith Bruce. Bruce, guided by a mixture of inquisitiveness, smarts, and a natural affinity for the slimy creatures, has not only learned how to raise, sell, and market worms and their castings (manure), but also learned what it takes to operate TK Worm Factory, the company he founded in 1997. In addition, Bruce has learned how to manage employees and maximize free publicity. On the other hand, he knows what it is like to have a down year because of circumstances beyond his control. And after having taken on a partner, he's learned what it is like to share the profits.

Bruce, by the way, is only 15, but already possesses the business acumen of someone at least twice his age. TK Worm Factory sold $7000 worth of earthworms and castings in 1999, and though this year's figures will fall short of that mark because of drought conditions in the area, Bruce is unperturbed. "This actually gives us time to work some problems out and raise more worms," says Bruce.

Bruce's introduction to earthworms came when his grandfather took him fishing. His interest grew, however, after accidentally reading information about earthworms on the Internet. "I was looking for data about a video game that had 'earthworm' in the title and wound up reading about the lives of worms and their positive impact on the environment. Earthworms like to eat garbage and have been promoted as a possible answer to overfilled landfills. I already knew that people had businesses selling worms as bait, but I didn't know it was that profitable," notes Bruce.

After finding a supplier that sold grain, which earthworms love to eat, Bruce started raising them in his basement. What started out as a hobby soon grew into a venture that required rented space in a warehouse.

Business picked up when Bruce participated in a garden show at the state fair and the local newspaper ran an article about his company. "Business wasn't as easy as I thought it was," remembers Bruce. "All this stuff started happening and you have to keep track of it. Like every businessperson, I want to expand and get repeat business. I want people to understand the usefulness of worms."

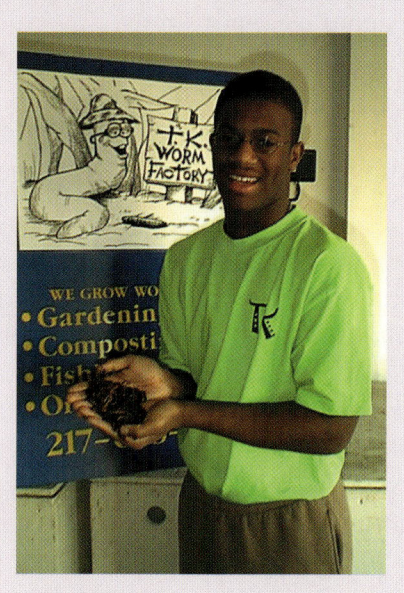

Exploring

1. What opportunity did Bruce identify?
2. Apply what you have learned about evaluating ideas to Bruce's idea. Should he continue with this venture? Why or why not?
3. What does Bruce reveal about himself in this Venture Profile?
4. Bruce says that he finds keeping track of his business more difficult than he expected. What advice would you give him?

ACTIVITIES

FLASHBACKS

Later in this book, you'll have an opportunity to plan a personal venture. Review the information below and then answer these questions:

1. What trends do I see in my community?
2. What personal ventures would I be interested in pursuing that would meet needs associated with these trends?

- Venture ideas can only be successful if they address opportunities in the market. Either the idea or the opportunity can come first.
- Entrepreneurs keep track of trends because the patterns and changes they see can help them identify opportunities.
- Information about trends may be plotted in line graphs. The slope of the line indicates growth, decline, or a stable situation. Changes shown on a line graph can be linear, curved, irregular, or cyclical.
- Primary and secondary research are both used to evaluate ideas and identify opportunities.
- Identifying a window of opportunity is part of the evaluation process for ideas.
- Intrapreneurship and innovation within a corporation improve productivity and give the organization a competitive edge. In today's economy, a workplace must be enterprising in order to survive.

LESSONS LEARNED

1. Explain the difference between market-pulled entrepreneurship and product- or service-driven entrepreneurship.
2. Explain the difference between a trend and a fad. Give two examples of each.
3. How can people forecast trends?
4. What can forecasting reveal about an idea or an opportunity?
5. Review the seven research steps. Where else could these steps be applied?
6. Why is it important to conduct research before you establish a venture?
7. How could you use each of the Six Thinking Hats to evaluate an idea for a new venture?
8. Why is it essential for corporations to be intrapreneurial?

VENTURING OUT

1. Choose one of the statements below.
   a) New technology will continue to change our lives at home and at work. Soon, machines that can think will be as commonplace as machines that fly.
   b) Changing age clusters will be a significant factor in defining business and social opportunities in the future.
   c) People are living longer. As they grow older, their psychological and physical needs change.

   With a small group, use primary research to gather information you can use to identify venture opportunities related to the statement you chose. For example, you could design a questionnaire to send to a select group of people, or prepare a list of questions to interview fellow students or individuals in your community.

2. With your group, choose a different statement from the list in Question 1. Use secondary research techniques to find opportunities that might exist for innovation and entrepreneurship. You may wish to search for related newspaper or magazine articles on the Internet or use statistics available from the Statistics Canada Web site by following the links at www.business.nelson.com.

3. Write a fictional newspaper report that describes the effect a group of innovative people, inside or outside the workplace, might have on a business in one of the following industries:
   a) retailing
   b) health and fitness
   c) food and drink
   d) furniture and housing

4. The number of women and the cultural diversity in the work force have increased steadily in the last 20 years. What are some of the venture opportunities that might be available as a result of this trend?

5. Meet with a partner to identify a trend in Canadian society. Describe the trend in a statement, such as: "People in Canada are becoming more aware of the need to protect the environment." Post your statement on a bulletin board. Join another pair to form a group of four. Select one statement from the board and list venture opportunities that would meet needs or wants that might result from this trend.

POINT OF VIEW

Would you describe your school as an enterprising environment? Why or why not?

E-Bits & Bytes

Suggest four ways in which corporations can encourage innovation. Visit www.business.nelson.com and follow the links to "intrapreneurship" to research several successful corporations to see how they encourage innovation. Prepare a chart outlining the strategies used by each company.

CHAPTER 7

The Venture Plan

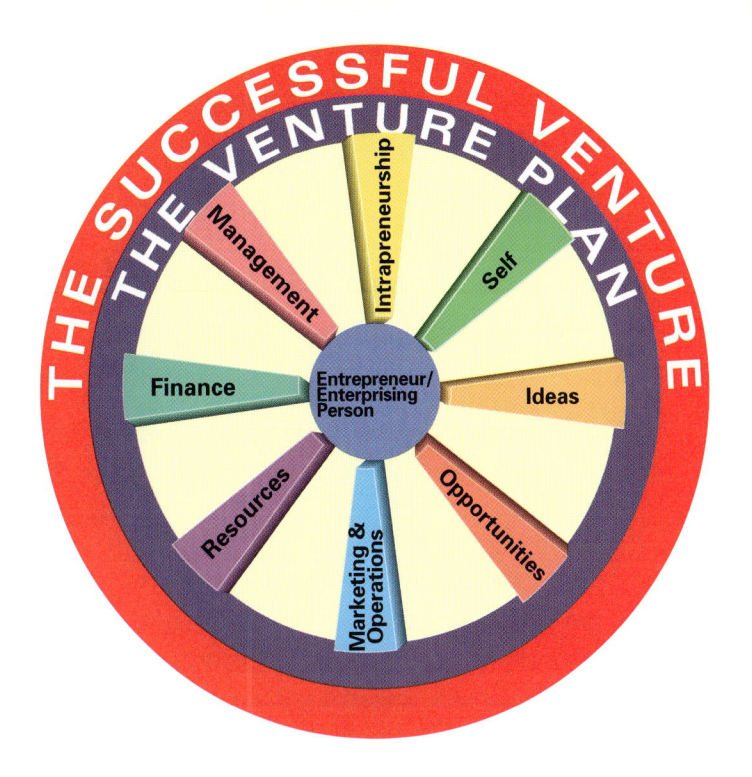

LEARNING OPPORTUNITIES

By the end of this chapter, you should be able to
- understand the stages in the life cycle of a business
- describe the research required to develop a venture plan
- outline the key steps in preparing a venture plan
- describe the elements of a mission statement (e.g., business philosophy, vision, goals, objectives)
- analyze the components of the business venture plan (e.g., executive summary, market analysis, resource analysis, operating strategy, and financial strategy)
- explain how mentors can contribute to the evaluation and revision of a business plan

Entrepreneurial Language

- break-even point
- total monthly revenues
- total monthly costs
- fixed overhead
- asset
- liability
- liquidation
- venture plan
- project plan
- executive summary
- needs assessment
- market analysis
- resource analysis
- material resources
- human resources
- financial resources
- consumable resources
- fixed resources
- operating strategy
- Gap Analysis
- financial strategy
- capitalize

The word "resource" is a key part of several of the terms on this list. Look up this word in a dictionary. How many different meanings can you find? Which one(s) relate to a small business?

Venture Profile

ENTREPRENEURS FOR THE NEEDY: WHIZ KIDS TRIO LANDS BLUE-CHIP BACKERS

John Spears, The Toronto Star

The idea came to Aaron Pereira as he watched the offering basket being passed at church. As a child of the Internet age, 20-year-old Pereira thought it would be better to make his contributions to charity in private, at home, and at a time when he knew money was at hand. That was the first glimmer of CanadaHelps.org, a new, not-for-profit Web site that will allow Canadians to send money to any of the country's 78 000 registered charities via the Internet. They may also offer their service as volunteers.

The first thing Pereira did after the initial brainwave was to talk the idea over with two friends from Appleby College, Ryan Little, 19, and Matthew Choi, 21. "We thought that it was a real cool idea to say the least," recalls Choi. The three friends realized that they needed some help to build and operate a Web site that could channel donations to thousands of different destinations quickly and securely.

The first opportunity came at a conference in Kingston, where Pereira and Little are now students at Queen's University. Pereira noticed that a team from Oracle Corp. of Canada Ltd. was making a conference presentation. He dropped in, collared John Davies of Oracle at the end of his session, and "gave him the 30-second overview." Davies asked him to put it in writing; Pereira had an e-mail on its way in 30 minutes. The proposal soon worked its way up to Bill Bergen, president of Oracle. Encountering 20-something whiz kids is routine.... Their age was not a worry. What intrigued him was their response to the questions, "Why are you doing this? What's in it for you?" The reply was, "I'm bright enough. I'm going to make money when I get older. Lots of people donate when they retire. We're going to donate now, then go out and get real jobs."

After Oracle, the trio went on to enlist a string of corporate heavy hitters including the CIBC, Nortel, Hewlett Packard Canada, and the law firm of Osler, Hoskin & Harcourt.

All charities listed with Revenue Canada have their names and addresses listed on the Web site. Canada Helps wants charities to get in touch so they can pass on information about their programs, finances, and need for volunteers on the site. The charities will also be able to e-mail newsletters to supporters through the site. The trio estimates the annual

CONTINUED →

budget for running the site will be $300 000 to $500 000: They'll raise that as a charity themselves. They've hired two staff members, and need several more to operate the site from a Toronto base. But they insist that it will be a not-for-profit site, which will not deduct any money from donations. Donors using the site will have to pay only their credit card transaction fee.

The young **philanthropists** have one other problem—finding time for schoolwork. They've played hooky this semester, they concede.

> ### *Exploring*
>
> 1. What steps did Pereira take to get the venture started?
> 2. When do you think Pereira and his friends needed to create their business plan? Why do you think so?
> 3. What ideas can you suggest for new not-for-profit ventures that could help people in need?
> 4. Choose one of the not-for-profit venture ideas you listed for Question 3. How could someone get help and financing to develop this venture?

Starting Up

Over the next few chapters, you'll have an opportunity to plan a venture of your own. Meet with a partner to talk about ideas for your venture. What needs could your venture meet? Who will be in your target market? Record your ideas and add to or refine your list as you read Chapter 7.

Life Cycle of a Business

All ventures, including not-for-profit organizations, go through a life cycle—a series of stages that begin when the business idea is initially conceived. An entrepreneur or enterprising person needs to learn to recognize these stages in order to anticipate and address the problems that can occur with each one.

Figure 7.1 Life Cycle of a Business

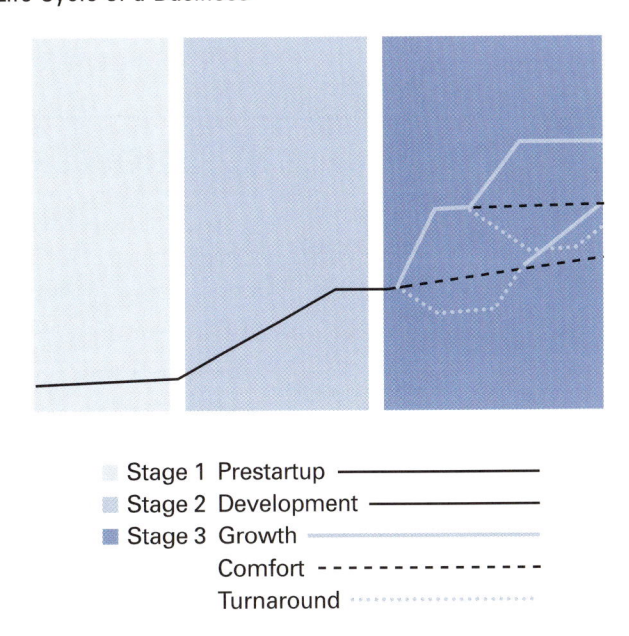

Stage 1 Prestartup
Stage 2 Development
Stage 3 Growth
         Comfort
         Turnaround

Agents of Change

Employment opportunities have sometimes been hard to create on Prince Edward Island. Carol Livingstone founded the not-for-profit West Point Development Corporation. Her organization has helped people tackle the challenges of business startups, improved the local craft industry, and encouraged tourism in the area. By focusing on one problem, Carol created solutions to many more.

What do you think motivates someone to start a not-for-profit venture?

Why is taking on new partners important for a small business?

Prestartup Stage

This is the stage where preparations for launching the business are made. It is a time for generating and investigating ideas, initiating research, and identifying and solving problems. At this stage, you need to review resources, consider how best to allocate them, and write a business plan. Careful budgeting and timing are important. If you want your venture to succeed, you need to take the time to plan thoroughly, to seek advice from others, to revise your plans if necessary, and to test the market's response to your ideas. Consider all the commitments you will need to make as you decide whether or not to move your idea on to the next stage.

Development Stage

By now, your research is complete. You have finalized your business plan, completed your market testing, reviewed the results, and made arrangements to get the funds you need. Your goal for this stage is to reach the **break-even point**—the point where your **total monthly revenues** are equal to your **total monthly costs**. The total monthly revenues include all the money that comes into the business from sales or other sources. The total monthly costs include all the money paid out by the business, including labour and production costs, as well as **fixed overhead** costs such as your rent, telephone lines, computers, and office staff. Reaching the break-even point can take much longer than you expect. Good management, weekly goal setting, and accurate record keeping are essential. Follow up on customer concerns, make sure orders are filled on time, and stay in touch with customers who are slow to pay their bills. If your venture is for profit, keep your profit goal in mind.

Growth Stage

Your business has passed the break-even point and is now earning a profit. It's time to consider bringing in experts to share the workload and to help your business expand. You might decide to add new product lines or services, broaden your customer base through e-commerce, or open a new location. As you consider your many options, you may decide to conduct research and write a new venture plan that can help you acquire the financing you need for your planned expansion. This is a good time to consider forming a joint venture, taking on a new partner, or taking a risk by adding something new to your business.

COMFORT STAGE

By now, your venture is secure and continuing to grow, although at a slower rate of less than 10% per year. You are enjoying the benefits of success—a comfortable income and an enjoyable lifestyle. By now, your business may own the building it operates from, as well as its production equipment and materials. The **assets** of the business are worth more than its **liabilities**. Although this stage seems secure, it can be a dangerous one for the entrepreneur who forgets that growth and change are essential to future success.

TURNAROUND STAGE

If you reach this stage, your venture is in financial trouble. The financial records reflect losses for more than two years, your competition is attracting customers away from your business, and your working capital has evaporated. If you want to save the venture, you will need to act now. Start by eliminating any nonproductive people, products, and services—no matter how difficult this seems. Payroll is often the highest cost of operation and is therefore the easiest to reduce. Consider the role of each employee in your organization. Whose work is nonessential? Whose work could be done by someone else? Terminating people is never easy, but it may be better than having everyone end up without a job.

Liquidation of some assets may also be necessary to generate cash. Reduce your inventory and make arrangements with your banker and suppliers for modified payment schedules. Seek help from a mentor who understands your situation.

What Is a Venture Plan?

Although most entrepreneurs are action-oriented, those who are most successful recognize that planning is a very important part of the action process. A **venture plan** is a road map for running a venture—a written summary of what the venture can accomplish and how. It should include

- a mission statement that describes your vision for the venture, including your aims and objectives
- the marketing research you have done, and a detailed description of your target market
- a list of the financial, material, and human resources you need to make your plan work

Worth Repeating

"I never see what has been done; I only see what remains to be done."

Marie Curie, Nobel Prize winning chemist

A good venture plan acts as a bridge between thinking and doing.

E-Bits & Bytes

Visit www.business.nelson.com and follow the links to "mission statements" to see examples of mission statements from companies like IBM, Microsoft, as well as middle- and small-size companies.

Worth Repeating

"Our number one priority is quality and service. What we do best is to provide good quality signs, quickly."

*Perry Brooks,
Advantage Signs Ltd.*

What makes this a good mission statement?

- an explanation of how the business will operate
- a plan for raising the money you need to start the venture

Since your venture plan is a tool you can use to communicate with potential investors, bankers, partners, and employees, it should include both words and numbers. It must provide a detailed description of the products or services you will offer, where the venture will operate, when it will start, and what resources are needed. Potential supporters will look at your plan to see what experience you bring to the venture, and whether your plan includes strategies for addressing problems that might occur.

A good venture plan acts as a bridge between thinking and doing. It will not only help you during the prestartup and development stages of your venture, but will continue to help you make day-to-day operating decisions as you move into the growth and comfort stages. For an enterprising employee, the goal may be a successful project rather than an entire venture. In this case, the plan might be called a **project plan**, but the components are similar.

If your venture is a for-profit undertaking, preparing a venture plan will help you predict future profits and make financial plans that will carry your business through the first few months after startup. If the venture is a not-for-profit enterprise or a community service, a venture plan can still help you weigh the costs and benefits and put plans in place that will make the venture a reality. If the project is being developed within an organization, the plan will help you determine the resources you need, analyze costs and benefits, and assess how the project will help move the organization toward its goals.

THE MISSION STATEMENT

Your venture plan should open with a mission statement that will capture the attention and interest of people who may be able to help you, for example, by investing money in your business. A good mission statement clearly identifies the type of venture you are planning, the products or services it will deliver, and the overall philosophy or purpose that has guided its development. It should also explain how the venture will meet the needs and wants of prospective customers. A clear understanding of purpose is an important step toward success.

THE RESEARCH ASSISTANCE GRID: A BASIC PLANNING TOOL

Entrepreneurs use the creative problem-solving model and the Six Thinking Hats described in Chapter 5 to help them organize

> **Worth Repeating**
>
> "The only place where success comes before work is in the dictionary."
>
> Vidal Sassoon, international hair stylist

resources to create a venture that will meet the needs of the market. While every venture plan is unique, each plan should outline specific goals and objectives, and describe planning strategies. It should also help the planner identify and assess potential risks.

A good planning model will help the entrepreneur or intrapreneur identify the right questions to ask before beginning a venture. The Research Assistance Grid that follows (Table 7.1) shows how to use six basic question stems—what, why, where, when, who, and how—to identify some of the questions that will need to be answered in the venture plan.

Table 7.1 Research Assistance Grid

What?	Why?
• What good or service will I produce? • What do people need and want? • What can my venture provide to meet these needs and wants? • What can I do to control production costs? • What can I do to maintain high, consistent standards? • What is the venture's potential for growth? • What is the potential impact of the project?	• Why should I spend my time and energy on this venture? • Why will others buy my product or service? • Why should investors finance my venture? • Why is it necessary to start this venture from scratch? • Why should my employer allocate resources to this project?
Where?	**When?**
• Where will I find a suitable site? • Where will I find the equipment I need? • Where will I find the right people? • Where will I find supplies at competitive prices?	• When is the demand greatest for my good or service? • When will I be able to start my venture? • When should I order the inventory I will need? • When should I change my selling price? • When should I recruit my team?
Who?	**How?**
• Who will my customers be? • Who will my major competitors be? • Who will help me do the things I can't do myself? • Who will be my mentor?	• How large is the market and what share can I get? • How strong is the competition now and how strong will it be in the future? • How will the competition react to a new competitor? • How will my product or service be unique? • How will my project align with the goals of the organization I work for?

Success Tips

- Your plan is a working document—don't be afraid to make changes.
- Be honest.
- Go straight to the point.
- Use clear and simple language.
- Appearance matters—use word processing software and check for errors.
- Include charts, graphs, and tables.
- Stick to the main points in the body and include details in the appendices.
- Have your plan professionally bound.
- Don't be afraid to ask for help.

Six Reasons to Prepare a Venture Plan

1. The plan helps you identify your market, understand your customers, choose the best pricing strategy, and get to know the competition.
2. The plan shows that the venture can work. It forces you to take a realistic view of your idea and logically assess your goals.
3. The plan introduces you to others as someone who is a careful planner. First impressions are very important.
4. The plan helps you determine how much financing you will need and when you will need it.
5. The plan identifies benchmarks or targets that will help you evaluate and improve the performance of your venture.
6. A written plan makes day-to-day management easier, since procedures can be reviewed and adjusted as necessary.

Table 7.2 The Contents of Venture and Project Plans

What Should Be in the Venture Plan?	What Should Be in the Project Plan?
• a description of the product or service to be offered	• a description of the purpose and goals of the project
• well-supported forecasts about sales and cash flow	• well-supported forecasts about income, costs, and cash flow
• a plan for obtaining the necessary financial resources	• a plan for obtaining the necessary financial resources
• a description of the human and material resources you will need	• a description of the human and material resources you will need
• an assessment of the strengths and weaknesses of the venture	• a description of how the project will benefit the organization
• a short-term plan for the venture	• a timeline for completing the project
• a long-term plan for the venture	• a plan for communicating results to others in the organization
• planned marketing and sales strategies	• well-supported information about the impact of the project on the company's bottom line
• a production plan	
• an evaluation of the competition	
• the risks	• risk assessment

YOUR TURN

1. What are the stages in the life cycle of a business?
2. At which stages in this cycle might someone need a venture plan? Why?
3. What is the relationship between the break-even point and total monthly costs? Why does an entrepreneur need to know this?
4. Why is it important for a venture to have a mission statement?
5. With a small group, create a mission statement for one of the following types of ventures: an in-line skating league, a recreation centre for seniors, a fitness centre for all ages, or a public library. Use the criteria for a good mission statement described on page 148.
6. Make an hour-by-hour plan of how you will spend tomorrow. What are some of the advantages and disadvantages of this kind of planning?

Sections in a Business Venture Plan

Whether a venture is large or small, it needs to begin with a venture plan. Plans are written not only for new business and community-service ventures, but also for established ventures that want to try something new. Small ventures have simple plans, while the plans for larger ventures are more complex. No matter what the venture is, the plan usually includes these five sections:

- Executive Summary
- Market Analysis
- Resource Analysis
- Operating Strategy
- Financial Strategy

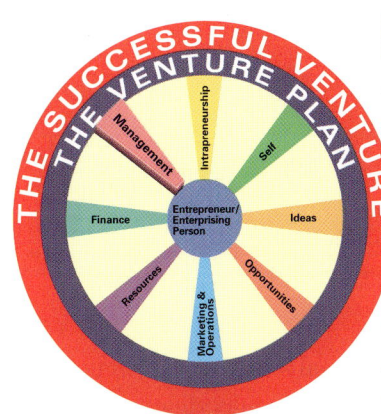

SECTION 1: EXECUTIVE SUMMARY

The **executive summary** is a one- or two-page summary of the most important points in your plan, intended to introduce the venture and to capture the attention of the reader. This is your chance to make a first impression, and, as such, it should be flawless and to the point.

A great executive summary opens with a mission statement that encourages the reader to read on and learn more about your venture. After the mission statement comes a description of the business. This description must be accurate and should tell readers enough for them to decide whether they are sufficiently interested in the ideas behind the venture to read further. Each area addressed in the executive summary will be explained in more detail later in the plan.

Chapter 7 ◆ The Venture Plan 151

Although the executive summary appears at the beginning of the plan, it cannot be written until all the other sections of the plan are complete. The executive summary should include

- names of the contact person and management team members, and how these people can be reached
- the name of the venture and a description of its nature and objectives
- information about goods or services offered, what makes the business unique, the location of the business, and proposed timelines for its development
- information about any security that can be offered to investors in exchange for their investment
- information about any business loans that are required
- key highlights of the business plan

Section 2: Market Analysis

Before you develop your venture, it's important to determine if the goods or services you intend to provide will satisfy the needs of the market. **Needs assessment**, or, as it is more often called in commercial business ventures, **market analysis**, can help you identify potential customers, analyze your competition, set prices, and plan ways to advertise your venture.

The market analysis section describes the marketing research you conducted and the conclusions you drew from your research. It should include

- the demographics of potential customers (age, gender, location, buying habits, etc.)
- the types of products or services you think your customers will buy and how you know
- a description of trends that suggest this is the right time to introduce your product or service
- who your competitors are, where they are, and how successful they are
- how you plan to make your product or service better than or different from your competitors'
- how much you will charge for your product or service
- how you plan to advertise your product or service to your target market

Pricing is an important part of market analysis that can make or break a new venture. If the price is too high, this may discourage sales. If it's too low, your customers may perceive your product or service as low quality, and your profit margins may not be enough to

Studying the demographic characteristics of potential customers is crucial to market analysis.

E-Bits & Bytes

Visit www.business.nelson.com and follow the links to "promoting your venture" to find sites that let entrepreneurs advertise their new ventures free of charge.

cover your costs. Ask yourself: How can my price be competitive and still give me a suitable profit margin? Could I offer cash or volume discounts? What will I need to charge for shipping and delivery?

How you advertise your product is also important. Your advertising plan should include an assessment of the various forms of advertising available, the types of customers you hope to reach, and the costs involved. Be sure to register the name of your venture to make sure that no one else is already using the same name for a similar business.

REGISTERING A BUSINESS NAME

To register your business name, you should first determine the form of ownership you will adopt for your company. You can register your business name in each province as a sole proprietorship, partnership, or corporation. Different forms of ownership will be discussed in detail in Chapter 9. If you are going to have a sole proprietorship, that is, if you are going to be the only owner of your venture, and if you will use your own name as the name of the company, you are not required to register the name (e.g., Kim Lee). If you choose to add any words to the name (e.g., Kim Lee Café), it is necessary to register the business name and pay a fee before you use it.

Registering your new business name ensures that only you can use this name for advertising and legal purposes. If you want to operate your business outside of one province, and you are incorporating your company, you should register it as a federally incorporated business. The name will then have national protection. You can obtain more information on the registration process from your local Canada Business Service Centres.

YOUR TURN

1. Why is it important to have a very good executive summary in your venture plan?

2. In Chapter 8, you will begin to write a venture plan for a personal venture you have chosen. Identify a venture that you would be interested in developing. Then create a Research Assistance Grid like the one on page 149 by listing specific questions you would need to answer during the planning process.

3. Which of the De Bono thinking hats did you use as you created the Research Assistance Grid for Question 2? How did you use them?

4. With a small group, discuss what you will need to do in order to prepare a market analysis of the venture you chose for Question 2. Consider the points outlined on page 152 as well as the following questions:
   - What specific needs will be satisfied by this venture? Whose needs are they?
   - What are your sales objectives for your first year of operation?
   - How might your venture grow in the future?

5. Chapter 5 outlines the three steps in the creative problem-solving process. What stage of the process were you in as you worked on your answers to Question 4? Explain.

SECTION 3: RESOURCE ANALYSIS

All good ideas need resources to make them work. In the **resource analysis** section of the plan, the entrepreneur needs to consider the **material resources**, **human resources**, and **financial resources** that will be needed for the venture.

Material resources include all the materials that are needed to operate the venture, both raw materials and finished products. For a particular venture, they might include equipment, storage bins, plastic, paper, extension cords, computers, software, printers, screws, flour, ovens, delivery trucks, and so on. Some of these are **consumable resources** while others are **fixed resources**, which can be used over and over. You will need to decide how to get the material resources you need and whether it's better to buy or lease them.

Human resources are the people needed to operate the venture—perhaps the most important resources of all. Without the right people, the venture is unlikely to succeed. Start by looking at the skills you and your partners possess. Then look for people whose skills will complement your own and fill in where there are gaps. How many people will you need to start your business? to help it grow? For example, you may be a great disc jockey, and your partner may be a great promoter, but without a professional accountant, your party music business won't get far.

The term "financial resources" means the money needed to start and operate the venture. This includes money to buy equipment and materials, to pay staff, and to pay other expenses such as rent,

Worth Repeating

"We know that in the shakeout for resources, it's the best business models, the best teams, and the most tightly focused execution plans that will attract the capital, the partners, and the customers long term."

Laura Rippy, CEO of Handango

electricity, and advertising costs. These resources will be dealt with in more detail in Section 5 of the venture plan.

In the resource section of your business plan, you will need to consider

- what tools and equipment you will need, and where you will get them
- what human resources you will need
- where your venture will be located
- how much space you will require
- the kind of space you will require
- whether you plan to buy or rent your facility, or whether your business can be operated without a bricks-and-mortar site
- whether you will manufacture your products yourself or hire a contract organization to do it for you
- which sources of raw materials you intend to use and how much these materials will cost
- how often your suppliers will deliver materials and what return and refund policies they offer on their products
- the total cost of all the resources you will need to start and operate your business

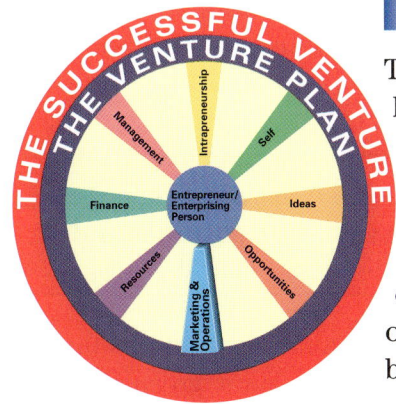

Both material resources and human resources play a part in the successful venture.

SECTION 4: OPERATING STRATEGY

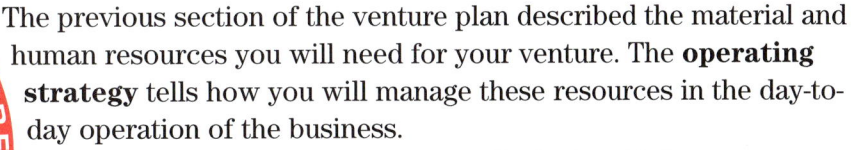

The previous section of the venture plan described the material and human resources you will need for your venture. The **operating strategy** tells how you will manage these resources in the day-to-day operation of the business.

The first part of this section usually deals with human resources management. It details people's responsibilities, channels of communication, the different departments that will exist in the organization, how work groups will operate, and how the work will be supervised.

Agents of Change

When West Coast developer Terrence Hui arrived in Canada more than a decade ago, he quickly shelved his college degrees in physics and electrical engineering, and launched a megadevelopment on Vancouver's waterfront, including Canada's first smart community. The new downtown suburban community is surrounded by six kilometres of fibre-optic cables that turn each residential and office unit into an interactive communications centre. Hui is set to pour billions into Toronto's long-neglected railway lands near Lake Ontario.... By the end of the decade-long megaproject, the barren site west of the SkyDome will be transformed into an upscale community of 12 000.

What is a "smart" community? What human resources do you think Terrence Hui might have needed to build a development like this?

An organizational chart is a good way to present a visual plan for human resources management.

Figure 7.2 Organizational Chart

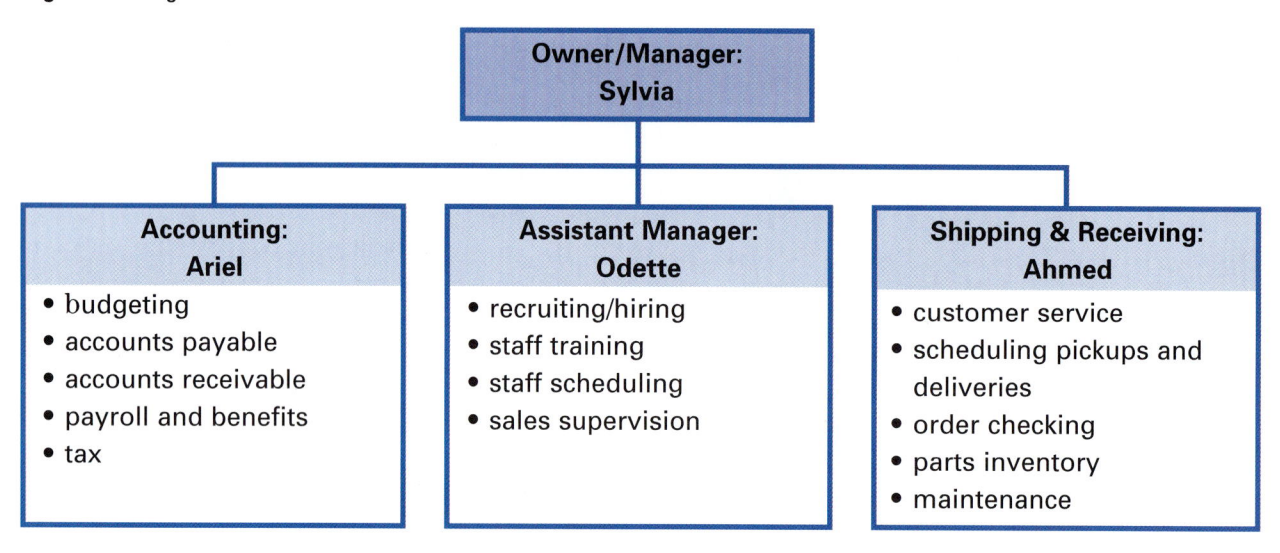

```
                    Owner/Manager:
                        Sylvia
          ┌───────────────┼───────────────┐
   Accounting:      Assistant Manager:   Shipping & Receiving:
      Ariel                Odette                Ahmed
  • budgeting         • recruiting/hiring   • customer service
  • accounts payable  • staff training      • scheduling pickups and
  • accounts          • staff scheduling      deliveries
    receivable        • sales supervision   • order checking
  • payroll and                             • parts inventory
    benefits                                • maintenance
  • tax
```

The operating strategy also deals with the production process and how the necessary supplies will be obtained. It describes how the facility will be set up, including its size, location(s), special needs, the ownership terms, or, if the facility is leased, the terms of the lease. The plan also describes the facility's present and potential production capacity, the minimum levels of production needed to sustain the operation, and any overhead operating costs.

This section also deals with inventory needs and record keeping. It tells who your suppliers will be, who will order and monitor supplies, how much you will spend on an average supply order, and what **contingency plans** you have made in case your regular suppliers can't fill your orders.

Your plan should also address any environmental policies that might affect day-to-day operations—your company's "green plan." Environmental awareness is an increasingly important goal for successful ventures in the 21st century.

The operating strategy should explain

- who will do each job and how the work will be supervised
- how people will work together
- what the operating facility will be like
- how the production process will be organized
- where the supplies will come from and who will be in charge of ordering them
- what records must be kept and who will keep them

Worth Repeating

"Nothing in life just happens. It isn't enough to believe in something; you have to have the stamina to meet obstacles and overcome them, to struggle."

Golda Meir, Israeli political leader

How does having a venture plan help you "meet obstacles and overcome them"?

- how the venture can keep its costs to a minimum
- what rules and regulations, including environmental ones, apply to the venture

Many venture plans also include a **Gap Analysis** to point out the difference between what is already in place and what ideally should be in place once the venture is successfully underway.

YOUR TURN

1. Why do you think some people consider human resources to be the most valuable resources?

2. In the previous Your Turn section, you began planning a small venture. Make a list of 10 material resources you would need for the venture you chose.

3. What human resources would you need to operate the venture you chose? Tell why you need each person.

4. Sometimes a small business can't afford to hire a large full-time staff. Given the venture you chose, how could you acquire the human resources you need without hiring everyone full-time?

5. Make an organizational chart to show how the human resources for your venture would be organized.

6. Write a list of questions you would need to answer before you could write the resource analysis for the venture you chose. Write another list of questions that would help you plan your operating strategy.

7. How would you solve any of the following problems in your business plan?
   a) lateness into the market
   b) lack of experience
   c) lack of team work
   d) lack of expertise

SECTION 5: FINANCIAL STRATEGY

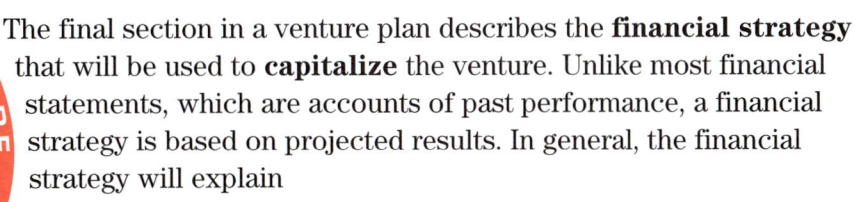

The final section in a venture plan describes the **financial strategy** that will be used to **capitalize** the venture. Unlike most financial statements, which are accounts of past performance, a financial strategy is based on projected results. In general, the financial strategy will explain

- how much it will cost to start the venture
- how much it will cost to keep the venture going after startup
- the expected costs and revenue for the venture
- how much capital will be required, and when it will be needed
- what sources of capital are available

The financial strategy of any business plan involves research and preparation. There are a number of possible sources of capital for a venture. They include bankers, government agencies, credit unions, venture capitalists, or friends and family. Whether you are starting a new business or buying an existing one, you will need to prepare a number of financial papers, which include information about the details listed in Figure 7.3 on page 158.

Chapter 7 ♦ The Venture Plan 157

Figure 7.3 Financial Information

- detailed cash-flow projections
- sales forecasts
- anticipated selling costs
- expected gross profit
- administrative costs
- expected pretax profit
- balance sheet
- rate of return on investment
- working capital
- repayment proposal
- collateral

A financial strategy must provide specific details about how much money is needed. Consider showing both a high and a low estimate for the future, for example, when you are forecasting sales or developing a repayment proposal. This lets potential investors see both the worst-case and the best-case scenarios.

It helps to include a breakdown of where funds will be needed. For instance, a new venture might need $10 000 to buy equipment and $30 000 for consumable raw materials. A lender might be more willing to lend money for the equipment, which can be resold if the business gets into trouble, than for consumable materials. Don't forget to include information about when the loan will be repaid, when the payments will be made and how large they will be, and what rate of interest you expect to pay.

This section of the venture plan is critical to your success. Without the numbers you provide in your financial strategy plan, no one will be willing to help you capitalize your venture.

YOUR TURN

1. Your class wants to sell something to the community to raise money for a class trip.
   a) With a small group, discuss what you need to know about the market. If this were a real venture, how would you gather this information?
   b) With your group, prepare a Research Assistance Grid filled with questions you need to ask in order to prepare an operating strategy and a financial strategy.
   c) Discuss how your team can share the task of finding the answers to the questions you described in part (b). You may need to estimate for some answers, since this is an imaginary venture.
   d) Write an operating strategy and a financial strategy for your class venture.
   e) Compare your plans with those of another group. What similarities and differences can you find?

2. Some students at your school are planning to organize a fashion show and have asked for your advice. Using the structure of a venture plan, list the questions they will need to answer in order to get their project off the ground. Beneath each question, jot down any related suggestions you have.

Venture Case

STEPS TO LAUNCH A SUCCESSFUL BUSINESS

Paul Tulenko, The Globe and Mail

Have you been selling your products or services to your friends and come to feel you should expand your horizons? Are you concerned that striking out on your own may not produce enough income to feed your family, much less make you a success? Do you wonder just what you are getting into and, more importantly, what your chances for success really are?

It would be nice if we could have a magic wand to find out how successful we will be as entrepreneurs, but that's beyond our ability. Fortunately, there are enough statistics to form guidelines that may be able to predict success. While having all of the attributes of success will not assure you of instant success, not having them could spell failure.

Money

Having enough money (beyond what it takes to start your business) to survive the first year is a major success factor. Successful business owners understand it takes money to exist as a person or family while the business income is building.

Existence money means rent, car payments, food, and similar items. Saying, "I'll pay for those out of profits from my business," is usually fatal. New businesses seldom generate enough cash to keep the doors open for the first year or so of operation, much less provide a profit for the owner.

A good rule of thumb is to have nine months of personal expense money and six months of business operating money on hand in addition to the basic cash startup funds. If that sounds like a lot of money, measure it against losing your home, car, and dignity.

Record Keeping

A couple of years ago, the Ohio Business Institute studied 5000 businesses to determine whether bookkeeping was an important ingredient for success. Their study indicated that 70% of successful business owners had a fundamental understanding of basic accounting while only 10% of failed business owners had the same understanding.

These facts indicate that ignorance of accounting could mean a nine in ten chance of failure, while taking a basic bookkeeping class could provide a seven in ten chance of success. This means that you should start your own business with a knowledge of bookkeeping before you spend a nickel on your business.

Start Small

If at all possible, start your business from your home. Practically any business can be started from a basement, garage, spare room, or even the kitchen table. Let's not get ourselves tied up with ego—be pragmatic. If you absolutely must go outside the house for your business,

CONTINUED➡

try sharing a location with a similar or complementary business.

Your goal in the first year should be to concentrate on establishing a presence in your community. Only then should you consider expanding your business to generate a larger market share.

Personal Traits

Successful business owners spend much of their waking time running their businesses. This means anywhere between 50 and 80 hours a week. Running a business can be fun, and the best scenario is where it is hard to separate the work part from the fun part. Families of successful owners understand this factor and expect a certain degree of isolation.

You will have to deal with impatience with the way that money comes in, overeagerness to make a sale, immaturity in handling adversity, poor judgment of people, and a feeling that the big guy is out to get you. Successful owners overcome these feelings and go on to manage successful businesses.

Planning for Success

Good planning means success. If you doubt this, interview a couple of startup successes in your area, and do the same with a couple of failures. There are plenty of the latter. They show up in the bankruptcy columns of your local newspapers. You will discover that a comprehensive business plan is the success factor. Help with planning can come from your banker, lawyer, or accountant. Don't start without a business plan, unless you plan to fail.

Exploring

1. According to Paul Tulenko, what is the most important thing an entrepreneur needs to do to achieve success?
2. How can prospective entrepreneurs predict their chances for success?
3. List all the points in Paul Tulenko's analysis that have to do with money. Why is it so important to prepare a financial strategy for your business?
4. Use the ideas in this Venture Case to predict your own success as an entrepreneur. List your strengths and weaknesses. What could you do to overcome the weaknesses?

Worth Repeating

"You really have to believe in what you're doing. You should talk to people in business because they know the ins and outs. Try for some funding programs—they could really get you on your feet."

Lori-lee Hollett, Hollett Visual Communications

Mentorship

Mentorship occurs whenever an experienced person, the mentor, offers advice and support to a less experienced person. In the business world, mentorship can be an invaluable help to an entrepreneur during the early stages of a venture.

Mentorship can be done either formally or informally. The mentor is usually a volunteer with personal experience in the field, although some mentors are paid consultants. Connecting entrepreneurs with experienced mentors has become a viable venture itself. As you read in Chapter 1, incubators—organizations that foster and nurture new ventures—often provide mentors for their clients, along with other services such as business training, shared office space, shared technology, and administrative assistance.

International NEWS

The UNIDO Online Inquiry Service, set up by the United Nations Industrial Development Organization, offers entrepreneurs in developing countries access to up-to-date business information provided by professionals from around the world. The clients pose their questions at the UNIDO Web site. Their questions are forwarded by UNIDO to experienced businesspeople from both developing and developed countries. The professionals respond directly to the clients, forming a relationship that can sometimes lead to online mentoring.

To learn more about how UNIDO works, visit www.business.nelson.com for links to the organization's Web site.

Cool Stuff

Pamela Wallin, best known as a TV host and interviewer, is also president of Pamela Wallin Productions. Here's her advice for other entrepreneurs: "Sometimes you don't recognize that you're already connected. When I left the CBC, I thought about starting my own production company. I knew a lot about TV journalism and people, but not a lot about business. I'd interviewed many businesspeople, but the penny hadn't quite dropped—I didn't realize I had access to this wealth of mentors! It took a helpful conversation with Adam Zimmerman, who used to head Noranda, to make me see that good advice was all around if I just asked."

Hilary Davidson, Chatelaine

Venture Profile

HELPING HAND FOR EARLY DAYS

National Post

When it comes to cutting hair, Patrick Trudeau and his colleague, Jayson Van Ee, are confident of their skills. But when the two of them decided to launch their own salon two years ago, they found themselves in uncharted waters. Both knew that they could navigate an established business and bring in new clientele but neither had experience with building a business from the ground up.

At first, the enthusiastic business partners worked on their own to develop a business plan. They turned to the Canadian Youth Business Foundation (CYBF) for help after a friend suggested the mentor program to them. Within months of their first meeting, Trudeau and Van Ee received a loan, encouragement, and plenty of guidance through the foundation's mentoring program. Today, the partners are the proud owners of Atelier Hair Salon, a trendy boutique near the downtown core of Calgary, Alberta.

"We would never have got this business off the ground without the help of our mentor,

CONTINUED➔

Derek Boniecki," admits Trudeau. "Joining the mentor program was one of the best business decisions we've ever made."

As a mentor, Derek Boniecki, a chartered accountant, volunteers his business expertise and time to these young entrepreneurs. With his help, Trudeau and Van Ee got more than just investment advice and an introduction to the local business community; they received plenty of encouragement and understanding during the stressful startup phase.

"Mentoring has always played an important role in the traditional corporate environment," says Boniecki, whose firm serves small- and medium-sized businesses, "But today's new economy does not allow for the natural mentoring relationships that once took place in business."

Gone are the days when a new employee would be taken under the wing of a superior. In today's job environment, terms such as downsizing, outsourcing, and relocation are part of the everyday business language. Young workers do not expect to experience the career stability that their parents' generation has had. Recent statistics support this change in the social and economic landscape.

A 1998 Angus Reid survey suggests that over 30% of young people expect to be self-employed at some point in their lives. Defined as the Nexus Generation—born in the 70s and 80s—this group rated entrepreneurship ahead of traditional careers such as law or medicine. They are optimistic about the possibility of self-employment, and half of those surveyed consider job satisfaction and risk taking to be critical to career success.

For new entrepreneurs, the absence of a mentoring relationship can make establishing a new venture an even more challenging process. "Not only can it be lonely and a little frightening when you're starting, but you find there are so many questions you need answered," recalls Justin Poy, president of Justin Poy Media, a firm that specializes in multicultural advertising. "Mentors play a critical role in helping to steer you in the right direction, and they enable you to operate efficiently."

CYBF decided to establish a mentor program after hearing about the success of a similar program in Ireland. The success rate of a young entrepreneur's business was 40% prior to introducing the mentor program. After just three years of offering the mentoring initiative, the success rate had climbed to 75%. It is statistics like these that have encouraged the Foundation to work equally hard to provide mentors for the thousands of enterprising young people who have come to them for help. Entrepreneurs between the ages of 18 and 29 can qualify for loans of up to $15 000 and, in lieu of collateral, they are required to work with a mentor during the startup and early years of operating their business. During the startup phase, protégés and mentors meet at least once a month to review the performance

Trudeau (left) and Van Ee (right) with their mentor Derek Boniecki (middle)

CONTINUED

of the enterprise and to work on achieving goals for the business. They also meet regularly with Foundation staff to see how the relationship is going. "We are careful to pair young people with individuals with whom they can develop a trusting relationship."

One of the key principles of the program is mutual selection. Loan recipients can use a mentor they selected themselves, or they can have the Foundation match them with one. Not only do young entrepreneurs learn from these mentors, they become more self-confident about their abilities to forge their own career paths. This alone makes the program worthwhile, says Judy Andrigo, executive director of the London Entrepreneurial Education Association. The organization, which has been working with CYBF for nearly two years, provides mentors for business people and not-for-profit organizations. "We've met so many people who don't know how to find the appropriate networking avenues.... With mentoring, they find out whom they might call in the local business community for help, and that gives them a feeling of control over their situation."

Volunteer mentors also find that they get personal satisfaction as a result of their involvement. "It feels good to know that I've played a part in helping two entrepreneurs establish themselves," says Mr. Boniecki. When Mr. Boniecki started working with Trudeau and Van Ee, there were just the two of them. Today they employ 10 others and there is a six-week wait for an appointment. Atelier Hair Salon is a respected member of Calgary's business community. Trudeau insists that, business experience aside, to be a great mentor one must be patient with the people with whom one works. He credits his mentor with having that quality. "What I found most helpful was having a patient and compassionate mentor, because starting a business is very frightening, even if you have experience in the field."

> **E-Bits & Bytes**
>
> Visit www.business.nelson.com for links to the Canadian Youth Business Foundation. Besides mentorship, what other services does this organization provide?

> **Exploring**
>
> 1. What skills did Trudeau and Van Ee bring to their venture? What skills did they lack?
> 2. What are some of the roles of a mentor?
> 3. How does society benefit when mentors help young entrepreneurs?
> 4. If you were planning a venture, what qualities would you want your mentor to have? Why?
> 5. Why might a successful business person decide to become a mentor?

The Importance of the Venture Plan

Planning and organization are vital to the success of any venture. Due to inadequate planning, some ventures have been started that should never have seen the light of day. Some were not based on a good idea. Sometimes the good or service produced was no better than what was already available. Perhaps the huge market the entrepreneur expected to find existed only in his or her imagination.

Perhaps people were just not willing to pay the price that had to be charged in order to make the venture worthwhile.

Other ventures have started smoothly, experienced some growth, and eventually failed. Perhaps they ran out of capital. Perhaps new competitors stole the market. Perhaps the entrepreneur was not interested in, or good at, managing and allocating resources. Perhaps the market simply vanished; customer needs and interests can change quickly.

Preparing a venture plan will take you through the process of assessing potential risks and identifying potential problems. It will force you to project future profits and to decide whether you have enough capital to make your plans work. It will help you anticipate some of the seasonal, market, and labour trends that can directly affect your bottom line.

Venture plans are useful even if the venture is well established. Many businesspeople have found that the venture plans they initially prepared for startup have proven to be even more helpful as their ventures grow and develop. They provide a framework against which to monitor progress, and can be useful when a business is planning to expand, add new lines, or even sell out completely.

A venture plan is a dynamic, living document that is constantly revised as circumstances change. Under extreme circumstances, the plan might need to be abandoned altogether and replaced with something else. The venture plan is a means to an end—not an end in itself. It exists only to benefit the venture.

Putting your plan in writing provides a record of what has been decided. This can help you save time, resolve disputes, and provide clear direction for future decisions. Putting a plan in writing ensures that the details have been thought through, and gives you a document you can use to impress others and gain their support. For all these reasons, a business with a written venture plan is much more likely to succeed.

Think About It

Motivational speaker Joel Barker says, "The ultimate function of prophecy is not to tell the future, but to make it. Your successful past will block your visions of the future."
How does this statement relate to venture planning? Do you agree or disagree with Barker's point of view?

YOUR TURN

1. List five possible reasons for the failure of a venture.
2. Describe a scenario in which an established business might require a venture plan.
3. Why does the venture plan need to be flexible?
4. Suppose a friend told you he was planning to open a small business without making a written venture plan. What reasons might he have for this decision? What advice would you give him?

ACTIVITIES

FLASHBACKS

Graphs and diagrams can sometimes communicate information more quickly and effectively than words. Review the different parts of a venture plan and then list some types of graphs or diagrams that you could put into each part. Keep this list handy. It will help you when you begin writing your personal venture plan in Chapter 8.

- The life cycle of a business includes the prestartup stage, the development stage, the growth stage, the comfort stage, and the turnaround stage.
- A venture plan is a written account of all the thinking and research that has been used to plan the venture.
- A Research Assistance Grid is a way of organizing questions you need to ask about your venture in order to write your venture plan.
- A mission statement captures the purpose of the venture and explains how the venture will meet the needs and wants of prospective customers.
- A venture plan consists of five sections: the executive summary, the market analysis, the resource analysis, the operating strategy, and the financial strategy.
- The executive summary introduces the venture.
- The market analysis defines the size and characteristics of the intended market.
- The resource analysis identifies the material and human resources the venture will require.
- The operating strategy explains how the resources will be organized and used.
- The financial strategy forecasts costs and revenues to determine how much capital will be required to start and maintain the venture, and when the capital will be needed.
- Mentors are experienced people who can help and guide new entrepreneurs.

E-Bits & Bytes

Visit the Nelson Web site at www.business.nelson.com and follow the links to "mentors" to connect with business specialists who can help you with your business plan.

LESSONS LEARNED

1. Why is a mission statement important to an entrepreneur?
2. What can a mentor do to help a new entrepreneur during the business planning stage?
3. Describe three possible uses of a venture plan that don't involve the launch of a new business.

4. Why is making a Research Assistance Grid a good way to start working on a venture plan?

5. What kinds of help might you need to ask for as you develop a business venture plan?

6. Draw a mind map to show the advantages of writing a thorough venture plan before starting a business.

VENTURING OUT

1. With a small group, use brainstorming to choose a venture you think could succeed at your school or in your community. It can either be a for-profit or a not-for-profit venture, but it must be different from the venture chosen by each other group. Then, continue to work with your group to complete Questions 2 to 5.

2. Create a mission statement for your venture.

3. Make a Research Assistance Grid and record all the questions your group will need to answer during the planning process for your venture.

4. Develop an executive summary to introduce your business plan. Include visuals and information that will help convince others to invest in your venture.

5. In a role-playing situation, present your proposal to a banker or to a group of potential investors. After each presentation, the class will select the best executive summary and give reasons for its choice. The selection should be based on criteria from this chapter.

> Remember to update the database you began in Chapter 2 to include the people you met in this unit.

POINT OF VIEW

Which of the following quotations do you think best captures the importance of writing a venture plan? Explain your choice.
   a) "Take the first step in faith. You don't have to see the whole staircase, just take the first step."
      (Dr. Martin Luther King, Jr., U.S. cleric and civil rights leader)
   b) "The best preparation for tomorrow is to do today's work superbly well." (Sir William Osler, Canadian physician and educator)
   c) "A vision statement is like the sun. You can't ever get there, but it's an attractive force that stimulates the growth of many things." (Greg Steltenpohl, founder of fresh juice company Odwalla, Inc.)
   d) "If I had eight hours to chop down a tree, I'd spend six sharpening my axe." (Abraham Lincoln, the 16th president of the U.S.A.)

UNIT 3
Moving into Action

What Does "Moving into Action" Mean?

This unit will provide you with the tools you need to bring your ideas to life. Your goal may be a business venture, or it may have to do with a job, a community activity, or your personal life. No matter what your goal is, working through the planning process will bring you face to face with many questions. The time you spend asking and answering these questions is well worthwhile, since it will help you shape and refine your ideas.

Self-discipline will also be necessary to help you keep yourself and your work on track. As you move into action, you will discover that the new economy has much to offer a new enterprise. Carrying small and medium ventures forward on a wave of technology, today's economy provides multiple possibilities for startups and business development. A venture that is destined for success will position itself to take advantage of change as it occurs. Always keep your goal in mind as you make and carry out your plans.

Now that you've moved through many turns of the Venture Creation Wheel, it's time to put all of your plans into action. You've already learned about the **Entrepreneur** and the **Enterprising Person** at the hub of the wheel, and you've assessed your own entrepreneurial potential. Also, you've learned about **Intrapreneurship** and labour market trends. You know how to spot enterprising employees, and you've explored changes that are occurring in the workplace.

You understand innovation, invention, and the creative edge that sustain the **Ideas** spoke of the wheel, and you've explored the trends, fads, and opportunities represented by the **Opportunities** spoke. In Chapter 7, you learned about the structure of the **Venture Plan** that will hold the venture wheel together as it carries you toward your goal.

As you turn the wheel in the last unit, you will learn about the **Marketing and Operations** spoke in Chapter 8, and **Management** of your **Resources** in Chapter 9. In Chapter 10, you will find out how to **Finance** your dream. In Chapter 11, you will pull all of these components together to create your own venture plan. Finally, in Chapter 12, you will learn to build and manage your venture in a way that will allow it to grow and thrive.

Remember that you, the enterprising person or entrepreneur, are the most important part of a successful venture plan, and that your place is at the hub of the Venture Creation Wheel. When you are ready to take this position, you will have at your disposal the motivation and knowledge that guided many of the successful ventures you've read about in profiles throughout this book.

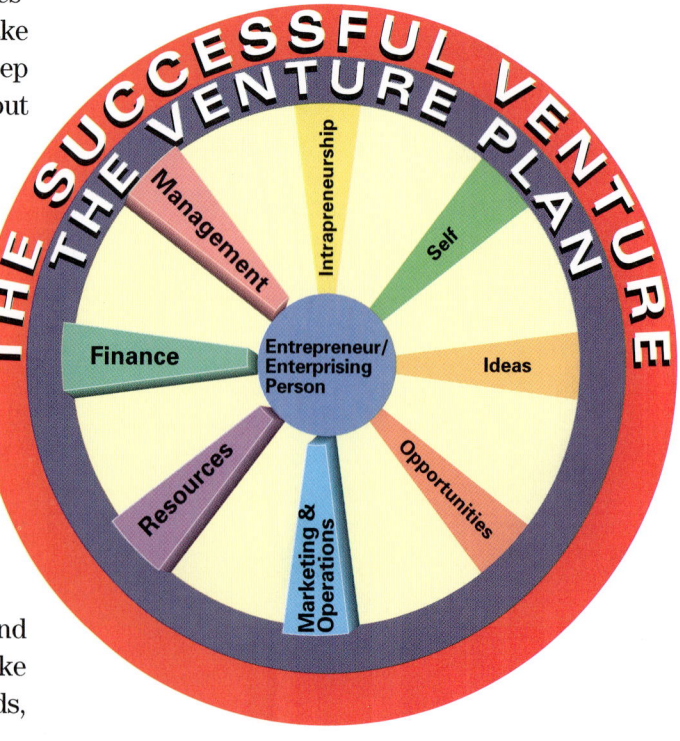

CHAPTER 8

Analyzing Your Market

LEARNING OPPORTUNITIES

By the end of this chapter, you should be able to
- explain how to determine whether the demand for a good or service exists
- identify and use the three forms of marketing research (exploratory, specific, causal)
- understand the Four Ps of Marketing (product, place, price, promotion)
- describe how and why target markets, market segments, and life cycles need to be identified
- describe the characteristics (demographic, geographic, socioeconomic, psychographic, etc.) of potential target markets
- analyze the impact of competition on a new product or service
- use the profit formula to predict profits

Entrepreneurial Language

- survey
- observation
- experimentation
- product sampling
- census
- sample
- marketing strategy
- marketing elements
- marketing mix
- promotion
- target market
- market segment
- life cycle
- profit formula
- fixed cost
- variable cost
- AIDA formula

The terms "survey," "observation," "experimentation," "product sampling," and "census" all represent ways of gathering information. Tell a partner about a time when you participated in one or more of these activities.

Venture Profile

YOU CAN'T SELL BROCCOLI TO CHILDREN

Hilary Davidson, Chatelaine

Virginia Marshall had such a great idea for a company name—Mark It—that she registered it before she knew what her business would do. Then, she began scouting for a niche to fill in serving the business community of Oakville, Ontario, where she lives. "I thought there's no sense starting something that can't float," she says. "You can't sell broccoli to children."

In order to find out what local firms needed, Marshall asked Statistics Canada for information about the number of small businesses in her area, which types were turning a profit, and other trends. Human Resources Development Canada handed over a labour market overview and details on the kinds of jobs being downsized. The local chamber of commerce shared community demographics.

Marshall's research told her there was a demand for a newsletter for small businesses. So, she asked more than 50 local companies and business associations if—and what—they would pay for such a newsletter. She also surveyed them about their businesses. Everyone who responded received a free year-long subscription to *In Pursuit*, a quarterly newsletter with articles on marketing, networking, and technology—and all of their company information went into Marshall's database. She targeted her survey and other business-related mailings for maximum impact after a friend in the direct-mail business showed her how to select postal codes in affluent areas.

Marshall's detailed research has allowed Mark It to expand into other ventures, such as Web page design, computer training, and database management. The lesson? "You need to give people what they want, rather than try to get people to buy what you want," advises Marshall.

Exploring

1. What was the niche that Virginia Marshall was looking for?
2. Why do you think the author of this article chose the title "You Can't Sell Broccoli to Children"?
3. How did Virginia use the information about labour markets?
4. How did she identify the needs of local businesses?
5. What kind of venture did Mark It become? How has it expanded?
6. How did Virginia target her survey?
7. What is the key message in this profile?

Starting Up

Have you ever participated in a survey? What was its purpose? How was it conducted? How do you think businesses use the survey information they gather?

■ Knowing Your Market

It is important to the success of your enterprise that you know who will be buying your products or services. This is your market. Marketing research involves learning about your customers by systematically and objectively collecting, recording, and analyzing data. Virginia Marshall talked to more than 50 companies in her community, analyzed labour market information obtained from the federal government, and talked to a friend about how to address her survey to postal codes in affluent areas. As a result of her research, Virginia Marshall was able to develop a successful marketing plan for her venture.

A good marketing plan should answer these questions:

1. What needs will be satisfied?
2. Whose needs will be satisfied?
3. How many people could benefit from my product or service?
4. How will consumers choose which product or service to buy?
5. Who are my competitors?
6. What will my competitors be doing?
7. What other factors could affect a business like mine?

Magazines are a rich source of information.

To find answers to these questions, you will need to explore as many sources of information as you can. Check out some of the following:

- industry associations and journals
- newspapers and magazines
- trade shows
- conventions
- newsletters
- trade publications
- local chamber of commerce
- local board of trade
- suppliers and customers
- competitors
- provincial and federal government agencies or departments, including Statistics Canada

Venture Profile

PUTTING A NEW SPIN ON TOYS

Diane McDougall, Financial Post

Anton Rabie, CEO of Spin Master Toys says, "Our goal is to create the most magical toys in the world. We believe that product is king, and our passion is product selection and marketing strategy."

Two other partners, Ronnen Harary and Ben Varadi, help lead Spin Master, a success story of global proportions. Award-winning toys, such as Air Hogs, Sky Sharks, and Flick Trix, are sold in over 25 countries.

The Toronto-based company sets itself apart with high-calibre, talented young people. One of the newest initiatives is the addition of a top-notch team of vice presidents. These new team members have the same youthful energy, but have come to the company with a great deal of experience. "There were a lot of things in the company that we were doing that had no rhyme or reason," says Mr. Rabie. "We've concentrated on hiring people who have done it before, can jump in and build processes and an infrastructure. Our approach is to hire strong people who have an entrepreneurial spirit. We wanted people who were looking to break out and have a massive impact on a smaller company." The three partners challenged everything that they could see and touch. "We told people to just go ahead and make changes. We said that we didn't want to have long meetings."

Spin Master also has an advisory board consisting of outside members from various disciplines including advertising, retail, venture capital, and finance. "I think the greatest thing about our board is how much they care about our organization. They know their input is valued and we implement their ideas," he says.

Key toy buyers give feedback from the marketplace. "We have focus groups including a group of kids on the Internet with whom we maintain constant dialogue," says Rabie.

Mr. Rabie's advice on exporting is: "If you've got the right product or service, it will go. Focus on your bread-and-butter market first. For us, it's in the U.S. But once you've had a chance to develop that, then go into other markets. We're now at the stage where we can put time into international business. It's really a very small world," he says.

Exploring

1. What is the key to success for Spin Master Toys?
2. What kinds of marketing research does Spin Master use and why?
3. What are Spin Master's target markets and what demographics are appropriate for its products?
4. How does Spin Master Toys know what its customers want?
5. Describe the company culture and staffing policies. What impact do you think these have on the success of Spin Master Toys?
6. Why is the advisory board important to this venture?
7. What kind of advisory board would you like for your venture? Who would you invite to be on it?

Advantages of Marketing Research

If an entrepreneur creates a product or service without considering who the potential customers will be, there is a much greater risk of failure. Good marketing research can show how many customers there are, who they are, and what they actually want or need. With this information, the entrepreneur can create a product or service that people will buy.

Marketing research can be used to

- provide data about customers, products, services, prices, advertising, and consumer behaviour
- project future sales
- tell entrepreneurs what products or services are in demand, what the main features or characteristics should be, and how the product or service should differ from the competition's
- help entrepreneurs refine and adapt their products or services to appeal to more customers

In Chapter 6, you learned how marketing research helps identify the right opportunity. Virginia Marshall took the time to identify the right opportunity *and* the right customers. This research paid off when it was time to launch her venture.

> *Good marketing research can show how many customers there are, who they are, and what they actually want or need.*

Knowing Your Product or Service

Successful entrepreneurs know their products or services inside out. They need to have answers at their fingertips when their customers ask questions such as

- Why is your product or service better than what the competition offers?
- How easy is it for me to get the product or service? Exactly how much will it cost?
- How does your company handle problems with the product or service?

One way to get to know your product or service thoroughly is to survey your existing customers. This type of marketing research will help you identify the strengths and weaknesses of your business. The better you understand the needs of your customers, the better your business will be able to meet those needs.

> ### Worth Repeating
>
> "Even if you are on the right track, you will get run over if you just sit there."
>
> Will Rogers, American author and movie star

How does Will Rogers's comment apply to entrepreneurs and intrapreneurs?

KNOWING YOUR CUSTOMERS

Getting to know existing customers can also help an entrepreneur identify others who might be interested in the same products or services. Questions to ask include

- Who are my customers and how do they fit into various demographic categories?
- How did they find out about my business?
- Where else have they purchased, or could they purchase, products or services like mine?

When you find the answers to these questions, you may have a better idea of how you can reach more people like the ones your business already serves.

FORMS OF MARKETING RESEARCH

Marketing research can take a variety of forms. Virginia Marshall used a **survey** or questionnaire to find out about small businesses in her area. A survey can be conducted by telephone, in person, by mail, or on the Internet.

Observation is another form of marketing research. When Peter Oliver, current owner of a chain of restaurants in Toronto, Ontario, opened his first restaurant, he sat outside the selected location every day for a week, counting the number of pedestrians and cars that passed. From that number, he estimated the location would be successful, and it was.

Experimentation or **product sampling** is another option. Entrepreneurs sometimes make a small number of sample products and provide them, for the purpose of experimentation, to a small group of people. The results of this experiment can then be used to determine how well the product meets consumer needs.

Agents of Change

Although he may not have been familiar with the term "marketing research," Thomas Edison devoted a great deal of thought to people's needs and wants as he created his inventions. After he developed the incandescent electric light bulb, he realized that people who wanted to replace their gas lighting with electricity would need a source of electric current. The next step for Edison was to develop and install the world's first large central electric power station in New York City in 1882.

Thomas Edison was a visionary who saw a need that others couldn't see. He also took risks and made things happen. At a time when most people thought the idea of electric lighting replacing gas lighting was "madness," how did Edison know that his idea would sell? How was he an agent of change?

PURPOSES OF MARKETING RESEARCH

Three main classifications of marketing research are **exploratory research**, **specific research**, and **causal research**.

Table 8.1 Types and Characteristics of Marketing Research

Classification/Example	Purpose/Characteristics
Exploratory Research — If a company is planning to introduce a new breakfast cereal, marketing staff might meet with focus groups to find out what types of cereal people like, and why they like them. This would help the company develop a product people would want to buy.	• Clearly defines a problem and leads to possible solutions. • Is usually conducted through in-depth interviews with a relatively small number of people. • Often includes open-ended questions designed to generate ideas or identify opportunities for the entrepreneur.
Specific Research — If a company is planning to change the design on a cereal package, they might survey a large group of consumers to find out which of several proposed package designs the consumers like best.	• Yields specific information regarding a clearly defined problem. • Is typically used with a large group of consumers. • Often includes multiple-choice questions.
Causal Research — If cereal sales suddenly declined, the company could try to determine what factors caused people to change their buying patterns.	• Explains the relationship between a particular cause and its effect. • Is typically used in situations where a particular incident has caused a particular result, for example, where sales have increased or decreased because of changed prices.

Agents of Change

Dr. Frederick Banting identified the need to help people suffering from diabetes. With his assistant Charles Best, he conducted experiments to isolate a substance that would help diabetics live longer and more normal lives. Their discovery, insulin, has helped millions of people who would otherwise have died.

Besides marketing and medicine, what other purposes are there for research?

YOUR TURN

1. Would you classify Virginia Marshall's research as exploratory, specific, or causal? Explain your reasoning.

2. Select a product or service that you might like to sell. Answer the seven questions in "Knowing Your Market" on page 171 to assess the demand for your product or service.

3. Do some research about the venture you chose for Question 2. Identify three helpful sources of information. Tell what you learned from each one.

4. With a small group, choose an issue of particular importance in your school or community. Design exploratory, specific, and causal questions that might provide data to help resolve the issue.

5. Invite students from other groups to respond to the questions you wrote for Question 4. Analyze the questions and answers to determine the following:
   a) What new ideas did you get from answers to your open-ended exploratory questions?
   b) What suggestions for resolving the issue resulted from your specific research questions?
   c) Looking at responses to your causal questions, try to explain why the issue emerged in the first place.

6. What did you learn about marketing research from your work with Questions 4 and 5?

Conducting Marketing Research

Marketing researchers use the most suitable means available to achieve the results they need. There are three types of marketing research they use to get these results.

PRIMARY, SECONDARY, AND INTERNAL RESEARCH

Chapter 6 introduced two forms of research: primary research and secondary research. Primary research is the term used when researchers gather information directly through observation, experiments, interviews, and surveys. Secondary research refers to the use of data collected by someone else. Such data may, for example, be published in a trade magazine or be posted on the Internet.

Primary research is very reliable, but it also takes a lot of work. For instance, if you decide to conduct a survey, you will have to begin by writing appropriate questions. You will also need to decide who will respond to your questions, and how you will distribute the survey and collect the responses. When the results come back, you will need to analyze and summarize the data.

Secondary research is easier to use, but you can't always rely on what you read. It's very important to find out how the data was gathered, and by whom, so you can decide how valid and/or useful it is.

Internal research involves using a business's own records to gather information about sales, products, customers, or complaints. It works best for a venture that has been operating for a number of years. Internal research is easy and inexpensive to conduct.

Businesses may either conduct their own survey or hire a marketing research company to design, conduct, and analyze the custom-made survey for them.

Whether you use primary, secondary, or internal research, it is critical to structure the research so it will yield the results you need. (Refer to "Designing a Questionnaire for Primary Research" in Chapter 6.)

SELECTING A SAMPLE

A survey conducted using the total population of a country is called a **census**. Statistics Canada conducts a census every five years. Marketing research, however, is usually conducted with a much smaller group. People who have been carefully selected to represent a segment of the whole population are referred to as a **sample**. The composition of the sample depends upon the objectives of the marketing research project and the size of the population to be represented. Marketing research usually follows a systematic procedure in order to remain effective and objective. This procedure is described in Chapter 6.

Cool Stuff

You might think that it would take a pretty large sample to represent the population of a whole country accurately, but you'd be wrong. In fact, to represent the entire population of Canada with a 5% margin for error, you would need to sample only 384 people. The important thing is to choose people for the sample who accurately reflect the characteristics and opinions of those people who make up the whole population.

When you survey people in a sample group, are you using primary or secondary research? How do you know?

Chapter 8 ♦ Analyzing Your Market 177

Venture Profile

THE BAD BOY STORY

The cofounders of Bad Boy Furniture and Appliances Warehouse Ltd., Blayne Lastman and Marvin Kirsh, recognized the potential in the dormant name and image of the Bad Boy stores that had gone out of business in 1976. In 1991, Lastman and Kirsh launched the new Bad Boy in Ontario. They opened their first store in the midst of the worst recession in years. Their marketing strategy was to continue to improve upon the public perception of the original Bad Boy chain. Lastman and Kirsh noticed that furniture stores that cater to the average-income household usually offered little in the way of customer service. Special orders were not accepted and price negotiating was not even considered—in spite of the hard financial times. The pair saw an opportunity to respond to a void in the market. Since then, the competition has been compelled to respond to Bad Boy's leadership in these areas.

The goodwill associated with the name, coupled with aggressive, zany, and innovative marketing strategies, and the unshakeable drive of the owners combined to provide Bad Boy with a comfortable market share from the outset. The stores grew from a startup in Scarborough to Mississauga, North York, Whitby, and Barrie, with plans to open a new store every year for the next five years in all major Southern Ontario urban centres, and to actively pursue franchising opportunities in smaller communities.

The global marketplace is changing and, with it, the expectations of consumers. The "warehouse" stores taught retailers that customers would educate themselves about a product if they could purchase it at a lower cost by not having to pay for high overhead. As this philosophy caught hold, consumers began to expect lower prices everywhere—not just from the "warehouses." Retailers like Bad Boy, in order to stay on top, have to offer a high level of service at a low cost. This is the wave that follows the "warehouse phenomenon."

A lean and flat organizational structure, coupled with on-site ownership, permits the entrepreneurs to stay on top of customer requirements and respond quickly to the market.

Successful marketing strategy for Bad Boy includes unique and catchy advertising. The phrase "Nooobody!" is a readily identified slogan that has considerable "quotability." As a result, it continues to appear in news stories, editorials, and political cartoons in ways in which the phrase was never intended to be used. Each quote benefits Bad Boy through reinforcing its presence in the marketplace. The famous U.S. president Bill Clinton lookalike promotion used by Bad Boy caused a worldwide sensation. The World Wrestling Federation (WWF) cooperated in a promotion to hold in-store autograph sessions with high-profile wrestlers at Bad Boy stores. Bad Boy also invited hockey legends like Johnny Bower and Bobby Baun to promote the business. Bad Boy runs successful coordinated giveaway programs with McDonald's, Loblaws, and Pizza Pizza. Affiliation with homebuilders has provided opportunities to completely furnish new homes. Capitalizing on the Beanie Baby craze, Bad Boy gave away popular baby-sized key chains that shouted "Nooobody!" when they were squeezed. Over a short period of time, Bad Boy has inundated its market with high-powered, effective marketing.

Toronto is the most culturally diverse city in the world, with over 160 countries and 100 languages represented in its populace. In this environment, Bad Boy has striven to ensure that all customers will be comfortable in its stores. To make all its customers feel welcome, it has hired a mix of representatives who reflect the diversity of the community. Bad Boy feels that this kind of personal attention—so markedly absent in other "big-box" retailers—is especially appreciated by New Canadian customers.

Bad Boy recognizes that, in today's market, change is the only constant.

Exploring

1. According to Kirsh and Lastman, what void in the market was Bad Boy developed to fill?
2. What are the key points in Bad Boy's marketing strategy? How did it result in a high profile for Bad Boy?
3. How do Bad Boy stores meet the needs of their customers?
4. What has the success of the "warehouse" stores taught retailers?
5. Explain the features of Bad Boy's business approach that enable it to respond quickly to market changes.
6. Do you think that advertising that uses people who are unrelated to the product or service is effective? Why or why not?

Identifying a Marketing Strategy

A **marketing strategy** or plan is important to any kind of venture, even if the venture is not undertaken for profit. Whenever something of value is offered in return for something of value, a specially designed marketing strategy has probably been used to achieve success. Business organizations offer products or services, and accept financial rewards in return. Fundraisers offer special services and accept donations in return. Politicians offer promises and accept votes. Special government health campaigns, such as an antismoking campaign, offer a healthier population in return for leading a healthier way of life.

Table 8.2 Three Functions of a Marketing Strategy

Function	**Identify target customers and define the product or service they are prepared to buy.**
Details	• Classify or group the customers into relatively **homogeneous** segments according to common, identifiable characteristics. • Identify where potential customers are located and what they expect in terms of price, quality, or service. • Track potential customers who have expressed an interest in a product or service. Describe why they have indicated this interest.
Function	**Indicate the size of the potential market and outline possible trends.**
Details	• Identify any competition that may serve the potential market. • Document the strengths of the proposed product and determine how the product differs from the competition. • Outline ways to take the idea for a product or service from the production stage to the consumer, or **final user**, stage.
Function	**Identify sales expectations for a particular product or service, and the kind of promotion or advertising activity that would be necessary to achieve those sales.**
Details	• Determine the number of units to be sold based on the size of the potential market and the market share held by the competition. • Develop a promotional strategy that targets the "right" customer to ensure an appropriate level of sales.

YOUR TURN

1. Explain the difference between primary and secondary research. Give an example of each.
2. Why would a new venture be unlikely to use internal research?
3. Explain the difference between a census and a sample.
4. Identify the three major functions of a marketing strategy.
5. You are researching an e-commerce venture that sells DVDs on the Net. Select one of the functions of a marketing strategy and state how you can use this to be successful.

Figure 8.1 The four marketing elements in the marketing mix

The Marketing Mix

Every marketing plan needs a target market and a good mixture of marketing elements. The right combination of these elements enables the venture to differentiate its products or services from the competition.

THE FOUR PS OF MARKETING

The success of any marketing strategy depends on whether or not the entrepreneur has planned the right combination of **marketing elements**. These elements are referred to as the **marketing mix**, or often as the Four Ps of Marketing. The elements are product (or service), place, price, and **promotion**. To establish a successful marketing mix, an entrepreneur has to ask the right questions:

Product (or service)
- Is the product or service something customers will want to buy?
- Will it be of benefit to them?
- Will it meet their needs?

Place
- How will the product or service get to the customer?
- What channels of distribution are needed?
- When should the product or service be in stock or ready?
- Where will the product or service be made available?

Price
- How much are customers willing and able to pay?
- What is the best price to charge to earn a maximum profit?

Promotion
- How will customers be made aware that the product or service is available?
- Which of the following promotional activities will be best for this venture: advertising, personal selling, publicity, sales promotion, or e-marketing?

Worth Repeating

"Even if the product isn't that different, better, or special, it's the job of the marketer to make people think that it's different, better, and special."

Sergio Zyman, The End of Marketing As We Know It

How do consumers, knowingly or unknowingly, participate in this marketing process?

Confirming a Target Market

Whether your idea for a venture involves a product or a service, you should start by using all the available marketing research techniques at your disposal to confirm a **target market**—those individuals or organizations that are likely to want to use what you can provide.

In Chapter 6, you examined trends and identified opportunities that might arise as trends change. You discovered that one person's problems could become another person's opportunities. Confirming a market involves identifying those people who have a particular need or want for a product or service. When you write your venture plan, you will need to explain who will be the target market for your product or service, and why you chose this group.

Market Segmentation

The market is made up of people who fit into many different groups. When a product or service is targeted toward groups of people who share common characteristics, the group is called a **market segment**. Market segmentation helps entrepreneurs match their products and services to the needs of a specific group.

Many products or services appeal only to a small segment of a country's total population. The Canadian market, for example, consists of more than 30 million people. These people live in different parts of the country, work at different occupations, have different access to the Internet, and have different lifestyles, needs, wants, and consumer behaviours. They range in age from newborn to elderly. They may have a very small income, or a very large one. Few products or services can be designed to appeal to everyone in Canada.

Consumer behaviour is also affected by culture. Culture is a combination of beliefs, understandings, morals, values, customs, and habits. Canada is considered to be extremely multicultural: The population is made up of people with roots in many different ethnic and religious groups from around the globe. Bad Boy stores have achieved success in part because they have tailored their approach to this multicultural market.

Each consumer is a member of a number of different groups or market segments. It is useful to identify these segments because consumers who share common characteristics can be expected to follow similar patterns of behaviour and make similar purchases.

People may be grouped in a market segment because they

- belong to the same culture
- have similar tastes and preferences
- share the same values or goals
- have the same socioeconomic background
- respect their group's norms or rules of conduct

To confirm a target market, you must first identify a group of consumers with common characteristics, and then prepare a description of a typical consumer in this market. This description is often referred to as a customer profile.

Common Market Segments

Market segments can be defined by any number of common characteristics:

- demographic
  People of the same sex, age, marital status, or family size, or in the same stage of the family life cycle.
- **socioeconomic**
  People of similar occupation, education, income, social class, or culture.
- **geographic**
  People who live in regions of the country that could be defined by a specific climate, or by provincial or regional boundaries.
- **psychographic**
  People with similar lifestyles or personality attributes.
- behaviour patterns
  People who can be identified by when, where, and how often they shop, as well as by their media habits.
- consumption patterns
  People who can be identified by their knowledge about, and loyalty to, particular products or brands.

It is important to note that even though members of a target market may share particular characteristics, these characteristics may not be measurable and meaningful in relation to the product or service being offered. For example, people who share the same birth date would be difficult to identify and measure in the marketplace. Moreover, for most products and services provided, a particular birth date would probably not be a very meaningful characteristic.

A target market should be one that can be reached easily, and that is large enough to be worth the effort required to identify it.

Worth Repeating

"Niche marketers win over their competition because they

- know who their primary customers are
- know what those primary customers want
- give those customers what they promise."

Susan Carter, CanadaOne Magazine

Is this approach different from that of businesses targeting wider markets? Explain.

Life Cycles and Competition

Most products and services pass through various stages over time. These stages make up a **life cycle**. Although the rates of change, and the length and intensity of each stage may vary, most life cycles follow roughly the same pattern. In the introductory stages of a product's life cycle, the focus is on the product. Later, the focus changes to promotion and price.

Entrepreneurs need to know as much as they can about their competition and about the probable life cycle of their product or service. This knowledge will help them identify any competitive advantages that their venture might have.

Stage 1: Introduction

The introduction stage is when a product or service first appears in the marketplace. If the product or service is successful at this stage, it will show a profit and its sales will increase. There is little or no competition during this stage because the product is a new idea.

Stage 2: Growth

As it begins to establish a presence in the marketplace, the product or service is in a growth stage. Some competitors move in at this point, and entrepreneurs need to be aware of the competition. They can emphasize the uniqueness of the product, reduce prices, or increase the advertising and sales promotion to hold onto or increase their market share.

Stage 3: Maturity

The maturity stage occurs when a product or service has reached its peak of popularity and has established itself in the marketplace. Competition is at its peak at this stage. Promotion and advertising campaigns need to be in full gear.

Stage 4: Decline

When sales begin to drop off, a product or service is considered to be in its decline stage. Many competitors have already left the scene. It is at this point that the company must decide whether to abandon the product entirely or modify it to meet new demands in the market. Modification would move the product or service to a different stage in the life cycle.

E-Bits & Bytes

Experts predict that the Internet economy could reach $155 billion in revenue and create 180 000 jobs by 2003.

What would the creation of these new jobs mean for the Canadian economy? How does revenue result in new jobs?

YOUR TURN

1. What four elements make up the marketing mix?
2. Select a product or service that you like. Use what you know about this product or service to answer the questions on page 181.
3. What is a target market? Give an example.
4. Explain the difference between these measures for defining market segments:
   - demographic and socioeconomic
   - behaviour patterns and consumption patterns
5. Describe stages in the life cycle of a product and give an example of a product that is now in each stage.

The Six Ps of Entrepreneurship

Just as the Four Ps of Marketing point the way to a successful marketing campaign, the Six Ps of Entrepreneurship help entrepreneurs articulate their visions and begin a process that will help them make their visions a reality.

The starting point for any venture is the venture plan. A specific plan for implementing the Six Ps shows investors that the entrepreneur understands how to start the venture and how to ensure that the product or service will reach its target market.

In Chapter 7, you learned how to use the Research Assistance Grid to formulate a course of action for each of the Six Ps of Entrepreneurship. Answers to the questions on the grid help entrepreneurs develop a viable venture plan.

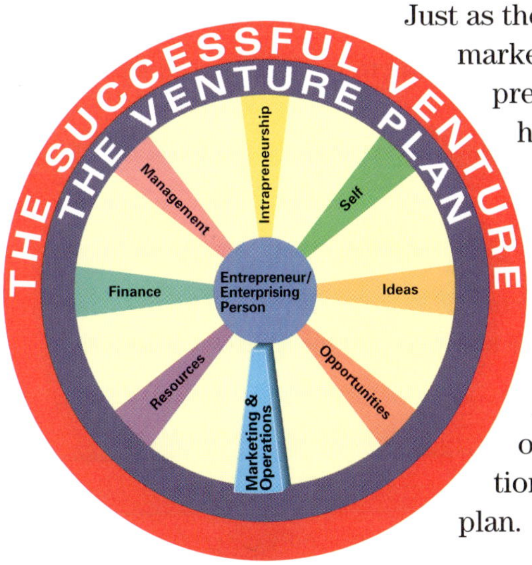

Figure 8.2 The Operations section of the Marketing and Operations spoke draws together the Six Ps of Entrepreneurship: profit, price, production, people, productivity, and promotion.

PROFIT

Profit, the first P of Entrepreneurship, is the major goal of the entrepreneur. It is the primary incentive for mobilizing resources, taking risks, and starting ventures. Without profit as a goal, few entrepreneurs, except perhaps those involved in not-for-profit social or community service ventures, would produce goods and services to satisfy consumer wants and needs. Even not-for-profit organizations must be concerned with creating an income that more than covers their operating expenses and provides funds for their ultimate goal. For instance, hospitals are not usually run for profit and most are funded provincially, but even those that receive government funding may use lotteries or other fundraising activities to increase their income.

Chapter 8 ◆ Analyzing Your Market **185**

> *The amount of profit is dependent on the price of the good or service, the quantity that is sold, and the costs of producing it.*

To earn profits, entrepreneurs must produce goods and services efficiently, without wasting economic resources such as land, labour, and capital. Efficient use of resources lowers production costs. If prices are lowered as a result, consumers benefit. Society also benefits by having a greater number of economic resources available to produce other goods and services.

For many entrepreneurs, profit is like a scorecard for measuring success. If the venture is meeting the needs and wants of the target market, the scorecard will reflect a high profit. If the score is low, there may have been a change in the market's perception of the product or service. It may be time to review the production and distribution processes, the pricing policy, or the promotional materials.

Profits indicate a demand for the product or service and encourage entrepreneurs to continue their efforts. The amount of profit is dependent on the price of the good or service, the quantity that is sold, and the costs of producing it.

The **profit formula** provides a way to project profits from known information:

$$\text{profit} = (\text{price of each unit} \times \text{quantity}) - \text{costs}$$

The quantity sold depends on the demand for the product or service, and the number of customers who are willing and able to pay the price for it. Decisions made by both the entrepreneur and his or her competitors, as well as the level of risk assumed, will influence the level of profits.

YOUR TURN

1. Outline the Six Ps of Entrepreneurship.
2. Use the profit formula. Which entrepreneur made the greatest profit?

Entrepreneur	Price	Quantity	Costs	Profit
Ali	$3	2000	$500	
Sarah	$2	4000	$1000	
Kannipani	$2	3000	$750	

3. Ms. Singh and Mr. Anderson are both in the landscaping business. They design, plant, and market gardens. Their philosophies on how to run a business differ. This is reflected in the following figures:

Item	Ms. Singh	Mr. Anderson
Labour Costs	$160 000	$80 000
Cost of Materials	$90 000	$50 000
Utilities	$10 000	$10 000
Advertising	$40 000	$20 000
Rent	$60 000	$40 000
Income	$400 000	$240 000

   a) What is the total cost for each venture?
   b) Which entrepreneur will make the greater profit?
   c) Comment on the different ways they operate their businesses.

PRICE

The price that a venture receives for its goods or services is used to pay for production and distribution costs. Sometimes selling a large quantity will be more profitable, but not always.

> total profit = total revenue − total cost
> total revenue = price of each unit × quantity sold

What will happen to the quantity sold if the price goes up? The answer to this question depends on consumer behaviour. If consumers perceive the increase in price as an indication of improved quality or popularity, the demand will probably remain steady or increase, resulting in a higher profit. If, however, the price increase makes the unit price higher than consumers are willing and able to pay, the quantity sold will drop, and so will the profit. The best price to charge is the one that allows you to earn the maximum profit, not sell the most. Knowing what the customer is willing and able to pay is essential in determining price.

PRICE AND QUANTITY SOLD AND THEIR EFFECT ON PROFIT

The amount of profit that can be earned in a venture depends on many factors. The price of the good or service, the quantity sold, and total revenues and costs are the most important factors that determine profit.

Table 8.3 Factors That Affect Profit

Price per Unit	Quantity Sold	Total Costs	Total Revenues	Total Profits
$100	100	$5 000	$10 000	$5 000
$80	120	$6 000	$9 600	$3 600
$60	150	$7 500	$9 000	$1 500
$40	200	$10 000	$8 000	$(2 000)

> **Think About It**
>
> Explain how, in Table 8.3, the item that sold in the greatest quantity generated the least profit—in fact, a loss.

To set a reasonable price for a product or service, an aware entrepreneur will ask the following questions:

1. What does the customer perceive the value of the good or service to be?
2. Are there any similar products on the market?
3. What price is the competition asking?

A few years ago, Tyco developed a toy called Tickle Me Elmo, based on a popular character from the television series *Sesame Street*. When the toy was first introduced, demand was so great that Tickle Me Elmo was constantly in short supply. The perceived value was higher than the actual value of the toy. There were no substitutes for the product, so the price increased significantly.

It is interesting to note that small ventures generally tend to be **price takers**—they set their prices by following the existing prices in the market. When competition exists, both prices and profits are lowered. Sometimes, the entrepreneur can regain some control over price by differentiating his or her product or service from the competition, and offering something unique.

Tyco's Tickle Me Elmo is a good example of how customer perception affects the price of a product.

Pricing Strategies

Costs, the target market, competition, and demand are all important factors in determining which pricing strategy to use. The pricing strategy you select has to give your product a competitive edge, while still yielding enough profit to maintain market share after the venture is launched.

Your pricing strategy will depend on the product or service, on consumer behaviour, and on your objectives for the business. It must be carefully thought out before you launch your venture. The pricing plan has to show potential investors that you have thoroughly considered such factors as the quality and costs of your product or service, your target market, the demand, and the competition.

Entrepreneurs can choose from several pricing strategies shown in Table 8.4.

YOUR TURN

1. Why is pricing important to the success of a venture?
2. What three questions must an entrepreneur ask before setting the price for a product or service?
3. Tickle Me Elmo is one example of a product that had a perceived value higher than its actual value. Give another example and explain your reasoning.
4. For a new small business venture, what are the advantages and disadvantages of using a price-taker strategy?
5. What are four important factors you would consider to determine a pricing strategy?
6. Work with a small group. Choose three products and two services. Determine what might happen if you use penetration pricing for these products and services. (See Table 8.4.) Compare your answers with those of other groups.

Table 8.4 Pricing Strategies

Cost-plus Pricing	A markup is added to the cost price to ensure a profit. markup = selling price − cost price $$\text{markup \%} = \frac{\text{selling price} - \text{cost price}}{\text{cost}} \times 100$$
Follow-the-competition Pricing	The price of the product or service is set equal to or slightly below a competitor's price. This pricing can increase market share, but it is important to be aware of your operating costs so you do not set a price that will result in a loss.
Penetration Pricing	A new product or service is priced significantly below a competitor's price. This pricing allows the newcomer to win market share from the competition and attract new customers. Selling large volumes at low prices can result in significant profits.
Skimming	When there is no competition, a new product or service can enter the market with a high price. This situation may result in short-term profits, but these profits will drop when competition moves in.
Psychological Pricing	Prices are chosen to give the impression that they are less than they actually are. An example might be pricing a product at $299.99 instead of $300.00.
Loss-leader Pricing	Selected products or services are sold at cost or less than cost to attract customers who will then make other purchases to compensate for the loss of profits.

PRODUCTION, PEOPLE, AND PRODUCTIVITY

Production is the mobilization of resources to yield a product or service that consumers want or need. The entrepreneur has to organize his or her resources—employees, materials, and equipment—to begin and sustain production.

An entrepreneur's resources are often limited, so they must be used as efficiently as possible to maximize productivity. Productivity is typically measured in terms of output per worker employed.

output per worker = total output ÷ number of workers

Entrepreneurs have to streamline their operations to produce the best quality goods, in sufficient quantity, using the resources available to them.

> **International NEWS**
>
> Canada enjoys many advantages that position it to compete effectively in electronic commerce. Canada has the highest postsecondary education enrolment in the world and is ranked first in knowledge workers by the World Economic Forum. Its telecommunications infrastructure is world-class, and its cost of using the Internet is among the lowest in the world.
>
> *The Canadian Electronic Commerce Strategy, published by the Government of Canada*
>
> How can Canadian entrepreneurs make the most of these advantages?

Every business has **fixed costs**, such as mortgage payments or rent and the cost of equipment, tools, or vehicles. Fixed costs are the same amount every month, regardless of how much the venture produces or sells. Businesses also incur **variable costs** for labour, raw materials, inventory, electricity, and gas. Variable costs differ every month, depending on the demand for, and output of, the product or service. The greater the demand, the higher the variable costs. More raw materials and labour will be required to meet increasing demands.

$$\text{total cost} = \text{fixed costs} + \text{variable costs}$$

When writing the operating strategy section of a venture plan, the entrepreneur should describe in some detail the production facility required and the personnel needed to operate the facility. Most ventures are designed with a specific number of employees in mind. This is the optimum number needed to generate maximum use of the facility. If the facility is already producing at full capacity and more personnel are hired, productivity (output per worker) may be lowered. Motivating employees to be as productive as possible will help the business maximize its profits without incurring additional costs.

PROMOTION

Before consumers in a target market can make the decision to buy, they must know that the product or service is available. Promotion is the vehicle most entrepreneurs use to tell consumers their message. It is a key element in the success of any new venture.

With the results of their marketing research, entrepreneurs can use promotion to bring their product or service to the attention of their target market. Promotional activities include advertising, personal selling, publicity, and sales promotion.

All the components of promotion depend on effective communication. Entrepreneurs communicate with customers in their target market to let them know about a new product or service, to persuade them to try a product or service, and to remind them that the venture is around and thriving.

ADVERTISING

How do you tell customers and prospective customers about your product or service? Advertising is a message paid for by the venture and directed toward the target market. The purpose of advertising is to move customers through the **AIDA formula**—Attention, Interest, Desire, Action. Advertising should attract the attention of

One of the most influential ways of promoting a product or a service is through advertising.

the customer, create an interest in the product or service, stimulate a desire to have the product or service, and encourage the customer to seek out and buy the product or service.

Answers to the following questions will help shape an effective advertising campaign:

1. How do customers currently find out about my product or service?
2. What strategies, such as personal referrals, advertisements, or flyers, would help me reach more potential customers?
3. How willing are people to try my product or service? What would encourage more people to try it?
4. What is the competition doing? How can I do it better?
5. According to others, how does my product or service compare with the competition?

Advertising can be delivered through a variety of media—newspapers, magazines, radio, TV, the Internet, direct mail, signs in or on transit vehicles, directories, or outdoor billboards. The medium you select will depend on the following factors:

- the audience you want to reach
- the number of people who will see the advertising
- the trading area to be covered (a neighbourhood, a city, a province, a country, many countries)
- the budget
- the suitability of the medium to the product or service, and to the target market

If the product is in-line skates, for example, suitable media might include television, magazines, the Internet, and transit advertising. This is because the target market for in-line skates is largely made up of young people aged 10 to 25. People in this age group watch television, read magazines, use computers, and travel on public transit. No matter which medium is chosen, advertisers will need to select television shows, publications, or Web sites that address the right audience. For example, an advertisement in a magazine like *Teen People* would reach more potential skate buyers than one in *Chatelaine*.

Chapter 8 ◆ Analyzing Your Market   191

E-Bits & Bytes

"The Net is tearing down the barriers that kept small businesses from challenging their largest competitors. New businesses can spring up instantly and compete nationally or internationally almost as quickly as they can design their Web pages.... Today's companies are fast!"

Marty Lippert, chief information officer, Royal Bank

Besides a speedy startup, how can new businesses use the Internet to stay competitive?

Coupons encourage customers to try new products or switch brands.

The cost of advertising in the medium will be a budget consideration. National advertising on prime-time television is very expensive because it reaches a large viewing audience. An advertisement aired on a local affiliate may be less expensive. Radio advertising spots cost less than television ads, and advertisements in specialized language or regional newspapers cost even less than those on radio and may target specific markets more effectively. If a newspaper is the most suitable medium, the type of newspaper, page location, size of the advertisement, and length of time the advertisement will run will all affect the cost. Most advertising media print rate cards that show the cost of advertising.

Internet advertising is an attractive option for many advertisers. The Internet is readily accessible to people from many demographic groups, and Web site development is offered at very reasonable rates by a number of organizations. Through the use of e-commerce, interested customers may be able to move directly from an Internet advertisement to a site where they can make their purchase immediately using a credit or debit card.

PERSONAL SELLING

Selling is what keeps a venture alive and well. A good salesperson makes the customer feel like the most important person around. The salesperson's job is to show the customer how the features of a product or service meet his or her needs. This requires a thorough knowledge of the product so the salesperson can answer any questions customers might have. A salesperson who demonstrates a sound knowledge of product features and benefits will add to the reputation of the venture.

PUBLICITY

Publicity is an unpaid message delivered by the media to the target market when the media decide that a product is newsworthy. A reporter gives a factual account of the product or service without trying to persuade customers to buy. One example is the worldwide publicity Bad Boy got when they used the Bill Clinton look-alike in their advertisement.

SALES PROMOTION

Sales promotion is any activity undertaken to increase sales and support advertising. Free samples are sometimes distributed to encourage customers to try a new product. Coupons offer everything from reduced prices on merchandise to free giveaways, and encourage consumers to try new products or switch brands. Coordinated programs with other businesses or with charities may give promotions a larger impact and a chance to share costs.

Sales promotion on the Internet is easy, adaptable, inexpensive, and fast. Users can print coupons, sometimes with large values, directly from Web sites.

Customer Expectations

In today's fast-paced economy, entrepreneurs and enterprising people need to think beyond the functional aspects of marketing. Customers have high expectations for the quality of the products and services that they buy. They also expect a fair price and easy access. To distinguish themselves from their competitors, entrepreneurs and enterprising people should consider the relationship they have with customers. Customers want to be rewarded for their business. The American Express slogan "Membership has its rewards" demonstrates that this company understands its customers' needs. American Express cards do not have any preset charge limits and customers who use them are rewarded with points that can be accumulated to purchase products or services. These features help differentiate American Express cards from those of competing companies. Marketing research identifies what customers are looking for—function or relationship, or a combination of the two.

Technology plays an important role in diversifying the marketing strategy. Today, businesses can use the Internet to market their products, build relationships, and differentiate themselves from competitors, extending their opportunities far beyond what was traditionally possible. Technology enables entrepreneurs and enterprising people to customize how they offer products or services on a **mass production** scale.

YOUR TURN

1. What is the relationship between production and productivity?

2. What is promotion? Why is it a key element in the success of a venture?

3. What is advertising? What are some of the effects of using and not using advertising on a new venture?

4. What does the acronym AIDA stand for? What is its purpose?

5. Explore the Internet to see what types of advertising strategies you can find. Record your observations. What can Internet advertising offer that more traditional forms of advertising cannot?

Activities

Flashbacks

Make up a quiz based on the following statements. Exchange with a partner. Answer the questions; then, discuss the answers.

- Marketing research involves collecting, recording, and analyzing data in order to make decisions about marketing-related issues.
- An effective marketing mix provides the right combination of the Four Ps: product, place, price, and promotion.
- Target markets are defined in order to identify customer needs and wants, and to focus selling efforts on people who are likely to buy.
- Markets can be segmented according to the following characteristics: demographic, socioeconomic, geographic, psychographic, behaviour patterns, and/or consumption patterns.
- Products go through four stages of development: introduction, growth, maturity, and decline.
- The Operations spoke of the Venture Creation Wheel depends on the Six Ps of Entrepreneurship: profit, price, production, people, productivity, and promotion.
- Efficient use of resources increases profits for the entrepreneur and benefits society.
- Pricing a product or service is dependent upon fixed and variable costs, demand, and profit objectives.
- Reaching the target market involves choosing the right mix of advertising, personal selling, publicity, and sales promotion.

Lessons Learned

1. What is marketing research?
2. Name the three main classifications of marketing research. Describe the purpose and characteristics of each one.
3. What are the three main forms of marketing research?
4. List and briefly explain the four elements of the marketing mix.
5. Define a "target market."
6. Why is it important for entrepreneurs to plan for each of the Six Ps of Entrepreneurship?
7. How do price, demand, productivity, and efficiency influence profits?
8. Explain the difference between fixed and variable costs.
9. What should a business owner consider when selecting the best medium to use to advertise a product or service?

10. Give examples of four types of sales promotion activities designed to increase sales.

VENTURING OUT

Later in this book, you will have an opportunity to plan a personal venture. Use marketing research to help you decide what that venture will be, and to develop the market analysis section of your venture plan.

1. List some ideas for ventures that you might like to develop. Consider demographic trends in your community, needs or wants a venture could satisfy, and problems a venture could solve. Include not-for-profit ideas as well as potential moneymakers.

2. Evaluate each idea from Question 1 to determine
    a) what skills and interests you could bring to the venture
    b) how practical it would be for you to start the venture

3. Choose the best venture idea to develop in detail. Conduct research to find out whether others have tried the same type of venture, and whether they succeeded. Identify a list of contacts who might help you with your venture, and some sources of useful information, such as business services or government agencies.

4. Use the following steps to help you write the market analysis section of your business plan.
    a) Create a survey you can use to find out who your potential customers will be, and what types of products or services you think they will buy. Conduct your survey and analyze the results. Write a profile of a typical customer for your venture.
    b) Find out who your competitors are, where they are, and how successful they are. Explain how you plan to make your product or service different from or better than theirs.
    c) Estimate the cost of producing your product or service. Then conduct a survey to determine the price your customers would be willing to pay. Does your venture have the potential to make a profit?

E-Bits & Bytes

After you decide what your venture is going to be, check out www.business.nelson.com for the links to useful information sources.

POINT OF VIEW

Visit www.business.nelson.com and follow the links to "advertising" to conduct secondary research about some different ways in which a product or service might be advertised. How would you promote your product or service? Gather rate cards from the media you intend to use in order to estimate the cost of promotion. Include your promotion plans in your market analysis.

CHAPTER 9

Rolling Up Your Sleeves: Resource Allocation and Management

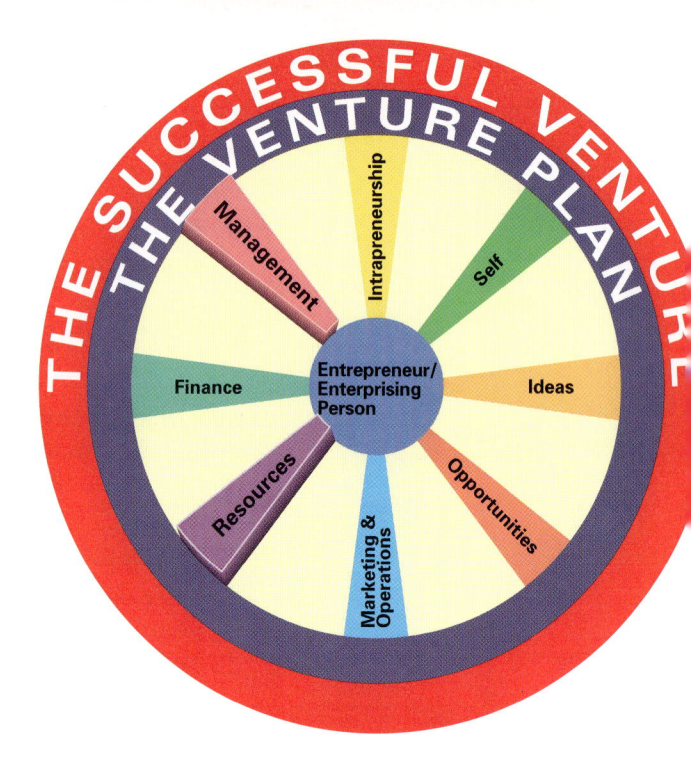

LEARNING OPPORTUNITIES

By the end of this chapter, you should be able to
- identify the resources that could be required to create a new venture
- determine the human resources and related supports a venture would require
- describe management styles, leadership qualities, and methods of employee recognition that contribute to the development of enterprising employees
- compare the various types of ventures and the various forms of business ownership
- develop the resource analysis and operating strategy sections of a venture plan

Entrepreneurial Language

- expense good
- capital good
- depreciate
- grant
- internal human resources
- external human resources
- external recruitment
- internal recruitment
- remuneration
- mobilize
- long-range objective
- computerized inventory control system
- quality control
- cash flow
- laissez-faire leader
- sole proprietorship
- partnership
- corporation
- general partnership
- joint venture
- limited partnership
- silent partner
- corporate charter
- share
- franchise
- vendor's permit

Write a paragraph that uses as many of these words as possible in meaningful sentences. If some words are new to you, look up their meanings in the Glossary or read to find out how they're used in the chapter.

Venture Profile

BRUCE POON TIP: THE GREAT ADVENTURE PERSON

Bruce Poon Tip is not an ordinary entrepreneur. Bruce's venture, G.A.P (or Great Adventure People), is one of the fastest-growing companies in Canada. The company is unique in many ways, including how Bruce got his start and how he runs his company. Bruce started G.A.P when he was 21 years old, with a great idea and no startup capital. Bruce was not new to entrepreneurship; he had run a successful venture as an elementary school student in Calgary. (He had a team of students making knitted weather worms in his parents' Alberta home as part of a Junior Achievement activity.) After completing a business degree at university, Bruce sought a way of combining a venture with something that he loved to do, and travel was his answer. Because there were already thousands of tour companies operating throughout the world, Bruce wanted to offer something unique. Bruce's plan was to rethink conventional travel, and to take people to exotic destinations in non-traditional ways where they would stay in bed-and-breakfasts or guest homes, and travel in small groups, enjoying local customs and cuisine. He would show countries to visitors from the perspective of the people who live there, not just from a tour bus or the lobby of a multinational hotel. With a vision but no money, Bruce did something that he does not advise: He financed his startup on his credit card. Today, however, G.A.P sends travellers on over 600 adventures to over 100 countries, from a camel brigade across India to a trek in the Andes, or traversing the plains of Africa.

The focus of G.A.P is on sustainable tourism, where conservation of local communities comes first. G.A.P partners with Conservation International in its efforts to protect fragile ecosystems. The company uses community-based, low-impact tourism to encourage local communities to support ecotourism, which depends upon a healthy environment. Bruce believes that by linking small communities in ecosystem hotspots with income-generating tourism projects, a greater chance for the long-term preservation of the ecosystem will result. Thousands of tourists agree.

G.A.P has won awards from the U.N., the World Bank, Ethics in Action, and many other organizations. Bruce has also won an award for operating one of the 50 best-managed companies in Canada. His basic philosophy of "sticking to the original values and goals, and redefining ourselves" has resulted in minimal staff turnover. When asked "How do you keep

CONTINUED→

people happy?" Bruce answered, "Fringe benefits, four weeks' holidays, one free trip a year, recognition for effort, an exciting high-growth company, and opportunities for everyone." Qualities of good employees, according to Bruce, are energy and a passion for both people and culture.

Bruce's advice to young entrepreneurs is "Now is the time! Nothing to lose! When you have no other commitments, take a chance."

Exploring

1. What is unique about G.A.P?
2. Why do you think G.A.P has won awards and international recognition?
3. What kind of leader do you think Bruce Poon Tip is? Give evidence from the profile to support your ideas.
4. Why might an enterprising person like working for G.A.P?
5. In Chapter 8, you did marketing research for a venture you might be interested in starting. How could you make this venture more environmentally friendly?
6. Most ventures need material resources such as raw materials, equipment, and office supplies. What questions could you ask your suppliers to find out how concerned they are for the environment?

Starting Up

Resources are the people, materials, technology, and money you need to start a venture. What resources would you need to start the venture you've been planning?

Resources for a Successful Venture

Most ventures require many types of resources to get off the ground and to grow. Some resources, such as furniture, equipment, raw materials, parts, technology, and inventory, can easily be purchased. Others, such as advice, expertise, and financing, may be harder to locate. In either case, financial resources will be needed to pay for what's required.

The costs of the resources needed for a venture can be either fixed or variable. Fixed costs for resources are the same every month, and might include salaries for paid staff, rent, or equipment lease payments. Conversely, costs for items such as heat, electricity, and raw materials are variable costs that change from month to month.

Resources generally fall into one of the following categories: material resources, technological resources (including information technology), financial resources, or human resources.

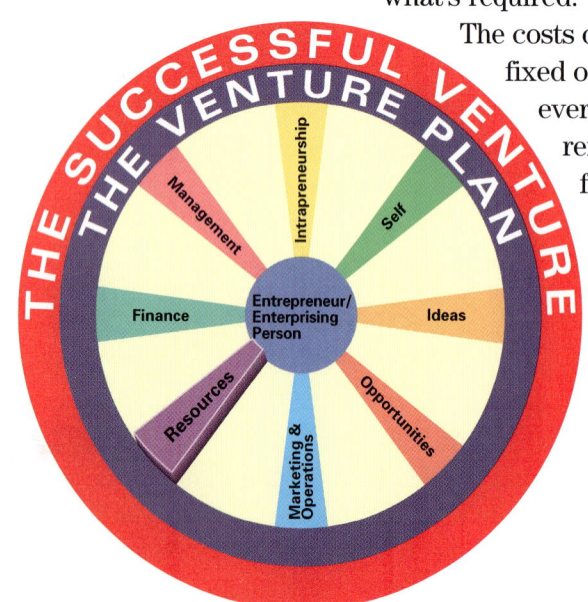

198   Unit 3 ◆ Moving into Action

MATERIAL RESOURCES

Material resources are the materials a business needs to operate, and will vary depending on the nature of the venture. If the venture involves manufacturing, raw materials and parts will have to be purchased from suppliers. For a Web-based business, the only needs may be for office supplies and equipment.

Material resources can be either consumable or fixed. Consumable resources or **expense goods**, such as paper, oil, gas, or telephone service, are used up in the process of doing business. Fixed resources or **capital goods** last a long time, although their value gradually **depreciates**, or decreases. Examples of capital goods include buildings, trucks, machinery, and office equipment.

TECHNOLOGICAL RESOURCES

In the new economy, information technology is considered to be a resource on its own. With widespread access to the Internet, ventures are constantly updating the ways they operate. Laptop computers and digital cellular phones have revolutionized the way we communicate. Today, decisions and discussions can take place anywhere, anytime, with anyone. With virtually instant access to events and economic changes taking place around the world, people are finding themselves part of a huge, global community.

Most businesses require technological resources of one type or another, and these resources are becoming less expensive all the time. Some technological resources, like computers and telephone systems, are purchased to improve communication and provide access to needed information. Others, like Computer Assisted Design (CAD) programs, make it possible to revolutionize the way engineers design products and processes. In one way or another, technological resources are key to nearly every venture.

FINANCIAL RESOURCES

Financial resources are the funds required for the startup and operation of the business. Sources of money might include financial institutions such as banks or credit unions, government agencies that provide loans or **grants**, or people who invest in the venture. In order to get financing to start a new venture, or to make changes to an existing venture, the entrepreneur will need to show carefully-researched projections about the potential revenues and costs. You'll find details about how to finance your venture in Chapter 10.

E-Bits & Bytes

Did you know that the acronym URL stands for Universal Resource Locator? Thanks to Internet technology and URLs (Internet addresses), entrepreneurs can locate resources from around the world at the touch of a keyboard.

What types of resources can entrepreneurs locate on the Internet?

HUMAN RESOURCES

Human resources are the people who make the venture work. **Internal human resources** are people who are part of the venture, such as the entrepreneur, the partners, and the employees. **External human resources** are people outside of the venture, such as accountants, business or technology consultants, lawyers, marketing advisers, bankers, insurance agents, suppliers, and mentors. To succeed, entrepreneurs need to know how to find people with the right skills.

Asking the right questions is part of the process of finding the right people. These questions might include

1. What needs to be done?
2. What can I do myself?
3. What can be done by people who are already on my team?
4. If I need someone else to do the job, what level of expertise and experience does the person need to have?
5. Will one person be enough to do the job? If not, how many people will I need?
6. Do I need people to work full-time or can they work on contract or be paid on a part-time or piecework basis?
7. Why will these people want to work for me?

Once you've decided what jobs need to be done and how much you can afford to pay, you can write job descriptions. A job description explains what the person will do and what responsibilities she or he will have. It also lists the qualifications needed to do the job. After you've written the job description, the next step is to let people know the job is available. You can do this by

- placing a classified ad
- enlisting the help of an employment agency or a professional recruiter
- telling people you know about the job, and asking them to pass on the information to others
- advertising the job through Human Resources Development Canada
- posting the job on career-related Web sites
- posting the job at a college or university placement centre

College or university career centres are a good place to post jobs, especially if you want to hire new graduates.

Whenever you hire others to work for you, there are many things to consider. How will you train them? How much should you pay them? What deductions are you required by law to make from their paycheques? What tax and employment regulations will apply to you and your employees? Will you offer your employees benefits such as a health or dental plan?

When you are considering questions like these, it may help to ask for advice from outside experts, such as lawyers, business consultants, or experienced mentors, who can guide you through the maze of rules and regulations that apply to your venture.

YOUR TURN

1. Read some job descriptions in the career ads section of a newspaper. Then create a description for a job that might exist with Great Adventure People (G.A.P). Be sure to describe the tasks that would need to be done, as well as the qualifications the person would need to do the job.

2. Visit www.business.nelson.com and follow the links to the Web site of G.A.P. Using information from the Venture Profile and from the company's Web site, list some of the resources that Bruce Poon Tip might have needed to launch G.A.P. Classify each one as a material resource, a technological resource, a financial resource, or a human resource. Identify the resource in each category that was likely the most expensive to acquire.

3. Review each of the following Venture Profiles. List the capital goods, expense goods, and human resources that were likely required to launch each venture.
   a) "Three Blondes Cook Up Sweet Success" from Chapter 1
   b) "Technological Innovator" from Chapter 2
   c) "Turning a Problem into an Opportunity" from Chapter 3

4. Consider the venture that you would like to launch.
   a) Describe the skills you would bring to the venture.
   b) List the jobs that would need to be done in the early stages.
   c) Classify each job according to whether you could do it yourself or whether you would need to hire someone else to do it.
   d) Describe the human resources you would need to launch your venture. Include a list of skills that each person would need to do his or her job.

Finding and Keeping Good Employees

It's easy to find people to work for you. It's not so easy to find the right people. When you have the right people working for you, the venture and the workers both benefit. The customers get the best possible service and the workers find their jobs challenging and rewarding.

To find the right people, you need to plan your recruiting and selection process in detail. You need to make sure your job advertisements will be noticed by people with the right qualifications and interests, and you need to interview and screen the respondents carefully. You may decide to look for the right people outside the venture (**external recruitment**) or to offer the job to somebody who already works for you in a different capacity (**internal recruitment**).

There are advantages and disadvantages with both approaches. When you recruit externally, you invite people with new and exciting ideas, experiences, and knowledge into your business. However, you are also taking a chance by hiring someone you don't know, and current employees may be hurt that they were passed over. When you recruit internally, you have the advantage of already knowing the skills, abilities, and work habits of your employees. New opportunities inside the organization will help motivate staff and encourage intrapreneurial attitudes. However, internal recruiting means that you are limiting your choices to existing staff, and this may mean that you are not hiring the best possible person for the job.

Choosing the Best Person for the Job

Prospective employees will submit résumés that describe their qualifications and experience. Review the résumés to narrow down the list of candidates to those who have the right qualifications. Skill testing may also be necessary.

Most candidates will include references—usually names of previous employers. Always check references, since these people can provide information that may help you make the right decision.

After you've checked the applicants' skills, consider their personal characteristics. In a comfortable atmosphere, conduct interviews to get a sense of what each person would bring to the job. Mix questions that test knowledge and skills with questions that will help you get to know the candidate and his or her personal goals. When you finally decide to offer someone the job, make sure that you clearly state the salary, the start date, and any benefits that will be provided.

Whenever a new employee joins the venture, take time to guide him or her through an **orientation period** during which she or he will get to know the job, the work environment, and the equipment. Introduce coworkers and talk about your mission. Training a new employee may be time-consuming and costly, but an effective training program is more than worthwhile, since it will help prevent errors that could seriously affect your business.

Worth Repeating

"The new entrepreneur is about partnership, surrounding yourself with people who complement your skills, seeking advice, asking questions, and approaching business methodically."

Ellie Rubin, Bulldog Group Inc.

Building Employee Loyalty

An employee who excels will likely receive job offers from other employers. If an employee is not happy working for you, then she or he will move on. Here are a few simple rules that help enterprising employers attract and retain enterprising employees.

Keeping Good Employees

- Treat employees with respect.
- Value their ideas.
- Ask for their opinions.
- Be honest about future opportunities.
- Ask for input and give feedback.
- Clearly communicate policies and expectations.
- Be flexible.
- Encourage employees to constantly upgrade skills.
- Provide opportunities for ongoing staff development.
- Offer pay incentives for improved performance.

The key to keeping good employees is loyalty. Allow your employees to make decisions for themselves in the areas they know most about, and they will begin to feel that they, too, have a personal stake in the success of the venture.

To attract and retain enterprising employees, employers need to be flexible about the types of **remuneration** they offer. Pay incentives such as the following may be attractive to employees, and may encourage them to increase their productivity.

Kinds of Pay Incentives

Entrepreneurs who keep their employees involved in the progress of the company, committed to its goals and objectives, and satisfied with the reward system in place will avoid employee–management problems that can take up time and energy, and ultimately affect the progress of the business.

Here are the different kinds of pay incentives adapted from the Bank of Montreal's publication for small businesses, *Becoming a People Manager*:

1. Gain sharing: Workers share a percentage of the revenues that result from increased productivity.
2. Profit sharing: If the venture makes a profit, part of this amount is shared by the employees.
3. Group incentives: Targets are set and team awards are given when targets are met.
4. Individual incentives: Individual workers are given awards when they meet productivity targets.

> **Worth Repeating**
>
> "If you're not doing the best for your employees, you're not doing the best for your customers."
>
> Maxine Turner, Cuisine Unlimited

5. Pay for knowledge: Employees are paid more as they acquire new skills.
6. Key contributor program: One-time awards are given to workers who have been critical to the success of a particular project.
7. Long-term programs: Incentives are given for long-term performance over more than one year.

The External Venture Team

The external venture team is made up of the advisers, consultants, and support groups who can offer advice and services to help the entrepreneur. Entrepreneurs should recognize the potential benefits of seeking expert advice and deliberately search it out whenever there is a gap in their own knowledge or experience. Successful entrepreneurs not only know how to acquire the right resources, they also know how to **mobilize** them, or use them, in the most effective way.

The Lawyer

A lawyer can offer advice on

- choosing the best form of ownership for your venture
- registering a name
- finding out about and applying any federal, provincial, and/or municipal laws and bylaws that relate to your venture

The Banker

The right banker can be an important asset to an entrepreneur who is just starting out. Bankers not only lend money, they also provide financial advice. Competition in the Canadian banking industry is keen, so it's a good idea to shop around for the financial help you need. See Chapter 10 for more information about how to finance a venture.

> **Worth Repeating**
>
> "Entrepreneurs have to look outward and network with the right people. The key is to be identified as bright, smart, and expert-oriented."
>
> Diane Hollett, Media Touch Technologies

Cool Stuff

In the race to hang on to talented employees, companies are trying very hard to create incentive programs that work. Bonuses and employee-of-the-month awards just don't have the impact they used to. The Ontario-based communications giant, Nortel Networks Corp. came up with a plan that lets employees choose their own rewards. A thank-you for work well done at Nortel is given in the form of points. The points can be redeemed for merchandise, cash, and even trips. Why waste money giving an employee a clock or a plaque for her office when what she really wants is a snow blower? One employee recently added a deck onto his house; he converted his reward points into lumber and supplies. Nortel's tailor-made rewards are immediate, concrete, and memorable. The program is one aspect of the company that sets it apart from the competition.

> Would an incentives program like Nortel's work equally well for a small venture with about 10 employees? Give reasons for your answer.

THE ACCOUNTANT

An accountant should be hired early in the planning stages of a venture, when the entrepreneur must prepare financial statements needed to acquire financing. He or she may even aid the entrepreneur in writing the financial section of the venture plan. Later, an accountant can help keep financial track of the venture as it grows, and assist with tax planning.

THE REAL-ESTATE AGENT

If your venture operates from a bricks-and-mortar physical location, the real-estate agent is a key external team member. In many cases, especially if the venture deals with the public, the right location can make or break the new venture. The real-estate agent's job is to be familiar with potential business locations in your community, and to help you find the right one. For this reason, it's essential that the agent know as much as possible about your venture and how it will operate. How much space will you need? What special features, such as shipping doors, access to public transit, or lots of customer parking, will your venture require? Once you find the right location, the agent will also assist you in negotiating a lease with your new landlord.

The site you select will depend on the nature and size of your business. A community service, for example, should be located close to the people it serves. A business that interacts with customers primarily by telephone or e-mail can be set up in an extra room in your home.

If you plan to store an inventory of special material or equipment, you will need storage space. If you are launching a retail business, you will need a location that is easy for your customers to find. As you decide on a location for your business, think about the following questions, and discuss your ideas with a real-estate agent.

- Who are my customers?
- Is it important for my customers to get to my business? If so, where should I locate?
- What, if any, parking facilities will I need?
- What kinds of businesses do I want to be near?
- What kinds of businesses do I want to stay away from?
- What kind of interior and exterior space should I be looking for?
- What kind of window space will I need?
- What infrastructure, such as light, heat, electricity, and communications technology, will I need?
- What rent can I afford?

Worth Repeating

"The three most important things in real estate are location, location, and location!"

Anonymous

Identify a business in your community that has a great location. Why is this location so good for this business?

Location is everything for a retail business.

Worth Repeating

"We can no longer accept the notion that suppliers provide only goods. We also want knowledge from them so that we can work together to meet the increasingly tough demands we face in the market.... By pooling knowledge we can all improve our products and our processes."

Lyse Thibault, I. Thibault Inc.

If your business is to be exclusively Web-based, you may not need to worry about customer access. E-commerce has made it possible for people to buy every conceivable kind of product or service without ever leaving their homes or offices, and has given businesses access to customers all over the globe. We now have borderless markets.

Even though e-businesses sell their wares via computer, they may still need storage space, shipping facilities, and an office where the administrative staff can work. Questions about location, interior and exterior space, infrastructure, and rent are often just as important for e-businesses as for other types of ventures.

▌ THE INSURANCE AGENT OR BROKER

Every careful entrepreneur plans for the unexpected. This includes arranging for suitable types of insurance coverage, such as protection in case of fire, flood, theft, or personal injury. Business interruption insurance can often save a venture from failure if its premises, records, or equipment are destroyed, because the insurance will pay employees' wages and other costs until the business can be restarted. Insurance can be obtained from an agent, who works for one insurance company, or from an insurance broker, who deals with several insurance companies to obtain the best coverage for the best price.

▌ THE MANAGEMENT CONSULTANT

Management consultants are in business to help entrepreneurs manage all phases of their ventures, and particularly startup and growth. They offer a wide variety of services, from conducting market surveys to preparing financial statements and assisting with the acquisition of startup capital. Management consultants use their network of specialists—lawyers, accountants, real-estate agents, bankers, and insurance agents—to ensure that the venture is securely placed on the road to success.

YOUR TURN

1. Prepare a class list of questions that would help you find out how each of the following people can assist an entrepreneur in creating a new venture. Then interview one person using the questions you prepared.
   a) a banker
   b) a lawyer
   c) an accountant
   d) a real-estate agent

2. Invite a representative from each of the following fields to speak to your class about his or her role in helping new entrepreneurs.
   a) a credit union manager
   b) a chamber of commerce representative
   c) an insurance agent
   d) a management consultant

3. Explore the real-estate listings in a local newspaper and watch for "For Sale" or "For Lease" signs in key locations as you investigate four possible sites for a retail gourmet coffee shop in your community.
   a) Use the Location Evaluation Chart below to record the facts about each location.
   b) Based on your research, which site would you choose? Why?

4. Look in the provincial government pages of a telephone book to find government departments and agencies that serve small businesses. With a small group, select one department or agency and describe the type of support it offers. Invite a representative to speak to the class about how they may be able to help you get started in business.

5. Contact an entrepreneur in your community. Ask the following questions:
   a) What outside advice did you get when you were planning and launching your venture?
   b) Who advised you?
   c) What outside advice do you still need now that the venture is established?

	Site A	Site B	Site C	Site D
Location (Corner/Strip Plaza/Mall/Town Centre)				
Surface Area (square units)				
Storage Available				
Parking				
Rent				
Nearby Competitors				
Customer Traffic				
Type of Heating/Air Conditioning System				
Plumbing/Electrical Systems				
Other				

Venture Profile

WEB SIGHTS INTERNATIONAL: ADAM'S STORY

What was a clever university student with a vision and no business degree going to do to put his dream into action? Adam Rumanek sees himself as an ordinary guy who has had an entrepreneurial spirit since his teen years. His first venture as an entrepreneur—selling souvenir T-shirts in downtown Toronto, with a staff of four working for him—combined his natural sales ability with his high energy. In 1995, when the World Wide Web was in its infancy, Adam and a friend noticed that the few Web sites online were mostly universities, governments, and other large organizations, and that the sites tended to give the user information in a very confusing and convoluted way. Adam asked himself, "If I can give the user that information in a clear and concise way and make it look good at the same time, can I make a living?"

The answer, naturally, was yes, and Web Sights International was incorporated in 1996. Most of Adam's problems at the start of the venture concerned the philosophy behind the Internet and how his company could adapt and grow with it. Practical problems were easier to deal with: Technical staff handled computer programs, language, and applications; accountants gave financial advice; and a lawyer was needed to draw up the contracts and advise on business issues, because Adam was busy working on Web sites almost from the start of his venture.

Adam recalls that it was an exciting time, because the idea of the Internet was still new and people key to Web Sights' success were eager to participate. Adam has since sold Web Sights International for a considerable sum, and is working on contract for the company that purchased it. Who knows what his next venture will be?

Adams's advice to young entrepreneurs is, "Stick to your original idea and do not change just to meet goals imposed on you by your bank or business plan. Also, know your limits and never try to be everything to everybody. Don't be afraid to say no!"

On leadership, Adam says, "Always listen to what people have to say. This is the hardest thing to learn, but I think once a leader gets this, he or she will be able to lead and build leaders within the organization."

Exploring

1. What gave Adam his venture idea?
2. What external human resources did Adam rely on?
3. What strengths and weaknesses might potential investors have seen in his proposal?
4. What do you think of the advice Adam gives to young entrepreneurs? Would it work for you or not? Discuss.
5. Adam says that good leaders always listen to what people have to say. What else do good leaders do? Brainstorm a list of ideas with a partner.

The Functions of Management

Creative energy, charisma, and strong motivation may help someone launch a venture, but a different set of skills is needed for the day-to-day management of the venture once it becomes established. Managers are required to plan, organize, lead, and control all available resources, and facilitate the achievement of the organization's goals.

PLANNING

Planning for an established venture should be seen as the bridge between where the venture is and where it wants to be. Managers need to look at the **long-range objectives** of the venture and plan how to get there. Planning starts with the articulation of the venture's objectives, policies, programs, budgets, and procedures. It incorporates all aspects of the operation—from the purchasing of supplies to the production process, sales and service, and finance. Planning is important when a venture starts up, but is equally important as the venture begins to grow.

Table 9.1 Functions of Management

Planning
• setting goals
• deciding how goals can best be achieved
Organizing
• finding the right people to do the work
• deciding who will do what
• organizing human, financial, material, and technological resources to achieve a goal
Leading
• motivating individuals or teams to work at achieving goals
• inspiring people to consistently give their best
• earning the respect of others
• providing direction to others
Controlling
• monitoring the employees' performance and results
• checking to see if goals are being reached
• taking action to correct problems

> **Worth Repeating**
>
> "Failing to plan is planning to fail."
>
> *Effie Jones, educator*

Formal planning integrates short-range plans (less than a year) with long-range plans (between three and five years.) If a long-range plan involves selling a particular product across Canada three years from now, immediate or short-range plans would have to be developed to include "steppingstone" goals to establish a wider distribution network, train more personnel, and expand the manufacturing operation.

Computer software programs have made the planning process easier and more efficient. Managers and employees use spreadsheet software to establish and manipulate cost figures, sales forecasts, and operations budgets. Project management software enables managers to organize and manage each component of a special project, and to assign individual responsibilities and timelines, as well as allocate available resources.

Figure 9.1 Planning Functions

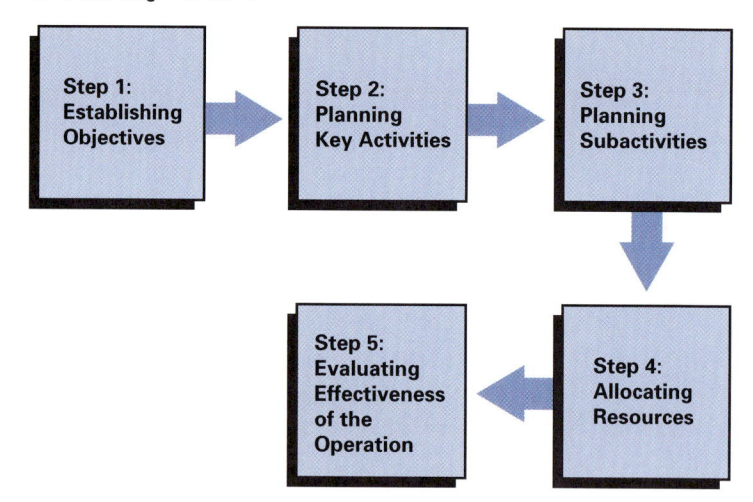

Step 1: Establishing Objectives → Step 2: Planning Key Activities → Step 3: Planning Subactivities → Step 4: Allocating Resources → Step 5: Evaluating Effectiveness of the Operation

ORGANIZING

When a venture is operated by only one person, the organizational tasks are relatively simple. The venture that involves more than one person needs a manager who can organize the operation of the venture, bringing together the human, material, financial, and technological resources needed to meet its objectives. As the venture grows, it becomes more important to organize the people involved. An organizational chart like the one in Chapter 7 can be used to show the hierarchy of management and to highlight lines of communication.

> **Worth Repeating**
>
> "If you treat a person as he is, he will become what he is; if you treat a person as he could be, he will become what he can be."
>
> *Anonymous*
>
> How do good leaders make others feel strong and capable?

LEADING

Management is required to direct, lead, and motivate people to perform to the best of their abilities. Managers must also learn to delegate responsibilities for specific tasks, to ensure that people performing these tasks are trained effectively, and to encourage interpersonal communication at all levels.

Leaders have a vision. They anticipate change and they are prepared for change. They are willing to experiment with new ideas, new methods, and new opportunities. Although they have a strong desire to make things happen, good leaders depend on others to help them achieve their goals. They encourage collaboration and make others feel strong, capable, and committed to their vision.

Leadership in the business world is a challenging role. A leader has to ensure that employees meet deadlines and that customers receive their orders on time. At the same time, a leader must motivate employees to give their best. Only by balancing these roles can a leader ensure that the goals of the venture will be reached.

CONTROLLING

The control function of management allows the manager to monitor all functions of an organization to ensure that plans are being implemented effectively. Effective control requires an analysis of what is happening in the business, and adjustments or corrections to keep the operation on target. Projected sales forecasts should be used to determine how much to produce, when it should be produced, and what processes should be used for production, sales, and distribution. This, in turn, will indicate what inventory is needed for production and what equipment and other facilities are required.

INVENTORY CONTROLS

Inventory control systems must be established to ensure that the costs of ordering and storing materials are kept to a minimum. Inventories should be ready to use when needed, and not left sitting in warehouses waiting to be used. Accurate records must be kept of raw materials, work-in-process, and finished inventories. Materials in stock should be clearly labelled and easy to locate. Many companies use a **computerized inventory control system**, which records goods received and automatically removes goods no longer in inventory from the inventory files.

PRODUCTION CONTROLS

The production of a particular product or the provision of a particular service must be managed in such a way that it is produced, sold, and serviced effectively and efficiently. Every product made by a company, or every service provided, must be produced and delivered to meet a set of predetermined standards. A good **quality control** program must be in place to ensure that

- appropriate standards have been set for production
- raw materials meet the necessary industry and company standards
- work is being checked by supervisors or team members
- products are inspected for quality

FINANCIAL CONTROLS

It is impossible to overemphasize the importance of keeping accurate financial records. Not only does the government require you to keep such records for tax purposes, but knowledge of where money is coming from and going to is essential to the success of your business. If you don't keep accurate records of **cash flow**, you may not have enough money in the bank to pay your bills, even though your products or services are selling well. It is also important to keep up-to-date and accurate information about topics such as potential suppliers and government rules and regulations.

Agents of Change

Ralph Nader, a prominent American consumer advocate, brought national attention to many problems involving product design and production standards. With the help of a group of students and volunteers called Nader's Raiders, Nader has helped bring people safer cars and airplanes, cleaner air and water, and better working conditions. In 2000, Nader ran in the U.S. presidential election as the candidate for the Green Party.

How might poor production standards affect a business? its employees? its neighbours? its customers?

YOUR TURN

1. It's been said that there are two kinds of people—those who can make money and those who can save it. Money-makers are typically entrepreneurs while money-savers are more typically managers. What kind of person are you? What makes you think so?

2. Given the characteristics you identified in Question 1, what role could you successfully play in the venture you're planning? What roles would you leave to hired employees or outside contractors?

3. What aspects of good management do you see in the operation of your school or of a sports team or club?

4. Visit a local retail or manufacturing business. Interview a representative of the business to determine what types of controls the company has put in place.
    a) What strategies are used for inventory and financial control?
    b) If it's a manufacturing business, what production controls are in place?

Venture Case

SUCCESS FOR SMALL BUSINESSES ACROSS ALBERTA

Alberta Venture

For small businesses across Alberta, success is anything but accidental. Talk to the individuals at the helm of respected small enterprises and you can almost taste the sweat, almost see the midnight monitor burning as the ledger is checked again….

The 21st century small business is an orchestra, not a kazoo; success requires a multiplicity of talents, united. The definition of success is as varied as the individuals who pursue it. It's clear the bottom line remains crucial. "There's no point going into business unless your business makes money," notes Pat Elemens, assistant dean of the faculty of Management at the University of Lethbridge. But she adds, "To have a positive bottom line, you need to pay attention to excellence."

What, then, makes a small business excellent? The benchmarks may be as diverse as the small businesses who make up the bulk of Alberta's economy, notes Kate Thrasher of KTG Enterprises Inc., winner of the 2000 Alberta Chamber of Commerce Small Business Award of Distinction for helping nearly 400 entrepreneurs launch new businesses. "For some of our clients, making 'x' number of dollars is excellence. Others, if they're able to be home with a child and still keep a roof over their head and food on the table, that's excellence."

Despite that diversity, themes emerge as Alberta's respected entrepreneurs describe their work. Leadership is the first and foremost benchmark for success. The best have a clear vision and dynamic plans. They pay careful heed to quality, teamwork, finances, and processes. They understand the primary importance of their relationships with customers and suppliers. They're always innovating. And they strive to balance work with family and community.

And certainly, smart entrepreneurs borrow insights from other high-performing companies rather than reinventing the wheel. It's the rare entrepreneur who does all things well. The wise one fills personal gaps by building a team, whether its members are partners, employees, consultants, or advisers. "Every one of our client businesses has an advisory board," says Kate Thrasher. "If they are not good at finances, we tell them to go out and find someone who is, so the expertise that is not their strong suit is sitting there."

Exploring

1. According to Kate Thrasher, what constitutes excellence in a small business?
2. Why do good leaders usually have success as entrepreneurs?
3. What should an entrepreneur consider when building a team?
4. What is your personal definition of success for the venture you're planning?

Effective Leadership

Every leader has a personal leadership style. Although there are a variety of theories about how leaders should behave, there do seem to be certain patterns that define particular styles. At one end of the scale, there's the goal-oriented leader who just wants to get the job done. At the other end, there's the people-oriented leader who is more concerned about the satisfaction of the people involved than about achieving goals.

Autocratic leaders are entirely goal-oriented. They make all the decisions for their organization and expect employees to do as they are told. Leaders with this style may lack confidence in their employees and be convinced that if they don't make all the decisions personally, nothing will be done correctly. They may clash with enterprising employees who want to make their own decisions and do the job in their own way.

Democratic leaders encourage employees to participate in the decision-making process as the organization proceeds toward its goals. They delegate the authority to make decisions to subordinates and foster an atmosphere of trust.

Collegial leaders are democratic leaders who tend to regard everyone as an equal, rather than as a part of a hierarchy. They prefer to use team decision-making processes, demonstrate a high degree of loyalty to employees, and respect the skills each person brings to the team.

Laissez-faire leaders ignore the specifics of a task or job and concentrate on giving employees the freedom to determine what they should do and how they should do it.

Although leaders have their preferred styles, there are certain tasks that every leader must perform in an organization. These include

- motivating others
- resolving conflicts
- facilitating communication
- managing personal stress

MOTIVATING OTHERS

It's important for leaders to recognize the needs of the people around them and to encourage them to pursue personal goals that are compatible with the goals of the venture. Successful leaders reward their employees appropriately and demonstrate to them that the work they do is meaningful and worthwhile.

According to Abraham Maslow, a noted behavioural psychologist, people have five levels of needs, and these needs exist in the form of a hierarchy.

Worth Repeating

"The role of leadership is to find, recognize, and secure the future."

Joel Barker, motivational speaker and author

Figure 9.2 Maslow's Hierarchy of Needs

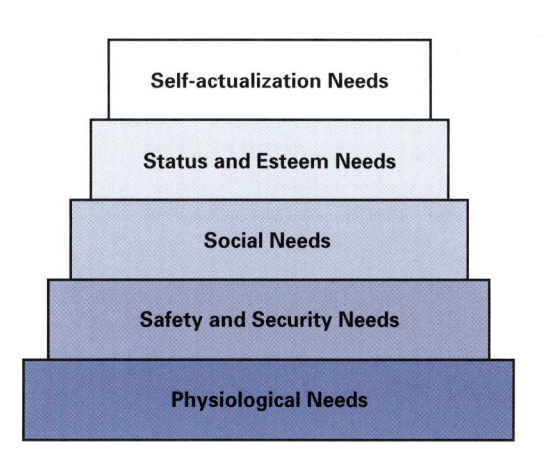

- Self-actualization Needs
- Status and Esteem Needs
- Social Needs
- Safety and Security Needs
- Physiological Needs

> **Think About It**
>
> Maslow believed that people have to satisfy the needs at one level before they can move up to the next. Why might he have thought that all other types of needs would have to be satisfied before someone could focus on self-actualization, which he defined as the freedom to make life choices according to personal values?

The leader who can identify the kind of reward that motivates an employee and then provide it will have an enthusiastic and committed work force. Some people are motivated by financial remuneration. A raise in pay will help an employee satisfy many types of personal needs. However, pay raises are not always possible or necessary.

The motivating factor might be recognition in the form of an award like The Employee of the Month, or added responsibility on the job. Awards like this work well for people whose needs are at the Status and Esteem level of the hierarchy. Being asked to take on a leadership role or manage a project does not necessarily bring more money, but it does provide status and recognition, and perhaps an opportunity for self-actualization. It's important to note that movement through the various levels is not always upward. Sometimes individuals may encounter significant changes in their lives that cause their needs to descend to a previous level.

FACILITATING COMMUNICATION

It's the role of a leader to make sure that lines of communication in the organization are working efficiently, and to present a communication model for others to follow. Human beings instinctively and constantly communicate with each other; this is one of the significant characteristics of our species. Men and women who excel in any field are almost always described as "good communicators," whether their communication skills are verbal, written, or artistic.

Effective communication is vital for the smooth operation of any venture—imagine the number and variety of messages that are sent and received even in a small business in the course of a single day. People communicate with each other about everything from products and services to financial issues to the future growth of the venture.

> **E-Bits & Bytes**
>
> Which give more clues—visual or audio signals? To find out, watch a television show with no sound and try to figure out what the characters are saying. Then turn up the sound, close your eyes, and try to figure out what the characters are doing. Discuss your conclusions with the whole class.

Ability to communicate effectively is a vital necessity in a workplace.

Messages are relayed by e-mail or by phone, both within the organization and to people outside, such as suppliers and customers. Schedules and agendas are often sent electronically. Letters to customers and clients, as well as proposals, reports, and research or contract documents need to be transmitted, both electronically and on paper.

Spoken communication occurs during informal meetings and conversations with coworkers, and in more formal situations, such as presentations to bankers or meetings with customers. A good communicator speaks clearly and concisely and also uses body language to emphasize a point.

Successful leaders are not only good at communicating their ideas, they are also good listeners. They understand that their employees often know more about the day-to-day functioning of the venture than they do themselves, so they constantly listen and learn.

It's important to remember that true communication takes place only when a message is both sent and received. Communication goes far beyond simply reading or hearing a message—it means thinking about the meaning of what has been communicated and making sure you completely understand what the other person is trying to say.

Analyze Your Communications Skills

1. Categorize these communication skills according to whether you practise them all the time, some of the time, or never.
   a) When I give instructions, I make sure my message is clearly understood.
   b) I plan what I am going to say to people.
   c) I listen carefully even when I do not agree with the message.
   d) I actively listen to all opinions.
   e) I wait until others finish speaking before I start to speak.
   f) I ask questions when I'm not sure I understand what others are trying to say.
   g) My body language shows that I am listening.

2. Analyze your answer to Question 1. How could you improve your communication habits? Why would these changes make you a better leader?

Agents of Change

Marshall McLuhan was concerned with the impact of media on culture. He argued that while the print culture (books, papers, etc.) locked each individual into his or her own consciousness, the electronic media had the opposite effect of creating a "global village." McLuhan's work changed the way we look at our world and how we relate to it; he once said, "There are no passengers on Spaceship Earth. We are all crew."

What would Marshall McLuhan say about the explosion of written communication over the World Wide Web? Is an e-mail message with an attached digital photograph different from a written letter enclosing a print of the same photograph? Explain.

Resolving Conflicts

Conflict is a natural extension of communication that occurs whenever individuals do not agree. Whether it poses a serious stumbling block to effective management depends on whether people treat it as an obstacle or as an opportunity.

Managers are often expected to act as mediators when conflict arises. In order to understand the conflict, you must listen carefully to both sides and build an accurate perception of the issue. Once you understand the problem, you then need to be able to communicate your understanding clearly to others.

The ability to listen to both sides, to identify any distortions, to understand what the true problem or cause of conflict might be, and to use sensitive and effective communication skills is crucial when trying to resolve situations where conflict is interrupting the progress of work.

Think About It

Describe three different situations in which you have been in conflict with someone. Describe the issue in each case and tell whether the conflict was resolved and, if so, how. Think about the strategies you tend to use when conflicts occur. What are these strategies? What do they tell you about yourself?

Managing Personal Stress

Busy entrepreneurs are constantly trying to balance their commitment to their ventures with the need to find time for their families, friends, and personal endeavours—a situation that may lead to physical and emotional stress. There are two kinds of stress: distress and eustress. Distress is the negative effect we often associate with the word "stress." Eustress is good stress caused by excitement. It is what drives many entrepreneurs. This problem of stress is compounded when an entrepreneur uses personal finances to start and run the venture. Financial stress affects every detail of people's lives—from where they live to how they relate to family members.

There are several keys to managing the personal stress that comes with launching and nurturing a venture.

- Take care of yourself first. Try to eat the right foods, get enough sleep, and make time for physical activities that will help you keep in shape.

- Respect the personal needs of your employees. If you show understanding about their need to make time for their families, then they will allow you the same privilege.
- Involve your family in your venture by inviting them to help out. Even small children can do simple jobs, such as packing boxes, that will help them feel as though they have a stake in the venture's success.
- Avoid relying on a new venture for all your personal financial needs. Make sure your venture plan includes a viable strategy for paying personal expenses during the startup phase.

International NEWS

Leadership for Environment and Development (LEAD) is an independent, not-for-profit organization that helps educate future leaders from countries around the world about issues related to the environment. According to its mission statement, LEAD exists to "create and sustain a global network of leaders who are committed to promote change toward patterns of economic development that are environmentally sustainable and socially equitable." LEAD branches are located in 14 countries, including Canada. Each year, the LEAD program in each country selects 15 young professionals (ages 28 to 40) who are expected to become agents of change in their fields. They are recruited from many different careers, including academics, business, government, and the media. LEAD associates spend two years in the training program, which is mostly conducted outside regular working hours so associates can continue doing their jobs. By 2000, there were more than 1000 graduates and students of the program in place around the world.

YOUR TURN

1. With a small group, discuss the statement "Leaders are made, not born."

2. With your group, discuss situations where each of the four leadership styles might be appropriate.
   a) What kind of venture would benefit from each style?
   b) How would each style look from the employee's perspective?

3. Prepare a list of rewards that would motivate individuals at each level of Maslow's Hierarchy of Needs.

4. Prepare a list of the factors that motivate you to work harder.

5. Think of an experience you've had where you were in charge.
   a) Where did it take place?
   b) Who initiated the experience?
   c) What was your role?
   d) What changes did you make while you were in charge?
   e) What risks did you take?
   f) In what ways did you motivate others to do better than before?
   g) How did you help others feel strong and capable?
   h) What were your feelings at the beginning, during, and at the end of the experience?

6. Share your answers to Question 5 with another student in your class. In what ways were your experiences similar? In what ways were they different?

7. How could you use your leadership experience in an entrepreneurial situation?

Choosing the Right Form of Ownership

Before you decide on a form of business ownership for your venture, you should review the possible forms of business organization and select the one that will best meet your needs. The form you choose should maximize your organization's strengths and help it operate efficiently.

A new venture can be established as a **sole proprietorship**, a **partnership**, or a **corporation**.

SOLE PROPRIETORSHIP

A sole proprietorship is the simplest form of business ownership and the easiest to enter. There is only one owner, who is entitled to all profits and responsible for all liabilities. Any type of business can be a sole proprietorship. Usually, all that is legally necessary is that the business be registered and that proper licences be obtained. The owner is held responsible for debts, contracts, leases, or other legal obligations.

Some people choose sole proprietorship because losses incurred during the first few years of operation, which are regarded as part of the proprietor's personal income, can be deducted from previous years' income. This strategy can yield tax refunds, which can then be used to help finance the business.

A sole proprietor assumes unlimited liability for the business. This means that if the business is in any financial trouble, the owner's personal assets, such as a home or car, may be seized to cover any business debts. However, a lawyer may be able to arrange to have your personal assets held in trust to protect them from your business liabilities.

> **Worth Repeating**
>
> "The secret of getting ahead is getting started."
>
> Anonymous

Table 9.2 Sole Proprietorship

Advantages	Disadvantages
• quick, easy, and inexpensive to establish	• limited in terms of employee compensation plans
• only requires registration and appropriate licences	• all business income is taxable
• owner makes all decisions	• profits may be taxed at a higher rate than for an incorporated organization
• owner includes all business profits/losses with personal income	• harder to raise capital than for a partnership or a corporation

PARTNERSHIP

A partnership is a formal commitment between two or more people to work together to achieve the objectives of a business venture. All partners may or may not be actively involved in the day-to-day operation of the venture. Partners share profits and losses according to the percentages laid out in their partnership agreement.

Each partner contributes something toward the partnership. This contribution may be in the form of startup money, material resources, talent, skill, experience, knowledge, or business contacts.

TYPES OF PARTNERSHIP

Partnerships can be either general or limited. A **general partnership** (or unincorporated partnership) is registered in the same way (and for about the same cost) as a sole proprietorship. At income tax time, the profits or losses of the partnership are divided according to each partner's percentage of interest or ownership in the venture. Each partner then applies that amount of profit or loss to his or her personal income for tax purposes. However, all debts and obligations of the partnership, regardless of whose responsibilities they were, are still the responsibility of each partner. If, in the event of a bankruptcy, one partner does not have enough personal assets to cover his or her share of the losses, creditors can file claims on the personal assets of any of the other partners in the **joint venture**.

> ### Worth Repeating
>
> "In a small business, the most important decisions you make are the things you decide *not* to do. So find what you're good at, and recognize where your weaknesses are. Then bring on an appropriate partner who can fill in the gap."
>
> Laura Rippy, CEO of Handango

Table 9.3 Partnership

Advantages	Disadvantages
• quick, easy, and inexpensive to establish • each partner may deduct business losses (in proportion to the amount invested in the business) from whatever is earned within the business or from other sources • favourable tax treatment, especially for startup losses • combines the talents and resources of two or more people	• general partners assume unlimited liability for all debts/obligations incurred by the partnership • both business and personal income are taxed • profits may be taxed at a higher rate than for an incorporated organization • unless otherwise stated in a partnership agreement, the partnership is automatically dissolved when one of the partners dies • if the partners can't agree on the day-to-day operation of the partnership, decisions become difficult to make

A **limited partnership** consists of one or more partners, whose liability is limited to the amount they invested in the venture. It may also, depending on the terms of the partnership agreement, include one or more general partners who have unlimited liability with respect to the debts and obligations of the partnership. **Silent partners**, who invest money in the partnership but do not take an active part in the management of it, may also be involved in a limited partnership. For more specific information on partnerships, you can refer to the limited partnership legislation of each province, or consult a lawyer.

People who depend on "handshakes" and "good friend" agreements in their partnerships often end up with regrets. The most important procedure in setting up a partnership is the writing of a partnership agreement, which is a legally binding contract.

THE PARTNERSHIP AGREEMENT

A partnership agreement is a legal document that allows members of a partnership to establish rules for their relationship and to specify the conditions that will cause the partnership to dissolve. Although the agreement regulates the relationship between the partners, it may not deal with relationships to third parties, such as clients and creditors. This is because these relationships are regulated by government legislation and can't be altered in the agreement.

A partnership agreement may include any or all of the following:

- the goals and aims of the partnership
- the initial contribution made by each partner
- each partner's continuing roles and responsibilities
- the amount of money each partner may draw out of the business
- authorizations for financial commitments
- procedures for
  - distributing profits/losses
  - admitting new partners
  - releasing (or buying out) one of the partners
  - dealing with the death or extended illness of one of the partners
  - selling or liquidating the partnership
  - the appointment of authorized persons for signing cheques and other documents
  - dealing with disagreements between or among the partners

CORPORATION OR LIMITED COMPANY

A corporation or limited company is a legal entity created by law, and established by **corporate charter**, that stands apart from the people who own it. Just like a person, the corporation is able to enter agreements, own land and property, and hold contracts. It can

---

Worth Repeating

" 'No' is an unacceptable answer. It is all attitude. The moment you say 'I can,' you've got a fighting chance. The moment you say 'I can't,' you are defeated."

Debbi Fields, founder of Mrs. Fields Cookies

be sued and incur debts. A corporation is called a "limited company" because, just as with limited partners, the liability of the shareholders or owners is limited to the amount of money that they originally invested in the corporation (or what they paid for the **shares** that they purchased.) By forming a corporation, you spread the risk of failure among a group of people rather than assuming it all yourself. In return, you give these people a small share in the future profits of your venture.

A corporation is often managed by a board of directors, which is elected by the shareholders. The board then appoints the president and other executives. Profits are given out to the shareholders based upon the number of shares each person holds. A corporation can have a very simple share structure, such as one single share owned by the former sole proprietor, or there can be hundreds or even millions of shares of different types and classes. When a corporation files the appropriate documents and gets approval to "go public," the shares can be publicly traded on a stock exchange. Trades on the stock exchange will set the price of the shares, and therefore the value of the company, from day to day.

In a corporation, the personal assets of shareholders can't be claimed to cover debts or obligations that the corporation incurs. Likewise, shareholders can't deduct from their personal income any losses that the business might experience. As an owner of a corporation, you may adjust the amount of personal income you take out of the business, and this will be reflected in how much of the income you're required to pay in tax.

Table 9.4 Incorporation

Advantages	Disadvantages
• corporations have an unlimited life, so day-to-day business continues despite the illness or death of their owners • ownership is easily transferred and does not affect the licences held by the company • profits can be removed from the corporation in the form of dividends, which can be a tax benefit to the owner • the corporation can arrange for employee benefits such as group insurance or registered pension plans • personal liability of the owner is limited	• more costly to set up because of government fees, name searches, legal fees • requires more formal annual activities (e.g., an annual meeting with formal minutes and an annual report) • losses cannot be used by the owner to offset personal income • business losses incurred during the startup period can be deducted only against future profits of the corporation • owner's personal assets can still be seized by the lending agency if he or she has put up personal collateral for a business loan

Venture Profile

THE FRANCHISE BIZ:
THINKING ABOUT BUYING OR SELLING A FRANCHISE? HERE ARE A FEW THINGS THAT YOU SHOULD KNOW!

Chris Daniels, Realm magazine

Lifelong best friends Jeff Pylypchuk, 29, and Peter Tofinetti, 30, never thought they could turn their love of bike riding into a business. Just four years ago, the two were socking away cash at menial jobs in Thunder Bay, Ontario.... Today, their bike shop, Cyclepath, pulls in an impressive $750 000 a year in sales.

How did they do it? By purchasing a franchise business that matched their interest. "We started cycling together—road racing—when we were about 13, and we had always been unimpressed with the service we received in bike shops," says Pylypchuk. "So, we thought about starting our own business."

With their combined savings of about $75 000 they considered opening an independent business, but that meant starting from scratch—coming up with a store name, finding real estate, and attracting customers. Then, they discovered Cyclepath, which at the time was a successful bicycle franchiser with 50 franchises. Pylypchuk and Tofinetti decided to buy into the system. They paid $40 000 for their franchise and took out a small business loan to help with expenses such as rent and merchandise. "It took off from there."

Did it ever! Their Cyclepath franchise opened in 1996 and was almost immediately profitable. Halfway through its second year, the store was pulling in half a million dollars, "which is double what we ever imagined," says Tofinetti.

They credit their success, in part, to the franchise system. "There was good advertising by a professional ad agency. The store looked polished; you could tell a lot of research had gone into these stores," says Pylypchuk. "There were a lot of things we could have figured out over time, but by buying into a franchise, we basically bought the package, and boom, it was set up."

Therein lies the allure of the franchise business: It's the same adrenaline rush that comes when starting an independent business, but with the instantaneous advantage of being associated with a larger brand-name company.

Franchising occurs in industries as diverse as food and beverage, travel, automotive, and high tech and is a booming business in Canada, raking in $100 billion in annual sales. There are 1300 franchisers and 76 000 franchisees across the country, with a new franchise going up every 90 minutes. You can buy

CONTINUED➡

a high-end franchise, like Choice Hotels, for about $1.5 million. Or you can buy a low-end franchise, like Jani-King International Laundromat, for just $1000.

According to the Canadian Franchise Association (CFA), the average startup fee for a franchise is between $25 000 and $35 000. While every franchise system is different, franchisees generally have to pay franchise fees, annual renewal fees, and sometimes advertising fees. "When you are making these payments, you are doing so for the brand name recognition, for expansion of the system, and for national advertising campaigns," explains the public relations coordinator at the CFA.

> ### Exploring
> 1. Why did Jeff and Peter choose Cyclepath as their business venture?
> 2. A franchise is a licence to start an independently owned business, like a Cyclepath store, that will be part of a chain.
>   a) What facts about franchises can you find in the article?
>   b) What were the advantages of purchasing a franchise over starting a new bike shop?
>   c) Create a diagram to show the advantages and disadvantages of buying a franchise.

Franchises

Food service represents 40% of all franchised units in Canada.

A **franchise** allows the owners of a successful business to duplicate it in another location without having to raise additional money or capital themselves. Each independently owned franchise operates like a part of a large chain. Each uses the same trademark, equipment design, and operating procedures. Each franchise produces the same standardized product or service. It doesn't matter how many Harvey's restaurants you eat in, the burger will taste the same in every one of them.

A franchise can be bought by a sole proprietor, a partnership, or a corporation. The purchase is a continuing agreement between the franchiser (the company that originated the venture) and the franchisee (the person buying the right to operate a copy of the venture). The franchiser's knowledge, image, success, manufacturing, marketing, and management techniques are part of the agreement. Generally speaking, franchisees are not free to run the business as they see fit. They must follow the franchiser's policies, standards, operating procedures, and product lines exclusively. They may also be required to pay regular royalty fees to the franchiser. In return, they gain the franchiser's knowledge and support in setting up the business. They may also pay less for material and technological resources because the franchiser is able to buy these in bulk.

YOUR TURN

1. With your class, prepare a list of restaurants in your community and identify whether each is or is not a franchise. Select one or two restaurants from each category and ask the owner why he or she chose that particular approach in starting the business.

2. Review your database of entrepreneurs to find at least one venture of each type (sole proprietorship, partnership, corporation, franchise). Remember to look for the abbreviations Corp., Inc., and Ltd. in the names of businesses, since these indicate that the ventures are corporations.

E-Bits & Bytes

With a small group, investigate franchise opportunities. Start by looking at newspaper advertisements, contacting the Canadian Franchise Association, or visiting the Nelson Web site at www.business.nelson.com and following the links to "franchises." Select two franchise ventures that you think might succeed in your community and prepare a comparison chart on the costs and benefits of each. Discuss and compare the information you gathered.

Laws and Regulations

Before you launch your venture, you'll need to find out about all the municipal, provincial, and federal laws and regulations that will affect its operation. If you plan to hire unionized employees, you will also need to know about any union regulations that apply. In Chapter 5, you learned how to register and protect your ideas; and in Chapter 7 you learned how to register a business name.

You should also determine if you require a business permit or tax licence, if any special building code regulations or labour laws apply to your industry, and what zoning bylaws govern your planned location. If you plan to open a retail business, you will need to obtain a **vendor's permit** (or retail sales tax licence) from your Provincial Ministry of Revenue. If you plan to be in manufacturing, you will need to contact the local office of the Customs and Excise Tax Division of the Canada Customs and Revenue Agency (formerly Revenue Canada) to ask about federal sales tax requirements. You should also contact the Canada Customs and Revenue Agency for information about salary, benefits, and deductions for prospective employees.

Since regulations vary from province to province, and in some cases from municipality to municipality, it is best to investigate these questions yourself, with the help of a lawyer, banker, accountant, or your local chamber of commerce.

Cool Stuff

Think of the symbols that best represent Canada: snow, hockey, bilingual cereal boxes, and the maple leaf. Now, add franchising to the list. Canada is the franchise capital of the world. The sector employs at least one million people and has sales of $100 billion a year. Fully 1300 franchisers count nearly 64 000 outlets, giving Canada more franchised units per capita than any place on the planet. Another 2500 units will open this year. "It's a wonderful time to be in franchising," says Richard Cunningham, president of the Canadian Franchise Association.

Profit magazine

ACTIVITIES

FLASHBACKS

Read the following statements. Then meet with a small group and talk about the experiences you've had with part-time and summer jobs. Based on what you've learned in this chapter, what improvements would you suggest to your former employers?

- Entrepreneurs need to mobilize their resources effectively in order to launch a successful venture.
- Key resources include material resources, technological resources, financial resources, and human resources.
- A startup team should represent a balance of abilities that complement the entrepreneur's personal strengths.
- Lawyers, bankers, accountants, real-estate agents, insurance agents or brokers, and management consultants are effective advisers for a beginning entrepreneur.
- Management includes the functions of planning, organizing, leading, and controlling.
- Effective leadership involves motivation, communication, and conflict resolution.
- Your business can be set up as a sole proprietorship, a partnership, or a corporation.
- A franchise is an independently owned business that operates like part of a large chain.
- It's important to know the regulations that apply to your venture before you open your doors.

LESSONS LEARNED

1. Define each term in your own words.
   - **a)** capital goods
   - **b)** expense goods
   - **c)** human resources

2. What strengths, including your own, should you have on the startup team for the personal venture you're planning?

3. How can each person help you launch your personal venture?
   - **a)** lawyer
   - **b)** banker
   - **c)** real-estate agent
   - **d)** accountant
   - **e)** insurance agent or broker
   - **f)** management consultant

4. Which members of the external team would be most crucial to the success of your venture? Why?

5. What types of controls will you need to put in place for your personal venture?

6. Explain when you would need a vendor's permit and how you would get one.

7. What is the difference between being a leader and being an organizer?

8. List the four leadership styles. Which type of leader are you likely to be? Why?

9. Review the Venture Profiles about Maureen Mitchells (Talking Success, Chapter 2), Phil Knight (The Nike Story, Chapter 4), and Guy Laliberté (The Method Behind the Magic, Chapter 6).
    a) What leadership characteristics did each entrepreneur display?
    b) In what ways were these entrepreneurs able to motivate the people around them?

10. Why is it useful for a manager to know about Maslow's Hierarchy of Needs?

11. Give three reasons why effective communication is important to the smooth operation of an organization.

12. Describe the advantages and disadvantages of each of the three main forms of business ownership. Give an example of each one from your community.

13. Explain why someone might opt to buy a franchise. Give an example of a franchise from your community.

Venturing Out

In Chapter 8, you developed the market analysis section of your personal venture plan. Now you're ready to complete your resource analysis and operating strategy. You may wish to review parts of Chapter 7 before you start, to see what should be included in these sections of your plan. (Don't worry about financial resources. You can add those to your plan after you've read Chapter 10.)

1. Decide what form of ownership you will use for your venture and give reasons for your selection.

2. Gather information that will help you identify the laws, insurance requirements, and government regulations that apply to your venture. List these and describe how you will take them into account as you develop your personal venture.

3. Prepare the resource analysis section of your venture plan. Ask yourself
   a) What equipment and technology do I need?
   b) What human resources do I need?
   c) What supplies do I need?
   d) Where do I want to locate? Why?
   e) How much will it cost to launch my venture?

4. Prepare the operating strategy section of your venture plan. Ask yourself
   a) What is the most productive way to organize the people who are working for me and their tasks?
   b) How will people's work be supervised?
   c) What supports, such as training, compensation, and benefit plans, will I provide for my employees?
   d) What will my working facilities be like?
   e) If I am producing something, how will the production process be organized? What controls will I put in place?
   f) Where will the supplies come from? Who will be in charge of ordering them?
   g) What records will I need to keep? How will I keep them?

5. In a Gap Analysis (see Chapter 7), explain how you expect your business to operate when you first start out, and how this will change as the business grows.

POINT OF VIEW

1. What else do you need to find out before you can start your venture?

2. Where could you get this information?

CHAPTER 10

Financing Your Dream

LEARNING OPPORTUNITIES

By the end of this chapter, you should be able to
- identify the seven steps in financial planning
- demonstrate how a venture can establish clear, specific, and measurable financial objectives
- demonstrate an understanding of the financial statements required by a new venture (e.g., personal budget, income forecast, balance sheet)
- demonstrate the purpose and structure of a cash-flow projection
- identify possible sources of capital
- compare the advantages and disadvantages of different kinds of business financing (e.g., debt and equity financing)
- prepare a financial strategy for a venture plan

Entrepreneurial Language

- cash-flow projection
- balance sheet
- income forecast
- profit margin
- return on investment
- startup cost
- bankruptcy
- dividend
- equity
- capital gain
- net cash
- surplus
- deficit
- net worth
- creditor
- equity financing
- venture capital
- credit rating
- minority position
- share purchase
- stock option plan
- consignment
- debt financing
- tax deductible
- fixed asset
- Six Cs of Credit
- line of credit
- term loan
- mortgage
- guarantee

In business, there are many words to describe money coming into or held by a business, and many words to describe money going out. Look at this list and record as many terms as you can in each category. Add others you've thought of on your own.

Venture Profile

MAKING IT: BREAKING THE BARRIERS
MANZI METALS INC. PRESIDENT AND CEO TALKS SHOP WITH THE BEST OF THEM

Bridget McCrea, Black Enterprise magazine

Today, as president and CEO of U.S. $4.3 million Manzi Metals, Inc., Barbara Manzi runs the only black female-owned metals distribution company in the U.S. Her eight-employee company supplies manufacturers with specialty raw metals and alloys for use in the aerospace and commercial industries. The client roster of Manzi Metals includes Lockheed Martin Corp. and Boeing Defense and Space Group.

After nine years of experience in the aerospace industry, Barbara Manzi founded the company that would become Manzi Metals in 1993 in her spare bedroom with about U.S. $45 000 in personal savings. A bank loan, used to hire staff and fund business operations, followed.

Learning the alloys and specifications necessary for quality control in the metals industry was a challenge. Manzi relied on knowledge from her past position and her own research.

The only downside to doing business with a company the size of Manzi Metals is that large contracts can be difficult to finance. "They are relatively disadvantaged financially," says Chris Gardner, a purchasing manager who buys from Manzi. "That makes it difficult to give them a $1 million order for metal, because you know they probably can't get the funding."

As advice to other small business owners, Manzi admonishes, "The best way to succeed is by paying keen attention to detail, quality, service, and competitive pricing—and don't ever take no for an answer."

Exploring

1. Describe the sources of funding that Manzi used to launch her venture.
2. Chris Gardner says, "That makes it difficult to give them a $1 million order for metal, because you know they probably can't get the funding."
   a) Why would Manzi need financing to fill an order like this?
   b) Why might this financing be difficult to get?

Starting Up

With a partner, discuss the main costs that would have to be paid before you could launch the personal venture you've been planning. How could you get the money you need?

Planning a Financial Strategy

To obtain the resources she required, Barbara Manzi needed to communicate effectively with financial professionals and show them a venture plan that included a sound financial strategy. She likely approached the bank with sales projections, **cash-flow projections**, **balance sheets**, and **income forecasts**.

Developing a sound financial strategy requires a detailed plan. Once completed, the financial plan forms an important part of the foundation on which a successful venture can be built.

The process of financial planning consists of seven steps:

1. Establishing financial objectives.
2. Preparing a personal budget.
3. Estimating revenue and expenses.
4. Preparing a cash-flow projection.
5. Calculating startup costs and operating expenses.
6. Preparing a personal balance sheet.
7. Preparing income forecasts and projected balance sheets.

STEP 1: ESTABLISHING FINANCIAL OBJECTIVES

Every venture needs money, no matter whether it is a not-for-profit cooperative or a profit-making private corporation, a new startup or a well-established corporation. It will, therefore, require financial objectives. A small business specializing in desktop publishing might have a financial objective of purchasing $20 000 worth of sophisticated computer equipment. A neighbourhood food cooperative might have a financial objective of reducing food bills by 20% through bulk buying. A community hockey league run by volunteers might aim to raise just enough money to have each team play one game and have one practice per week. All three will require money to pay for their costs, in this case computer equipment, food, or ice time. All ventures must aim to break even at the very least. Total revenues of all money flowing into the venture must equal or exceed the total costs of providing the good or service. Total revenue for a venture is determined by multiplying the selling price by the number of units sold. (See Chapter 8 for the formula.) Adding together all fixed and variable costs determines total cost. As you studied in Chapter 7, the point at which total revenues equal total costs is known as the break-even point.

YOUR TURN

1. If the XYZ Company's total cost of production was $1000 and the selling price of its product was $5, how many units would it have to sell to reach the break-even point?

2. What would the XYZ Company's break-even point be in each of the following total cost and selling price scenarios?

Total Costs	Selling Price	Number That Must Be Sold to Reach Break-even Point
$1000	$10.00	
$1000	$2.00	
$1000	$0.50	
$3000	$5.00	

3. The ABC Company calculated that for a total cost of $5000 it could produce 200 units. What would it have to sell each unit for, in order to break even?

4. What happens to the number of units sold as the selling price decreases? Why?

Units Sold	Total Costs	Selling Price
100	$800	$15
200	$1400	$10
300	$1800	$6
400	$2000	$3

5. Spreadsheet software allows you to complete calculations very quickly. Each cell in the spreadsheet is identified with a letter and a number, and you can enter formulas that allow you to calculate with information from several cells.
   a) Enter the information from the chart in Question 4 in a spreadsheet. Use a formula to create a fourth column that shows the total revenue the company would generate in each case. (Most spreadsheet programs allow you to enter the formula in the first cell, and then use a command such as "Fill Down" to extend the same formula to other cells in the same column.)
   b) What selling price should the company set for each unit in order to break even? make a profit?

WAYS TO EXPRESS FINANCIAL OBJECTIVES

Financial objectives can be expressed in terms of capturing a defined market share, attaining a particular **profit margin**, earning a certain **return on investment**, or reaching a specific level of profit.

Market share is a way of representing one company's sales as part of the total volume of sales of a particular product made by that company and its competitors, and is usually expressed as a percent. If a venture has a market share of 18%, this means that its sales represent 18% of the total sales made by all companies producing the same good or service.

The profit margin is the percent of the final selling price that represents the profit—the amount left over after the cost of producing the item is paid. If a good costs $15 to produce, and sells for $20, then the profit margin is $5/$20 or 25%. To calculate the profit margin, you can use this equation:

$$\text{profit margin} = \frac{\text{selling price} - \text{cost price}}{\text{selling price}} \times 100$$

Return on investment is the amount of profit that investors earn in return for the capital they have invested in a venture. If someone invests $10 000 in a venture and is paid $15 000 at the end of the first year, then the return on investment is $5000/$10 000 or 50%. To calculate the return on investment, you can use this equation:

$$\text{return on investment} = \frac{\text{amount returned} - \text{amount invested}}{\text{amount invested}} \times 100$$

Most people who invest in a new venture expect a return on their investment that is substantially greater than what they could earn by putting the money in the bank or buying government bonds. The higher return compensates them for the greater risks they take.

YOUR TURN

1. This year, the market is expected to spend $850 000 on products like yours. If you hope to capture 25% of the market, what amount will the total value of your sales have to reach?

2. What will your sales target be if you aim for a market share of 20% instead?

3. Use what you know about profit margin to solve each problem.
   a) If the selling price of each unit is $10 and your profit margin is 25%, how much does it cost to produce each unit?
   b) If it costs $20 to produce each unit and you want to have a 50% profit margin, what selling price will you set for your product?

4. Use what you know about return on investment to solve each problem.
   a) A venture has total revenues of $142 000 and total costs of $120 000. The profit is used to repay an investor who invested $20 000 in the business. What rate of return does the investor receive on this investment?
   b) If you invest $10 000 in a venture and you want to earn a return of 25% per year, how much must you receive from your investment each year?

Think About It

Why is it better for your business if you can pay the operating expenses with sales revenues, rather than with money you got from a bank loan or an investor?

COVERING COSTS

When you plan a financial strategy, you must have the financial resources available to cover both the **startup costs** and the **operating expenses**. The startup costs are the expenses that must be paid in order to get the business up and running. They include all the fixed costs of production, plus any variable costs incurred in providing the good or service during the startup phase.

Operating expenses are the expenses needed to keep a venture going once it has successfully completed the startup phase. These costs can be fixed or variable.

It's important that all operating expenses, or as many as possible, be paid for from sales revenues. When a venture does not have sufficient funds to cover its expenses, it may go into **bankruptcy**. The financial plan needs to anticipate any factors that could cause this to happen and include a contingency plan for how extra costs could be covered should they arise.

Venture Profile

DROWNING WITHOUT CASH FLOW

Chatelaine

Michelle Secours thought she had made it: Fresh from school in 1997, she got a $3000 loan to create seven prototype sweaters. On a two-week sales trip, she secured $35 000 in orders for her company, Frëtt Design. And that's when the now 26-year-old Montrealer's trouble began.

Secours watched her knits sell swiftly in stores but waited 60 to 90 days to get paid, a common problem in the retail clothing industry. When money finally came in, she immediately handed it over to pay off supplies and dug herself further in debt each time she needed materials. "It was a vicious circle," says Secours. By the end of its first year, the company was going bankrupt.

Secours turned to Jack Boisaubert of the Groupement Québécois des Chefs d'Entreprises, an association that, in part, provides young entrepreneurs with networking opportunities and confidential forums in which to discuss sensitive business issues. "All the suppliers know that we are in a trade where business is difficult," says Boisaubert. Instead of repaying a debt in one lump sum, Frëtt asked to stretch payments over a maximum of six months, leaving Secours cash to keep the business running. Suppliers generally agreed, especially when Frëtt's growth potential was highlighted.

Negotiating extended payments has made it easier for Secours to build her company's three labels—Frëtt, Ë, and Kreo—without losing sleep. "I try to respect my word, but if I try to pay everything off all at once, there won't be a business," she says. "You need to go priority by priority."

Exploring

1. Describe the scenario that led Secours to the brink of bankruptcy.
2. Secours opted to extend her payments to her suppliers over a period of up to six months. How did this financial strategy help her business?
3. What other options might have been available to help Secours save her business?
4. What should Secours do to make sure a similar problem doesn't occur again?

Step 2: Preparing a Personal Budget

If an entrepreneur is depending on a venture for money to pay living expenses, then breaking even isn't good enough. A careful look at the entrepreneur's personal financial affairs will show how much income the venture must generate to meet his or her expenses. This analysis needs to be done during the planning stages for the venture, since it may help the entrepreneur decide if the venture is a viable one.

White hat thinking helps someone gather the facts, figures, and objective information needed to complete a personal budget.

Entrepreneurs who start a successful business may earn money from a venture by taking a wage or salary, by selling the venture for a profit, or by taking their share of the profits in the form of a **dividend**. A dividend is an amount of money paid out to people who own shares in a business.

Wages or salaries are referred to as **personal drawings**. While these represent income for the entrepreneur, they are a cost to the venture and are included as such in the venture's cash-flow statements.

An entrepreneur, especially one who is just starting out, may decide to reinvest profits in the venture to make it grow. Reinvesting profits increases the value of the entrepreneur's **equity**, or personal financial investment, in the venture. The value of the venture increases but this increased value can only be turned into cash when the venture is sold. The profit acquired as the result of selling a venture is called a **capital gain**.

Table 10.1 A Personal Budget

Expense	Amount
1. Fixed Monthly Payments	
a) Rent/Mortgage	
b) Car	
c) Appliance	
d) Television	
e) Personal Loan	
f) Life Insurance Premiums	
g) Other Insurance Premiums	
h) Miscellaneous	
Total Fixed Monthly Payments	
2. Household Operating Expenses	
a) Telephone	
b) Gas/Electricity	
c) Water	
d) Repairs	
Total Household Operating Expenses	
3. Transportation Expenses	
a) Public Transportation	
b) Gas/Car Repairs	
Total Transportation Expenses	
4. Food Expenses	
a) Food at Home	
b) Food Away from Home	
Total Food Expenses	
5. Personal Expenses	
a) Clothing/Cleaning	
b) Drug Store Purchases	
c) Doctor/Dentist	
d) Education	
e) Gifts	
f) Travel	
g) Miscellaneous	
Total Personal Expenses	
6. Total Monthly Expenses	

How the money will be derived from the venture is for the owners to decide. They will often choose the method that yields the most income after taxes.

Some entrepreneurs rely on money from their businesses to pay their personal expenses, while others have income from other sources.

YOUR TURN

1. Create a personal budget that details the expenses you currently face in a typical month. If possible, use a spreadsheet to calculate the totals in each category, and the total monthly expenses.

2. Imagine a time in the future when you have left home and are attending college or university. Create a new monthly budget to reflect these circumstances.

3. From a financial point of view, what are the advantages and disadvantages of wanting to start your own venture when you are still in high school?

4. What does your personal budget tell you about the financial strategy you might use to start a venture?

Agents of Change

It's fitting that William Mariani produces movies as CEO of Blackwatch Communications Inc., because his own start is straight out of a Hollywood script. Mariani quit university to make a movie he hoped to finance with a public offering. Prospectus in hand, all he needed was people to pitch to. No problem: "I was seeing 30 people a night delivering pizza," says Mariani, "So I started delivering prospectuses to them." If they couldn't give money, he says, "they'd refer me to someone who could." One customer contributed $15 000—enough to get Mariani's film, *Obstruction of Justice*, off the ground. Now, the successful Montreal-based firm produces and distributes films. Blackwatch's total sales in 1999 were $4.5 million.

Use your red thinking hat. Describe what your reaction would have been if Mariani had delivered pizza and a prospectus to your home.

Step 3: Estimating Revenue and Expenses

Estimating revenues and expenses of a venture requires close attention to detail.

The purpose of a cash-flow projection is to predict the timing and amount of revenues and expenses. It projects when money will actually flow into the venture, for example, from cash sales and **accounts receivable**. It also projects when money will flow out of the venture, for example, for salaries, expenses, and **accounts payable**. A cash-flow projection shows the entrepreneur when the venture will be cash rich and when it will be cash poor.

A venture becomes cash rich when revenues are greater than expenses. When expenses exceed revenues, the venture becomes cash poor. The entrepreneur must make sure that there is always enough money on hand in its cash reserve to cover cash-poor periods. If this precaution isn't taken, the venture will be unable to pay its bills and will be forced to cease operations. Frëtt Design is an excellent example of what can happen when entrepreneurs do not anticipate cash-flow problems.

Estimating Revenue

In Chapters 6, 7, and 8, you learned how to use market analysis methods to find the demand for a particular good or service, and to choose a price that will maximize sales. This information is contained in the market analysis section of your venture plan.

Once you know how much you can expect to sell, and how much you plan to charge for each unit, you can estimate the total revenue your venture might generate over a period of time. While this analysis is basically straightforward, it does require some careful calculation. With cash sales, the money flows into the venture immediately. With other sales, where credit buying is involved, the purchase may not be paid off for months, or even years. A cash-flow projection does not record revenue until it actually arrives. Money earned from credit sales is recorded when the payments are received, not when the initial sale is made.

Estimating Expenses

To estimate expenses, you need to determine the cost of all the resources the venture will need. This process depends on information contained in the resource analysis section of the venture plan.

Worth Repeating

"Why do businesses fail? One hundred percent bad management. Not paying attention to inventory, receivables, and monthly financial statements. People forget that a sale is just a gift until they get paid."

Jon Close, Community Futures Network Society of Alberta

Most entrepreneurs have limited startup funds and must doggedly seek out potential suppliers, negotiating the best possible price and terms for the resources the venture needs. A venture's suppliers can be its best friends or its worst enemies. Helpful suppliers can provide information about customers, or offer production advice and special financial terms, such as discounts and credit. On the other hand, they may fail to deliver on time or provide shoddy materials. Sometimes, as with Michelle Secours's company, a venture has to pay its suppliers before it has received payment for its output. Making sure there is always enough cash to cover expenses can be a tricky balancing act.

Why is it important for an entrepreneur to have a good relationship with suppliers?

YOUR TURN

1. This partial cash-flow projection shows the revenues and expenses of a new venture in its first four months of operation.

	Total Value of Sales	Total Monthly Expenses
Month 1	$10 000	$12 000
Month 2	$12 000	$9 000
Month 3	$20 000	$15 000
Month 4	$25 000	$20 000

   a) Calculate the venture's profit or loss for each month.
   b) Calculate its total profit or loss after four months of operation.

2. Now assume that the venture described in Question 1 receives only half of its sales revenues in cash, and that the remainder is paid in 30 days. Further assume that it must pay all its expenses in cash as they are incurred. (This is not unusual for a new venture.)

   a) Revise the projection to show the actual amount of money received and paid out each month. Recalculate the venture's profit or loss for each month, and its total profit or loss after four months.
   b) How much capital will the entrepreneur need to have on hand to make sure all the bills will be paid during these four months?

3. Expenses do not always have to be paid as they are incurred. Assume the entrepreneur has friendly suppliers who are willing to take half of each monthly payment in cash, and to wait 30 days for the other half. Revise your calculations again to find out whether the venture is cash rich or cash poor at the end of each month.

STEP 4: PREPARING A CASH-FLOW PROJECTION

A simple cash-flow projection has three components—the cash that comes into the business (**cash in**), the cash that flows out (**cash out**), and the **net cash** (cash in – cash out).

Table 10.2 A Simple Cash-Flow Projection

	Time Period (months or years)
	1 2 3 4 5 6
Part 1: Cash In This section keeps track of the money that is actually received by the venture from sources such as sales, loans, and contributions. Income is recorded only when it is received. (If a firm sells something in Month 1 but does not receive payment until Month 3, the cash is registered in Month 3.)	
Part 2: Cash Out This section keeps track of all expenses as they are paid. If supplies are purchased in Month 1 but not paid until Month 2, this expense would be listed under Month 2.	
Part 3: Net Cash This section records the balance of cash flow for the individual period. The value of the Cash Out is deducted from the value of the Cash In to determine whether a surplus or a deficit exists for that period. The balance is recorded as either a monthly **surplus** (when revenues exceed expenses) or a monthly **deficit** (when expenses exceed revenues). The last line in the forecast records the cash surplus or deficit since the beginning of the accounting period under the heading of Cumulative.	

Agents of Change

Debbi Fields, founder of Mrs. Fields Cookies, was one "smart cookie" when she opened her first retail cookie outlet. Debbi used a recipe for chocolate chip cookies that she perfected when she was 13 to build a U.S. $425 million cookie empire in 11 countries around the world.

Why do you think such a simple concept has been so successful?

A Sample Cash-Flow Projection

Assume that you are planning a venture that will specialize in house-painting services. To prepare a cash-flow projection, you first have to make a list of your expenses:

Purchase of Equipment:
- used pickup truck $4500
- ladders $300
- miscellaneous $200
- total $5000

Rental of Equipment: • sprayer, extension ladder

Labour Expenses: • hiring one employee for April and September, two employees during busy months ($9.00/hour for wages plus employer's contribution to UI and CPP)

Materials: • paint, turpentine, primer, etc. used in providing services

Business Licences: • for registering the company name

Advertising: • community newspaper advertisement, flyers, and lawn signs

Insurance: • for the truck and business liability

Office Expenses: • business phone and answering machine

Other: • allowance for gas and truck repairs

Then, you have to estimate when your expenses will occur in order to prepare the following cash-flow projection. Let's assume that you will purchase everything on a cash basis.

Table 10.3 A Cash-Flow Projection for a House-Painting Service

	April	May	June	July	Aug	Sept	Total
Cash In							
Estimated Sales of Goods or Services	$2 400	$7 280	$9 800	$9 800	$5 800	$1 600	$36 680
Cash Out							
Purchase of Equipment	$5 000						$5 000
Rental Expenses	$150	$150	$150	$150	$100	$50	$750
Labour Expenses	$400	$3 200	$4 800	$4 800	$1 200	$300	$14 700
Personal Drawings	$100	$400	$500	$500	$300	$200	$2 000
Materials	$200	$400	$600	$600	$400	$200	$2 400
Business Licences and Fees	$20						$20
Advertising	$300	$200	$200	$100			$800
Insurance	$1 500						$1 500
Office Expenses	$400	$100	$100	$100	$100		$800
Other (gas and truck repairs)	$250	$200	$500	$400	$150	$100	$1 600
Total	$8 320	$4 650	$6 850	$6 650	$2 250	$850	$29 570
Net Cash (Cash In – Cash Out)							
Monthly Surplus		$2 630	$2 950	$3 150	$3 550	$750	$13 030
Monthly Deficit	$5 920						$5 920
Cumulative (to date)	–$5 920	–$3 290	–$340	$2 810	$6 360	$7 110	$7 110

240 Unit 3 ◆ Moving into Action

Venture Profile

STARTUP AWARD GOES TO MEDICARD FINANCE INC.

Rotman School of Management, University of Toronto, Canadian Woman Entrepreneur of the Year Awards

In August 1996, Medicard Finance Inc. of Vancouver, BC, was formed by Ann Kaplan to offer financing to persons seeking elective medical procedures. At the time, there was a growing demand for reconstructive surgery, laser eye treatments, skin resurfacing, cosmetic dentistry, and other procedures not covered by the public health care system. The increase in demand was attributed to advances in technology, a decrease in recovery time, and increasing acceptance of cosmetic procedures. In fact, the private sector market expenditures showed a staggering increase of 35% per year.

As the president and CEO of Medicard, Ann's goal was to become the facility that Canadians would think of when seeking finance or information for medical procedures. She wanted Medicard to be "Canada's medical finance and information company."

Ann presented Medicard to financial institutions for funding. It was a tedious process, yet the research and **pro formas** showed a demand and an ability to work with third parties while recognizing a comfortable profit. Her business model, associations with Canada's financial wizards, and the support of the Canadian financial community in general enabled her to open doors to larger institutional lenders. Ann borrowed money to take her through the six-month **due diligence** process that resulted in a decision by Bank of Montreal to back Medicard.

By December 1997, legal and licensing requirements had been met and physicians were registering for the program. A significant investment in computer accounting software and technology to manage the business had been made. A marketing package was ready. Ann had a country to conquer. Through appearances at trade shows and utilizing physicians to market to patients, the business grew. It took thirteen months to book the first million dollars in loans. It took a month to book the second million.

Exploring

1. In pairs, brainstorm a list of possible expenses for Ann's business startup.
2. Why do you think the Bank of Montreal decided to offer financial support to Medicard?
3. People who need elective procedures borrow money from Medicard and pay it back slowly over months or years.
   a) What financial challenges might this present for the company?
   b) How might the company meet its expenses?

Step 5: Calculating Startup Costs and Operating Expenses

Ann Kaplan needed to have sufficient startup capital to last more than a year until her revenue started to flow in. That is not unusual for startup ventures. Other ventures, like Frëtt Design, are seasonal. They have revenue flowing in during specific times of the year, yet their expenses are spread out over the whole year. Understanding how cash flow works is essential for any entrepreneur.

Startup costs must be calculated accurately. Experience shows that many people underestimate the amount of time and money it takes to get a venture operating efficiently. Entrepreneurs need to be honest with themselves and others about how long this process will take, the amount of money that's likely to come in, and the amount they will have to pay for expenses. Only careful planning will ensure a successful transition from startup to established organization.

Step 6: Preparing a Personal Balance Sheet

At the start of a venture, it is often effective and less expensive to use personal savings for startup funds. There is no interest to pay, and the profits don't have to be shared. The entrepreneur also retains control over the venture and maintains greater freedom of action. Interestingly, ventures in which the owner has a personal stake are usually more successful than those where the owner has not invested.

However, many entrepreneurs don't have the savings they need to finance the startup phase. An important part of financial planning involves determining how much capital can be drawn from personal savings, and how much will have to be obtained from other sources.

Researching and writing a personal balance sheet will provide this information. A personal balance sheet consists of three sections. The first section lists the entrepreneur's assets. Assets include everything the entrepreneur owns that has a cash value. The second section lists the entrepreneur's liabilities. A liability is a debt—a sum of money the entrepreneur owes. The third section is a calculation of the entrepreneur's **net worth**. Net worth is determined by subtracting the value of liabilities from the value of the assets.

An entrepreneur's net worth will help determine how much capital can be raised from personal sources, and will help lenders decide how much capital it is safe to lend. However, it's easy to overestimate this amount, since not all assets can be sold quickly for the full amount they are worth. Lending institutions, such as banks, credit

---

Think About It

What reasons can you identify for the fact that ventures in which the owners have invested money are more successful?

unions, and government agencies, may also be unwilling to accept some assets as collateral for a loan.

The personal balance sheet will indicate the personal financial resources that are available to finance a venture, and will also show the entrepreneur what sacrifices need to be made in order to make the dream a reality.

Table 10.4 A Personal Balance Sheet

Assets	Value (dollars)
Cash	$ .00
Bank Accounts	$ .00
Stocks, Bonds, and Other Securities	$ .00
Money Owed	$ .00
Life Insurance Cash Value	$ .00
Income Tax Refunds	$ .00
Vehicles	$ .00
Real Estate	$ .00
Pension Plan/Retirement Accounts	$ .00
Personal Assets (furnishings, jewellery, etc.)	$ .00
Other	$ .00
Total Assets	$ .00

Liabilities	
Bank Loans	$ .00
Mortgages	$ .00
Credit Card Debts	$ .00
Income Tax Owing	$ .00
Life Insurance Loans	$ .00
Other	$ .00
Total Liabilities	$ .00
Net Worth (Total Assets − Total Liabilities)	$ .00

YOUR TURN

1. Suppose your friend Tazim is in the following financial situation. Construct her personal balance sheet.
   a) She has $165 in her bank account.
   b) She has a $5000 term deposit.
   c) She owns a motorbike worth $1200 but still has to make payments to the bank totalling $500.
   d) She lent her younger brother $200.
   e) She owns a stereo system worth $400.
   f) She expects to get an income tax refund of $150.
   g) She owes her father $600, which was the cost of additional insurance so she could drive his car.

2. Which of Tazim's assets could easily be sold for cash or accepted as collateral for a loan?

3. Suppose Tazim decides to go to university. What might her personal balance sheet look like at the end of her first year?

4. Suppose that when Tazim is 40 she has two children. What might her personal balance sheet look like then?

5. When it comes to raising personal capital, what are some advantages of being young? of being older? Prepare a Venn diagram to compare the advantages you found.

STEP 7: PREPARING INCOME FORECASTS AND PROJECTED BALANCE SHEETS

No matter what type of financing you decide to use to raise money, you will need to convince potential investors and financial institutions that your venture is sound and attractive. To do this, you will need to prepare both an income forecast and a projected balance sheet. These two documents will help prospective **creditors** or owners assess the risk of the investment and the size of the potential return.

Risk assessment is very important to creditors because their return is limited to the interest that they can earn on the outstanding balance of the loan. They want to make sure that the venture is likely to be able to repay its debts. Owners are more interested in the potential benefits offered by the venture, for example, the possibility of receiving a share of the profits in the form of dividends, or having a potential capital gain as the assets of the successful venture increase in value.

THE INCOME FORECAST

The income forecast estimates what the total income and total costs of a venture will be for a specific period of time and helps determine whether the company will earn enough to pay its debts. It also estimates the amount of the profit or loss for the venture. The income forecast follows the same format as a cash-flow projection, except that it includes income that has not yet arrived, such as sales that will be paid for in 30 days, and also shows cumulative totals. An **income statement** is like an income forecast, except that the figures reflect what has happened in the past, rather than what the entrepreneur thinks will happen in the future.

■ THE PROJECTED BALANCE SHEET

The projected balance sheet forecasts what a venture will own and what it will owe on a given date. Even more important, it shows the estimated value of the owner's equity, or personal investment in the business.

As with the personal balance sheet described earlier in this chapter, a projected balance sheet is divided into three main sections: assets, liabilities, and owners' equity. The owners' equity, or net worth, is what is left after the liabilities of a venture are deducted from its assets.

Preparing realistic and sound income forecasts and projected balance sheets is crucial for the credibility of the potential venture.

Cool Stuff

WHERE VENTURE CAPITALISTS ARE PLACING THEIR BETS

Venture capitalists put their money into growth industries where they can get the best return. Here is where they invested money in 1998.

According to this table, what are the two most attractive and two least attractive sectors to invest in?

Industry	Amount Invested (millions)	Number of Financings
Computer-related	$387	244
Biotechnology	$235	123
Medical/Health	$153	85
Manufacturing	$194	149
Electronics	$182	93
Communications	$150	69
Consumer-related	$98	74
Industrial Automation	$34	27

MacDonald & Associates Ltd., Toronto

Chapter 10 ◆ Financing Your Dream **245**

Venture Profile

HANDLED LIKE A PRO

Melba Newsome, Success magazine

When her husband, the founder of All Pro Construction died of lung cancer, Georgia Buchanan took over the firm out of desperation, not desire—and found herself at the helm of a business she knew nothing about. "A lot of people asked if I was concerned about running a business in which I had no experience," says Buchanan. "I wasn't just concerned. I was terrified!"

The Kansas company was desperately in need of cash for its day-to-day operations. Despite U.S. $7 million in pending contracts, Buchanan found herself struggling to make payroll and keep the lights on. Bids on pending contracts had been grossly underestimated. The first two projects completed under her watch lost U.S. $220 000.

Buchanan scoured the company's books looking for ways to save the business. With the aid of a few small-business advisers, Buchanan drafted a new business plan, detailing how she planned to turn the ailing company around. She hired new employees who had experience in the areas she lacked. She shifted the company's focus from interior finishing to concrete construction, asphalt paving, and steel work. And she established a procedure to check and recheck bids to avoid making the kinds of errors that had cost All Pro big in the past.

Still she needed money. For that, she turned to her bank. "I showed my banker my new business plan and the kind of work we were contracted to do, and I explained how we would pay off the debt," she says. The presentation impressed the banker enough to increase All Pro's line of credit.

Within three years, all her efforts paid off. All Pro had developed a reputation in the industry for quality work that was completed within budget and on schedule.

Those days of robbing Peter to pay Paul taught Buchanan the benefits of long-term planning. Her detailed business plan maps out where she wants to take the company and how she plans to get there. Instead of putting the plan in a desk drawer to collect dust, she reviews it monthly to make sure she stays on track.

Exploring

1. What do the entrepreneurs profiled in this chapter have in common?
2. How might Georgia Buchanan use a line of credit to help with the day-to-day operations of All Pro Construction?
3. Explain the meaning of the expression "robbing Peter to pay Paul."
4. If Buchanan had been unable to get money from the bank, where else could she have gone?

Ways to Raise Capital

It takes capital to start a venture. Often this capital is more than the entrepreneur has on hand. Ann Kaplan and Georgia Buchanan were able to secure their financing from traditional banks. However, there are many other potential sources of money for a venture.

Looking for financing can be very frustrating. To catch the interest of potential lenders or investors, entrepreneurs need to generate excitement about their ideas, and show a strong commitment to the venture, and a belief in its success. Georgia Buchanan did just that. She increased her line of credit based on her outstanding presentation to the banker.

The process of creating a venture plan takes entrepreneurs out into the community to talk to people, to do research, to seek advice, and to interact with other entrepreneurs. They will gradually develop a network of contacts who may be able to help in the search for financing, or even become investors themselves. Entrepreneurs may have to knock on many doors before they find the financing they need. William Mariani made his pitch to everyone on his pizza delivery route.

It's important to note that investors will rarely lend money without thoroughly researching the venture. The venture plan must provide carefully considered answers to the following questions:

- How will the venture earn revenue?
- What is the potential profit?
- How long will it take to reach this profit level?
- How much money will the investor need to provide?
- Is the investment secured? If so, how?
- Can the investment be converted to cash at any time?
- Who will be involved in the day-to-day management of the venture?
- Will the investor have any say in the management of the venture?

A detailed and well-presented venture plan will attract investors, inspire their trust, and encourage them to commit to the venture.

Equity Financing

Equity financing is a form of financing in which the investor receives some ownership in the venture in exchange for a financial contribution. The investment may come from the entrepreneur's personal savings or from friends, relatives, or business partners. It may be acquired by forming a partnership, establishing an incorporated business and selling shares, or through **venture capital**,

---

International NEWS

Thirty women entrepreneurs attended the Women's Venture Capital Forum in Boston in November 2000. The forum sought to give women access to the capital they need to launch and sustain businesses. Several people at the event said women have been excluded from the venture capital "network." As with most "old boy" systems, the network is intangible and built on relationships between lawyers, investors, and other service providers, they said. Women make better entrepreneurs "because they're tougher and have to jump through more hoops," observed Oliver Curme of Battery Ventures.

Metro

How might attending such a forum lead to obtaining venture capital?

private placement, or business employees. Weighing the advantages of equity financing against the disadvantages can help entrepreneurs determine if this is the best form of financing for their venture.

Sources of equity financing include personal savings, friends and family, partners, selling shares, venture capitalists, private placement, employees, suppliers, and customers.

Table 10.5 Advantages and Disadvantages of Equity Financing

Advantages	Disadvantages
• A large capital investment by the owner(s) increases the venture's borrowing power. • Suppliers may offer more generous credit terms to ventures that are equity-financed. • More people share ownership of the venture, so the individual risk is less. • Investors have a genuine interest in the success of the venture.	• The entrepreneur may become the employee of the other investors. • The entrepreneur may lose some of his or her independence. • Investors share in the profits according to their investments. • Additional expenses may be incurred, for example, for legal fees or auditing expenses.

> **Worth Repeating**
>
> "Money is just money. Who invests is more important than how much is invested."
>
> Regis McKenna, The McKenna Group

> **E-Bits & Bytes**
>
> Visit www.business.nelson.com and follow the links to "financing your venture" to find sites that help entrepreneurs find financing.

PERSONAL SAVINGS

Entrepreneurs who have sufficient personal savings and who do not wish to share the decision making, profits, or ownership of the business may choose to use their own savings to start the venture. Using personal savings can be a great financial and personal sacrifice for the entrepreneur. However, it conveys a high level of confidence in the venture and that may make it easier to obtain a personal loan.

FRIENDS AND FAMILY

Friends and family may wish to invest money because they believe in the entrepreneur, they can envision the success of the venture, and they are willing to risk some of their savings to help start the venture. This type of investment is commonly referred to as **love money**. The inventors of the board game Trivial Pursuit, for example, obtained their startup capital from friends and relatives. They had tried unsuccessfully for several months to raise capital. Some people they approached thought the board game was not a marketable idea, others thought the inventors' lack of business

248 Unit 3 ◆ Moving into Action

experience was a deterrent. But these young entrepreneurs persevered. They approached friends and relatives and asked for only a small investment—$1000 in exchange for five shares of equity in the business. They were finally able to raise $75 000 to test market the game. The rest of the story, as they say, is history. The friends and family members who invested have made huge returns on their initial investment.

The potential disadvantage to investment from friends or family is that the personal relationship could be hurt if the money is lost or not repaid. To prevent this from happening, there should be a shareholder's agreement in writing that outlines the terms of the investment. Regular reporting to investors should be done as a matter of course.

▌ PARTNERSHIP

As you read in Chapter 9, a partnership is formed when two or more entrepreneurs get together to start a venture. With each of the partners making a financial investment in the venture, there may be no need to raise additional capital. However, if further capital is required, partnerships will generally receive a higher **credit rating** that will increase borrowing power. A written partnership agreement should include a formula for dissolving the venture or for partners to buy each other out.

▌ INCORPORATING AND SELLING SHARES

If the venture requires a great deal of capital, incorporating the business and selling shares may be the wisest route to take. The advantages and disadvantages of this choice have been examined in Chapter 9.

▌ VENTURE CAPITALISTS

Venture capital comes from private individuals or companies who are interested in investing in new ventures that will likely provide a high return on their investments. Some look for a return of 25% or more. The venture capitalist, often introduced to the entrepreneur through a network of contacts, sets goals for the level of return he or she is looking for and will make investment decisions based on the projected ability of the venture to reach these goals.

Venture capitalists like to see a precise breakdown of how much money is required, how much the entrepreneur has committed, and the potential growth of the venture. They will then weigh this against how much they are prepared to invest.

Venture capitalists usually bring expertise in planning, in financial control, and in taking the venture public. Venture capital typically comes in the form of equity and the investors usually want a

---

Worth Repeating

"A strong, positive self-image is the best possible preparation for success."

Dr. Joyce Brothers, psychologist

substantial **minority position** in the venture. Having a minority position means to own a small or minor share of the business. The money these minority shareholders invest may come with conditions, such as

- representation on the board of directors
- monthly financial reports
- a life insurance policy that will repay the investor in the event of the entrepreneur's death
- input into the budgeting process
- a clause in the investment agreement outlining buy-sell arrangements

▌ PRIVATE PLACEMENT

Private placement is similar to venture capital; however, it is generally used to raise large amounts of capital from a group of investors after a venture is past its startup phase. Investors interested in private placement might include pension fund managers, wealthy individuals, trust companies, and some venture capitalists. These investors are generally looking for a return on their money in two to three years.

▌ EMPLOYEES, SUPPLIERS, AND CUSTOMERS

Employees who have been with a company for a specified period of time or who are in senior positions may be invited to invest in a venture on a limited basis. Inviting employees to become owners in a venture can have beneficial results. **Share purchase** and **stock option plans** often serve to motivate employees to work more productively, to resolve problems more efficiently, and to be more committed to the venture.

Suppliers are another often-overlooked source of capital. Marianne Bertrand, president of Muttluks, High Quality Boots for Dogs, found that during her off seasons it was difficult to pay her suppliers on time. She approached her largest supplier and asked for special terms. Her supplier agreed. Suppliers are often willing to provide special terms during seasonal lulls, sometimes without charging interest. Some suppliers may even be willing to provide goods on **consignment**, charging only for the goods that are sold.

Customers can also help finance a venture. Consider the roller hockey league founded by Brett and Devon Cranson. Customers pay for the service before it is provided, giving the venture all the cash flow it needs to meet its commitments. Customers may be willing to pay cash up front or to make a deposit and follow up with payments as the work is completed.

> **Think About It**
>
> With a small group, interview three local entrepreneurs or research three businesses on the Internet. Discover where the startup funds for each venture came from.

DEBT FINANCING

Debt financing means that money is borrowed to finance a venture. The entrepreneur borrows money for the startup or to finance growth, improvements, or investments, and the loan is paid back gradually over time. It's a relatively easy process to obtain a business loan. Most lenders will approve a loan within a few days. Compare this to the challenge of finding a partner to share your vision and you can see why many entrepreneurs use debt financing to finance at least part of their startup costs.

It's important to note that all the costs incurred in borrowing money for the venture are **tax deductible**. This means that interest on the loan and any costs associated with setting up the loan reduce the amount of income tax the venture has to pay. This actually reduces the effective interest rate of the loan in terms of after-tax dollars. The entrepreneur must ensure, however, that he or she does not borrow more than can be repaid from the income generated by the venture.

It's the entrepreneur's responsibility to find a lender who is compatible with the venture. The lending institution with the lowest interest rate is not always the best one. Some lenders place limits on what the entrepreneur can and cannot do. The lender must understand the requirements of the venture and must be able to assess the financial risk with a fair degree of knowledge.

New ventures pose a special risk to a lender because the venture has no track record and the lender may not know if the entrepreneur can be relied upon to repay the loan. Lenders usually feel more comfortable lending to entrepreneurs who have previous business experience and some expertise. They also like to feel confident that the entrepreneur understands financial management. It is important, too, that the entrepreneur has invested his or her own money or has some form of equity in the venture as security.

Depending on the lending institution, the individual involved, and the particular venture, lenders will look for a **debt to equity ratio** of anywhere from 1:1 to 4:1. This means that the amount of debt will be at least equal to the equity, and, at most, four times as great as the equity. Government agencies tend to have a 1:1 lending ratio for such programs as New Venture Loans or Youth Venture Loans. This is because the government is taking a significant risk and will be responsible for repaying the loan to the financial institution should the entrepreneur be unable to do so. A 4:1 debt to equity ratio might exist where the entrepreneur has considerable financial and management expertise, a proven record of past earnings, and a **fixed asset**, such as real estate, as security for the loan.

E-Bits & Bytes

Visit www.business.nelson.com to research the types of help offered to entrepreneurs by the municipal, provincial, and federal governments. Once you have the information, prepare a chart listing each agency and the type of support it offers.

When applying for a loan, the entrepreneur must be prepared for a full investigation. Lenders want to know about the entrepreneur's character, capital, collateral, capacity, circumstances, and coverage. These are known as the **Six Cs of Credit** and are used as the basis for evaluating any loan application.

Table 10. 6 The Six Cs of Credit

Character	Is the entrepreneur honest? reliable? trustworthy?
Capital	How much has the entrepreneur invested in the venture?
Collateral	What personal assets does the entrepreneur have that could be sold to pay off the loan if necessary?
Capacity	Can the entrepreneur manage the venture effectively?
Circumstances	What product or service will the venture offer? What competition is there for the venture? What is the state of the economy? the current inflation rate?
Coverage	What insurance protection is in place in case something happens to the entrepreneur?

Possible sources of debt financing include banks, credit unions, and government agencies.

Banks

Chartered banks are financial institutions organized under federal legislation. Banks can offer the entrepreneur a **line of credit**, a **term loan**, or a **mortgage**. A line of credit allows the entrepreneur to draw money whenever it is needed for a short period of time. The repayment schedule is flexible as long as the interest is paid every month. Georgia Buchanan was able to increase her line of credit when she presented her plan for managing All Pro Construction more efficiently. A term loan is usually made to purchase equipment and there is a defined payback period with specified payments. For example, if the entrepreneur borrows money to purchase a delivery truck, the loan will have to be paid back before the value of the truck has depreciated to nothing. A mortgage is a loan made for the purchase of real estate. The term on a mortgage is much longer than on most other types of loans and the real estate purchased is used as collateral for the loan. Canadian laws regulate the maximum rate of interest that the bank can charge on any type of loan. Interest rates

International NEWS

When you're selling goods or services outside your own country, special financing may be necessary because the time between production and payment is usually longer. The Canadian government offers several programs to assist small businesses in exporting their products. For instance, the Export Development Corporation and Canadian Commercial Corporation offer help with financing, and the Business Development Bank of Canada offers financial and consulting services. Details about these and other government programs can be found at the Industry Canada Web site.

are also influenced by the rates charged by the Bank of Canada, which lends money to the banks.

CREDIT UNIONS AND *CAISSES POPULAIRES*

Credit unions are financial institutions organized under provincial legislation. *Caisses populaires* are located mainly in Quebec and other places in Canada where there's a significant French-speaking population. To obtain a loan from a credit union, the entrepreneur must be a member. Members have a common interest, that is, they work in the same industry or live in the same neighbourhood. Credit unions operate like banks. They offer lines of credit, term loans, and mortgages. The manager of the credit union will evaluate each loan application on the basis of the Six Cs of Credit; however, sometimes credit unions will take a risk on a member that other financial institutions might not. Because the credit union is operated for its members, the borrowers may receive a rebate on their loan interest if the credit union has a surplus of money at the end of the year.

GOVERNMENT AGENCIES

Both the federal and provincial governments provide money to new ventures that have the potential to create jobs, develop a new technology, or provide a domestic product to compete against a foreign product. This money may come in the form of a grant, a **guarantee**, or a loan. If the entrepreneur obtains a grant, it generally does not have to be paid back. Loans and loan guarantees do need to be repaid.

A number of government agencies provide support in the form of money or advice for entrepreneurs. Some provide a "matchmaking service"—matching the investor with the entrepreneur. Some provide loan guarantees—providing collateral to the bank so the loan will be made. Others provide direct funding, while still others offer advice.

Credit unions operate very much like banks, except that all the customers, called members, have a common interest.

YOUR TURN

1. Interview a local bank manager or loans officer, a representative of a credit union, and a representative of a government agency that lends money to entrepreneurs. Ask each person questions such as
   a) What types of loans do you offer to entrepreneurs?
   b) What rate of interest do you currently charge on each type of loan?
   c) What advantages are there for entrepreneurs who borrow from your organization?
   d) What information do you ask for on a loan application?
   e) What types of collateral do you require?
   f) What factors do you consider when you are deciding whether or not to lend money to an entrepreneur?
   e) How do you review a loan application?

2. Look up Credit Unions in the Yellow Pages. List the credit unions in your community. A class volunteer can call each of these credit unions to identify what the customers of each one have in common.

Why Plan a Financial Strategy?

The Finance spoke of the Venture Creation Wheel is vital to the creation of a successful venture for two reasons. First, completing the required financial research will help you synthesize or pull together the planning you did as you worked through each other spoke of the wheel. Secondly, expressing your ideas in terms of dollars and cents will help you define and assess all aspects of your venture in very specific terms.

Start by examining your needs and objectives. Then state those objectives in precise, measurable terms, describing break-even points, profit margins, market share, and projected return on investment. Ask yourself

- How many people will purchase the good or service? What price will they be willing to pay?
- What specific resources are required? How much will they cost?
- How much capital will my venture require?
- How much profit can I expect? Are the returns worth the risks?

When the financial analysis is done, you will have a forecast of what your venture can be, described in specific detail. Bankers, and other investors who have the financial resources you need, can relate to this forecast. A good financial strategy is the best promotion for your idea. It is also a blueprint you can use to guide your venture through the startup stage.

ACTIVITIES

FLASHBACKS

Write a letter to a "potential investor" to explain why you think it would be a good business decision to invest in the personal venture you've been planning. Make sure each of the Six Cs of Credit is covered in your letter.

- No venture plan is complete without a thoroughly researched financial strategy that establishes the specific financial objectives of the venture.
- If the venture is intended to generate income for the entrepreneur, a personal budget will show how much income is needed.
- As part of the financial strategy, the entrepreneur needs to prepare accurate estimates of production costs and projected revenues. This information is recorded in a cash-flow projection that can be used to determine how much capital will be needed to cover startup costs and short-term operating expenses.
- The entrepreneur should prepare a personal balance sheet to determine how much of the needed financial capital can be supplied from personal savings, and how much will need to be raised elsewhere.
- Entrepreneurs need to prepare an income forecast and a projected balance sheet to show potential investors.
- Entrepreneurs can raise money for their ventures through equity financing or debt financing.
- Equity financing is provided in return for ownership in the venture. Sources of equity financing include personal savings, investments from friends or family, partners, incorporation and selling shares, venture capitalists, private placement, employees, suppliers, or customers.
- Debt financing is a loan to the venture that must be paid back. Loans usually come from banks, credit unions, or government agencies.
- Most lenders use the Six Cs of Credit when they consider whether to make a loan. The six Cs are character, capital, collateral, capacity, circumstances, and coverage.

LESSONS LEARNED

1. Describe a scenario in which an entrepreneur makes a decision about his or her business because of a financial objective.

2. Describe how you could use each of the six thinking hats to help you plan a financial strategy for a business.

3. Entrepreneurs can obtain money for business startup and development in two different ways, and from many different sources. Describe the advantages and disadvantages of each alternative.

4. How might an accurate cash-flow projection be helpful to an entrepreneur? List several possible answers.

5. Briefly explain why a financial strategy is vital to the creation of a successful venture.

6. The first loan or investment is often the most difficult for the entrepreneur to obtain.
   a) Why is this the case?
   b) What advice would you give to a new entrepreneur who is having trouble finding the money to start a venture?

7. How can a venture plan help an entrepreneur obtain outside funding for a venture?

8. Assume you are trying to finance a new venture. List the first three places you would go to find the money you need and explain your choices.

Venturing Out

1. In Chapter 8, you identified a venture that you would like to pursue and planned the resources you need. Now is the time to begin planning your financial objectives.
   a) Briefly describe what your venture will be like.
   b) Prepare a personal budget for yourself and any others who may be involved in the venture to determine how much income the venture must generate.
   c) State the specific financial objective(s) your venture will pursue.
   d) Research the market to find out what your competition is offering, how much people are willing to pay for your product or service, and how much you can expect to sell in the first year. Specifically calculate projected revenues by month for the first 12 months for each of these scenarios: least favourable, most likely, and most favourable.
   e) Refer to the list of resources you made in Chapter 9. Calculate all costs of production month by month for the first 12 months using these three headings: least favourable, most likely, and most favourable scenario.
   f) Complete a cash-flow projection to show how your projected revenues relate to your projected costs.

g) Draw up a personal balance sheet for yourself and each partner to determine whether you have enough capital to cover the startup and operating costs or whether you will need to find financing.
   h) Prepare an income forecast for your venture.
   i) Prepare two projected balance sheets—one for the end of the first six months and the other for the end of the first year of operation.

2. Consider whether it would be better to use equity financing or debt financing for your venture. Briefly assess the pros and cons of each in a chart and then write your conclusion.

3. Review the information an investor would require for the type of financing you chose. Write a proposal to include in the financial analysis section of your venture plan to obtain the money you need for your venture.

4. After your proposal is written, review it to ensure that you have included everything you want to say. Then plan how you would present your proposal to someone who can help you get the financing you need. Practise your presentation with a classmate.

POINT OF VIEW

Entrepreneurs and small-business owners often complain about a lack of support from banks. Investigate this complaint.
   a) Do owners of certain types of businesses make this complaint more frequently than others?
   b) What do the banks say about their support for small businesses?

CHAPTER 11

Vision to Action: Writing the Venture Plan

LEARNING OPPORTUNITIES

By the end of this chapter, you should be able to
- evaluate the key components, appropriate formats, and presentation styles of venture plans
- develop the appropriate production, marketing, human resources, management, and financial components of your venture plan
- identify and list the critical risks involved with your venture
- describe contingency plans that an entrepreneur should have for a new venture
- use various types of computer software to assist you in writing a venture plan
- generate a draft version of your venture plan using appropriate software
- organize ways for selected individuals to help you assess your venture plan
- produce a revised and edited version of your venture plan

Entrepreneurial Language

- contingency plan
- critical risk
- exit strategy
- go/no-go decision
- title page
- copyright statement
- disclaimer statement
- table of contents
- letter of transmittal

The first three terms on this list all have to do with "What if...?" situations. Read the definitions of these three terms in the Glossary. Then list some "What if...?" questions you will need to consider as you develop and finalize your personal venture plan.

Venture Profile

THE HELICOPTER COMPANY INC.

Julia Henderson is flying high as the president and cofounder of The Helicopter Company Inc., a dynamic new tourism-oriented rotorcraft operation in Toronto. The Helicopter Company offers romantic flights, historical flights, city tour flights, picnic flights, and other helicopter adventures that have never before been available in Canada. Through creative alliances and partnerships with acclaimed cultural, leisure, and entertainment attractions, Julia and her partner, Kevin Smith, have dedicated their services to quality customer service and dynamic packaging. They have received many awards and considerable media recognition.

Julia did not just decide one day to become a pilot and start a helicopter company. She set long-term goals for herself at an early age, beginning with saving her babysitting money at the age of 14 so that she could pay for her university degree and, eventually, for the training required to obtain her helicopter pilot's licence.

When asked how she and Kevin created their business plan, Julia tells the story. The Helicopter Company began as the dream of two pilots who wished to have control over their flying careers. "Like so many entrepreneurs-at-heart, we sought the perfect niche market to fit our goals, and when we found it, we went after it full bore."

The business plan was created on an ongoing basis. Initially, Julia and Kevin modelled their plan after a sample they found in a library book. In the second year, they dedicated their efforts to developing a "master plan." The experience they gained in their first year helped shape and fine-tune their particular goals.

The partners sought planning help from various sources, including the Internet, government business assistance and training programs, the Canadian Youth Business Foundation, business seminars, and mentors. According to Julia, as the business grew, so did the size of the business plan. The basics of the plan have not changed, but the content and details have expanded dramatically. Sections that were initially just sketched-out headings are now filled with ideas and content. Today, Julia believes in updating her plan every year to keep it current, and she recommends referring to the latest business planning resources, such as those offered on the Industry Canada Web site.

"We believe in developing our plan with experience," says Julia. "The process keeps our business in touch with reality, and prevents that overwhelming effect of biting off more than we can chew."

Julia had her share of the usual trials and challenges of startup, which included finding

E-Bits & Bytes

Visit www.business.nelson.com for links to the Web site of The Helicopter Company to see how it markets its services to a worldwide clientele. What strategies might be outlined in the company's marketing plan?

CONTINUED➡

Chapter 11 ◆ Vision to Action: Writing the Venture Plan 259

resources to support the initiative, the ideal location, and the right support partners—including an external resource team of legal, accounting, and computer experts. She also faced the challenge of "copycat" businesses that want to imitate her success. A strong business plan has helped Julia anticipate and deal with the problems posed by would-be competitors. Above all else, Julia reminds new entrepreneurs that any venture will make enormous demands on its owner's physical and mental energy.

Julia's secret for success is to "Do what you love to do." She advises young entrepreneurs, "Get the education you need and look for experience in your field in any kind of related work—perhaps as a volunteer or through summer or part-time work. Network and keep in mind that it's not what you know, it's the people you know and how they perceive you that will make a difference. Go out into the community and join community groups, volunteer associations, charities, and industry associations. Learn! Learn! Learn! Seek the experiences that are relevant to your future business dream."

When asked about goal setting, Julia says, "If you split your focus you will lose your focus. Try to focus on the long-term plan. Short-term opportunities and temptations will only distract you from your ultimate goal."

The result of this focus, research, passion, and planning is a truly exciting Canadian business that attracts both local and international clientele.

Exploring

1. What advice does Julia Henderson have for young entrepreneurs?
2. What connection does Julia see between the entrepreneur's focus and the business plan?
3. How did Julia and Kevin begin their business plan?
4. How did the concept of their business plan evolve over time? Why was this evolution necessary?
5. How do Julia and Kevin market their business? What does this strategy tell you about their marketing plan?
6. What ideas from The Helicopter Company could you use in your personal venture plan?

Starting Up

You have already written draft plans for marketing, managing, and financing your personal venture. What do you still need to do in order to complete, improve, and polish your venture plan?

The Venture Planning Process

The profile of The Helicopter Company describes what many entrepreneurs go through during the venture planning process. As Julia Henderson discovered, the foundation of a successful venture is a comprehensive and carefully thought out venture plan. In Chapter 7, you learned that this plan has several purposes. It is designed to help you

- set realistic goals and keep track of how the venture is progressing
- plan what products and/or services you will provide, how your venture will operate, and what resources (human, material, technical, and financial) you will need
- describe how resources will be used on a day-to-day basis

- summarize and analyze your marketing research and present information about your industry
- identify and assess the target market(s) for your venture and evaluate the competition
- identify the management team, and the internal and external human resources you will need
- project costs and revenues, and obtain the financing you need to operate your venture
- provide people with background information and support material about your venture that will demonstrate its strengths

The venture planning process is not haphazard, but is made up of a series of sequential steps that may be repeated over and over as the document evolves.

Figure 11.1 The Steps in the Venture Planning Process

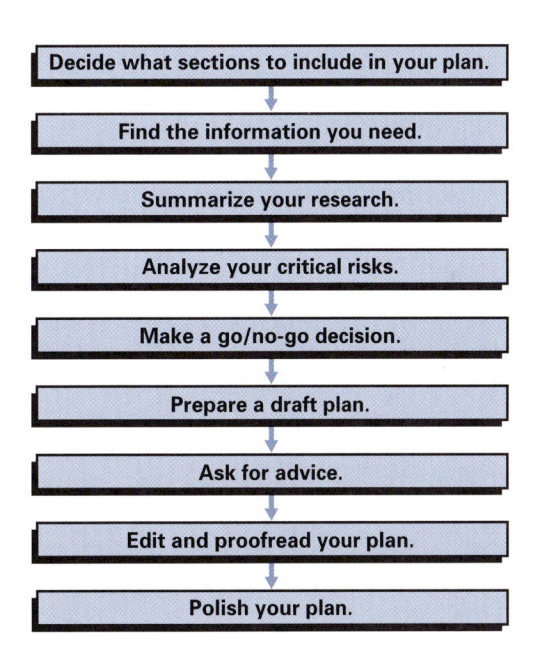

```
Decide what sections to include in your plan.
            ↓
Find the information you need.
            ↓
Summarize your research.
            ↓
Analyze your critical risks.
            ↓
Make a go/no-go decision.
            ↓
Prepare a draft plan.
            ↓
Ask for advice.
            ↓
Edit and proofread your plan.
            ↓
Polish your plan.
```

STEP 1: DECIDE WHAT SECTIONS TO INCLUDE IN YOUR PLAN

Each venture is different, and so is each venture plan. The size, nature, and scope of the venture, the amount of startup capital, the projected timeline, the number of staff, and the projected profits are just a few of the characteristics that will help shape the venture plan.

As you learned in Chapter 7, certain information needs to be included in almost every plan. The standard sections include an executive summary, a market analysis, a resource analysis, an operating strategy, and a financial strategy. However, within each section, you will need to include a number of subsections. What you decide to include in each section will depend on the nature of your personal venture. Here are some possible subsections you might include in your plan.

Table 11.1 Subsections of a Venture Plan

Executive Summary	Market Analysis	Resource Analysis	Operating Strategy	Financial Strategy
Company Description • Business History and Description • Current Status • Future Plans • Key Management **Mission/Vision Statement** • Mission Statement • Company Vision • Company Values and Approach **Product/Service Description** • Description • Advantages of Product/Service • Product Development Activities • Product Liability	**Industry Analysis** • Industry Overview • Industry Participants • Industry Trends and Growth Patterns **Marketing Plans** • Target Market Demographics • Market Trends and Growth Patterns • Market Size and Potential • Pricing Strategy and Position • Advertising Plan • Public Relations and Promotions **Competition** • Direct/Indirect Competitors • Strengths and Weaknesses • Competitive Market Niche • Market Share Analysis • Entry Barriers **Sales Strategy** • Sales Process • Distribution • Service and Warranty Policies • Sales Incentives	**Human Resources Team** • Key Management Personnel • Board of Directors • Advisers • Consultants **Material Resources** • Own or Lease Location • Equipment • Raw Materials • Major Milestones **Technological Resources** • Hardware/Software • Other Technology Needs • Technology Upgrades • Technology Training • Technology Staff	**Management Controls** • Quality Controls • Administrative Procedure Controls **Human Resource Management** • Staffing and Training • Labour Considerations • Management Control Systems • Organizational Chart **Material Resource Management** • Suppliers • Purchasing Policies	**Financial Plan** • Financial Summary • 3–5 Year Projected Financial Statements • Financial Assumptions • Break-even Analysis • Financial Ratios • Funding Request/Term of Investment • Sources and Uses of Funds **Exit Strategy** • Sell Public Shares • Merger/Acquisition • Buyout by Partner • Franchise • Hand Down the Business to Family Member • Sell Business • Close Business

Step 2: Find the Information You Need

You may already have done substantial research as you completed the Venturing Out sections at the ends of Chapters 8, 9, and 10. Now it's time to take a look at the information you've gathered to see how it will fit into the overall structure you've chosen for your plan. What information do you already have? What do you still need to find out?

It may also help to compare your plans with those other students have written, or with sample plans you've found, since these may give you ideas to include in your own work. Sample plans and templates are available from local banks, accounting firms, government agencies, and on the Internet. Examine these plans critically and note how each plan presents its information, and how this presentation builds an overall impression of the venture.

This is the time to make use of the network of contacts you've been building. Talk with possible mentors, and with professionals such as bankers, real-estate agents, or insurance brokers who can help you find the detailed information you need to complete your plan.

Sample venture plans and templates are available from local banks.

Agents of Change

When Kim Campbell replaced Brian Mulroney as the leader of the Progressive Conservative Party of Canada in 1993, she became the first woman to lead a federal political party, and the first woman Prime Minister in Canadian history. In a policy speech in 1993, Kim Campbell made the following comment about the nature of business in Canada: "The trend is toward industry that adds value. The trend is toward provision of services, rather than the production of goods. The trend is away from the idea of harvesting to the harvesting of ideas."

Do you think that the business trends Kim Campbell identified in 1993 still exist? If so, explain how your personal venture adds value, provides service, and/or harvests ideas. If not, explain how you think these trends have changed, and how your venture will address the changes.

International NEWS

If you plan to sell products outside Canada, or buy products from people outside Canada, you need to research the rules and regulations that govern international trade. The best place to start is with the Canada Customs and Revenue Agency (CCRA) or with a Canadian embassy in the country where you plan to do business.

Worth Repeating

"Our senior managers try to be explicit about our vulnerability and failings. We talk to people about the bad decisions we've made. It demystifies senior management and removes the stigma traditionally associated with taking risks. We also talk about the limitations of our knowledge, mostly by inviting other people's perspectives."

Robert D. Haas, CEO of Levi Strauss & Co.

STEP 3: SUMMARIZE YOUR RESEARCH

When you did your initial research for each section of the plan, you compiled the results and organized them in a draft document. The same type of organizing will need to be done with any data you collect as you revise and develop your plan.

When all the other sections of your plan are complete, it's time to write the executive summary. This summary will not only introduce others to your business plan, it will also help you crystallize your own ideas and make major decisions about your business. Before you write this summary, compile all of your research and prioritize the information that you think is most important.

As you learned in Chapter 7, the executive summary is a one- or two-page summary that opens with a mission statement. After the mission statement comes a description of the business that is designed to capture the interest of people who may be able to help you, either financially or as customers, suppliers, or advisers.

See page 151 in Chapter 7 for a more detailed description of the executive summary.

STEP 4: ANALYZE YOUR CRITICAL RISKS

No venture plan is complete without a written assessment of potential risks. If your venture is to achieve success, you need to identify any problems you might encounter and make **contingency plans** to minimize or avoid them. Realistically dealing with **critical risks** shows potential backers that you understand the environment in which your business will function and that you have sufficiently planned for the challenges that might arise. These challenges can occur in many different areas, including

- competition
  What will you do if your competition decides to cut its prices or offer improved service?
- sales
  How will you minimize the effect of lower-than-projected sales figures?
- management
  Where will you get key management personnel if someone leaves the team? What will happen to the business if something happens to you or the manager? What non-competition agreements are in place to prevent key personnel from joining your competitors?
- legal factors
  What legal protections such as patents, copyrights, or trademarks

are in place? What licences must be obtained and how often do you need to renew them? What laws or regulations do you need to know about?

- human resources
  How can you compensate for an inexperienced management team or for a lack of skilled employees? What human resources needs will the venture have in the future and how will you meet them? How will you compensate workers to encourage maximum efficiency and productivity?
- operational
  How will you cover any losses caused by shoplifting, liability to the public, or property damage?
- financial
  How will you compensate for capital shortages or customers who don't pay their bills?
- other areas of vulnerability
  How can you make sure your products won't become obsolete? What will you do if a foreign competitor offers a product like yours at a cheaper price? How will you deal with periods of low sales that result from cyclical changes or economic downturns? What **exit strategy** will you use if and when you decide to leave the venture?

These questions address only a few of the risks that entrepreneurs commonly have to face. The risks that threaten each venture depend on the nature of the venture itself. For example, if goods are stored in a warehouse, it might be prudent to purchase insurance to minimize possible losses from theft, fire, or water damage. If a business experiences seasonal highs and lows, losses could be offset by acquiring another product line with a different cycle. If a venture is starting out with an inexperienced management team, a professional consultant could be added to the team to compensate.

Understanding the risks associated with your venture and addressing them early can make the difference between success and failure. Consultants and specialists can help you find the answers to these types of questions.

STEP 5: MAKE A GO/NO-GO DECISION

By now, you have defined a target market and confirmed an opportunity for your venture. You have a good appreciation of the human, financial, material, and technical resources you will need, and you have decided on a financial strategy for startup and continued operation. You have a clear picture of the cost of production as well as the revenue that will be required for you to operate at a profit.

E-Bits & Bytes

Canadian small businesses are adopting e-commerce at an increasingly fast rate, according to a survey conducted by SES Canada Research, which surveyed 1000 small businesses. Although the number of businesses using the Internet is levelling off, the intensity of activity among those users continues to increase. The survey asked who has bought or sold over the Internet (yes or no). Here are the results:

	Spring 1999	Spring 2000
Yes	27%	41%
No	73%	59%

SES Research, Web Entrepreneurship Surveys

At this point in the planning process, you'll need to review your plans and decide whether to proceed with the venture or give it up. Your critical risks analysis should help you put things in perspective as you make your **go/no-go decision**. Making a "no-go" decision is not failure. Instead, it is an excellent decision based on the information that you gathered and discussed. By making this decision, you may have saved yourself untold agony, money, and precious time. All is not yet lost, you can always go back and review your venture plan and modify where necessary to make your concept work. You can always make use of your detailed research and study as reference for your new concepts.

Cool Stuff

OPENING A NEW BUSINESS? BE BIG, FAST, AND READY TO RELOCATE!

If you are starting a new business, Statistics Canada says that there is a one in four chance that your venture won't reach its first birthday. The best way to beat the odds is to start big—relative to the average for your industry.... Grow fast while getting those first crucial years of experience under your belt. Statistically, it also helps if you live in Ontario, Quebec, Alberta, or British Columbia.

Startup companies are important because they play a role in economic change by offering consumers innovative goods and services, often by developing new market niches.

Agents of Change

Loren Freid was watching a Blue Jays game in the '80s and wondered what they did with all of the unsold hotdogs when there were hungry people in Toronto. Inspired, Loren eventually founded the North York Harvest Food Bank to help feed needy families in Toronto. The food bank began as an emergency response to social problems spawned by the recession. Now it is an institution in Toronto. Loren runs one of the largest food drives in North America. Most of the recipients are children, single mothers, and the elderly.

Loren Freid has turned a social need into a successful community venture. What were some possible risks he might have considered as he planned this venture?

YOUR TURN

1. Review the material you prepared for the Venturing Out sections at the ends of Chapters 8, 9, and 10. Check for completeness and accuracy. Then review the list of possible subsections on page 262 to see what additional information might be needed.

2. List the strengths and weaknesses you see in each section of your personal venture plan. Then revise each section to emphasize its strengths and minimize its weaknesses. Rethink anything you feel may not have been adequately researched or prepared in sufficient detail.

3. Think through your particular venture and identify any possible risks. Discuss these risks with a small group and determine what you could do to eliminate or minimize each one. Then add a risk analysis to each section of your plan.

4. Create an executive summary for your plan. This summary should include a mission statement and it should answer the following questions:
   a) What are your objectives for your venture?
   b) What goods or services will you provide?
   c) What is unique about these goods or services?
   d) Where will the venture be located?
   e) When and for how long will it function?
   f) Who will be most involved in starting and managing the venture?

5. You should now have enough information to decide whether your venture will be a go or a no-go. Give reasons for your decision in either case and share them with the class.

Venture Profile

SENDING THANKS WITH ACME HUMBLE PIE

John Schreiner, National Post

If apologizing with a fresh apple pie strikes you as, well, flaky, it's just because you haven't met Jessica Chen, the effervescent "face" of Vancouver's Acme Humble Pie Co. "Our mission is to be known as the Canadian way of apologizing," she says.

It's a new company, set up in the summer of 2000 by a small group of investors who prefer to be silent. They put the execution of the idea into the expressive hands of Chen, 25, plucking her straight from the graduating class of the British Columbia Institute for Technology. "I wanted something that I could put my hands to and that affected people," she says.

Chen, a high-energy charmer with a silvery laugh, is marketing director of Acme Humble Pie Co. but she does just about everything at the company except bake the succulent 2 kg volcano-shaped pies made with tart Granny Smith apples (a professional baker does that).

Chen laughs that she "had caramel sauce all over me" after helping pack a large order recently in the big wooden gift cases used for delivery. The pies—there's a Merci Beaucoup as well as a Humble pie—cost $55 each, including the box and the reusable pie plate.

The idea behind Acme Humble Pie is that flowers or chocolates don't have the impact

CONTINUED➡

they used to. Vancouver City Savings Credit Union recently sent a pie to employees at each one of its 65 branches to thank them for fundraising. "We've done chocolates in the past and, well, it doesn't seem very special," says communications director Leslie Boldt. "We wanted to do something to catch people's attention."

How's this for impact? A woman was snubbed by a boyfriend, who said he never wanted a letter, a phone call, or an e-mail from her again. She sent a pie instead. "Their relationship is back on track," Chen says. An individual was so depressed after major surgery that she secluded herself for two months—until a friend sent a pie. "It's just so unexpected and unique," Chen says.

She tells of two lawyers who had a heated argument about rules during a round of golf. Later, one of them looked up the rules and saw that he was wrong; so he sent a Merci Beaucoup pie and thanked the other for the "information learned." "A neat thing about lawyers," Chen says, "is that they don't admit they're wrong."

It is early days yet in the business, but, totally confident in their idea, she and her partners are researching other food products that could be used to send a variety of high-impact messages.

Exploring

1. What market need prompted the launch of Acme Humble Pie Company?
2. What is the company's market niche?
3. Using information from the article and your imagination, create a point-form summary of what might have been in each section of the venture plan for this company.
4. Imagine that you have been hired to help the silent investors find financing to research other products and markets, and to expand the company's product line. Explain how you would change the venture plan you sketched out for Question 3 to fit this purpose.

Worth Repeating

"What kind of [person] would live where there is no daring? I don't believe in taking foolish chances but nothing can be accomplished without taking any chance at all."

Charles Lindbergh, first to fly solo across the Atlantic Ocean

STEP 6: PREPARE A DRAFT PLAN

By now, you have likely completed all the main sections of your venture plan. If you haven't already done so, this might be a good time to explore some of the different types of desktop publishing software you can use to incorporate these sections into a draft plan. Using this type of software will allow you to develop an effective layout, select an interesting print style, and introduce visuals such as graphs and diagrams.

Many software programs are available to make your plan look good. Select one that you feel comfortable using and that has the features you need to create an outstanding plan. Your venture plan should be logically organized, with large bold headings that make it easy for the reader to understand the purpose of each section. You will need to include a title page at the beginning of your plan, followed by a table of contents and a schedule for the development of your venture. Each of these pages presents important information that will help the reader make sense of your plan. You may also decide to include appendices at the end that contain details to support information in the plan.

TITLE PAGE

The **title page** is the page that greets the reader when the plan is first opened. The name of the venture should be instantly visible, set off in a way that makes it stand out. In smaller type, the page should list the names of the people proposing the venture, the date, a **copyright statement**, and a **disclaimer statement**.

The copyright statement is necessary to keep the information in your venture plan confidential. As an entrepreneur, you will want to prevent unauthorized copying or distributing of your plan. A disclaimer statement protects you from challenges to your credibility or questions about the accuracy of the data you used. Although you have done your best to check the information in your plan for accuracy, there may still be a few factual errors or inaccurate forecasts and projections. The copyright and disclaimer statements may be worded like this:

> No part of this venture plan may be reproduced or used in any form or by any means—graphic, electronic, or mechanical—without the prior written permission of the authors.

> While every effort has been taken to include accurate and up-to-date information, the authors recommend that members of the legal, financial, and business fields be consulted for professional advice before any action is taken.

TABLE OF CONTENTS

The **table of contents** helps the potential investor or financial officer find relevant sections of the plan quickly and easily. It also shows that the plan has been well organized. It should be neat, with the text carefully aligned, to indicate that a great deal of thought and effort has gone into the plan.

Every business plan is different and will need a customized table of contents. The major headings should be shown in larger type than

---

E-Bits & Bytes

Investigate three to five electronic templates designed to help people write venture plans. These are available from Industry Canada and financial organizations; they can sometimes be downloaded from the Internet. Compare and contrast the templates you find.

Worth Repeating

"The success of most things depends upon knowing how long it will take to succeed."

Baron de Montesquieu, French philosopher

the subheadings, so the reader can see at a glance how the plan is organized.

It's very important that the table of contents be complete and error free. Every section must be listed and the page numbers must be correct. For this reason, the table of contents will need to be added after the rest of the plan has been finalized.

The Overall Schedule

Effective venture plans include an overall schedule or timeline that shows when each major step in the development process will occur. Creating this schedule will help you finalize your plans for your venture and get them up and running. The timeline will not only help you stay on target and on time, but will also ensure that you are progressing toward your goal. Including the schedule in the business plan will help others see at a glance how you see your venture developing.

Appendices

The major sections of your venture plan should contain only summarized findings and highlights. If you tried to include every piece of information in the body of the plan, you would overwhelm your readers with too much information.

Support documents such as detailed research results, lists of resources you used in writing the document, and other related data can be included in appendices placed after the financial strategy. By moving these items to the end of the document, you can maintain the flow of information, while still including the necessary details. Label each appendix with a letter (Appendix A, Appendix B, etc.) and refer to the appendices wherever they apply in the main text. For example, a note on a page about marketing survey results might say "See Appendix A for detailed results."

Information to present in appendices might include

- marketing research forms
- survey results
- résumés of people on the management team
- photos of the product or drawings of proposed packages
- copies of purchase orders
- floor plans
- marketing and promotional materials
- details of the manufacturing process

Worth Repeating

"Business, more than any other occupation, is a continual dealing with the future; it is a continual calculation, an instinctive exercise in foresight."

Henry R. Luce, cofounder of Time Magazine

STEP 7: ASK FOR ADVICE

If there are others on your startup team, you likely invited their input as you were researching and drafting the plan. Now everyone involved in the venture should have an opportunity to review the plan and suggest revisions. A team effort is more likely to produce a plan that everyone can live with.

When you have finished drafting your venture plan, have it reviewed and critiqued. No matter how good you and your team are, you will probably have overlooked some issues or treated a particular aspect of your venture inadequately. Good reviewers can point out such deficiencies and offer an objective evaluation. They can act as a sounding board to help you develop alternative solutions to some of your venture's problems. They can also provide answers to some of the questions that investors might ask.

Circulate copies of your plan to classmates, teachers, advisers, possible investors, bankers, relatives, and business professionals. In some cases, you might want to take your plan to a lawyer to ensure that there are no misleading statements. One of the advantages of using word-processing software to prepare your venture plan is that it's easy to make changes.

As you make your revisions, carefully consider what investors might be looking for in your venture plan. They will be especially interested in how much profit they can expect to earn on their investment and when you will be able to repay them. They will likely want assurance that your financial projections are reasonable and based on careful marketing research studies, and will want to see that you have a clearly defined target market.

Think About It

Why is it important to keep revising your venture plan?

YOUR TURN

1. Contact a representative from the local chamber of commerce, a manager or loans officer from a bank, or someone else in your community who is familiar with venture plans. Invite this person, or a panel of experts, to speak to your class about the kind of information that should be included in a venture plan.

2. Review your venture plan and identify people who can help you verify the information in each section.

3. Use computer software to consolidate the writing you've done so far into a draft plan. Remember to include a title page, a table of contents, a schedule, and any necessary appendices.

4. Share your draft plan with other students or groups in your class. Ask them to help you check that your content appears under the appropriate headings, that you have included all the information necessary for a complete plan, and that you have presented your information in a logical manner. Write down any suggestions for improvement.

5. Show your draft plan to a knowledgeable person such as a bank manager or business leader, someone who operates a venture similar to yours, or someone who acts as a consultant to entrepreneurs starting up or expanding their ventures. (Many universities and community colleges offer student-run consulting services.) Invite advice about how to improve your venture plan. Don't forget to takes notes.

STEP 8: EDIT AND PROOFREAD YOUR PLAN

When your venture plan is finished and ready to be presented to a potential investor, banker, or adviser, you will want it to look professional and to represent as complete a picture of your proposed venture as possible.

Professionally prepared venture plans do not have to be long. In fact, they should be kept as short as possible without compromising the description of the venture and its potential. All key issues should be covered and every major step outlined. Only information that is unnecessary should be eliminated.

Ambiguous or unsupported statements should be avoided. They will only make you seem like a shallow or fuzzy thinker. An entrepreneur seeking additional funding to expand a particular venture, for example, should not claim in the venture plan that his or her markets are growing rapidly without providing concrete support for such a statement. Past, present, and future expectations of performance and market size should be identified.

Editing and rewriting take time and require careful attention to details. There are a number of excellent reference books available to help you use an effective style and correct language in your writing. It might also be useful to have someone proofread your plan to catch the things you've missed.

Worth Repeating

"The new organization is edgeless, permeable, amorphous ... constantly re-forming according to need."

The Virtual Corporation,
W.H. Davidow and M.S. Malone

PROOFREADING AND EDITING STEPS

1. Read for content.
   Does what you said make sense? Is it complete?
2. Read for style.
   Have you used an effective writing style?
   Have you avoided unnecessary repetition?
3. Read for language usage.
   Have you used jargon or too much technical language?
4. Read for spelling errors and grammar.
   Are there any typing or spelling errors?
   Is the writing grammatical?
   Have you used punctuation correctly?
   Have you double-checked everything that didn't sound quite right?
   Have you used available software tools to check spelling and grammar?

Worth Repeating

Bill Gates's Success Factors for Microsoft

1. Long-term approach
2. Passion for products and technology
3. Teamwork
4. Results
5. Customer feedback
6. Individual excellence

Note: 1 and 4, 2 and 5, 3 and 6 should work to balance each other.

STEP 9: POLISH YOUR PLAN

The first impression readers receive will often determine the frame of mind they'll adopt when reading through your venture plan. Be sure to print your final plan on good quality paper and present it in an attractive binder or folder that will open easily and lie flat for reading.

Your plan should be neither too fancy nor too plain. Leave plenty of white space on each page so that it is easy to read, attractive to look at, and convenient for the reader to make comments and references. If you want a potential investor or adviser to take your plan home, it will have to fit into a regular-sized file folder and briefcase.

Your pages should be numbered and should be printed in black ink on the front of each page. (One-sided printing makes the pages look neater and leaves room for comments on the backs of the pages.) Reserve colour for highlighting graphs, charts, and illustrations. Label and/or number each graphic, and remember to indicate sources for your data.

Spreadsheets and cash-flow projections that have a number of columns might be difficult to present. Sometimes large forms can be reduced to regular size through photocopying so that they will fit into the printed plan. If this is not possible, spread them out over a double page and fold to size.

> *The first impression readers receive will often determine the frame of mind they'll adopt when reading through your venture plan.*

> **Worth Repeating**
>
> "It's a very funny thing about life; if you refuse to accept anything but the best, you very often get it."
>
> W. Somerset Maugham, British author

Even though you have carefully edited your plan, you will need to give it one final check before you place it in the folder. Make sure that

- the pages are numbered and in sequence
- the table of contents is accurate and complete
- the graphics have been numbered in sequence and the sources are cited
- the appendices have been numbered in sequence and cited in the right places in the main text
- your work has been checked for grammar, punctuation, and spelling

Your venture plan is the most important tool that you have at your disposal in your quest to achieve your goals. An effective plan will show people who can help you that you have thought through your proposed venture carefully and considered every aspect, including possible situations that could place your venture at risk. A strong, organized, well-written plan will help you as you move forward on your journey toward success.

LETTER OF TRANSMITTAL

The **letter of transmittal** accompanies your plan when it is sent to a potential investor. Two or three paragraphs are usually enough. The first paragraph should introduce your proposed plan and briefly describe one or two of its unique features. The second paragraph should outline why your reader should be interested in your proposal. The third paragraph should explain what you want your reader to do about your proposal. Letters of transmittal are most effective when they are simple, short, and honest.

> **E-Bits & Bytes**
>
> Compare your personal venture plan with plans other people have written. For more options, visit www.business.nelson.com and follow the links to "venture plans." What ideas can you find for ways to improve your plan?

YOUR TURN

1. Exchange venture plans with a classmate. Proofread and edit each other's work using the steps outlined on page 273.

2. Meet with a small group to compare and contrast several venture plans you found on the Internet. (See E-Bits and Bytes activity above.) What do you find attractive about each one? What impressions about the venture does each one create?

3. Prepare a draft letter of transmittal for your venture plan. Share this draft with a classmate and discuss how it might be improved. Then, write a final draft.

Venture Profile

SECURITY SOLUTIONS: AN ENTREPRENEUR WITHOUT A BUSINESS PLAN

Ben Kayfetz has been entrepreneurial since his preteen years. At age 12, Ben bought a supply of large plastic Coke cups for 10¢ each and took a booth at the Thunderbird Flea Market in Fort Lauderdale, where his family had a vacation home. Ben sold the cups for $1 each, earning a tidy 900% profit. As Ben grew older, his fascination with computers led him into his second business venture—Ami Support Computers. At age 17, Ben was selling computers to family and friends from his home. After taking a course in computer technology, Ben was ready to venture out on his own. He sold computers for a year and then realized that some business education would be helpful, so he enrolled in the Scarborough Student Venture program.

With a Royal Bank Student Venture loan of $3500, Ben started Security Solutions of Canada Inc. Recognizing that there was a high demand for theft prevention at computer labs in schools and libraries, he devised a way to secure the CD-ROMs in school library computer labs. Then, he expanded into other product lines as his school lab business grew. Ben ultimately moved his business out of his home into an office and warehouse and has hired an office manager. Ben still does much of his business on the phone, but he's already planning ways to use his Web site to expand his business through e-commerce.

When Ben started Security Solutions of Canada Inc., he didn't have the time to create an initial venture plan because he was so busy meeting the demand for his product. His financing came from a student venture loan, so there was no need to market his ideas to investors.

Ben Kayfetz (left) at a business convention

Now that Security Solutions is planning to expand into other types of systems, such as alarm systems and wireless tracking systems for business computers, Ben knows that he will need a written plan. His advice to other hopeful entrepreneurs is "Keep focused and have a business growth plan."

Exploring

1. What kinds of entrepreneurial experience has Ben had?
2. Why didn't Ben need a venture plan when he started Security Solutions?
3. Why does he need to have one now?
4. Why does Ben advise other entrepreneurs to have a business growth plan?
5. What changes in the future might make it necessary for Ben to update his business plan?

ACTIVITIES

FLASHBACKS

Meet with a partner to discuss what you learned from writing your personal venture plan. Which sources of information did you find most helpful? How did your vision of your venture change as your plan developed?

- There are nine steps in the venture planning process. These steps may be repeated again and again as the venture develops and grows.
- A venture plan should include a title page (with copyright and disclaimer statements), a table of contents, an overall schedule, an executive summary, a market analysis, a resource analysis, an operating strategy, a financial strategy, and any appendices necessary to support the data.
- Each major section of the plan can be divided into subsections that reflect the nature of the venture.
- An analysis of critical risks can help you make a go/no-go decision about the venture. It will also help you make contingency plans about what to do if a problem occurs.
- It's important to research your plan thoroughly before you begin to write.
- Make sure to allow enough time to complete each section properly.
- When you have finished drafting your venture plan, have it reviewed and critiqued by classmates, teachers, mentors, and professional advisers.
- Edit, proofread, and format your venture plan to make it look as professional as possible. Make sure it clearly addresses the concerns of the people for whom it is written.
- Include a letter of transmittal to introduce your plan to people who can help you and to briefly describe the unique features of your venture.

LESSONS LEARNED

1. List five reasons for preparing a venture plan.
2. Identify the nine steps in the venture planning process. Which of these steps do you think is the most important? Why?
3. Tell a partner how you divided your personal venture plan into sections and subsections. Explain why you chose this particular structure.

4. Why is it important to assess the critical risks for your venture?

5. What can the table of contents indicate about a venture plan?

6. What is the purpose of a disclaimer statement? What could happen if the disclaimer statement were left out?

7. Why is it important to edit and proofread your plan?

8. What did you do to make your venture plan easy to read? attractive?

9. Why is it important to include a letter of transmittal?

10. What do you like best about your venture plan? Give reasons for your choice(s).

E-Bits & Bytes

Visit www.business.nelson.com and follow the links to "business planning" to compare the types of planning assistance some of the sites like Industry Canada and Canadian Youth Business Foundation offer to entrepreneurs.

VENTURING OUT

1. Describe the characteristics of an exemplary venture plan.

2. Review the notes you took for Your Turn Questions 4 and 5 on page 272. Summarize the types of responses you got when you asked others for advice about your plan.

3. Identify some public and private sources of information that helped you as you developed your plan.

4. If you have not already done so, create a final version of your venture plan. Be sure to follow the proofreading and editing steps outlined earlier and to incorporate any suggestions you received from others.

5. Present your venture plan to a small group of classmates who are playing the part of investors. The "investors" can listen to your presentation, read the plan in detail, and then meet to tell you how they would likely respond and why.

POINT OF VIEW

Did you make a "go" or a "no-go" decision about your venture? Explain the reasons for your choice.
   a) If you made a "go" decision, describe what your next step will be and when you plan to take it.
   b) If you made a "no-go" decision, describe what your next step will be.

CHAPTER 12

Venturing as a Way of Life

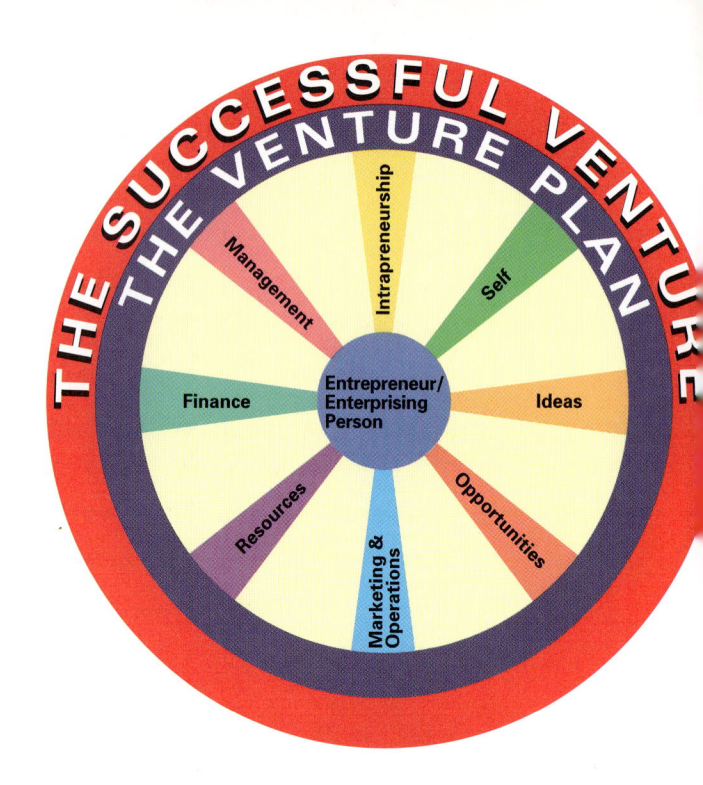

LEARNING OPPORTUNITIES

By the end of this chapter, you should be able to
- explain why some ventures succeed and others fail
- describe the tasks that need to be completed in each stage of the venture life cycle
- compare the advantages and disadvantages of pursuing continuous growth as a goal for a business venture
- describe effective growth strategies used by entrepreneurs
- explore the relationship between ethics and the law
- examine the values that guide decision making in business and in people's personal lives

Entrepreneurial Language

- demise
- undercapitalization
- inventive task
- innovative task
- entrepreneurial task
- managerial task
- administrative task
- bootleg
- management buyout
- code of ethics

With a partner, choose any three words from this list to look up in a dictionary. On each dictionary page, find at least one other word that relates to the entrepreneurial process. Record the words you found and explain your reasoning.

Venture Profile

SERIAL ENTREPRENEURS LEARN FROM THEIR PAST

Susan Strother Clarke, The Toronto Star

It wasn't the long hours, cleaning his own bathrooms, or even eating cold pizza every evening that made entrepreneur Karl Seiler feel lousy. Rather, it was when he had to dismiss 22 employees after an early software venture hit a rough patch.

"We had gone down a path with some of our product lines and the marketplace shifted," Seiler said, adding that firing people was "awful."

Even successful business owners like Seiler make mistakes. He is what is known as a serial entrepreneur—one of thousands who begin businesses, sell them, and start anew.

But business junkies don't always have the magic touch. Repeaters make mistakes just like ordinary operators who start a business and hang onto it for a lifetime.

Research from the University of Georgia suggests the probability of succeeding at entrepreneurship increases with each attempt at starting a business. Ten business failures, in fact, all but guarantee a successful eleventh attempt, according to the data.

Nothing breeds smarts like screwing up. Someone on the tail end of a failed business is likely to know next time about the importance of delivering a product on time, or the trouble with starting out with too little capital. The repeaters learn from their mistakes.

Seiler began Level Five, his first business, in his grandmother's garage apartment in 1984. He started selling software packages for U.S. $95, but within three years was making products that fetched up to U.S. $300 000.

While the company did well overall, Seiler made a miscalculation early on, producing a type of mainframe software that lost favour. The result: Employees lost their jobs.

But his experience taught him to keep an ear to the market and anticipate changes. And that has helped in his fourth venture, Affinity Logic. The company produces software that helps businesses create personal Web pages for their customers.

Exploring

1. What does the author mean when she says, "Ten business failures, in fact, all but guarantee a successful eleventh attempt"?
2. How might this information help entrepreneurs in the startup phase of their first venture? a subsequent venture?
3. If you were one of the employees Karl Seiler had to fire from his first venture, would you be willing to work for him again on a subsequent venture? Why or why not?
4. Describe a time when you learned from
   a) a mistake you made
   b) a mistake someone else made

Starting Up

Review your personal venture plan. What steps have you taken to reduce the risk that your venture might fail? If you do achieve success, how will you help your venture grow?

Worth Repeating

"Trying, even though you fail, breeds learning; wishing you had tried only breeds discontent."

Anonymous

Why Some Ventures Fail

According to statistics compiled by various government offices across Canada, between 70% and 80% of all business startups do not reach their fifth anniversary. Does this mean that all these businesses failed?

Some businesses disappear from government records because they have grown in size and taken advantage of their success by changing their name or moving to another location. Other businesses are designed for a short-term existence and are shut down at the end of this time so their owners can move on to something new. For example, an entrepreneur who puts a product on the market to catch a fad usually plans to stay in business only until the demand for the product wanes. These businesses have not failed. They have accomplished their goals, reached their objectives, and then closed down.

Studies of real business failures show that the overwhelming reasons for failure are poor management, lack of experience, and insecurity. In the case of Level Five, Karl Seiler made a miscalculation by developing a product for the wrong market. The company had to lay off 22 workers when sales did not go as planned and revenue was not sufficient to meet payroll costs.

In some failed business ventures, an entrepreneur's fear of failure can become a self-fulfilling prophecy. Entrepreneurs who let their inexperience or feelings of insecurity affect their business decisions sometimes make mistakes that will lead to the ultimate failure of the venture.

RECOGNIZING THE WARNING SIGNALS

Very few ventures will fail without showing some warning signs long before their actual **demise**. Some entrepreneurs ignore or fail to look for these signals. Even if they do see the signals, entrepreneurs don't always recognize their significance or realize that they pose a threat to the venture. An awareness of some common causes of failure can help entrepreneurs be more alert, so they can identify and fix what's going wrong before it's too late.

To anticipate possible problems, entrepreneurs need to monitor and recognize changes not only in their own ventures, but also in their industry or in the overall economy. Their goal should be to anticipate problems that might occur and to plan to avoid or at least minimize the risk of failure.

Recognizing early warning signals can help an entrepreneur

- identify small problems before they become big ones
- find out which products or services are profitable and which are not
- identify the best ways to cut costs or reallocate resources
- apply new ideas
- see the venture from different perspectives

RAPID GROWTH

Success brings its own kinds of problems. In some cases, the growing business may be so demanding that the entrepreneur has no time left for the important tasks of keeping accurate and up-to-date records, monitoring supplies or inventory, dealing with customer concerns, or pursuing customers who haven't paid their bills. When any of these tasks are left undone, the result can be an interrupted cash flow and the ultimate failure of the business. Companies that are growing very quickly need to ensure that they can maintain accurate and up-to-date information in order to make sound business and growth-related decisions.

RECORDS MANAGEMENT

Financial records are the internal yardsticks entrepreneurs can use to see how the venture's current status compares with its past performance. Today, these records can be compiled efficiently and effectively using automated systems.

Entrepreneurs need to check these records at regular intervals to look for warning signals that might predict trouble ahead. For example, examining a summary of the venture's accounts receivable (the money owed to the venture as a result of sales) could reveal that customers are taking longer on average to pay their bills than they did six months ago. This could be the result of a downturn in the economy or dissatisfaction with the product, or there may be internal reasons for this change, such as changes to collection procedures or terms of payment. Whatever the cause, a wise entrepreneur will stay well informed about the current status of the venture.

UNDERCAPITALIZATION

Entrepreneurs are often able to raise enough money to start a venture but not to keep it operating in the long term. This is referred to as **undercapitalization**.

When the venture is in the manufacturing or service industry, extra capital is needed to operate the business because cash flow may take some time to materialize. Without enough capital to cover the costs of inventory, production, and other operating expenses, the venture could go bankrupt even if it is experiencing healthy sales.

> **Worth Repeating**
>
> "There is a difference between noise and signal. You need to pay attention to the signal amid all the noise."
>
> *Anonymous*

> **Worth Repeating**
>
> "I am no longer what I was. I will remain what I have become."
>
> *Coco Chanel, fashion designer*

When the venture is not-for-profit, its income often depends on contributions or government grants. For the venture to continue to operate and pay its expenses after startup, it will require enough capital to cover employee costs, space and utility charges, and any operating costs or promotional expenses incurred until a regular flow of income is established.

▍INSUFFICIENT PROFIT MARGINS

Some entrepreneurs underprice their products or services in a misguided effort to increase sales. If revenues do not cover expenses, then the venture will fail. It's important to remember that prices will decrease naturally over the life cycle of a product, so initial profit margins need to be high enough that expenses can still be met when the prices are reduced.

▍FINANCIAL MISMANAGEMENT

Enthusiastic entrepreneurs who jump into a venture with unrealistic sales expectations will find themselves in the potential failure group, as will entrepreneurs who underestimate the costs that must be covered before the business can break even. The break-even point must be considerably less than the potential volume of sales if the business is to remain profitable and functioning. Keeping as many costs as possible dependent on sales achieved is a safer approach because the break-even point can be kept low. For example, if you pay salespeople with commissions rather than salary, your staff costs will decrease if sales go down.

▍POOR EMPLOYER–EMPLOYEE RELATIONSHIPS

Entrepreneurs who do not keep their employees involved in the progress of the company, committed to its goals, and satisfied with their rewards will find that employee–management problems take up a great deal of time and energy and ultimately affect the success of the business. Some entrepreneurs empower their employees to make their own decisions about customer issues. Such an approach helps employees feel that they are contributing to the company and leads to increased pride in their work and loyalty to their employers.

Measuring staff turnover and absenteeism is a concrete way of determining employee satisfaction. Many successful ventures have a policy of conducting "exit interviews" with employees who leave, in order to understand their reasons for leaving the job and to take advantage of their perspective on how the business operates and where it could improve.

Worth Repeating

"Being defeated is often a temporary condition. Giving up is what makes it permanent."

Marilyn vos Savant, American columnist and writer

CHANGING TECHNOLOGY

Entrepreneurs need to keep informed about technological changes in order to stay competitive. For example, when it first became possible for people to use debit cards to pay for their purchases in stores, the technology spread very quickly. Entrepreneurs recognized that this payment option provided greater convenience for customers and also encouraged people to make impulse purchases, since they no longer needed to limit their spending to the amount of cash they had on hand. A business that was unaware of this change, or slower to adopt the new technology, might have lost profits as a result.

OUTSIDE FACTORS

Sometimes a business fails because of outside factors. For example, there may be a downturn in the economy that causes sales to drop off or the government may change a policy that regulates the import or export of a certain product. Although these factors can't be controlled, they can be anticipated and planned for.

An entrepreneur's first defence against external challenges is information. Reading a daily newspaper and keeping up to date about events that affect the business world is an important way to stay informed about forces that may affect your venture. Membership in a trade organization or chamber of commerce is also a good way to stay informed.

Once potential threats are identified, it's important to plan for "just-in-case" scenarios. For example, if an economic downturn occurs, it may help to scale down production or to reduce staff in order to keep costs down. If a change in government policy will affect your business, then it might be wise to diversify into other product lines or distribution procedures that won't be affected by the change.

PERSONAL STRESS

No one has ever claimed that starting and operating a new business venture is easy. Regardless of how consuming the venture is, the entrepreneur must remember that every life needs a balance between work and time spent with family or friends.

There are many potential sources of physical and emotional stress in an entrepreneur's busy life, including strained personal relationships and financial difficulties. The entrepreneur must recognize that decisions made under stress are frequently bad decisions, so anything that reduces the entrepreneur's personal stress level—even something as simple as taking a night off to see a movie—is probably also good for the business.

Worth Repeating

"There are two ways of meeting difficulties. You alter the difficulties, or you alter yourself to meet them."

Phyllis Bottome, British novelist

YOUR TURN

1. With a small group, use the experiences of students who have been employed in part-time or summer jobs to prepare a list of good and bad policies for customer and employee relations.

2. Find case studies of business failures. Prepare a list of the reasons for each failure. Classify the reasons according to the categories outlined in the previous section.

3. Describe steps an entrepreneur could take during the startup phase of a business that would help to avert the types of difficulties outlined in the previous section.

Venture Profile

YOONTOWN

CBC's Venture

You've heard that people who live in glass houses shouldn't throw stones. But what about people who try to build them? Sebastian Yoon runs a high-end glass art studio in Calgary, Alberta. At 29, he's successful, by gallery standards, and hungry to grow. His dream is to build a combined restaurant, glass blowing studio, and gallery. To build it, he purchases a former nightclub on Calgary's once notorious Electric Avenue, an area better known for drunken brawls and all-night parties than for fine art. What's at risk?

"Financially, everything I have," says Yoon. The Electric Avenue strip has fallen on hard times, enabling Yoon to purchase the abandoned bar for relatively little, just over half a million dollars. He gets the money from a wealthy relative, an eight-month interest-free loan that must be repaid on time, no matter what. Sebastian has eight months to build his dream.

His projected budget is $1 million, half to repay the loan on the building and half to develop his project. The problem? He's about $1 million short of his goal. His first stop is the major banks, where he's dealt a bitter lesson in "there's the door" financing. "I went to every bank and they said 'no.' They said, 'What do you do, glass art? That could break, couldn't it?'"

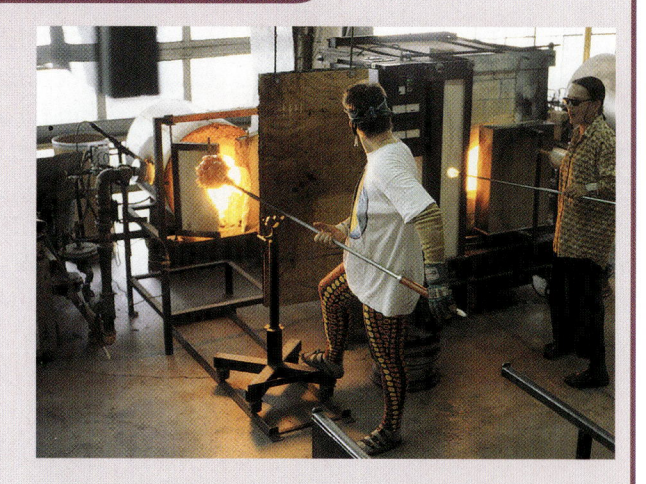

Next stop, individual investors. With the help of accountant Doug Porter, Yoon draws up a detailed business plan, and sets out to sell shares at $10 000 each.

After some initial success, he runs into problems closing deals. Many investors promise financial help, but, in the end, fail to come up with the cash.

Disappointed, he tries one more time to arrange a loan from a bank, and finds a sympathetic bank manager at Canada Trust willing to hear his story. He brings along Doug

CONTINUED →

Porter for support. Porter knows this is a long shot.

"You're probably dealing with traditionally the two most risky businesses, restaurant and retail.... From a risk profile, I think Sebastian's almost off the chart on the risky side," says Porter.

The Canada Trust loan officer likes Yoon's idea, but grows concerned when he can't provide adequate collateral to insure a loan. If Sebastian could put his clear title in the abandoned bar up against the loan, it would be sufficient. But he has promised his wealthy relative he won't do that. That leaves only his investors' equity.

"Maybe we can use not only their equity investment but their personal backing on the line of credit. That would open a lot of doors," says the loan officer.

For Sebastian, it means the deal just got tougher. Now he needs investors willing to put their own collateral on the line, if he wants help from the bank. As the deadline grows closer for repaying the loan, Sebastian begins to despair.

Despite his best efforts, he simply isn't able to convince investors to invest in his dream. Finally, with just weeks to go before the repayment date, his luck changes.

A surprise offer comes in to purchase the building. It means giving up on his dream, but it's just too good to turn down. All the while Sebastian has been struggling, the building has been gaining in value. He sells it for a profit of almost $300 000.

Sebastian still plans to build a glass blowing studio (without a restaurant) in a nice, cheap, out-of-the-way warehouse space. What did he learn? "Don't bank on goodwill."

Exploring

1. Why was Sebastian's dream venture viewed as such a high risk by potential investors?
2. How could Sebastian have eased their concerns?
3. If Sebastian had approached you as a potential investor, and you had $500 000 to invest, would you have invested it in Sebastian's venture? Why or why not?
4. Has Sebastian prepared adequately to invest his $300 000 in "a glass blowing studio in an out-of-the-way warehouse space"? Give reasons for your answer.

Worth Repeating

"If you are not failing every now and again, it's a sign you are not doing anything very innovative."

Woody Allen, American film director and actor

MINIMIZING RISKS

When an investor puts money into a business, he or she wants to know how safe the investment will be—or, in other words, how much risk is involved. For example, because Sebastian has to repay the $500 000 he used to buy the building at the end of eight months, investors might fear that there will not be enough cash flow during the startup stage of the business to buy supplies or pay staff, and that the business might fail as a result. This risk could have been averted if Sebastian had chosen a less expensive location for his business, or financed the purchase of the building in a different way, and investors might have been more willing to participate.

In order to minimize risks, the entrepreneur needs to do a critical risks analysis during the planning stages for the venture and implement risk reducing strategies as the business develops.

Agents of Change

Hugh Le Caine not only built the world's first voltage controlled music synthesizer (1945), touch-sensitive keyboard, and variable speed multi-track tape recorder, he also composed unique works that helped to popularize electronic music. "Dripsody," a composition produced through the electronic manipulation of the sound of a single drop of water, is considered to be a classic of the genre and the most-played example of this type of electronic music.

Suppose you had an idea for producing and selling a new musical instrument. If you needed support from investors to finance your idea, what concerns might they have? What could you do to reduce their perceived level of risk?

The Importance of Development Tasks

In Chapter 7, you learned about the stages in the life cycle of a business. As a venture develops from the prestartup stage through the comfort stage, five different development tasks come into focus. In the prestartup stage, the focus is on invention and innovation. The **inventive task** involves the creation of a new device or process as previously unrelated elements are joined in a new way. The **innovative task** takes a familiar idea and adds a new twist. These tasks require both creative and practical thinking. Creative thinkers can come up with lots of ideas, but it takes a practical thinker to match a new idea with a market need. A great many inventions and innovations never make it past a file in the Patent Office because no one has been able to find practical uses for them.

The **entrepreneurial task** begins in the prestartup phase and continues through the development phase. For this task, the entrepreneur must organize previously unrelated resources to build a venture that can produce and market a good or service to satisfy a need. The entrepreneurial task requires critical thinking and evaluation, because the entrepreneur must decide which creative ideas and innovations will satisfy needs that exist in the market, and must recruit the resources that will make the venture a success.

Once the business is launched, the **managerial task** begins. The manager directs operation of the venture by identifying day-to-day operating goals and any strategies needed to reach these goals. Hand-in-hand with the managerial task is the **administrative task**, which involves executing or carrying out strategies identified by management in an efficient and effective way.

The managerial and administrative tasks require someone who can plan and coordinate the day-to-day operation of a venture. These skills can be learned, just as entrepreneurial skills can be learned, but nobody is ideally suited to every job. A wise entrepreneur must recognize the point when his or her personal skills and energies are no longer what the venture needs most, and step aside to let someone with different skills take the organization to its next stage.

Cool Stuff

INVENTIONS EVOLVE THROUGH INNOVATION

Many of the objects we use every day have evolved through a series of innovations that would astonish the original inventor.

Do some research about the evolution of timepieces throughout history. How did each new innovation reflect the needs and resources of the people who created it?

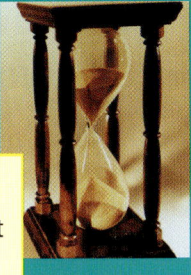

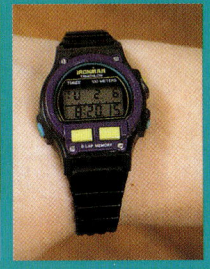

Agents of Change

Mary Pickford, a Canadian actress, is considered to be the world's first movie star. She made many films and won an Academy Award for her role as a small-town southern woman in *Coquette*, her first "talkie" film.

The introduction of "talkies" in the 1920s profoundly changed the film industry. Some jobs were lost while others were created. Actors and actresses had to develop new skills and the production process became more complex and expensive as sound technicians, musicians, voice coaches, and choreographers were added to production teams. Unlike many of her peers, Mary Pickford benefited from the transition to sound and went on to become one of the richest women in history.

Each major technological advance in the film industry leads to a repeat of the cycle of development tasks (inventive, innovative, etc.). List some advances in the film industry and describe how the industry was changed by each one. Where in the developmental cycle is the Canadian film industry today? Give evidence for your answer.

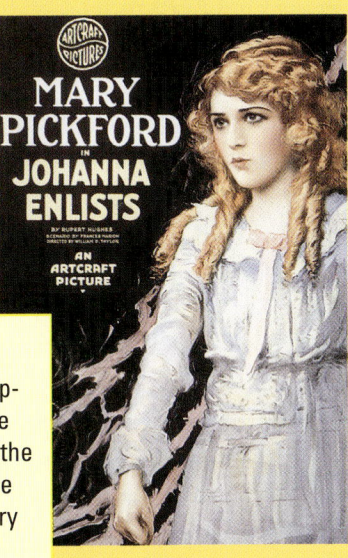

YOUR TURN

1. Make a chart with three columns. In the first column, list the five development tasks. In the second, list the De Bono Thinking Hat(s) the entrepreneur would use to perform each task. Complete the chart by explaining, in the third column, how the entrepreneur would use each hat.

2. Compare the chart you made for Question 1 with another student's. Discuss the similarities and differences you notice.

3. Review the self-assessment you completed in Chapter 3. Which of the five development tasks would be easiest for you to accomplish? How would you manage the remaining tasks?

Venture Profile

"LIKE MAMA USED TO MAKE"

Paul Delean, The Gazette

When the banquet hall that was supposed to host a surprise 25th anniversary party for Robert Dorazio's brother and sister-in-law burned to the ground the night before, Dorazio knew whom to call—Ada Gallo.

With just a few hours' notice, Gallo put together a selection of Italian foods that proved a huge hit with the 75 guests who ended up fêting the couple in a private home. Dorazio has been a fan of Gallo's food since he started visiting the Montreal-based bakery/restaurant/catering business, Boulangerie Pizza Motta, decades ago with his mother. "My mom brought me here for bread and I never stopped coming. This is a tradition—food like mama used to make."

For Gallo, it is a source of great pride. She doesn't do the cooking herself, but she's a stickler for taste, quality, and presentation, as she has been since she opened the business in 1975.

"I'm a perfectionist. I will have a recipe tested and retested before we sell it. I can spend a whole day getting across what I want. And I make a point of asking the customers what they think. The food has to taste good and look appetizing."

The idea for the business first came to her during a visit to her old neighbourhood, when she caught sight of a vacant shop. Suddenly, dreams of self-employment started to take shape.

"I had an aunt who used to come up from Boston around Labour Day every year and bring these big loaves of bread—we call them pagnottas—and as a kid, I joked with her that one day I'd open a bakery and make them here."

That's what she envisioned when she saw the shop for rent, and it's what she ended up doing, in partnership with her brother Claudio. She was 22.

She named the bakery after the Italian city where her husband was born. It opened, without fanfare, four days before Christmas, selling pizza, bread, and pastries. "The first day we had $371 in sales. Now, on a good day, we'll gross about $6000."

Over the years, the product line has expanded to include salads, pâtés, and sauces. The family eventually acquired the building, which has been renovated again and again. A wholesale division was started, but was abandoned after the last recession dealt the business a severe blow and left Gallo pondering a career change.

"A lot of restaurants went bankrupt and we had a hard time getting paid."

In the end, Gallo bought out her brother and set about repositioning the business. She closed the wholesale division, added a small bistro area and patio, and began placing a greater emphasis on catering.

After 26 years, Motta remains a passion for Gallo, who has changes in mind to keep the business growing in its next quarter-

CONTINUED →

century. She plans to dress up the restaurant and emphasize family-size orders on the take-out side.

"My philosophy has always been 'Whatever you choose to do in life, don't be wishy-washy. Commit to it and do it right.' "

Exploring

1. The stages in the life cycle of a business are outlined on pages 145 to 147 in Chapter 7.
   a) Draw a timeline to show some of the events that occurred as Pizza Motta developed through each stage.
   b) Tell which stage you think Motta is currently in and give reasons for your choice.
2. Review the timeline you made for Question 1. Explain how each of the five development tasks helped shape the growth of Motta.
3. If Gallo had anticipated the recession, how could she have protected Motta from the problems that occurred when her restaurant customers went bankrupt?
4. With a partner, brainstorm ways for Gallo to grow and expand her business over the next quarter-century.

Venture Profile

FRESHLIMESODA

Sarah Elton, The Toronto Star

When India's earthquake ripped through the northwestern province of Gujarat in January 2001, the Indian Web site freshlimesoda.com was awash with messages within minutes of the initial tremor. Parmesh Shahani, the site's founder and CEO, was on his way to work in Mumbai some 500 km away from the epicentre when the earthquake struck. By the time he arrived at his office, users of the Web site were already exchanging their experiences. For the rest of the day, news of the calamity kept trickling in. The site was an outlet that brought people from across the country together.

This is exactly what Shahani, 24, was hoping for when he started freshlimesoda.com, a Web zine for young English-speaking Indians. His goal was to create an online community for Indian youth. But in less than two years, the site has done more than bring together young people in his country. Today, it also acts as a headquarters for young South Asians around the world who are interested in everything from pop culture to Victorian literature to global politics. The site regularly gets thousands of hits from Canada, ranking Canadians the eighth most frequent visitors after those from India and countries like the United States, Great Britain, and Saudi Arabia. But it is not just Canadians of South Asian descent who like freshlimesoda.com. According to Shahani, people from all backgrounds are attracted to the site—something he hoped for when he first

CONTINUED→

thought up the Web zine. "We can share both the commonalities and differences of growing up in different parts of the world," he says.

And people come in droves. When the site first went up, they got 1000 page views a month. Today, they get close to half a million. The average visitor is between 13 and 25 years old and, from what staff can tell, equal numbers of guys and girls visit.

When you log on to the site, what strikes you first is green. Lime green. What is even more striking is the content. The site showcases the creative energy of computer-connected young people around the world. It is divided into various sections, including features, art, fiction, and reviews. There are witty columns, artwork, and all forms of creative writing. The site invites everyone to participate and submit any form of creative expression they've produced.

What really makes the site stand out is that it doesn't talk down to users. On the message board, participants tackle a range of meaty issues, including interfaith marriages and the literary merit of *Harry Potter*. Shahani started the site (in August 1999) on the premise that young people are intelligent and have something to say. As a young person working in the media, he realizes that people often assume his peers only care about pop culture icons like Britney Spears. Shahani wants to show that American cultural exports aren't the only entertainment option. He wants young people to know it's okay to read books and love poetry too.

Recently, Shahani agreed to sell part of the Web zine to one of the largest television companies in India, Sony Entertainment. While the site is run out of a converted boardroom at Sony headquarters in a city suburb, Shahani's vision for the site is truly international. "I'm aiming for global youth with an Indian flavour," he says. Shahani doesn't think Sony Entertainment's involvement will compromise his vision for the site. He says that the company is very hands-off and lets the creative team go to work. In addition, the site has recently started hosting advertising. "This isn't rocket science. We haven't invented something new. But we put something up and people found it and liked it."

Exploring

1. What was Parmesh Shahani's goal for freshlimesoda.com when the Web zine was first founded? How did this goal change over time?
2. Describe two ways in which Shahani has helped his business grow.
3. Why might Shahani have decided to sell part of his business to Sony Entertainment?
4. Why might Sony Entertainment have been interested in acquiring part ownership of freshlimesoda.com?

Think About It

What are some of the advantages and disadvantages a venture might experience if it pursues continuous growth throughout its life cycle?

Growing a Venture

Each of the five development tasks requires different abilities and strengths—a combination of characteristics rarely found in a single individual. The inventive, innovative, and entrepreneurial tasks will get a venture up and running, and carry it through the prestartup and development stages. They will also help the venture navigate the difficult turnaround stage, when it must either reinvent itself or face failure.

During the growth stage, however, it's the managerial and administrative tasks that become dominant. Understanding a venture's growth potential is a challenging task, especially for those entrepreneurs who have little interest in, or aptitude for, managing or administering a venture once it's past the startup phase. Many promising ventures have failed to grow because the entrepreneur could not, or would not, perform the managerial task. At the very least, entrepreneurs need to learn how to delegate tasks and authority.

Growth doesn't happen on its own. It needs to be carefully planned and nurtured. The manager of a growing venture needs to understand where the venture is in its life cycle and what its options are for development. The first step in planning a growth strategy is an analysis of the existing venture. What is its production capacity? What are the strengths of the management team? What is the venture's financial capacity? Where is it positioned in the market?

Once the management understands a venture's current position, the next step is to identify goals for growth and strategies for reaching those goals. For example, the company might decide to create new products, change its pricing structure, or explore new ways to distribute its existing products. At this point, the need for innovation and invention resurfaces.

When Apple Computer, Inc. wanted to create a powerful new computer that would be more user-friendly than existing models, Steven Jobs, the cofounder of the organization, created a separate and independent division within the company to attract and mobilize creative people. This investment in research and development paid off when the new division produced the Macintosh computer. Nortel Networks, a Canadian firm that is a world leader in the communication industry, is another example of a venture that pursues growth by continually searching for ways to accommodate individuals who are inventors, innovators, and intrapreneurs within its business environment.

During the growth stage, there is also a role for the entrepreneurial task. The huge 3M Company, known worldwide for its innovative attitudes, encourages its employees to **bootleg** a certain amount of their time and resources from current production tasks and devote them to the development of new products. This idea has been so successful that 25% of the company's sales in any given year come from products that did not even exist five years previously. Other large companies rely on smaller entrepreneurial firms to produce new ideas and technology. The larger firms then purchase the new technology or, in some cases, the firms that developed it, in order to acquire what they need.

The two keys to successful growth are the identification of new needs and the development of innovations designed to meet these needs. Sometimes this can be achieved by a venture working on its own. At other times, new business units are created as ventures expand, merge, acquire other ventures, or forge partnerships through strategic alliances. The growth strategy depends on the desired result. If a company wants to diversify its products or services, a merger or acquisition is often the quickest way. If the company wants to break into new territories, selling franchises or forming a strategic alliance may be an efficient answer.

> **Worth Repeating**
>
> "There is a way to look at the past. Don't hide from it. It will not catch you if you don't repeat it."
>
> Pearl Bailey, American singer and performer

Once the goals for growth are set, the final step is the development of a financial strategy that will help the company find the money it needs to pursue its objectives. The owner(s) of the venture may need to sell some of their assets or they may decide to identify private sources of funding. They may need to work closely with a bank or alternative financial source. Since the business is seeking further capitalization, it will be necessary to create a new venture plan for the growth phase.

Planning for growth requires a good understanding and a careful analysis of the venture's strengths and weaknesses.

Experienced entrepreneurs recognize that planning for growth will help a venture remain healthy and competitive, even during the comfort stage, when the business seems to be doing well. Complacency is dangerous and turnarounds can occur when they are least expected. By continuing to set and pursue goals, the management of the venture can ensure that the organization will have the strength and resources to survive the challenges that will inevitably arise.

E-Bits & Bytes

The number of host computers connected to the Net grew exponentially between 1993 and 1999. Yet distribution of host computers with Internet access has not been even across all countries. For example, Greece, with a population of 10.3 million, has 78 000 host computers, while China, with a population of 1.2 billion, has 72 000. Only 2.47 million adults in China now have access to the Internet. There truly is a divide between the world's information haves and have-nots.

Network Wizards, 2000

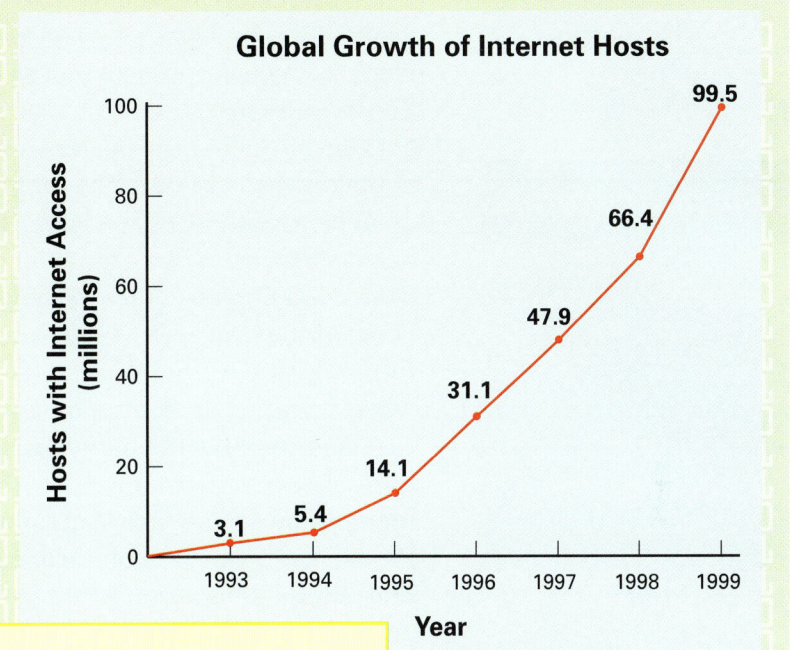

Global Growth of Internet Hosts

Hosts with Internet Access (millions) by Year:
- 1993: 3.1
- 1994: 5.4
- 1995: 14.1
- 1996: 31.1
- 1997: 47.9
- 1998: 66.4
- 1999: 99.5

The increase in global Internet access has provided a growth opportunity for some ventures and posed a threat to others. Describe some advantages and disadvantages of people's increasing reliance on the Internet.

Harvesting a Venture

The term "harvest" is appropriate because harvesting a venture is like harvesting a crop. Harvesting implies that a seed has been planted and nurtured into growth by the provision of the water, nutrients, and sunlight it needs to mature. The entrepreneur's seed is the idea and opportunity on which the venture is based. The entrepreneur nurtures the growth of the idea into a venture by providing it with the resources it needs. Both the farmer and the entrepreneur invest time and effort in the long-term process of creating something valuable. Once a crop has matured, the farmer harvests it by cutting it down and selling it. The entrepreneur harvests a venture in other ways.

FINANCIAL HARVEST

Many entrepreneurs choose to stay with their ventures and grow with them by learning the skills of management and administration. They receive a financial harvest in the form of the income they draw from their ventures. An entrepreneur can also realize a financial gain from the venture by selling all or part of it. As a venture grows, the value of its assets increases. As partial or complete owner of the venture, the entrepreneur can sell the venture's assets for a profit. The entrepreneur can sell his or her equity or share of the venture to existing partners or managers in the venture. This is referred to as a **management buyout**. The entrepreneur might sell the venture to another company, often a larger business in the same industry. Another choice is "going public," which involves selling shares of ownership in the venture to the general public on a stock exchange. Some of the proceeds of the sale of shares might be used to finance further growth or the venture might issue new shares as payment when acquiring another company.

Financial rewards in the form of profits represent an important form of harvest from a venture. High profits indicate that demand for a product or service is great and that a greater supply is needed. Profits can create a pool of capital to be used to expand production. The potential for a significant profit is what motivates an investor to put money into a venture and evaluating the profit potential is an important part of calculating the level of risk in an investment. Profits can also be used to measure how effectively one entrepreneur is running his or her venture in comparison with another.

Worth Repeating

"I discovered you never know yourself until you're tested and that you don't even know you're being tested until afterwards, and that in fact there isn't anyone giving the test except yourself."

Marilyn French, author

International NEWS

An International Space Station (ISS) is currently being constructed by a global team of partners led by NASA. Countries participating in the program include the United States, Canada, Japan, Russia, Brazil, and a number of European nations. The space station, the first components of which were placed in orbit in 1998, will provide a unique laboratory that will be used to conduct scientific research and to assemble satellites and space platforms in space.

Canadian robotic technology, supplied by MacDonald Dettwiler Space and Advance Robotics Ltd., will be used on virtually all of the shuttle flights that will deliver components of the station to their location in space. A key part of this technology is the Canadarm, which allows shuttle personnel to perform precise and delicate operations in space.

NASA and the Canadian Space Agency have invested nearly $100 million in the robotic system that will be used to transport and assemble the space station. Why might these government agencies have decided to invest this much money in a project that will yield no profits for them? What indirect financial benefits could Canadians receive as a result of the project?

PERSONAL HARVEST

While profits are important to entrepreneurs, most successful entrepreneurs say that making a profit is not their main reason for starting new ventures. Many entrepreneurs, financially successful to the point of being multimillionaires, will continue to risk their wealth on one new venture after another. Why do they take the risk? This is a question concerning human behaviour. It deals with the core of the entrepreneurial process and the hub of the Venture Creation Wheel. Entrepreneurship is, after all, fundamentally a human rather than a financial or technological process. All sorts of nonfinancial rewards exist, ranging from personal satisfaction to independence, self-respect, and even closer family ties (if the venture is a family business). All of these rewards can motivate and satisfy the entrepreneur. Entrepreneurial endeavours provide a way for individuals to express themselves and to grow as people. In the process, the wider community may also benefit greatly, as more jobs and greater wealth are created, new goods and services are offered, and more needs are satisfied.

Personal satisfaction and independence can be more important for an entrepreneur than making a profit.

YOUR TURN

1. What does an entrepreneur or manager need to look at in order to assess a venture's readiness for growth?

2. With a small group, discuss the advantages and disadvantages of each growth strategy.
   a) encouraging intrapreneurship
   b) establishing new divisions or locations
   c) merging with another company
   d) acquiring another company
   e) forming an alliance with another company

3. Choose a business currently operating in your community. Meet with a small group to assess the venture's potential, plan possible growth strategies, and develop a financial plan for financing this growth.

4. Describe the types of financial and personal harvest you hope to obtain from your personal venture.

Venture Profile

BLUEPRINT FOR A MUTINY

Nattalia Lea, Profit magazine

Shelly Tupper wanted to head up her own business. So when the silent partners who owned Calgary printing and photocopying company Copyright Reproductions Inc., which Tupper managed, put the $900 000-a-year business up for sale, Tupper and her entire staff of 11 put together a bid. But the owners rejected the $225 000 offer, even though it was the highest of three submitted.

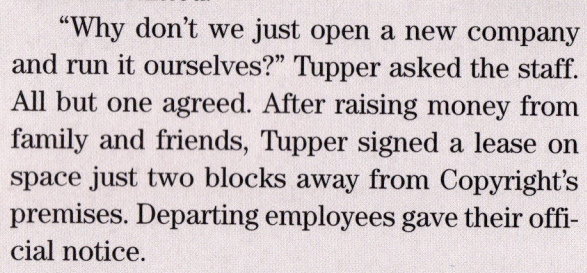

"Why don't we just open a new company and run it ourselves?" Tupper asked the staff. All but one agreed. After raising money from family and friends, Tupper signed a lease on space just two blocks away from Copyright's premises. Departing employees gave their official notice.

Tupper orchestrated a phone blitz to inform customers of the staff's plans. All but three of the regular customers jumped ship, too. "Business is about people and when the people move, so do you," says client Craig Robins, office manager for the Canadian Association of Professional Land Administration.

Most important, Tupper consulted lawyers, who vetted the resignation letters and advised her people not to take anything—even a pair of scissors—belonging to Copyright. So Tupper's team bought personal cellphones and used them to solicit customers on their own time, keeping records of all calls. They kept receipts for all purchases.

Naturally, Copyright's owners were not thrilled about Tupper and her plans. They even withheld wages; Tupper personally paid the staff. On September 1, 2000, First on Colour opened with $100 000 worth of second-hand equipment. Loyal suppliers extended credit: Supplier—and customer—Ken Hegert says, "I've heard a lot of business plans and dreams, but Tupper delivers what she says."

The following month, Tupper was sued by Copyright Reproductions for lost revenues and staff. She countersued over unpaid wages. The parties settled out of court. According to Tupper, getting good legal advice was critical to her success. "If we had not followed the advice to the letter, we would have been shut down," she says. "The courts would have ordered us to cease business until the legal points had been resolved."

Tupper and her staff logged 60-hour weeks to get First on Colour flying. First-year revenues were $800 000 and the company was profitable within 18 months. Tupper has kept an amicable relationship with Copyright's new owners, sending them work when possible.

Exploring

1. Shelly Tupper moved from being an intrapreneur to being an entrepreneur. How did this change occur?
2. In small groups, use the Six Thinking Hats to examine the launch of First on Colour from different points of view.
3. Aside from the legal issues cited in the article, what are some of the ethical issues Tupper likely considered as she made her decision?

Ethics, Integrity, and the Law

Ethical business practices are essential for any entrepreneur. Legal and moral standards need to be observed in all the dealings of the venture. Basing decisions on a **code of ethics** helps build trust with customers, suppliers, employees, investors, and potential partners. A code of ethics defines, often in written form, the moral and professional duties that the managers and staff of the venture have to each other and to the public. The code of ethics needs to be clearly articulated to and understood by every employee. Everyone who works in the venture makes decisions every day and should consistently apply and refer to the code of ethics in making them. Training employees to do so is the first step.

ETHICS AND INTEGRITY

The entrepreneur serves as a role model for employees. The entrepreneur's behaviour is important because he or she is in a position of power, control, and leadership. Often an entrepreneur began with a desire to escape the values imposed by some other job and some other boss. As a result, entrepreneurs have an interest in fostering higher standards in their own ventures and in their own employees.

If an entrepreneur solicits gifts from a supplier, then employees might think that this is an acceptable practice and do likewise. Such behaviour could easily damage the reputation of the venture and the code of ethics should address this issue. Similarly, if Tupper and her team had solicited customers for First on Colour while being paid by Copyright Reproductions, not only would that have been legal grounds for dismissal and a lawsuit, it would also have tainted the reputation of the new venture before it even got off the ground.

Some say entrepreneurs are ruled by the discipline of a marketplace that values and rewards honesty and fair dealing. Cheat your suppliers and you will not be able to get what you need to keep your venture going. Sell shoddy goods to your customers and eventually no one will buy your product. Word gets around!

Worth Repeating

"An ethical person ought to do more than he's required to do and less than he's allowed to do."

Michael Josephson, founder of the Joseph & Edna Josephson Institute of Ethics

Describe a situation where each part of this rule might apply.

YOUR TURN

1. With a small group, develop a code of ethics for Boulangerie Pizza Motta or First on Colour.

2. Brainstorm as many ethical problems as possible that might be faced by Gallo's or Tupper's employees during a normal work day. Discuss the possible solutions to each problem. Refer to the code you developed in Question 1 and add new points if necessary.

3. With a partner, role-play what you would do in each of the following situations:
   a) Your venture is a small manufacturing firm in serious financial trouble. A large order of your product is ready to be delivered to a major customer when you discover the product is simply not right and will likely cause problems for the customer.
   b) One of your suppliers tells you he or she can no longer supply you with an important raw material you need to produce your product.
   c) You are trying to sell a computer package to a major prospective client. On her desk, you see two copies of a competitor's proposal and cost outline. Your client leaves the room to use the washroom, leaving your competitor's proposals less than an arm's length away.
   d) You have been asked to prepare something for your boss that would be much easier if you had a certain piece of software. A friend you know at another firm has that software program. He has offered to make you a copy of the software.

Ethics and the Law

The basic beliefs we share as a community are reflected in the laws we make, but obeying the law represents only the minimum acceptable level of behaviour in a community. Even if something is allowable by law, it may not necessarily be right. We can look to the courts to see how to act but sometimes it makes sense to rely on our peers for guidance as well.

Some professions have developed their own codes of ethics, which may impose higher standards of behaviour than laws do. In fact, many professions write and enforce their own codes of ethics, with the government's approval. This releases the government from the task of creating detailed written laws to govern their actions and gives the group or profession more control over itself and its members. The Code of Ethics of the Canadian Marketing Association establishes guidelines (not laws) for sales and advertising. Table 12.1 highlights some of these guidelines.

Table 12.1 Selected Sections from the Code of Ethics of the Canadian Marketing Association

B1	Offers must be clear and truthful and shall not misrepresent a product, service, solicitation, or program, and shall not mislead by statement, technique of demonstration, or comparison.
B3	Test or survey data referred to shall be competent, reliable, and must support the specific claim for which it is cited.
B8	Testimonials and endorsements must be • authorized by the person quoted • genuine and related to the experience of the person quoted • not taken out of context so as to distort the opinion or experience of the person quoted
C1	The offer shall contain clear and conspicuous disclosure of the following terms: • the exact nature of what is offered • the price • the terms of payment, including any additional charges such as shipping and handling • the consumer's commitment and any ongoing obligation in placing an order
C2	Comparisons included in offers must be factual, verifiable, and not misleading. In addition: No offer shall include a deceptive price claim or deceptive suggestion of a discount, or exaggerated claim as to worth or value.
E2.2	All printed materials shall accurately and fairly describe the product or service offered. Type size, colour, contrast, style, placement, and other treatment shall not be used to reduce the legibility or clarity of the offer, exceptions to the offer, or terms and conditions.
E4.2	Marketers shall not transmit marketing e-mail without the consent of the recipient or unless the marketer has an existing relationship with the recipient.

Business and Personal Ethics

Are business ethics different from personal ethics? Should they be? Should we treat a competitor in the same way as we treat a friend, a neighbour, or a stranger in the street? These are difficult questions.

Ultimately, the entrepreneur is forced to rely on his or her own personal code of ethics in the workplace. The law defines the minimum acceptable standard of behaviour; the rest depends on the entrepreneur's personal values and on what he or she wants the new venture to stand for.

Entrepreneurs are agents of change in society. The values they express through their ventures and their philanthropic involvement in the community will have an important impact on society.

> **Think About It**
>
> If you had to write a personal code of ethics, what rules would you include?

Agents of Change

Michael Josephson is a former law professor and publisher who founded the not-for-profit Joseph & Edna Josephson Institute of Ethics, which he named after his parents. He is a writer and radio commentator who airs his views in a daily radio commentary called "Character Counts!" Through the Institute, Mr. Josephson founded the award-winning Character Counts! Coalition, a partnership of hundreds of communities, schools, and other educational and youth-service organizations. The Coalition helps kids live more responsible, honest, and safe lives by providing character-building programs based on core ethical values called the Six Pillars of Character: trustworthiness, respect, responsibility, fairness, caring, and citizenship.

> *The most satisfying entrepreneurial venture is one you've created yourself that allows you to live the life you want.*

ETHICS AND THE ENVIRONMENT

George Bernard Shaw once said, "We are made wise not by the recollection of our past, but by the responsibility for our future." People are gradually learning that some of what has been done in the past in the name of profit has been harmful to the environment and may threaten our future. Our natural resources are depleted and we face growing environmental crises resulting from pollution in our air and water.

Today, there are positive signs that a new environmental ethic is emerging. Businesses are becoming more aware of their responsibility to the environment and most are taking this responsibility seriously. There are laws that spell out the basic environmental obligations for any venture, but as Michael Josephson suggests on page 297, ethical people are those who do more than they're required to do. Therefore, as businesses are launched and developed, it's important for those at the helm to keep informed about environmental issues and to do their best to ensure that their ventures are doing no harm, and preferably, are helping to solve environmental problems. Remember that a problem, such as industrial pollution, can present an entrepreneurial opportunity for someone with a new technology.

INTEGRITY AND THE ENTREPRENEURIAL VENTURE

The ethics of the free market, with an emphasis on profit making, will always drive private enterprise. However, integrity and honesty have a strong and valuable role to play in venture creation.

The most satisfying entrepreneurial venture is one you've created yourself that allows you to live the life you want. The harvest you receive from any venture you undertake will depend as much upon your personal values and your own code of ethics as it will upon your entrepreneurial skill. Your venture, and your life, will be enhanced if you pursue it with integrity.

300   Unit 3 ◆ Moving into Action

According to the *Nelson Canadian Dictionary*, the word "integrity" has three meanings. The first meaning is the one that has been used throughout this chapter: "a steadfast adherence to a strict ethical code." However, the second and third meanings are revealing when you apply them in the context of a venture. Integrity means "the state of being unimpaired," and "the quality or condition of being whole or undivided." If you bring integrity to your venture, you will gain a sense of completeness. Decisions will be easier to make, and will be more likely to be the right decisions. When you base your venture on what you value most, you and your venture will become part of a whole, operating together without conflict.

E-Bits & Bytes

YottaYotta Inc. is the result of a merger last year between Seattle-based Seek (Storage) Systems Inc., and Edmonton's Myrias Computer Technologies. YottaYotta makes computer storage systems that can store and speed large amounts of data out onto the Internet. The name comes from the word "yottabyte," the equivalent of one trillion terabytes. To put this number in perspective, the contents of the entire U.S. Library of Congress is only about 10 terabytes. Since a storage system capable of holding a yottabyte would cost about $1 billion, the company is setting its sights a bit lower for the coming year. Their initial product, called the Net Storage Cube, will hold several petabytes, each of which is equal to 1000 terabytes. The cube is designed not only to store data, but also to protect it from system crashes and to speed it out onto the Internet.

Why might Seek Systems Inc. and Myrias Computer Technologies, two companies that made similar products, have decided to merge? Now that they've joined forces, how could they raise the financing they need to produce their new storage devices?

YOUR TURN

1. What are some of the values that guided the development of the Canadian Marketing Association's code of ethics?

2. Visit www.business.nelson.com and follow the links to "advertising codes of ethics" to find the codes for some other organizations related to advertising. What ethical values do these codes have in common?

3. Find four examples of advertisements from any media that you think might contravene the code of the Canadian Marketing Association or other advertising codes that you've discovered. Then find four examples of advertisements that do seem to follow the regulations.

4. Visit www.business.nelson.com and follow the links to "professional codes of ethics" to find codes governing professional behaviour, for example, for teachers, doctors, or lawyers. What ethical values do these codes appear to share?

5. Explain several ways in which the discipline of the marketplace encourages entrepreneurs to behave in an ethical way.

ACTIVITIES

FLASHBACKS

Although this chapter deals with the life cycle of a venture, many of the points below could be applied to life in general. Discuss the Flashbacks with a partner to see which points could be applied this way.

- Ventures fail for a variety of reasons, many of which result from poor management.
- At each stage of a venture's life cycle, different development tasks (inventive, innovative, entrepreneurial, managerial, administrative) become dominant.
- Continuous controlled growth is healthy for a venture. It can be achieved through strategies such as introducing new products, changing the pricing structure, or exploring new distribution channels.
- Growth can be achieved by a venture working on its own or through an alliance with another venture. Alliances can be achieved through franchising, mergers, acquisitions, or strategic partnerships.
- An entrepreneur can harvest financial returns from a venture in the form of income or by selling interest (shares) in its ownership.
- An entrepreneur might also gain a personal harvest through satisfaction with the venture and the opportunity for self expression, personal growth, and contributions to the community.
- Ethical business practices are essential for any entrepreneur but codes of ethics vary from one venture to another.
- It is important that every entrepreneur defines a personal code of ethics to use as a guide in his or her venture.
- Professional organizations often have their own codes of ethics. These codes usually impose a higher standard of behaviour than laws do.
- Entrepreneurs have an ethical obligation to keep informed about environmental issues and to make environmentally responsible choices for their ventures.

LESSONS LEARNED

1. Describe the warning signals that indicate that a venture might be heading for trouble.

2. Describe the characteristics of each of the development tasks a successful venture will go through.

3. What options do entrepreneurs have for growth once their ventures have become established?
4. What factors should be considered in developing a growth strategy?
5. The harvest the entrepreneur receives from a successful venture may take many forms. Describe at least four of them.
6. Explain the difference between the law and a code of ethics.
7. Comment on the relationship between personal and business ethics.
8. Why is it important for entrepreneurs to be socially responsible?

VENTURING OUT

> Don't forget to update the database you began in Chapter 2 to include the people you met in this unit. Review the information on your database and make some general observations about entrepreneurs' and enterprising people's characteristics and skills.

1. Describe several strategies you could use to help your venture grow after it becomes established.
2. Prepare a cost/benefit analysis for each strategy you suggested in your answer to Question 1.
3. Describe some ethical issues that apply to your personal venture. What steps could you take to make your venture more socially responsible?
4. Describe your vision of success for your venture after one year, three years, and five years.

POINT OF VIEW

1. In Chapter 3, you wrote a letter to yourself about your goals and included a timeline. Review the letter and timeline now. Make revisions to reflect any goals or plans that have changed since you wrote your letter.
2. Write an essay about the life you hope to have. Begin by describing the values that are most important to you and then show how these values might guide the choices you make for the future. The essay should have the following sections:
   a) development (from now to age 30)
   b) growth (from 30 to 50)
   c) maturity (after age 50)

   Good managers and enterprising people do not experience decline. Truly enterprising people learn how to grow and develop as long as they live.

Glossary

accounts payable Money that a business owes.

accounts receivable Money owed to a business.

administrative task The task of carrying out identified strategies or policies in an efficient and effective way.

Agricultural Age The historical time period, as described by Alvin Toffler, when most people gave up a nomadic lifestyle to establish stable, permanent communities based on farming.

AIDA formula A formula for good advertising; an acronym for Attention, Interest, Desire, and Action.

asset Anything the entrepreneur or business owns that has a cash value (e.g., accounts receivable, cash, and inventory).

attitude scale A scale used to rate consumers' attitudes toward certain aspects of products or services. The scale typically goes from 1 (poor) to 5 (excellent).

attrition A gradual reduction in the work force that occurs when people leave their jobs voluntarily (e.g., due to retirement or relocation).

autocratic leader A leader who makes all the decisions and expects employees to do as they are told.

balance sheet A financial statement that represents the assets, liabilities, and equity of the business at a specific date.

bankruptcy A state that is declared by a court of law when a business is unable to pay its debts and its assets are distributed among its creditors.

bootleg To transfer resources without specific approval to entrepreneurial projects within the firm other than those for which the employee was originally hired.

brainstorming A technique for exercising creativity that involves the generation of many new and unusual ideas.

break-even point The point where total monthly revenues are equal to total monthly costs.

bricks-and-mortar An actual location for a business that is in a store or other type of building. (*See also* **virtual business**.)

capital The funds that must be invested in a company in order to enable it to carry out its activities. Also, one of the Six Cs of Credit: The amount of money the entrepreneur has invested in the venture from his or her own savings.

capital gain The profit acquired (as a result of selling a venture) that reflects an increase in the value of the owner's equity.

capital good A fixed material resource that lasts a long time, such as buildings, machinery, and equipment.

capital investment Money that is used to acquire a capital good, such as a building or a piece of equipment.

capitalize To supply a venture with funds.

cash flow The amount of money that a business receives and pays out over a period of time.

cash-flow projection A prediction of incoming cash through sales or other receipts alongside outgoing cash to pay for the company's bills.

cash in The section of a cash-flow projection that keeps track of the flow of money that is actually received by the venture.

cash out The section of a cash-flow projection that keeps track of a venture's expenses as they are paid.

causal research A type of research designed to explain the relationship between a particular cause and effect.

census A survey conducted by contacting everyone in the total population (e.g., of a country).

certification mark A word or symbol that identifies goods or services that meet a defined standard.

code of ethics A statement (usually written) of the moral and professional duties that members of a specific profession have to each other and to the public.

collateral Assets that can be offered as security for a loan, or seized by the lender if the loan is not repaid.

collegial leader A democratic leader who tends to regard everyone as an equal, rather than as a part of a hierarchy.

command and control An Organization model in which the activities of employees are dictated by managers from a central office.

competency An ability or strength that enables a person to accomplish something.

computerized inventory control system A computer-based system designed to automatically maintain and update records of goods received and sold.

consignment A loan of merchandise for sale. Any items not sold are returned to the supplier.

consumable resources Material resources, also known as expense goods, that are used up in the process of doing business, such as paper, oil, gas, or telephone service.

contingency plan An alternative course of action that can be taken if needed.

copyright The legal protection of original literary, musical, and artistic works, software, industrial designs, and similar items from being copied or used by others without the permission of the owner.

copyright statement The assertion of the author's ownership of an original work, to deter unauthorized copying or distribution.

corporate charter A legal document that establishes a corporation.

corporation An artificial entity created by law, and established by corporate charter, that has an existence apart from the people who own it.

cost-plus pricing A pricing strategy in which the price of a product is based on its cost, plus a fixed markup.

creative-thinking skills The skills required to generate new alternatives, possibilities, and ideas; a type of thinking often referred to as right-brain thinking.

credit history The past borrowing patterns, including repayments, of an individual or business.

credit rating The financial standing and reputation of a company, used to determine the amount of money the venture may borrow and the terms of the loan.

creditor A person or institution that is owed money.

criteria The standards or measures that are used to evaluate the strengths and weaknesses of an idea.

critical risk A potential problem that could have serious consequences for a venture.

critical-thinking skills The skills required to analyze problems and evaluate proposed solutions; a type of thinking often referred to as left-brain thinking.

curved The shape of a line graph when the rate of change is increasing or decreasing.

customer profile A description of the target market for a particular product or service.

cyclical The shape of a line graph when there is a repeating pattern of increases and decreases.

debt financing Borrowing money from a lending institution to start a business; the money must be repaid with interest, and may be obtained only with specific terms and conditions imposed by the lender.

debt to equity ratio The amount of debt owed by a business compared to the amount of its equity.

declining trend A trend that is in a stage of decline or falling in magnitude.

deficit The amount by which more money was spent than was earned in a given period of time.

demand The amount of a good or service that customers are willing to purchase.

demise Death.

democratic leader A leader who encourages employees to participate in the decision-making process.

demographics Data about groups of people, including their age, ethnic origin, religion, family size, income, etc.

depreciate To diminish or reduce in value.

diorama A miniature replica of a scene.

disclaimer statement A warning to the reader of a venture plan not to rely on its assumptions or predictions without exercising caution and obtaining independent advice.

distinguishing guise The unique shape of a product or its package.

dividend An amount of money paid out by a corporation to people who own shares in it.

downsize To reduce operating costs in an organization by reducing the number of employees.

due diligence Following the appropriate legal or accounting procedures to verify that information is accurate.

e-commerce Business that is principally conducted electronically, especially over the Internet.

entrepreneur A person who takes risks and organizes resources in order to satisfy needs.

entrepreneurial task The task of organizing previously unrelated resources to build a venture that can produce and market a good or service to satisfy a need.

entrepreneurship The quality of being an entrepreneur; the act of identifying opportunities and mobilizing resources to bring about change in order to operate a venture.

equity Personal financial investment in a venture.

equity financing A form of financing in which the investor receives some ownership in the venture in exchange for a financial contribution.

European Union An affiliation of European countries that operates as a single market, with no barriers to people, products, and services moving between the countries.

executive summary A one- or two-page summary of the most important points in a venture plan, intended to introduce the venture and to capture the attention of the reader.

exit strategy A plan for ending or leaving a venture.

expense good A consumable material resource that is used up in the process of doing business, such as paper, oil, gas, or telephone service.

experimentation *See* **product sampling**.

exploratory research A type of research designed to define a problem clearly or obtain possible solutions to it.

external human resources People outside the venture who provide services to it, such as accountants, business or technology consultants, lawyers, bankers, suppliers, mentors, and insurance agents.

external motivator Something outside the individual that causes the individual to act, such as a salary increase.

external recruitment Recruiting people from outside the venture to fill a position, as opposed to offering the job to a current employee.

fad A product or service with a very short life cycle.

final user Consumer.

financial resources The money needed to start and operate a venture, including money to buy equipment and materials, pay staff, and cover other expenses.

financial strategy The final section of a venture plan that predicts how the venture will make use of its financial resources.

fixed asset Something owned by a company that is of a fairly permanent nature, such as real estate or equipment.

fixed cost A cost, such as rent, that is the same every month regardless of how much the venture sells or produces.

fixed overhead Costs such as rent, telephone lines, computers, and office staff.

fixed resources Material resources, also known as capital goods, that last a long time, such as buildings, trucks, machinery, and office equipment.

follow-the-competition pricing A pricing strategy in which a product or service is priced at or slightly below the price of competing items.

forecast A prediction of the future.

franchise A type of business ownership in which the purchaser buys the right to operate one or more units in a chain of similar businesses that all follow the same plan and sell the same products.

gap analysis An analysis that can be included in a venture plan to point out the difference between what is already in place and what ideally should be in place once the venture is underway.

general partnership An unincorporated partnership in which all the partners are liable for all the debts of the business.

geographic Relating to physical location, such as a specific climatic condition or provincial or regional boundaries.

globalization The expansion of businesses and markets based on worldwide interdependence.

go/no-go decision The final decision that an entrepreneur makes before actually implementing a venture plan.

goal A purpose or objective.

good A product produced or distributed for sale to consumers.

goodwill An intangible business asset, such as a good reputation or a satisfied customer base.

grant A sum of money given to a company by the government that does not have to be paid back.

gross national product (GNP) The total value of all the goods and services produced in a country in one year.

growth trend A pattern of consumption or production that increases over time.

guarantee An undertaking, often in the form of collateral, provided for a loan by someone who agrees to pay back the loan if the borrower does not.

hierarchy An organizational system that includes distinct levels of authority.

homogeneous A group whose members have common identifiable characteristics.

human resources The people needed to operate a venture.

IC product A product made with or from integrated electronic circuits.

idea finding A stage in the problem-solving process in which the entrepreneur tries to come up with different ways of solving the problem.

income forecast An estimate of the revenues to be earned by a venture.

income statement A statement that shows the profit or loss of a company over a specified period of time; revenue minus expenses.

incremental problem solving To move toward a solution by taking a series of small steps.

incubator An organization that fosters and nurtures new ventures.

Industrial Age The historical time period, as described by Alvin Toffler, when people gave up a rural farming way of life for an urban industrial lifestyle.

industrial design Anything that is made by hand, tool, or machine that has distinctive features, such as the shape of a chair.

Information Age The current time period, as described by Alvin Toffler, in which we are experiencing rapid change in our lifestyles and institutions brought about by new technologies and the explosion of information that can be turned into knowledge.

infrastructure An underlying system that helps accomplish a purpose.

innovation The application of new ideas, technologies, or materials to existing goods and services.

innovative task The task of applying a new technology, process, or idea to satisfy an existing need.

intangible asset An asset that has no physical existence, such as goodwill or the collective knowledge and experience of employees.

Integrated Circuit Topography Electronic integrated circuits or IC products that are configured and interconnected in a specific way; the originator or owner has rights to the design that are protected by law.

intellectual capital The information, knowledge, and thinking skills that employees bring to bear on their work.

intellectual property Original ideas and concepts that can be protected by law.

internal human resources People who are part of the venture, such as the entrepreneur, partners, and employees.

internal motivator Something within a person that spurs the person on toward the achievement of a goal.

internal recruitment Offering a job to a person who already works for the venture in a different capacity.

internal research Research that uses a business's own records to gather information.

interpersonal skills The skills required to communicate with, motivate, and encourage others.

intrapreneurship Entrepreneurship that occurs within an existing organization or corporation.

invention The generation of new ideas, technologies, or goods and services.

inventive task The task of creating a new device or process by joining together previously unrelated elements in a new way.

irregular The shape of a line graph when rates of increase and decrease change frequently.

joint venture A venture undertaken by two or more parties.

just-in-time A process by which necessary items are obtained at the moment when they are needed rather than stored in advance.

labour market The supply of and demand for workers in the economy.

labourer Someone whose work primarily involves physical effort.

laissez-faire leader A leader who ignores the specifics of a task or job and concentrates on giving employees the freedom to determine what they should do and how they should do it.

lateral thinking Generating ideas by being flexible and creative.

left brain The left hemisphere of the brain, that is said to function in a sequential, analytical, and linear way.

letter of transmittal A letter of two to three paragraphs that accompanies the venture plan when it is sent to a potential investor.

liability A debt; a sum of money the entrepreneur owes; the financial obligation of a business.

life cycle The various stages most products and services pass through over time.

limited partnership A type of partnership that consists of one or more partners whose liability is limited to the amount they invested in the venture.

line of credit A type of financing that allows the borrower to obtain funds as needed up to a set limit.

linear The shape of a line graph when the rate of increase or decrease is steady.

liquidation The sale of assets in order to raise funds.

long-range objective A goal that may take years to achieve.

loss-leader pricing A pricing strategy by which goods or services are priced at or below cost in the hope of attracting customers who will then buy other, more profitable items.

love money Money that an entrepreneur's friends and family invest in a venture.

management buyout The sale of an entrepreneur's equity or share of the venture to existing partners or managers.

managerial task The job of directing the venture on a day-to-day basis.

market analysis One of the five sections of a venture plan, that helps entrepreneurs identify potential customers, analyze the competition, set prices, and plan ways to advertise the venture.

market niche A specific segment of the market.

market-pulled entrepreneurship Entrepreneurship that first identifies a problem or an unsatisfied need in the market and then develops an idea to resolve or satisfy it.

market segment A group of consumers who share common characteristics.

market share A way of representing one company's sales as part of the total volume of sales made by that company and its competitors, usually expressed as a percent.

marketing elements Elements of a marketing strategy, also known as the Four Ps of Marketing or the marketing mix: product (or service), place, price, and promotion.

marketing mix *See* **marketing elements**.

marketing strategy A plan developed for the entire marketing process, from research to advertising, promotion, packaging, distribution, sales, and service.

mass production The making of products in large quantities, usually on an assembly line.

material resources All the materials that are needed to operate the venture, both raw materials and finished products.

mentor A person who nurtures and encourages others to achieve at a higher level.

merchant A type of job originating in the Agricultural Age; a person who buys goods and then sells them for a profit.

milestone A major event that marks one's progress toward a goal.

mind mapping A visual way of organizing and relating ideas using pictures and key words.

minority position A small or minor share of a business.

mission statement A statement describing the purpose and goals of the organization.

mobilize To organize resources so that they work in an effective way.

modification A change that one person has made to another person's idea.

mortgage A loan made for the purchase of real estate, secured by the real estate itself.

multiple-choice question A question that gives three or four possible answers to select from.

multiplier effect The phenomenon that occurs when the creation of new jobs leads to the creation of further new jobs because of an increase in the overall demand for goods and services.

need Something that is essential to life.

needs assessment *See* **market analysis**.

net cash The section of a cash-flow projection that records the balance of cash flow for a specified period.

net worth The dollar value of a company's assets, determined by subtracting the value of liabilities from the value of assets.

networking The ability to interact with people and develop business relationships with them.

new economy The current information-age economy, which is experiencing rapid change due to technology, globalization, deregulation, and a shortage of skills and talents.

not-for-profit Ventures that are created for social or community service purposes, not to make profits.

observation A method of collecting primary data by directly watching people or processes.

open-ended question A question that allows for a wide range of answers, such as "How do you feel about…?"

operating expense An expense needed to keep a venture going once it has successfully completed the startup phase.

operating strategy One of the five sections of a venture plan that indicates how the entrepreneur will manage the resources of the venture in its day-to-day operation.

opportunity A need, want, problem, or challenge that can potentially be satisfied by an entrepreneurial idea and venture.

opportunity cost The costs incurred as the result of choosing a course of action.

ordinary mark A word or symbol that distinguishes the goods or services of a specific firm or individual.

orientation period A period during which a new employee gets to know the job, the work environment, and the equipment.

out-of-the-box thinking Thinking beyond the first possible answer and looking in unusual places for solutions.

partnership A formal, legal commitment between two or more people to work together to achieve the objectives of a business venture.

patent A grant made by the government that gives the creator of an invention the sole right to make, use, and sell the invention for a set period of time.

penetration pricing A pricing strategy in which a new product or service is priced considerably lower than the competition in order to gain market share.

personal balance sheet An itemized listing of an entrepreneur's assets and liabilities, from which the entrepreneur's net worth can be calculated.

personal budget An itemized listing of all of a person's living expenses, such as rent, food, and utilities.

personal drawing A wage or salary paid to the entrepreneur by the venture.

philanthropist A person who gives time and/or resources for a good cause.

practical skills The skills required to follow instructions and to use specific tools or procedures in the entrepreneurial process.

price taker A venture that sets the price of its goods or services by following the existing prices in the market.

primary research The technique of gathering data firsthand through such methods as personal observation, interviews, and questionnaires.

private placement Money invested by a small group of investors into a startup or growing business.

pro forma Literally, "as a formality"; a financial statement that indicates what the position of the venture would currently be (or will be at some point in the future) under certain circumstances.

problem finding A stage in the problem-solving process in which the entrepreneur tries to define a problem by gathering observations, feelings, and impressions about the situation.

product-driven entrepreneurship Entrepreneurship that first develops an idea for a product or service, and then seeks out a marketing opportunity.

product sampling A method of conducting marketing research that involves providing a small group of consumers with a product or service to use and evaluate.

profit The amount by which revenues are greater than costs.

profit formula A way to project profits from known information: profit = (unit price × quantity) − costs.

profit margin The percentage of the final selling price of a good or service that represents profit.

project plan A plan to help an employee organize a successful project.

projected balance sheet A projected financial statement that shows the company's assets and liabilities and the amount of equity held by its shareholders.

promotion The process entrepreneurs use to deliver their message to consumers, by activities such as advertising, personal selling, publicity, and sponsorships.

proprietary Owned by someone or some organization.

proprietor Owner.

psychographic Relating to a group's lifestyles or personality attributes.

psychological pricing A pricing strategy that uses odd number amounts in order to lead the consumer to perceive that the price is lower than it really is.

quality control The process of monitoring and ensuring the quality of a product or service.

red tape Administrative processes that must be completed in order to accomplish a task or reach a goal.

remuneration Salary, wages, or other income paid to someone for doing a job.

research instrument A tool for marketing research, such as a questionnaire, telephone survey, or personal interview.

resource analysis One of the five sections of a venture plan, in which the entrepreneur considers the material, human, and financial resources that will be needed for the venture.

return on investment The amount of profit that investors earn in return for the capital they have invested in a venture.

revenue Income received by a venture from selling its goods or services.

right brain The right hemisphere of the brain that is said to function in a creative, imaginative, emotional, and intuitive way.

rightsize To reduce the number of employees in an organization to a certain number in order to meet current organizational or economic goals.

sample A survey conducted with a small, representative group of the population.

secondary research The techniques of analyzing and evaluating information that has already been gathered by other means, such as census data.

service The performance of an action that is useful to others.

service-driven entrepreneurship *See* **product-driven entrepreneurship**.

share A unit of ownership of a business.

share purchase A means by which managers encourage employees to buy ownership in the business.

silent partner A partner who invests money in the venture but does not take an active part in managing it.

308 Glossary

six Cs of credit The six things a lender wants to know about an entrepreneur who is applying for a loan: character, capital, collateral, capacity, circumstances, and coverage.

skimming A pricing strategy in which a new product or service is sold at a high price because it has no competition.

socioeconomic Relating to a group's occupation, education, income, social class, or culture.

sole proprietorship The simplest form of business ownership, in which there is only one owner who is entitled to all profits and responsible for all liabilities.

solution finding The final step in the problem-solving process, in which the entrepreneur evaluates each of the ideas created earlier.

specific research A type of research designed to gather specific information relating to a clearly defined problem.

stable situation A trend that shows no tendency to either grow or decline.

startup cost An expense that must be paid in order to get a business up and running.

steppingstone A minor objective that can be achieved within a relatively short period of time as one works toward one's goal.

stock option plan A means by which employees are given the opportunity to purchase shares in a corporation, usually at an advantageous price.

strike A legal refusal to work by employees, in accordance with a trade union agreement.

supply The amount of a good or service that is available for distribution or consumption.

surplus The amount by which more money was earned than was spent in a given period of time.

survey A questionnaire; a set of questions designed to obtain information.

SWOT analysis An analysis of the Strengths, Weaknesses, Opportunities, and Threats associated with a possible undertaking.

syndicated Sold or distributed through many channels of delivery.

table of contents An organized list of the chapters or other sections of a venture plan, including the page numbers where each one begins.

target date A date set to complete something or reach a goal.

target market Those individuals or organizations that are likely to want to use what you can provide.

tax deductible An expense that can be deducted from income and thus reduce the amount of income tax payable.

telecommuter A person who works somewhere other than the usual workplace, with access to files and people through communications and computer technology.

teleconferencing Working together via telephone or using collaboration software online.

term loan A loan that must be paid back in specified payments within a specific period of time.

Thinking Hats A phrase created by Edward De Bono to describe his six ways of thinking and problem solving.

time-series forecast A method of forecasting that involves plotting a trend from the past to the present on a chart, making comparisons to other trends, and projecting it into the future.

title page The first page of a venture plan; it includes the name of the venture, the names of the people proposing the venture, the date, and the copyright and disclaimer statements.

total monthly costs All the money paid out by the business in a month, including labour and production costs as well as fixed overhead costs.

total monthly revenues All the money that comes into the business in a month from sales or other sources.

trademark A word, symbol, design, or a combination of these used to identify a product or service and distinguish it from its competitors.

trade-off A compromise people make when they choose between two or more options.

trade union An organization of workers who have joined together to negotiate with management on a range of issues.

trend A pattern or direction in the way something is changing.

undercapitalization The condition of a venture that lacks sufficient capital for the startup and day-to-day operation of the business.

value-added A product or service that offers its customers more than they expected.

variable cost A cost such as labour, that fluctuates every month depending on the demand for, and output of, the product or service.

vendor's permit A licence that has to be obtained when opening a retail business.

venture A business startup or undertaking.

venture capital Money that is invested into a startup or growing business.

venture plan A written summary of what a venture can accomplish and how it intends to do so.

virtual business A business that is conducted electronically over the Internet rather than from a conventional physical or "bricks-and-mortar" location.

visualizing The creative process of closing one's eyes and imagining different scenarios to help solve a problem.

want A human desire that goes beyond basic needs and is not essential for survival.

war for talent The competition among organizations to find the right people to work for them in the new economy.

window of opportunity The part of the market into which a new product or service will fit; that length of time while unmet needs continue to exist.

word clustering A free association of ideas and words, used to stimulate right-brain thinking.

workplace culture The beliefs, morals, values, customs, habits, systems, and practices within an organization.

Index

A

Accountants, 205
Accounting, knowledge of, 159
Accounts payable, 237
Accounts receivable, 237
AC Dispensing Equipment Inc., 93
Acme Humble Pie Co., 267–268
Adherex Technologies Inc., 15
Adler, Kerry, 119
Administrative task, in venture development, 286, 291
Advertising, 190–192
Affinity Logic, 279
Agents of change, 27, 35, 71
    Adler, Kerry, 119
    Banting, Frederick, 175
    Bell, Alexander Graham, 71
    Best, Charles, 175
    Blackwatch Communications Inc., 236
    Bombardier, Joseph-Armand, 101
    Campbell, Kim, 263
    CarsDirect.com, 46
    Character Counts! Coalition, 300
    Corbin, Mike & Tom, 122
    Edison, Thomas, 174
    Eyeball.com Network Inc., 30
    Fields, Debbi, 239
    Ford, Henry, 13
    Freid, Loren, 266
    Fry, Art, 138
    Gisborne, Frederick, 72
    Gross, Bill, 46
    Gutenberg, Johannes, 109
    Hui, Terrence, 155
    insulin, 175
    Josephson, Michael, 300
    Kraft Dinner, 103
    Le Caine, Hugh, 286
    Lilith Fair, 36
    Livingstone, Carol, 146
    Mariani, William, 236
    McLachlan, Sarah, 36
    Mrs. Fields Cookies, 239
    Nader, Ralph, 212
    Painter, Scott, 46
    Picasso, Pablo, 109
    Piché, Chris, 30
    Pickford, Mary, 287
    Post-it Notes, 138
    printing press, 109
    Suzuki, David, 62
    Watson, Thomas, 71
    Webhelp.com, 119

Agents of Change (*continued*)
    West Point Development Corporation, 146
    Williams, Charles, 71
Agricultural Age, 69
AIDA formula, 190
All Pro Construction, 246
Ami Support Computers, 275
Apple Computer, Inc., 291
Assets, 147
    fixed, 251
    intangible, 70
    value of, 294
Attrition, 72, 73
Auger, Corey, 20
Autocratic leaders, 214

B

Baby boomers, 16
Bacile, Tony, 49–50
Bad Boy Furniture and Appliances Warehouse Ltd., 178–179
Balance sheets
    personal, 242–244
    projected, 244–245
Bankruptcy, 220, 233
Banks, 204, 252–253
Banting, Frederick, 175
Behaviour patterns, as market segment, 183
Bell, Alexander Graham, 71
Bertrand, Marianne, 250
Best, Charles, 175
Betty Flyweight, 126–127
Black hat thinking, 103
Blackwatch Communications Inc., 236
Blind faith operators, 80
Blue hat thinking, 104, 134–135
Bombardier, Joseph-Armand, 101
Boniecki, Derek, 162–163
Bookkeeping, knowledge of, 159
Bootlegging, 292
Boulangerie Pizza Motta, 288–289
Bowerman, Bill, 68
Brain, right vs. left, 107–108
Brainstorming, 110–111
Break-even point, 146
Bricks-and-mortar locations, 10, 205
Brinsmead, Candace, 6–7
Bruce, Travis Keith, 140
Buchanan, Georgia, 246
Budget, personal, 235–236
Burnham, Andy, 98–99
Business associations, 92

Businesses. *See* Ventures
Business name, registering, 153
BuyBuddy.com, 25, 52

C

Cachagee, Wade, 39–40
Caisses populaires, 253
Campbell, Kim, 263
CanadaHelps.org, 144–145
Canadarm, 294
Canadian Marketing Association, 298–299
Canadian Youth Business Foundation (CYBF), 161, 162–163
CanTalk Canada Inc., 24–25
Capital, 81
    intellectual, 79
    raising of, 247–254
Capital gains, 235
Capital investment, 70
CarsDirect.com, 46
Cash flow, 212, 237–238
    projections, 239–240, 273
Cash in, 239
Cash out, 239
Cash-poor periods, 237
Cash-rich periods, 237
Causal research, 175
Cell phones, 59
Census, 177
Certification marks, 96
Change
    agents of. *See* Agents of change
    in products, 116
    resisters, 80
    technological, 11–12, 84, 116, 199, 283
    ventures and, 91
Character Counts! Coalition, 300
CHART (Coastal Habitat Assessment Research Technology), 133
Chen, Jessica, 267–268
Choi, Matthew, 144–145
Cirque du Soleil, 117–118
Code of ethics, 297, 298–299
Collateral, 46
College courses, 92
Collegial leaders, 214
Command and control model, 70
Commercial laws, 13
Communication
    facilitating, 215–216
    spoken, 216
Community organizations, 92
Competencies, 81

Competition, 264
    technology and, 84
Compressed work week, 78
Computerized inventory control system, 211
Computer Professionals for Social Responsibility (CPSR), 61–62
Conference Board of Canada, 73
Conflict resolution, 217
Consignment, goods on, 250
Consumable resources, 154
Consumer behaviour, 182, 183
Consumer demand. *See* Demand
Consumption patterns, as market segment, 183
Contingency plans, 233, 264
Coolgirls.org, 26
Coolwomen.org, 26
Copyright, 95–96
    statement of, 269
Copyright Reproductions Inc., 296
Corbin, Mike & Tom, 122
Corporate charter, 221
Corporate logos, 97
Corporations, 221–222
Corriero, Jennifer, 25–26
Cost-plus pricing, 189
Costs, 134
    covering, 233
    estimating, 237–238
    fixed, 190, 198, 233
    fixed overhead, 146
    operating, 233
    opportunity, 135
    startup, 233, 238, 242
    total monthly, 146
    variable, 190, 198, 233
Cranson, Brett & Devon, 44, 45–46
Creative-thinking skills, 59, 100
Credit
    history, 46
    line of, 252
    rating, 249
    six Cs of, 252
Creditors, 244
Credit unions, 253
CREE-TECH Inc., 39–40
Criteria, 101
Critical risks, 264–265
Critical-thinking skills, 59, 100
Culture, 182
Customer profiles, 131
Customers
    access to location, 205, 206
    expectations, 193
    knowledge of, 174
    as source of capital, 250
    target, 180
Cyclepath, 223–224

D

Deblois, Elisabeth, 133
De Bono, Edward, 102
Debt financing, 251–254
Debt to equity ratio, 251
Declining trends, 124
Deficit, 239
Demand
    defined, 13
    labour market, 72
Democratic leaders, 214
Demographic market segment, 183
Demographics, 11–12. *See also* Population: trends
    entrepreneurship and, 16
Disclaimer statement, 269
Distinguishing guises, 96
Distress, 217
Dividends, 235
Dolan sisters, 115, 116
Dorazio, Robert, 288
Downsizing, 12
Duck, Michael, 93
Due diligence, 241
Dumas, Paul, 18

E

Earning power, 37
E-commerce, 10, 11, 111, 192, 206
Edison, Thomas, 56, 174
Educational level, jobs and, 73
Efinity Inc., 20
Einstein, Albert, 56
Employability Skills Profile (Conference Board of Canada), 73
Employees. *See also* Human resources
    bootlegging and, 292
    enterprising, 36–37, 79, 84, 137
    entrepreneur as role model for, 297
    finding and keeping, 201–206
    innovation and, 138–139
    key contributors, 204
    long-term performance, 204
    loyalty of, 203–204
    motivation of, 214–215
    orientation of, 202
    as owners, 250
    personal characteristics, 202
    references of, 202
    relationships, and venture failure, 282
    as source of capital, 250
    termination of, 147
    training, 202
Employment, home-based, 77–78
Enterprising people, 35–39

Entrepreneurial revolution, 12
Entrepreneurial task, in venture development, 286
Entrepreneurial ventures. *See* Ventures
Entrepreneurs
    characteristics of, 19, 27–30, 45–46
    defined, 9
    motivating factors, 32, 37
    as role models for employees, 297
    skills, 30–31, 54, 57–58
Entrepreneurship, 9
    approaches to, 18
    bones of, 35
    demographics and, 16
    economic benefits, 15
    history, 13
    impact on community, 15–16
    job creation and, 15
    market-pulled, 118
    new ideas and, 15
    political benefits, 15–16
    product-driven, 118
    service-driven, 118
    six Ps of, 185–193
    success in, 60
Entrepreneurship, L.P., 15
Environment
    ethics and, 300
    policies regarding, 156
Equity, 235
Equity financing, 247–248
Ethics
    business, 297
    environment and, 300
    law and, 298–299
    personal vs. business, 299–300
European Union, 137
Eustress, 217
Executive summary, 151–152, 264
Exit interviews, with employees, 282
Exit strategy, from ventures, 265
Expenses. *See* Costs
Experience.com, 136–137
Experimentation, with products, 174
Exploratory research, 175
External human resources, 200
External motivators, 37
External recruitment, 202
Eyeball.com Network Inc., 30

F

Facility, production, 190, 205–206
Fact finding, 100
Fads, 120
Family
    balance with work, 74–75
    involvement in venture, 218
    as source of capital, 248–249

Feng Shui, 88–89
Fibreglass Canada, 94
Fields, Debbi, 239
Final users, 180
Financial controls, 212
Financial mismanagement, 282
Financial objectives, 231–234
Financial records, 281
Financial resources, of venture, 154–155, 199
Financial strategy, 157–158, 231–246, 292
Financing
   by customers, 250
   debt, 251–254
   by employees, 250
   equity, 247–248
   by friends and family, 248–249
   by personal savings, 248
   by suppliers, 250
First on Colour, 296–298
Fixed assets, 251
Fixed costs, 190, 198
Fixed overhead costs, 146
Fixed resources, 154
Flexibility, of attitude, 51
Flexible work schedule, 78
Floren, Jennifer, 136–137
Follow-the-competition pricing, 189
Ford, Henry, 13
Forecasts, 120–121
   time-series, 123–126
Fox, Terry, 33–34
Franchises, 223–224
Free market, 300
Free trade, 137
Freid, Loren, 266
Freshlimesoda.com, 289–290
Frëtt Design, 234
Fry, Art, 138
Fujisawa Investments, 15
Furdyk, Michael, 25–26, 52
Furdyk, Paul, 52

G

Gain sharing, 203
Gallo, Ada, 288–289
Gap Analysis, 157
GATT (General Agreement on Tariffs and Trade), 11
General partnerships, 220
Geographic market segment, 183
Geomancy, 88
GirlsAreIt, 26
Gisborne, Frederick, 72
Globalization, 10, 84
Global Meeting of Generations, 121–122
Goals, setting of, 47–49

"Going public," 294
Go/no-go decisions, 265–266
Goods. *See also* Products
   defined, 10
Goodwill, 70
Government agencies, 92, 251, 253
Grants, 199
Graphs, 125
Green hat thinking, 103
Gross, Bill, 46
Gross national product (GNP), 10
Groupement Québécois des Chefs d'Entreprises, 234
Growth, of ventures. *See* Ventures: growth
Growth industries, 245
Growth trends, 123
Guarantees, loan, 253
Gupta, Susheel, 61–62
Gutenberg, Johannes, 109

H

Hammarubi Code, 13
Harvests
   financial, 293–294
   personal, 295
Hayman, Michael, 25
The Helicopter Company Inc., 259–260
Henderson, Julia, 259–260
Heward, Lyn, 117–118
Hickes, John, 76–77
Hierarchies, 84
Hodgson, Paul, 94
Home-based employment, 77–78
Hudson's Bay Company, 13
Hui, Terrence, 155
Human resources, 154, 200–201. *See also* Employees
   departments, 81
   external, 200
   internal, 200
   management, 155–156
Hutcheson, Bob, 107
Hutcheson's Sand and Gravel, 107
Hutchins, Wil, 20

I

IC products, 96
Idea-finding stage of problem solving, 100
Ideas
   development of, 91–92
   evaluation of, 134–135
   generation of, 110–111
   innovative, 89
   needs satisfaction and, 89
   new, 15, 90
   opportunities vs., 116, 118

Ideas (*continued*)
   protection of, 95–96
   ventures and, 89
Immigration, 16
!mprov at work, 98–99
Incentives, pay, 203–204
Income forecasts, 244–245
Income statements, 245
Incorporation, 249
Incremental problem solving, 56
Incubators, 12
Industrial Age, 70
Industrial designs, 96
Information
   gathering, 105
   interpreting, 106
Information Age, 71, 73
Information technology, 12, 84
Infrastructure, 205
Innovations, 15
   defined, 94
   employees and, 138–139
   to meet new needs, 292
Innovative task, in venture development, 286
Insulin, 175
Insurance agents, 206
Intangible assets, 70
Integrated Circuit Topographies (ICT), 96
Integrity, 300–301
Intellectual capital, 79
Intellectual property, 95
Internal human resources, 200
Internal motivators, 37
Internal recruitment, 202
International Properties Group Ltd. (IPG), 20
International Space Station (ISS), 294
Internet, 10
   advertising on, 192
   high-speed access, 32
   surveys, 128, 129
Interpersonal skills, 58
Interviews, personal, 128, 129
Intrapreneurs, 35, 79
Intrapreneurship, 17
Invention, defined, 94
Inventive task, in venture development, 286
Inventory controls, 211

J

Job(s)
   creation, 15
   descriptions, 200
   loss of, 12
   new, 73–74
   openings, 72–73

Job(s) (*continued*)
  sharing, 78
Jobs, Steven, 291
Joint ventures, 220
Josephson, Michael, 300
Just-in-case scenarios, 283
Just-in-time scheduling, 25

K

Kaplan, Ann, 241
Kayfetz, Ben, 275
Kirsh, Marvin, 178
Knight, Phil, 68
Kraft Dinner, 103
Kroc, Ray, 18

L

Labour, history of, 69–71
Labourers, 70
Labour market, 72
Lai, Albert, 25
Laissez-faire leaders, 214
Laliberté, Guy, 117
Lastman, Blayne, 178
Lateral thinking, 102–103
Lavergne, Anne, 50
Law
  business, 225
  ethics and, 298–299
Lawyers, 204
Leadership, 211, 214–216
Leadership for Environment and Development (LEAD), 218
Leave programs, personal, 78
Le Caine, Hugh, 286
Left brain, 107–108
Legal risk factors, 264–265
Letter of transmittal, 274
Level Five, 279
Liabilities, 147
Liability, of ownership, 219, 222
Life cycle
  of products, 184
  of services, 184
  of ventures, 145–147
Lifelong learning, 84
Lilith Fair, 36
Limited companies, 221–222
Limited partnerships, 221
Line of credit, 252
Linquist, Kevin, 39
Liquidation, of assets, 147
Listening skills, 216
Little, Ryan, 144–145
Livingstone, Carol, 146
Loans, 199, 251, 253
  term, 252
Logos, corporate, 97
Lone wolves, 80

Long-range objectives, 209–210
Loss-leader pricing, 189
Love money, 248
Loyalist Country Inn, 14

M

Madore, Josée, 49–50
Magazines, ideas from, 90
Management, 264
  functions of, 209–212
Management buyouts, 294
Management consultants, 206
Managerial task, in venture development, 286, 291
Manzi, Barbara, 226
Manzi Metals, Inc., 226
Marathon of Hope, 33–34
Mariani, William, 236
Marketing
  elements, 181
  mix, 181–182
  strategy, 180
Marketing research, 131–132, 171
Market-pulled entrepreneurship, 118
Market(s)
  analysis, 152–153
  niche, 7
  segmentation, 182–183
  share, 17, 232
  target, 182
  trends, 120–125
Mark It, 170
Marshall, Virginia, 170
Maslow, Abraham, 214–215
Mass production, 13, 193
Matchmaking service, 253
Material resources, 154, 199
Maxim, Judith, 82–83
McDonald's, 18
The McKinsey Quarterly, 75
McLachlan, Sarah, 36
Media, advertising in the, 191–192
Mediation, 217
Medicard Finance Inc., 241
Mentors, 25
Mentorship, 160, 162–163
Merchants, 69
Messages, 215–216
Meyer, Terry Lynn, 6–7
Milestones, 47
Mind mapping, 110
Minority position, 250
Mission Hockey, 126–127
Mission statement, 148
Mitchells, Maureen, 24–25
Mobilization, of resources, 204
Modifications, 18
Mohr, Tom, 8
Mortgages, 252

Motivation, 32, 37
  of employees, 214–215
Mrs. Fields Cookies, 239
Multiplier effect, 15
Municipal governments, 92
Muttluks, 250
MyDesktop.com, 25
Myrias Computer Technologies, 301

N

Nader, Ralph, 212
NAFTA (North American Free Trade Agreement), 11, 137
Nanuk Enterprises Ltd., 76
Needs
  assessment, 152
  classified, 9
  defined, 9
  hierarchy of, 214–215
  new, 292
Net cash, 239
Networking, 80, 247, 263
Net worth, 242
New economy, 71, 84
"New Perspectives on Nexus Generation" (Royal Bank of Canada), 45
Newspapers, 90, 283
Nexus Generation, 45, 162
Ng, Paul, 88–89
Nike, 68–69, 75
Nortel Networks, 291
North York Harvest Food Bank, 266
Not-for-profit organizations, 9, 148, 185, 282
Nova Cruz Products, 28

O

Observation skills, 90–91, 174
Operating expenses, 233, 242
Operating strategy, 155–157
Opportunities, 116, 118, 119
Opportunity cost, 135
Ordinary marks, 96
Organizational charts, 156
Orientation period, 202
Out-of-the-box thinking, 56
Ownership, forms of, 219–222
Oxenergy, 8
Oxyl'Eau Inc., 8

P

Pacific Rim countries, 137
Painter, Scott, 46
Parking, 205
Partnerships, 220–221, 249
Part-time work, 78
Patents, 95

Pay incentives, 203–204
Payroll, 147
Pearson, Dave, 69
Penetration pricing, 189
Penner, Curtis, 20
Pereira, Aaron, 144–145
Personal budget, 235–236
Personal selling, 192
Personal vs. business ethics, 299–300
Philanthropists, 145
Piatka, Nadja, 6–7
Picasso, Pablo, 109
Piché, Chris, 30
Pickford, Mary, 287
Plante, Jacques, 94
Poon Tip, Bruce, 197–198
Population
    sample, 177
    trends, 121–122. *See also* Demographics
Porter, Doug, 284–285
Post-it Notes, 138
Postsecondary education, 73
Poy, Justin, 162
Prefontaine, Steve, 68
Price takers, 188
Pricing, 152–153, 181, 187–188, 265
    cost-plus, 189
    follow-the-competition, 189
    loss-leader, 189
    penetration, 189
    psychological, 189
    skimming, 189
    strategies, 188–189
Private placement, 248, 250
Problem solving, 100–108
Product-driven entrepreneurship, 118
Production, 189–190
    controls, 211–212
    process, 156
Productivity, 190
Products, 10, 181
    knowledge of, 173
    life cycle of, 184
    obsolete, 265
    pricing, 265
    sampling, 174
Profit formula, 186
Profit margin(s), 152–153, 232, 282
Profit(s), 9, 185–186, 222, 294
Profit sharing, 203
Pro formas, 241
Project management software, 210
Project plans, 148, 150
Promotion, 181, 190–193
Proprietary software, 25
Proprietors, 96
Psychographic market segment, 183
Psychological needs
    defined, 9

Psychological pricing, 189
Publicity, 192
Pylypchuk, Jeff, 223–224

Q

Quality control programs, 212
Questionnaires, 128, 129, 130–131, 174

R

Rabie, Anton, 172
Real-estate agents, 205–206
Real needs, 9
Recruitment, of employees
    external, 202
    internal, 202
Red hat thinking, 103
Red tape, 46
Regulations, 225
Remuneration, 203
Rent, 205
Research, 128
    causal, 175
    exploratory, 175
    internal, 177
    marketing, 131–132. See Marketing research
    primary, 128–131, 176
    secondary, 131, 177
    specific, 175
Research Assistance Grid, 148–149
Research instruments, 128
Resource analysis, 154–155
Resources
    consumable, 154
    financial, 154–155, 199
    fixed, 154
    human. See Human resources
    material, 154, 199
    technological, 199
Résumés, 202
Return on investment, 232–233
Revenue estimating, 237
Rheaume, Manon, 126–127
Right brain, 107–108
Rightsizing, 12
Risk(s)
    assessment, 244
    from competition, 264, 265
    critical, 264–265
    financial, 265
    human resources, 265
    legal, 264–265
    management, 29, 264
    minimizing, 285
    operational, 265
    sales, 264
    taking, 27, 54, 146
Robotic technology, 294
Roller hockey, 44

Roméo & Juliette, 49–50
Royal Bank of Canada, 45
Rumanek, Adam, 208
Ruth, Nancy, 26

S

Sales, 264
Sales promotion, 192–193
Sample, population, 177
Sandberg, Duane, 111
Satellite Sisters, 115
Savings, personal, 248
Schurman, Jo-Anne, 14
Secours, Michelle, 234
Security Solutions of Canada Inc., 275
Seek (Storage) Systems Inc., 301
Seiko Corporation, 17
Seiler, Karl, 279
Self-esteem, 37
Selling, personal, 192
Service-driven entrepreneurship, 118
Services, 10, 181
    knowledge of, 173
    life cycle of, 184
    value-added, 24
Shahani, Parmesh, 289–290
Shareholders, 222
Share purchase plans, 250
Shares, 222
    selling, 249
Shaw, George Bernard, 300
Short-range planning, 210
Silent partners, 221
Silly Putty, 94
Skills
    assessment of, 57–58
    changes in, 79
    classification of, 58–59
    in communication, 216
    creative-thinking, 59, 100
    critical-thinking, 59, 100
    of entrepreneurs, 30–31, 54
    interpersonal, 58
    in intrapreneurship, 79
    networking, 80
    practical, 59
Skimming (pricing), 189
Skoronski, Steve, 20
SMART principle, 47–48
Smith, Kevin, 259
Socioeconomic market segment, 183
Software
    desktop publishing, 268–269
    for planning, 210
    for small enterprises, 12
Sole proprietorship, 219
Solution-finding stage of problem solving, 101
Sparrow car, 122

Specific research, 175
Spin Master Toys, 172
Spoken communication, 216
Spreadsheets, 210, 273
Stable situations, 124
Standard of living, entrepreneurship and, 15
Startup costs, 233, 238, 242
Statistics Canada, 73, 92
Steppingstones, 47
Stock option plans, 250
Storage space, 205
Stress
    management, 217–218. *See also* Work-life balance
    venture failure and, 283
Strikes, 70
Super-specialists, 80
Suppliers, 238
    as source of capital, 250
Supply
    defined, 13
    labour market, 72
Surplus, 239
Surveys, 174
    Internet, 128, 129
    telephone, 128, 129
Suzuki, David, 62
SWOT analysis, 53, 55
Syndication, 116

T

Table of contents, 269–270
TakingITGlobal, 25
Talent, war for, 75
"Talkies," invention of, 287
Target market, 182
Taxation, 219, 220
Tax deductibility, 251
Team play, 80
Teamwork, 107
Technological development
    changes following, 11–12, 116
    competition and, 84
    venture failure and, 283
Technological resources, of ventures, 199
Telecommuters, 77
Teleconferencing, 77
Telephone surveys, 128, 129
Term loans, 252
Thinking Hats, 102–104
Thrasher, Kate, 213
Three Blondes and a Brownie, 6–7
3M Company, 138, 292
Tickle Me Elmo, 187–188
Time management, 80
Time-series forecasts, 123–126
Tip, Bruce Poon. *See* Poon Tip, Bruce

Title page, 269
TK Worm Factory, 140
Tofinetti, Peter, 223–224
Total monthly costs, 146
Total monthly revenues, 146
Trade
    agreements, 11
    free, 137
Trademarks, 96
Trade-offs, 37
Trade shows, ideas from, 90
Trade unions, 70
Training programs, 202
Trends
    declining, 124
    forecasting, 120–121
    growth, 123
    labour market, 72
    market, 120–125
    population, 121–122
Trudeau, Patrick, 161–163
Tumie Tours, 76
Tupper, Shelly, 296
Tyco, 187–188

U

Ulrich, Karl, 28
Undercapitalization, 281–282
UNIDO Online Inquiry Service, 161
United Nations Industrial Development Organization, 161

V

Value-added services, 24
Van Ee, Jayson, 161–163
Variable costs, 190, 198
Vendor's permit, 225
Venture capital, 247–248
Venture capitalists, 245, 249–250
Venture Creation Wheel, 2–4
Venture plans, 147–151, 260–261
    appendices, 270
    draft preparation, 268–269
    editing, 272–273
    importance of, 163–164
    information for, 263
    letter of transmittal, 274
    polishing, 273–274
    proofreading, 272–273
    reasons for preparing, 150
    reviewing, 271
    sections in, 151–158, 261–262
    table of contents, 269–270
    timeline in, 270
    title page, 269
Venture Profiles
    AC Dispensing Equipment Inc., 93
    Acme Humble Pie Co., 267–268
    Affinity Logic, 279

Venture Profiles (continued)
    All Pro Construction, 246
    Ami Support Computers, 275
    Atelier Hair Salon, 161–163
    Auger, Corey, 20
    Bad Boy Furniture and Appliances Warehouse Ltd., 178–179
    Betty Flyweight, 126–127
    Boulangerie Pizza Motta, 288–289
    Bowerman, Bill, 68
    Brinsmead, Candace, 6–7
    Bruce, Travis Keith, 140
    Buchanan, Georgia, 246
    Burnham, Andy, 98–99
    BuyBuddy.com, 25, 52
    Cachagee, Wade, 39–40
    CanadaHelps.org, 144–145
    CanTalk Canada Inc., 24–25
    CHART (Coastal Habitat Assessment Research Technology), 133
    Chen, Jessica, 267–268
    Choi, Matthew, 144–145
    Cirque du Soleil, 117–118
    Computer Professionals for Social Responsibility (CPSR), 61–62
    coolgirls.org, 26
    coolwomen.org, 26
    Copyright Reproductions Inc., 296
    Corriero, Jennifer, 25–26
    Cranson, Brett & Devon, 44
    CREE-TECH Inc., 39–40
    Cyclepath, 223–224
    Deblois, Elisabeth, 133
    Dorazio, Robert, 288
    Duck, Michael, 93
    Dumas, Paul, 18
    efinity Inc., 20
    experience.com, 136–137
    Feng Shui, 88–89
    First on Colour, 296
    Floren, Jennifer, 136–137
    Fox, Terry, 33–34
    freshlimesoda.com, 289–290
    Frëtt Design, 234
    Furdyk, Michael, 25–26, 52
    Furdyk, Paul, 52
    Gallo, Ada, 288–289
    G.A.P (Great Adventure People), 197–198
    Geomancy, 88
    GirlsAreIt, 26
    Gupta, Susheel, 61–62
    Hayman, Michael, 25
    The Helicopter Company Inc., 259–260
    Henderson, Julia, 259–260
    Heward, Lyn, 117–118
    Hickes, John, 76–77
    Hutchins, Wil, 20

Venture Profiles (continued)
  !mprov at work, 98–99
  International Properties Group Ltd. (IPG), 20
  Kaplan, Ann, 241
  Kayfetz, Ben, 275
  Kirsh, Marvin, 178
  Knight, Phil, 68
  Lai, Albert, 25
  Laliberté, Guy, 117
  Lastman, Blayne, 178
  Level Five, 279
  Linquist, Kevin, 39
  Little, Ryan, 144–145
  Loyalist Country Inn, 14
  Manzi, Barbara, 226
  Manzi Metals, Inc., 226
  Marathon of Hope, 33–34
  Mark It, 170
  Marshall, Virginia, 170
  Maxim, Judith, 82–83
  Medicard Finance Inc., 241
  Meyer, Terry Lynn, 6–7
  Mission Hockey, 126–127
  Mitchells, Maureen, 24–25
  Mohr, Tom, 8
  MyDesktop.com, 25
  Nanuk Enterprises Ltd., 76
  Ng, Paul, 88–89
  Nike, 68–69
  Oxenergy, 8
  Oxyl'Eau Inc., 8
  Pearson, Dave, 69
  Penner, Curtis, 20
  Pereira, Aaron, 144–145
  Piatka, Nadja, 6–7
  Poon Tip, Bruce, 197–198
  Porter, Doug, 284–285
  Prefontaine, Steve, 68
  Pylypchuk, Jeff, 223–224
  Rabie, Anton, 172
  Rheaume, Manon, 126–127
  roller hockey, 44
  Roméo & Juliette, 49–50
  Rumanek, Adam, 208
  Ruth, Nancy, 26
  Schurman, Jo-Anne, 14
  Secours, Michelle, 234
  Security Solutions of Canada Inc., 275
  Seiler, Karl, 279
  Shahani, Parmesh, 289–290
  Skoronski, Steve, 20
  Smith, Kevin, 259
  Spin Master Toys, 172
  TakingITGlobal, 25
  Three Blondes and a Brownie, 6–7
  TK Worm Factory, 140
  Tofinetti, Peter, 223–224
  Trudeau, Patrick, 161–163

Venture Profiles (continued)
  Tumie Tours, 76
  Tupper, Shelly, 296
  Van Ee, Jayson, 161–163
  Web Sights International, 208
  Yoon, Sebastian, 284–285
Ventures
  acceptability, 135
  capitalization of, 157–158
  change and, 91
  characteristics of, 9–11
  comfort stage, 147
  controlling, 211–212
  costs. See Costs
  demise of, 280
  development stage, 146
  development tasks, 286–287
  employees. See Employees
  external team, 204–206
  failures of, 280–285
  feasibility of, 135
  financing. See Financing, and headings beginning Financial
  for-profit, 9, 148
  goods production, 10
  growth stage, 146, 291–292
  harvesting, 293–294
  ideas and, 89
  international, 10–11
  joint, 146
  large scale, 9–10
  leading, 211
  life cycle of, 145–147
  local, 10
  national, 10
  not-for-profit, 9, 148, 185, 282
  opportunity cost, 135
  organizing, 210
  ownership of, 219–222
  partners in, 146
  physical, 10
  planning, 160, 209–210
  prestartup stage, 146
  provincial, 10
  rapid growth, 281
  record keeping, 159
  selling of, 294
  service production, 10
  size of, 159–160
  small scale, 9–10
  timing, 135
  traits of owners, 160
  turnaround stage, 147
  usefulness, 135
  virtual, 10
Virtual business, 10
Virtual corporations, 82–83
Visualization, 111

W

Wakefield, Ruth, 95
Wallin, Pamela, 161
Wants, defined, 9
Warehouse phenomenon, 179
War for talent, 75
Watch industry, 17
Watson, Thomas, 71
Webhelp.com, 119
Web Sights International, 208
West Point Development Corporation, 146
White hat thinking, 103
Williams, Charles, 71
Window of opportunity, 134
Women's Venture Capital Forum, 247
Word clustering, 110
Work, alternative arrangements in, 77–78
Work-life balance, 74–75. See also Family; Stress: management
Workplace
  changes in, 84
  culture, 38
  enterprising, 137, 139
  flexibility in, 75
Wright, James, 94

Y

Yellow hat thinking, 104
Yoon, Sebastian, 284–285
YottaYotta Inc., 301

Credits

Every reasonable effort to trace the copyright holders of materials appearing in this book has been made. Information that will enable the publisher to rectify any error or omission will be welcomed.

Photographs

Cover Images
Top centre: Jim Craigmyle/Masterfile; top right: Laurent Delhourme; bottom right: Doug Menuez/PhotoDisc; bottom centre: Ryan McVay/PhotoDisc; fingerprint: Don Farrall/PhotoDisc; skyscrapers: Emma Lee/Lifefile/Photo Disc.
Table of Contents Images
vi Courtesy Corbin Motors Inc.; **vii** Wayne Karl, *Hockey Business News*; **viii l** Image Courtesy LEADnet Photolibrary; **r** Arista Records; **ix** Gail Harvey, Photographer and The Terry Fox Foundation.

CHAPTER ONE: 1 SW Productions/PhotoDisc; **6** John Ulan Photography; **7** Dick Hemingway; **11** MalcolmFife/PhotoDisc; **12** Courtesy The NRGGroup; **13** The Granger Collection, New York; **14** Courtesy The Loyalist Country Inn; **16** Steve Mason/PhotoDisc; **19** Keith Brofsky/PhotoDisc; **20** Roth & Ramberg; **CHAPTER TWO: 24** Greg Gerla Photography, Inc.; **26** Rick Madonis/*The Toronto Star*; **28** Courtesy Nova Cruz Products, LLC; **33** Gail Harvey, Photographer and The Terry Fox Foundation; **35** Created by Gary Rabbior © The Canadian Foundation for Economic Education; **36 t** Arista Records; **36 b** Lisette Le Bon/Superstock; **37** Steve Cole/PhotoDisc; **40** Courtesy Wade Cachagee, Cree-Tech Inc.; **CHAPTER THREE: 44** Peter Power/*The Toronto Star*; **47** Dick Hemingway; **50** Courtesy Tony Bacile, Roméo & Juliette; **52** Courtesy Michael Furdyk, Buybuddy.com; **54** Keith Brofsky/PhotoDisc; **56 l&r** The Granger Collection, New York; **59** Kwame Zikomo/Superstock; **62** CBC/Fred Phipps; **CHAPTER FOUR: 61** James Foord; **65** Steve Chenn/First Light; **68** Photographic Collection, Special Collections & University Archives, University of Oregon; **69** The Granger Collection, New York; **70** Corbis/Magma Photo News Inc.; **74** Buccina Studios/PhotoDisc; **76** James Darrell Greer/Northern News Services Ltd.; **79** Doug Menuez/PhotoDisc; **81** Keith Brofsky/PhotoDisc; **82** Corbis/Magma Photo News Inc.; **CHAPTER FIVE: 88** Courtesy Paul Ng; **90** Courtesy Reed Exhibition Companies; **91** Dick Hemingway; **93** © Peter D. Marsman, Courtesy Black Business Initiative (BBI); **94** Imperial Oil-Turofsky, Hockey Hall of Fame; **96** Dick Hemingway; **97** The Canadian Red Cross; **101** Musée J. Armand Bombardier; **98** Julie A.F. Timmins; **CHAPTER SIX: 115** Sara Krulwich, NYT Pictures; **117** CP Picture Archive/Paul Chiasson; **122** Courtesy Corbin Motors Inc.; **127** Wayne Karl, *Hockey Business News*; **129 bl** Dick Hemingway; **129 tr** Keith Brofsky/PhotoDisc; **133** © Rhonda Hayward; **136** © William Polo; **138** Jose L. Pelaez/First Light; **140** Courtesy Travis Keith Bruce; **CHAPTER SEVEN: 44** Tony Bock/*The Toronto Star*; **146** Ryan McVay/PhotoDisc; **153** Dick Hemingway; **155** Arthur S. Aubry/PhotoDisc; **159** Superstock; **161** CP Picture Archive/Peter Bregg; **162** Mathieson & Hewitt/Atelier Salon; **CHAPTER EIGHT: 167** Dick Hemingway; **170** © Susan King; **171** Dick Hemingway; **172** Courtesy SpinMaster Toys; **177** John Smyth/Superstock; **178** Dick Hemingway; **188** Dick Hemingway; **191** Dick Hemingway; **192** Dick Hemingway; **CHAPTER NINE: 197** Dick Hemingway; **200** Dick Hemingway; **206** Dick Hemingway; **208** Dick Hemingway; **213** Jose L. Pelaez/First Light; **216** Ryan McVay/PhotoDisc; **218** Image Courtesy LEADnet Photolibrary; **223** Cyclepath/Thunder Bay; **224** Dick Hemingway; **CHAPTER TEN: 230** © Skip Gandy; **234** © Suzanne Langevin; **236** Dick Hemingway; **237** Peter Beck/First Light; **238** David Buffington/PhotoDisc; **239** Mrs. Fields' Original Cookies, Inc.; **245** Tom Stewart/First Light; **241** Rotman School of Management, University of Toronto; **246** © 2000 Mike Fuger; **253** Dick Hemingway; **CHAPTER ELEVEN: 259** Julia Henderson; **263 t** Dick Hemingway; **263 b** CP Picture Archive/Fred Chartrand; **266** Colin McConnell/*The Toronto Star*; **268** Marina Dodis/*The National Post*; **271** Jeff Maloney/PhotoDisc; **275** Ben Kayfetz; **CHAPTER TWELVE: 279** Courtesy Karl Seiler; **282** Dick Hemingway; **287 tl** Spike/PhotoDisc; **287 tr** Dick Hemingway; **287 b** The Granger Collection, New York; **288** Ted Church/*The Gazette*; **290** Sarah Elton; **292** Rob Lewine/First Light; **294** NASA; **295** Rob Lewine/First Light; **296** Courtesy Shelly Tupper.

Text

CHAPTER ONE: 6–7 Donna Korchinski, www.netnewsinc.com; **7–8** *The National Post*; **14** Rotman School of Management, University of Toronto; **20** Julie Alnwick, *Canadian Business*, September 18, 2000; **CHAPTER TWO: 24–25** Susanne Baillie, from PROFIT Magazine, September 2000; **25–26** Sharlene Azam, August 2000. Reprinted with permission, The Toronto Star Syndicate; **33–34** Leslie Scrivener and The Terry Fox Foundation; **CHAPTER THREE: 49–50** Paul Delean, *The Gazette*; **52** Reprinted from the August 2000 issue of *Fast Company Magazine*. All rights reserved. To subscribe, please call 800-542-6029 or visit www.fastcompany.com; **54** Chips Klein, Chipco Canada Inc.; **58** Table 3.1 Originally published in *Orbit* magazine, "School-to-work Transitions" (Spring 2000); **61–62** As appeared in the October 2000 issue of *htc–Canada's HiTech Career Journal*. Reprinted with permission of the publisher. Brass Ring Canada Inc. To view the online version, visit www.Brassring.com/Canada; **CHAPTER FOUR: 68–69** Reprinted from the Jan/Feb 2000 issue of *Fast Company Magazine*. All rights reserved. To subscribe, please call 1-800-542-6029 or visit www.fastcompany.com; **76–77** James Darrell Greer, Northern News Services Ltd.; **80** Reprinted by permission of PROFIT, the magazine for Canadian Entrepreneurs © 2000; **81** By permission, *Canadian HR Reporter*, Carswell, Thomson Professional Publishing. "The Battle Escalates for All Levels of Talent," *Canadian HR Reporter*, September 11, 2000; **82–83** Material from *The Next 20 Years of Your Life* © 1997 by Richard Worzel. Reprinted by permission of Stoddart Publishing Co. Limited; **CHAPTER FIVE: 93** Dawn Calleja, *Canadian Business*, December 31, 1999; **105** *Insights: Understanding Yourself and Others*, C.M. Mamchur, 1984, OISE Press, University of Toronto Press; **CHAPTER SIX: 115** First appeared in WORKING WOMAN, November 2000. Written by Alissa MacMillan. Reprinted with the permission of MacDonald Communications Corporation. © 2000 by MacDonald Communications Corporation, www.workingwoman.com. For subscriptions call 1-800-234-9675; **116** "Technology keeps

Credits **317**

changing products we buy for everyday use." Human Resources Development Canada, "Canada Prospects, 1994," Reproduced with the permission of the Minister of Public Works and Government Services Canada, 2000; **117–118** Reprinted with permission from Tod Jones, *The Costco Connection.*
126–127 Reprinted with permission from Transcontinental Publishing; *Hockey Business News*, Wayne Karl; **133** Caron Hawco, NEW SHOES, Vol.1 #1, 1999; **134** "Steps to Evaluate Your Ideas," Canada Business Service Centres Network (www.cbsc.org); **136–137** Reprinted with permission of SUCCESS Magazine, November 2000; **140** © November 2000, Reprinted with permission BLACK ENTERPRISE Magazine, New York, N.Y. All rights reserved; **CHAPTER SEVEN: 159–160;** "Steps to launch a successful business" by Paul Tulenko. Reprinted with permission from Miller Features Syndicate Inc.; **161–163** Reprinted with permission of Canadian Youth Business Foundation and *The National Post*, May 25, 2000; **144–145** Reprinted with permission, The Toronto Star Syndicate; **CHAPTER EIGHT: 170** © Hilary Davidson, Courtesy of *Chatelaine Magazine* © Rogers Publishing Ltd.; **172** Diane McDougall/*The Financial Post*, December 13, 2000; **CHAPTER NINE: 223–224** Reprinted with permission from REALM. "Creating the Work You Want," published by YES Canada-BC. Available online at http://realm.net and in print by calling 1-877-REALM-99. For more information: Phone (604) 412-4147, Fax: (604) 412-4144, E-mail: info@realm.net; **213** Excerpted from article by Cheryl Mahaffy, with permission of *Alberta Venture* magazine.
CHAPTER TEN: 230–231 © November 2000, Reprinted with permission, BLACK ENTERPRISE Magazine, New York, N.Y. All Rights Reserved; **234** © Hilary Davidson, Courtesy of *Chatelaine Magazine* © Rogers Publishing Ltd.; **241** Rotman School of Management, University of Toronto; **245** "Where Venture Capitalists Are Placing Their Bets" Reprinted by permission of PROFIT, the magazine for Canadian Entrepreneurs © 2000; **246** Reprinted with permission of SUCCESS Magazine, November 2000; **CHAPTER ELEVEN: 266** Agents of Change: Reprinted with permission, The Toronto Star Syndicate; **266** "Opening a new business? Be big, fast, and ready to relocate" Reprinted with permission from *The Globe and Mail*; **267–268** John Schreiner, *The National Post*, December 2, 2000; **CHAPTER TWELVE: 279** © Knight Ridder Newspapers, Reprinted with permission, The Toronto Star Syndicate; **284–285** CBC *Venture*; **288–289** © Paul Delean, *The Gazette*; **289–290** © Sarah Elton 296 © Nattalia Lea, 2001.

Illustrations

CHAPTER ONE: Figure 3.1 Royal Bank Financial Group; **CHAPTER FOUR: Figure 4.1** Human Resources Development Canada, "Overview of Labour Market Trends," Reproduced with the permission of the Minister of Public Works and Government Services Canada, 2001; **Figure 4.2** This exhibit is taken from Elizabeth G. Chambers, Mark Foulon, Helen Handfield-Jones, Steven M. Hankin, and Edward G. Michaels III, "The War for Talent," *The McKinsey Quarterly*, 1998, Number 3, and can be found on the publication's Web site: www.mckinseyquarterly.com. Used by permission; **CHAPTER FIVE: Figures 5.6 and 5.7** Reprinted with permission of Simon & Schuster from *Teaching for the Two-Sided Mind* by Linda Verlee Williams. © 1983 by Linda Verlee Williams; **CHAPTER SIX: Figure 6.1** "Demographic Trends: The Numbers and the Issues They Raise," by Robert J. Berg, Managing Partner, Global Meeting of Generations, presented to the Global Meeting of Generations, January 1999, Washington, D.C. Available on www.idc/gmg; **Figure 6.2** United Nations Publications, "World Population 1998"; **Figures 6.5 and 6.6** "Subscribers with Mobile Devices," and "Number of Personal Computers Worldwide," eMarketer; **CHAPTER SEVEN: Figure 7.1** Reprinted with permission of the Bank of Montreal; **CHAPTER ELEVEN: 265** SES Canada Research Inc., www.sesresearch.com; **293** "Global Growth of Internet Hosts," eMarketer.